Sport in the Global Society

General Editor: J.A. Mangan

FREEING TH

D0143605

SPORT IN THE GLOBAL SOCIETY
General Editor: J.A. Mangan

The interest in sports studies around the world is growing and will continue to do so. This unique series combines aspects of the expanding study of *sport in the global society*, providing comprehensiveness and comparison under one editorial umbrella. It is particularly timely, with studies in the cultural, economic, ethnographic, geographical, political, social, anthropological, sociological and aesthetic elements of sport proliferating in institutions of higher education.

Eric Hobsbawm once called sport one of the most significant practices of the late nineteenth century. Its significance was even more marked in the late twentieth century and will continue to grow in importance into the new millennium as the world develops into a 'global village' sharing the English language, technology and sport.

Other Titles in the Series

Footbinding, Feminism and Freedom
The Liberation of Women's Bodies in Modern China
Fan Hong

Shaping the Superman
Fascist Body as Political Icon: Aryan Fascism
Edited by J.A. Mangan

Superman Supreme
Fascist Body as Political Icon: Global Fascism
Edited by J.A. Mangan

Making the Rugby World
Race, Gender, Commerce
Edited by Timothy J.L. Chandler and John Nauright

Sport in Australasia
Past and Present
Edited by J.A. Mangan and John Nauright

The Nordic World
Sport in Society
Edited by Henrik Meinander and J.A. Mangan

The First Black Footballer
Arthur Wharton 1865–1930: An Absence of Memory
Phil Vasili

Scoring for Britain
International Football and International Politics, 1900–1939
Peter J. Beck

Sporting Nationalisms
Identity, Ethnicity, Immigration and Assimilation
Edited by Mike Cronin and David Mayall

Cricket and England
A Cultural and Social History of the Inter-war Years
Jack Williams

The Games Ethic and Imperialism
Aspects of the Diffusion of an Ideal
J.A. Mangan

The Race Game
Sport and Politics in South Africa
Douglas Booth

Rugby's Great Split
Class, Culture and the Origins of Rugby League Football
Tony Collins

FREEING THE FEMALE BODY

Inspirational Icons

Editors

J.A. MANGAN
University of Strathclyde

and

FAN HONG
De Montfort University

FRANK CASS
LONDON • PORTLAND, OR

First published in 2001 in Great Britain by
FRANK CASS PUBLISHERS
Crown House, 47 Chase Side
London, N14 5BP

and in the United States of America by
FRANK CASS PUBLISHERS
c/o ISBS, 5824 N.E. Hassalo Street
Portland, Oregon 97213-3644

Copyright © 2001 Frank Cass & Co. Ltd.

Website: www.frankcass.com

British Library Cataloguing in Publication Data

Freeing the female body : inspirational icons. – (Sport in
  the global society ; no. 20)
  1. Feminism 2. Sports for women – Psychological aspects
  3. Exercise for women – History
  I. Mangan, J.A. (James Anthony), 1939– II. Hong, Fan
  305.4'2'0922
  ISBN 0-7146-5088-9 (cloth)
  ISBN 0-7146-8129-6 (paper)
  ISSN 1368-9789

Library of Congress Cataloging-in-Publication Data

Freeing the female body : inspirational icons / editors, J.A. Mangan and Fan Hong
  p. cm. – (Sport in the global society, ISSN 1368-9789 ; 20)
Includes bibliographical references and index.
"First appeared as a special issue of the International journal of the
history of sport (ISSN 0952-3367), vol. 18, no. 1, March 2001, published
by Frank Cass"–T.p. verso.
ISBN 0-7146-5088-9 (cloth) – ISBN 0-7146-8129-6 (paper)
1. Physical education for women–Social aspects–History.
2. Feminism–History. 3. Feminists–Biography. I. Mangan, J. A.
II. Hong, Fan. III. International journal of the history of sport.
IV. Cass series–sport in the global society ; 20.
  GV439 .F67 2001
  796'.082–dc21   00-012309

This group of studies first appeared as a special issue of
The International Journal of the History of Sport (ISSN 0952-3367), Vol.18, No.1, March 2001,
published by Frank Cass

All rights reserved. No part of this publication may be reproduced, stored in or introduced into a retrieval system, or transmitted, in any form or by any means, electronic, mechanical, photocopying, recording or otherwise, without the prior written permission of the publisher of this book.

Printed in Great Britain by
Antony Rowe Ltd., Chippenham, Wilts.

OLSON LIBRARY
NORTHERN MICHIGAN UNIV
MARQUETTE, MICHIGAN 49

Contents

List of Illustrations   vii

Series Editor's Foreword   ix

Prologue – Freeing Bodies: Heroines in History   **Fan Hong**   1

1. 'All the Freedom of the Boy':
   Elizabeth Cady Stanton, Nineteenth-Century
   Architect of Women's Rights   **Roberta J. Park**   7

2. A Martyr for Modernity: Qiu Jin,   **Fan Hong**
   Feminist, Warrior and Revolutionary   **and J.A. Mangan**   27

3. A Militant Madonna:
   Charlotte Perkins Gilman, Feminism
   and Physical Culture   **Patricia Vertinsky**   55

4. A Lifetime of Campaigning: Ettie Rout,
   Emancipationist beyond the Pale   **Jane Tolerton**   73

5. Breaking Bounds: Alice Profé, Radical
   and Emancipationist   **Gertrud Pfister**   98

6. At the Heart of a New Profession:
   Margaret Stansfeld, a Radical English
   Educationalist   **Richard Smart**   119

7. Alexandrine Gibb: In 'No Man's Land
   of Sport'   **M. Ann Hall**   149

8. A Glittering Icon of Fascist Femininity:
   Trebisonda 'Ondina' Valla   **Gigliola Gori**   173

9. Ignoring Taboos: Maria Lenk,   Sebastião Votre
   Latin American Inspirationalist   and Ludmila Mourão   196

10. In Pursuit of Empowerment: *Sensei*
    Nellie Kleinsmidt, Race and Gender
    Challenges in South Africa   Denise E.M. Jones   219

Epilogue – Prospects for the New Millennium:
Women, Emancipation and the Body   J.A. Mangan   237

Select Bibliography   251

Notes on Contributors   257

Index   261

List of Illustrations

1.1	Elizabeth Cady Stanton	11
2.1	Qiu Jin	31
2.2	Qiu Jin's monument	47
3.1	Charlotte Perkins Gilman	57
3.2	Charlotte Perkins Gilman in 1876, 1887 and 1898	58
4.1	Ettie Rout, group photograph	74
4.2	Ettie Rout, passport photograph	76
4.3	Ettie Rout with the Volunteer Sisterhood	78
4.4	Ettie Rout with soldiers	81
4.5	Ettie Rout in bathing costume	89
4.6	Belly dance from *Exercises for Women*	93
5.1	Alice Profé	113
6.1	Wylam Lodge, 1905	127
6.2	Student working with children, 1933	129
6.3	Wembley Festival of Youth, 1937	129
6.4	Margaret Stansfeld and students	135
6.5	Margaret Stansfeld with students and staff, 1904–5	137
6.6	Margaret Stansfeld with Swedish gymnasts, 1948	145
6.7	Men and women students, 1999	146
7.1	Alexandrine Gibb, Summer Olympics, 1928	162
7.2	Alexandrine Gibb in 1935	165
7.3	Alexandrine Gibb, Iran, 1935	165
7.4	Alexandrine Gibb, 1930s	167
7.5	Alexandrine Gibb in 1951	167
8.1	'Ondina' Valla, 1930	175
8.2	Valla and Italy's athletics team, 1930	175
8.3	Valla doing the high jump, 1934	177
10.1	Nellie Kleinsmidt in action	227
10.2	Nellie Kleinsmidt in action	227

Series Editor's Foreword

J.A. MANGAN

In his magisterial *Enlightenment: Britain and the Creation of the Modern World*,[1] Roy Porter quotes approvingly one leader of the Movement who, with colleagues of like mind, considered it 'our first concern, as lovers of our country ... to *enlighten* it'.[2] No less sincerely and with a wider audience in mind, *Freeing the Female Body* aims not only to enlighten its audience but to advance reflection on female emancipation, the body and power. This is how it should be. *Freeing the Female Body* itself is an outcome of the 'secular value system [the Enlightenment] to which most of us subscribe today which upholds the unity of mankind and basic personal freedoms, and the worth of tolerance, knowledge, education and opportunity'.[3]

Committed emancipationists of the female body, with justice on their side and passion in their prose, have accumulated important and impressive evidence in the following pages, of iconic figures who have challenged prejudice, denied the validity of custom and pushed aside the barriers to progress.

There is another side to the coin. It is considered in the final part of *Freeing the Female Body*. In some studies of women's liberation the terms oppression and exploitation are used perhaps rather too sweepingly. Patriarchal extremism, perhaps a little too often, is depicted as omnipresent. Powerlessness, perhaps a little too glibly, is sometimes seen virtually everywhere. There are clear dangers in this. The complexity of the nature of power can be forgotten, overlooked, ignored in the certainty of the denial of power. This is not how it should be.

Care must be taken, in the sober words of Roy Porter, 'to avoid making progressive voices sound too much like a caucus or a conspiracy'.[4]

In academia, subtlety is a *sine qua non*. It ensures that analysis reflects life rather than distorts it. It is time to abandon a less than analytically adequate subscription to 'heroines and villains' judgementalism and consider more completely the actual world of the oppressive, domineering and manipulative of *both* sexes, and confront the realities of power – overt *and* covert.[5] To do this we must be sensitive to chiaroscuro so as to read political, social and cultural contours correctly; we must resist seduction by impassioned, lopsided mantras; our vantage must be advanced; our perspectives capacious enough to embrace complexity.[6]

Nothing could be more unwise than to tightlace past men and women into today's sometimes inflexible and constraining conceptual corsets.[7] Subtlety of analysis should be a spur to completeness of analysis. Usefully there could be an adherence to the Horatian tag of Immanuel Kant: *sapere aude* ('dare to know').[8]

J.A. MANGAN
Director,
International Research Centre
for Sport, Socialisation, Society,
University of Strathclyde
January 2001

NOTES

This Foreword draws fully, and with gratitude, on the scintillating Introduction to *Enlightenment: Britain and the Creation of the Modern World* by Roy Porter and makes generous use of his metaphoric reflections and observations. They are considered particularly appropriate to our modern era of 'enlightenment' which rightly embraces, among other things, the emancipation of the female body.

1. Roy Porter, *Enlightenment: Britain and the Creation of the Modern World* (London, 2000).
2. Ibid., p.xvii.
3. Ibid., p.xxii.
4. Ibid., pp.xvii–xviii.
5. A useful start could be made by reading Margaret Crosland, *Madame de Pompadour: Sex, Culture and Power.* Pompadour was the *maîtresse en titre* (official mistress) of Louis XV. She was a king's mistress but she was no 'sex object'; she was sexually boring. She was a ruthless woman of cold intelligence but manipulative charm, who schemed for, and obtained extensive power which she used when necessary against both men and women. In short, she exploited far more than she was exploited! At the same time, by means of a judicious use of her influence she was as much creative as she was destructive: 'The sheer range of her patronage would always make her a figure of major interest. She was the moving spirit behind the creation of a French porcelain manufactory at Sevres; saw to the founding of the Ecole Militaire; supported Voltaire and the *philosophes*; made Boucher her favourite painter; encouraged Rousseau to write opera; and lived long enough to pay the nine year old Mozart to play in her salon.' See John Adamson, 'The Headmistress in her pomp', a review of Crosland's book in the *Sunday Telegraph*, 31 december 2000 (Review), p.13. Gender polemics sometimes can be simplistic; life sometimes can be complicated!
6. This paragraph adapts, and in a modern setting, makes use of Roy Porter's vivid observation about the Enlightenment, see *Enlightenment*, p.xxii.
7. See Porter, *Enlightenment*, p. xxiii.
8. Ibid., p.1.

Freeing Bodies: Heroines in History

FAN HONG

Interest in the body has swept like a tornado across the fields of social science and cultural studies since the 1980s. Books and articles on the body have been published and journals on the body have appeared. The body has been a topic discussed at numerous conferences. Consequently, Kathy Davis has claimed: 'The body has clearly captured the imagination of contemporary scholars'.[1] There are two major reasons for this. First, it is a logical requirement of cultural analysis, because the body is the 'only constant in a rapidly changing world, the source of fundamental truths about who we are and how society is organized, the final arbiter of what is just and unjust, human and inhumane, progressive and retrogressive'.[2] In short, the study of the body offers a useful starting point for the historical and contemporary investigation of our culture and society. Second, arguably, it is largely the feminists who have put the body on the intellectual map.[3] In the past two decades an enormous amount of feminist research on the female body has been generated from a diversity of disciplines, theoretical perspectives and methodologies. The female body has been the subject of numerous empirical studies from reproductive control and postnatal depression to anorexia nervosa and menopause.

However, Ann Hall has pointed out that 'Female bodies have always been central to feminism, but sporting bodies have not.'[4] Not only sporting bodies but also bodies in sport seem to pose a particular problem to mainstream feminism and women's studies. One explanation has been put forward for this: intellectual bias in Western culture. Traditional high culture has made a clear-cut distinction between play and work and between physical and intellectual activities. Sport has been viewed as trivial. In other words, because sport is a physical rather than mental activity, it has been viewed as a lower form of culture and unworthy of serious attention.[5] Feminists are no exception to this view. They have been more interested in women's political struggles and their economic independence than their physical freedom. Consequently, any research on the female body in sport has been, and is, marginalized. However, Bryan S. Turner has argued perceptively that 'The problem of the body is not simply an issue in epistemology and phenomenology, but a theoretical location for debates about power, ideology and economics.'[6] Too many feminists have overlooked the fact that for women, sport has been an instrument of liberation. This is not an exaggeration. Roberta Park has stated correctly that 'modern women's emancipation is intimately bound up with her athletic ability – and certainly with her physicality'.[7]

With the aim of deepening understanding of the significance of the female body and sport, and the role of women in sport in the cultural heritage of modern society, scholars from disciplines like history, sociology, social psychology and physical education have recently produced a proliferation of historical and cultural studies dealing with women's bodies. They have demonstrated an increasing interest in the role of sport as a means of maintaining, shaping and transmitting bodily images and moral values. The body in sport – and the female body in particular – is a location for debate about the changing nature of ideology, power, social structures and cultural systems. A history of women's sport is a history of women's struggle to free their bodies over the past centuries. Involvement in sport has symbolized women's desire for change. The liberation of their bodies has been, and is, an essential requirement for their wider physical, social, cultural, economic and political freedom.

As mentioned earlier, there is now a large number of publications devoted to women, their bodies and their sports. The intention here is to briefly make reference to six books which in the recent past have blazed new trails, stimulated strong interest and propelled inquiries into women in sport forward. In 1987 J.A. Mangan and Roberta Park provided an early, seminal and thought-provoking work entitled *From 'Fair Sex' to Feminism: Sport and the Socialisation of Women in the Industrial and Post-Industrial Eras.*[8] It brought together various leading scholars in a consideration of hitherto discrete perspectives on women's studies in the social history of sport and drew on research from Britain, North America and Australasia. The book critically confronted myths of the female body. While it argued self-evidently that women's bodies are socially as well as naturally constructed it argued further that they are substantially shaped by culture. The volume demonstrated that success in sport and the associated physical power posed a serious threat to women's traditional subordinate place in patriarchal society, and that sport had played a significant role in overcoming myths concerning female bodies in Western societies. 'It marked … a watershed in scholarship on women's sport history during the 1980s by focusing substantially upon analysis rather than description.'[9]

The connections between the female body, exercise and feminist analysis are well covered in Patricia Vertinsky's ground-breaking book *The Eternally Wounded Woman: Women, Doctors and Exercise in the Nineteenth Century* in 1990 and her later article 'The Social Construction of the Gendered Body: Exercise and the Exercise of Power' in 1994.[10] She examined the influence of late nineteenth century medical beliefs on the perceived risks and benefits of female exercise, and showed how biological determinism was a pernicious ideology that established and reproduced gendered bodies in sport. She argued that the medical profession idealized women as reproductive vehicles and focused upon pathology, limitation and disability, portraying the female body as a malfunctioning organism that embodied society's ills.[11] She suggested that the process by which a powerful alliance of male 'experts' in medicine, science and education exercises control over the female body is central to the analysis of the social construction of gender and the body. She wrote in 1994: 'The body, the sexed body, has become a particular site of investigation and re-theorizing in terms of its ability to provide explanations for women's social subordination and as a pathway into understanding women's attempts to transform and transfigure historical conditions of confinement and constraint.'[12]

In their exploration of the relationship between women, sport and the body in Western culture, feminist scholars offer social theories of the body in which gender and power is the core. In 1994 Jennifer Hargreaves' book *Sporting Females: Critical Issues in the History and Sociology of Women's Sports*[13] presented an comprehensive analysis of the extent to which women's sport has been, is, and will be, an instrument of both radicalism and repression. She argued: 'The history of women's sports show that patriarchal relations on their own do not explain women's subordination. Female sports are integral to the totality of relations of cultural power.'[14] Her explanation for this is straightforward: sport can be an important means of emancipation and is, therefore, a critical context for feminist intervention. She has discussed concepts of body, freedom and restriction which are crucial to an understanding of her historical critique, and to her extensive reflections on contemporary themes of women and bodily empowerment, eroticization, discrimination, and diversification in sport.

In 1996 Ann Hall's book *Feminism and Sporting Bodies: Essays on Theory and Practice* put female sporting bodies into the context of contradictory and limited feminist theoretical agendas. It was the first book which tried to bring feminist theory to bear on women's study of sporting bodies in a systematic way. In her view, logically to understand women and sport it is necessary to understand feminism and its application to the body, oppression and emancipation. However, Hall argued that we are in a new theoretical era, in which feminist theories are not enough for our analysis and understanding of the past and the present. We need theories from cultural studies, historical studies and sociology, and we need to construct new theories of power, social practice and cultural struggle. She claimed: 'Theory raises our consciousness level and helps us to provide an ongoing critique of our culture, in this case, our sporting culture.'[15]

While feminist scholars are busy investigating the enormous diversity in the appearance and comportment of the female body in Western culture[16] Fan Hong and Susan Brownell[17] have examined the female body and culture in the East. Their research on the body in sport in China reveals just how untenable the notion of a 'natural female body' is. Their work demonstrates that the female body is an ideal starting point for any consideration of social and cultural constructionism. They have examined the relationship between women's bodies, exercise and emancipation in China and tried to assess the impact of women's sport on the status of women in Chinese society. The dramatic and brutal patriarchal traditions of physical repression of the female body in Chinese history make the physical freedom of Chinese women an issue of special significance and a valuable case study in the history of the emancipation of the modern female body.

This balance, incidentally, of 'outsider' and 'insider' has special merit. It helps avoid the 'Père David syndrome'[18] of foreign 'discovery' of matters the indigenous Chinese have known about and understood better for generations, and it allows subtle consideration of 'opaque' issues sometimes unconsciously unintelligible to the external view. To paraphrase Fanon, the 'colonist', cultural or otherwise, when writing of the alien nation invariably writes the history of his own nation.

Research during past decades has offered us an understanding of the processes whereby the female body becomes sexualized, controlled and oppressed. More importantly, it has shown how sport paradoxically plays a vital role in both reinforcing the male–dominated status quo while emancipating women from traditional repression in both Western and Eastern worlds. Scholars now intend to extend their analysis of sporting bodies more extensively to race, class and ethnicity, disability and ageing. However, there remains a rich and untilled soil needing to be ploughed: the historical investigation of female icons, if we want to explore further the body in sport. We need detailed stories of individuals. Without individual effort evolution would never occur. Without many remarkable women who devoted their lives to the cause of women's physical liberation, women's political and economic freedom would never have been achieved. Such women are heroines of history. Although different cultures have produced very different heroines, in this book they have one thing in common: the ambition to free women's bodies through sport. They pursued this ambition with great passion and demanded it with great bravery. Their personalities created the reality of the history they dominated. Through their actions they extended the taxonomy of female types and revealed the potential of women's dynamism. It is important that the taxonomy is expanded further and that the heroic actions that women have historically performed be recognized, researched and recorded. This book is intended as a plea. Over and above the call of Hall and Pfister to write about, for example, women's sports organizations,[19] we make a plea for individual stories because the history of individual women and of their ambition has been, and is, in too short supply.

Picasso's masterpiece *The Race* shows two women pressing ahead through wind and storm. The strong wind, stormy sea and the dark clouds in the background suggest that there is a violent storm on the way. The held hands, the purposeful bodies and the joyful expressions seem to be saying 'let the storm become more violent'. The images of these women bring together many of the themes of this book. It is as well to recall, however, that the women in this book do not belong to the imagination of painters. They are flesh and blood heroines of history, who have run, or are still running, a good race! Qiu Jin, the Chinese heroine, once wrote:

> Don't say
> A woman can never make a knight,
> Do you hear
> The double-edged sword is singing
> On her wall day and night.[20]

NOTES

1. Kathy Davis, 'Embody-Ing Theory: Beyond Modernist and Postmodernist Readings of the Body', in Kathy Davis (ed.), *Embodied Practices* (London, 1997), p.1.
2. Arthur W. Frank, 'Bringing Bodies Back in: A Decade Review', *Theory, Culture and Society*, 7 (1990), 133.
3. Ibid. It should also not be overlooked that others have played their part. J.A. Mangan and James Walvin made an early contribution to the moral debate associated with the male body in their *Manliness and Morality: Middle-Class Masculinity in Britain and America, 1850–1940* (Manchester, 1987). Recently there have been two important contributions to the political analyses of the male body: J.A. Mangan (ed.), *Shaping the Superman: Fascist Body as Political Icon – Aryan Fascism* (London, 1999) and J.A. Mangan (ed.), *Superman Supreme: Fascist Body as Political Icon – Global Fascism* (London, 2000).
4. M. Ann Hall, *Feminism and Sporting Bodies: Essays on Theory and Practice* (Champaign, IL, 1996), p.51.
5. Jay J. Coakley, *Sport in Society: Issues and Controversies* (St Louis, 1990), p.6.
6. Bryan S. Turner, *The Body and Society* (Oxford, 1984), p.59.
7. Roberta J. Park, 'Embodied Selves: The Rise and Development of Concern for Physical Education, Active Games and Recreation for American Women, 1776–1865', *Journal of Sport History*, 5 (1978), 5.
8. J.A. Mangan and Roberta J. Park (eds.), *From 'Fair Sex' to Feminism: Sport and the Socialisation of Women in the Industrial and Post-Industrial Eras* (London, 1987).
9. Debbie Cottrell, 'A Broadening Common Ground in Women's History and Sport History', paper presented at 107th Meeting of the American Historical Association, Washington, DC, 1992, cited in Patricia A. Vertinsky, 'Gender Relations, Women's History and Sport History: A Decade of Changing Enquiry, 1983–93', *Journal of Sport History*, 21 (1994), 13.
10. Patricia A. Vertinsky, *The Eternally Wounded Woman: Women, Doctors and Exercise in the Nineteenth Century* (Manchester, 1990); and 'The Social Construction of the Gendered Body: Exercise and the Exercise of Power', *International Journal of the History of Sport*, 11 (1994), 147–71.
11. Vertinsky, 'The Social Construction', 150.
12. Ibid., 148.
13. Jennifer Hargreaves, *Sporting Females: Critical Issues in the History and Sociology of Women's Sports* (London, 1994).
14. Ibid., p.288.
15. Hall, *Feminism and Sporting Bodies*, p.30.
16. Since the 1980s many academics have tried to document the processes of women's physical emancipation and sport. Articles and books have been published. Among them are K. Dyer (ed.), *Catch Up Men: Women in Sport* (London, 1982), Bourlier San Giovanni, *The Sporting Women* (Champaign, IL, 1983), S. Fletcher, *Women's First: The Female Tradition in English Physical Education, 1880–1980* (London, 1984), H. Lenskyj, *Out of Bounds: Women, Sport and Sexuality* (Toronto, 1986), K. McCrone, *Sport and the Physical Emancipation of English Women 1870–1914* (London, 1988), E. Wimbush and M. Talbot (eds.), *Relative Freedom: Women and Leisure* (Milton Keynes, 1988), M. Burton Nelson, *Are We Winning Yet? How Women Changing Sport and Sports are Changing Women* (New York, 1991), R. Cashman and A. Weaver, *Wicket Women: Cricket and Women in Australia* (Sydney, 1991), A. Guttmann, *Women's Sport: A The History* (New York, 1994), D. Margaret Costa and S.R. Guthrie (eds.), *Women and Sport* (Champaign, IL, 1994), S. Birrell and C.L. Cole (eds.), *Women. Sport and Culture* (Champaign, IL, 1994), P.J. Creedon (ed.), *Women, Media and Sport* (London, 1994), S.K. Cahn, *Coming on Strong: Gender and Sexuality in Twentieth-Century Women's Sport* (Harvard, 1994), J. McKay, *Managing Gender* (Albany, 1997), A. Power-Allred and M Powe, *The Quiet Storm: A Celebration of Women in Sport* (Indianapolis, 1998), and S.J. Bandy (ed.), *Crossing Boundaries: An International Anthology of Women's Experiences in Sport* (Champaign, IL, 1999).
17. Fan Hong, *Footbinding, Feminism and Freedom: The Liberation of Women's Bodies in Modern China* (London, 1997); and Susan Brownell, *Training the Body for China: Sport in the Moral Order of the People's Republic* (Chicago, 1995).
18. Père David was the French missionary who, when in the interior of China, 'discovered' the Chinese deer then named after him in Europe, an animal known of course to the Chinese for thousands of years!
19. M. Ann Hall and Gertrud Pfister, *Honouring the Legacy: Fifty Years of the International Association of Physical Education and Sport for Girls and Women* (Nanaimo, BC, 1999), 1.
20. Qiu Jin, 'Gang Hui' (My Consciousness), in Zhonghua shuju (ed.), *Qiu Jin Ji* (The Collected Works of Qiu Jin) (Shanghai, 1960), p.91.

1

'All the Freedom of the Boy'[1]
Elizabeth Cady Stanton, Nineteenth-Century Architect of Women's Rights

ROBERTA J. PARK

Less than three weeks short of her 87th birthday, Elizabeth Cady Stanton passed away in the New York City apartment that she shared with her son Robert and her recently widowed daughter Margaret Lawrence.[2] The previous day (25 October 1902) 'the grand old woman' of the nineteenth-century 'woman's rights' movement had dictated a letter to Theodore Roosevelt in which she stated:

> As you are the first President of the United States who has ever given a public opinion in favor of woman suffrage, and when Governor of New York State, recommended the measure in a message to the Legislature, the members of the different suffrage associations in the United States urge you to advocate, in your coming message to Congress, an amendment for the enfranchisement of American women, now denied their most sacred right as citizens of a Republic.[3]

This, the last of the hundreds of letters, articles, and other writings that flowed from her active and perceptive mind, reflects the core of the various causes to which she had dedicated more than fifty years of her busy life. Her reform interests included, but were not limited to, abolition, property rights for wives, child custody rights for mothers, liberalization of divorce laws, coeducation, 'dress reform', and above all suffrage.[4] Although her interests were many, as Lois Banner has written: 'As a reformer and public figure, Cady Stanton was first and foremost a feminist.'[5]

She placed particular emphasis upon women learning to be self-reliant. Noting that among earlier societies women had engaged in strenuous agricultural labour and even fought alongside men, if they

now seemed physically weak and incapable of serious intellectual
endeavours (ideologies that were widespread during her lifetime) 'it was
because society had made them so by denying them an education, a
profession, exercise, and sensible clothing'.[6] Whereas social custom
(which assigned to 'the female sex' a separate and inferior sphere)
severely circumscribed their lives, existing laws rendered them even
more powerless. Therefore, gaining the franchise was an imperative. As
a young woman she had become attracted to abolitionist causes.
Nonetheless, she was incensed when the Fourteenth and Fifteenth
Amendments to the United States Constitution, enacted shortly after
the Civil War (1861–65), extended the franchise to black males while
denying this right to *all* females.

It would not be until 1920 that the passage of the Nineteenth
Amendment would grant the franchise to females, but in 1902
opportunities for women were considerably greater than they had been
when Stanton was born in the small town of Johnstown, New York. Her
voice and her pen had done much to bring such changes about. During
the twentieth century her friend and frequent collaborator Susan B.
Anthony would become the better-known advocate; but, as Elisabeth
Griffith and others have observed, among her contemporaries Elizabeth
Cady Stanton was widely recognized as *the* most powerful and articulate
American 'woman's rights' advocate:

> For almost fifty years she led the first women's movement in
> America. She set its agenda, drafted its documents, and articulated
> its ideology … Her statements and actions were recorded in the
> national press; her death in 1902 made international headlines.
> Newspapers called her 'America's Grand Old Woman'.[7]

Various histories and biographies have examined Stanton's social,
political, and religious thought. They have discussed her advocacy of
'dress reform' and her insistent demands that women have the right to
the liberation of their bodies in matters such as birth control. Few,
however, give more than a passing comment on her views regarding
exercise and 'physical culture'.

The middle daughter of Daniel and Margaret (Livingston) Cady's
ten children, Elizabeth was born on 12 November 1815. Childhood was
spent in comparative luxury; self-control and respect for parental
authority were stressed; daughters were instructed in those domestic arts
appropriate to their expected future role as genteel wives. Her father, a

distinguished New York lawyer and judge, served a term in the House of Representatives and also in the New York Assembly. Her son Theodore and daughter Harriot recalled: 'Abounding physical health was united in Elizabeth Cady Stanton with a striking mental virility. She enjoyed that rare combination bodily vigour and temperamental inclination to the sedentary life of the scholar.'[8]

As a child Elizabeth had played blind man's bluff and other games in garret, cellar, and out-of-doors. She roamed in the forests and sailed on the mill pond. In her autobiography *Eighty Years and More: Reminiscences, 1815–1897*, she recalled climbing up and down huge piles of ice-covered wood, building snow statues and forts in the winter, and playing jackstraws, chess, and other games with her sisters and her brother-in-law. Throughout her lifetime their mother had enjoyed games of chance and was, according to her children, 'as intense, as uncompromising, in a game as in a suffrage contest, and defeat was as painful to her in one situation as in the other'.[9]

At Johnstown Academy, where Stanton was the 'only girl in the higher class of mathematics and languages', girls and boys had mingled freely in running races, sliding downhill, and throwing snowballs.[10] Although today these would be considered exceedingly simple pastimes, it must be remembered that before the Civil War organized sport was a rarity.

In 1826, when Elizabeth was eleven, her brother Eleazer, whom she described as 'a young man of great talent and promise', died. The young graduate of Union College was the only one of the Cady's five sons who had survived childhood. His passing had a profound impact upon her life. Seeking to console her disconsolate father, her efforts were greeted with the response: 'Oh, my daughter, I wish you were a boy!' Whereupon she replied: 'I will try to be all my brother was.' She resolved to give less time to play and to devote herself to study because 'the chief thing to be done in order to equal boys was to be learned and courageous'.[11] To these ends, she learned to ride horseback, subsequently expressing pride in her ability to leap a fence or a ditch. A neighbour, the Reverend Simon Hosack, tutored her in Greek, mathematics, and chess. At Johnstown Academy she studied Latin, Greek, and mathematics with a class of boys. (At the time, and for many decades to come, intellectual as well as physical skills were considered fit only for males.) When she presented to her father the 'second' prize in Greek that she had received, he kissed her, sighed, and stated: 'Ah, you should have been a boy!' As she grew older her father (who initially had shown some encouragement for her 'academic and athletic achievements') found it increasingly uncomfortable to condone her more unorthodox activities.[12] Instead he suggested that she turn her attention to 'balls and dinners'; and, indeed, during her lifetime Stanton very much enjoyed both dancing and eating.

The young Elizabeth had read widely among the volumes in her father's library and had listened to debates about legal issues and pleadings in court. She recalled 'continually squabbling' with the law students who frequented her father's office over matters having to do with 'the rights of woman'.[13] It was through such activities, Banner holds, that 'she gained her first knowledge of her society's discrimination against women'.[14] Although her father often extended to them financial assistance, judge Cady was convinced that females had no *legal* redress – an attitude that Flexner and Fitzpatrick contend made a life-long impression on his daughter.[15] 'Nothing pleased me better', Stanton recalled, than arguing about woman's equality, 'which I tried to prove by the diligent study of the books [the law students] read and the games they played … I did not study so much for a love of the truth or my own development … as to make those young men recognize my equality'.[16]

Having graduated from Johnstown Academy, Elizabeth had wished to attend Union College. However, in 1830 no college would accept women. (Oberlin College, which also admitted blacks, did not admit women until 1837.) At age fifteen she began attendance at Emma Willard's Troy, New York Female Seminary. Although the curriculum was considered innovative, she found that few subjects offered to her new things to be learned. These included music, French, and dancing. She admired the fact that Mrs Willard taught her pupils physiology,[17] 'which marked Troy off from the usual young ladies' school of the day' (and created consternation for the girls' mothers). Contact with girls from other parts of the United States and from abroad 'cured' her provincialism; and the experience convinced her that it was ill-advised to educate boys and girls in separate schools. While at the Seminary, she engaged in occasional 'pranks' but missed the company of boys, with whom she had 'grown up, played with for years, and later measured [her] intellectual powers'. Nonetheless, she held Mrs Willard in high esteem, recalling in a 1892 address to the school's alumnae Willard's 'classic features, most genial manners, and profound self-respect (a rare quality

FIGURE 1.1

ELIZABETH CADY STANTON AT THE AGE OF 20

Courtesy: Brigham Young University.

in woman)'.[18] The years immediately following Troy Seminary, she recalled, were the most pleasant of her youth with their 'simple country pleasures … [and] brisk exercise, even with the thermometer below zero'.[19]

Although abolition had not been discussed in her home, Elizabeth was probably inclined in that direction from an early age. Her family's three black servants had been her friends and playmates; at church she had sat with Peter in the pew reserved for members of his race. Each year the Cadys visited the home of her well-to-do cousin Gerrit Smith and his family in Peterboro, New York. Smith was a prominent figure in various antebellum reform movements, especially abolitionism; and his home was one of the stations on the 'underground railway'. Here she was introduced to the views of William Lloyd Garrison, Wendell Phillips, former slave Frederick Douglass, Angela and Sarah Grimké, and other prominent abolitionists.

It was in Peterboro that she met Henry Brewster Stanton, a journalist and prominent speaker in the cause of the abolition of slavery. On the way home from one of their horseback rides Henry expressed his intentions; they were married in May 1840. Elizabeth was twenty-five; her husband was ten years her senior. Because she 'refused to obey one with whom I supposed I was entering into an equal partnership', she had had the word *obey* omitted from the ceremony.[20]

Henry was a delegate to the 1840 World's Antislavery Convention and the two immediately set sail for London. Before departure, Elizabeth and her brother-in-law Daniel Eaton had enjoyed another of their frequent games of 'tag'. Encumbered by her long skirts, she had chased him all over the vessel. During the voyage she read, conversed with the ship's captain and other delegates, played chess, and was hoisted up to the masthead on a chair – an act for which she was chastised by a male passenger who also objected to her calling her husband by his first name in public. (She recorded that both she and husband Henry were possessed of a high degree of self-esteem and were not overpowered by either blame or praise.) When their ship was becalmed off the south coast of England, the Stantons were among those who were rowed the two miles to shore in a small boat.[21]

The World Antislavery Convention marked another important juncture in her life and turned her interests more fully towards 'woman's rights'. Women were accustomed to speaking and voting at meetings of America's National Antislavery Society. At the 1840 London Congress they were denied this opportunity and relegated to the gallery. (William Lloyd Garrison joined them there on principle.) She was incensed! Discussing these and other grievances with Lucretia Mott (the liberal Quaker minister from Philadelphia, who also was in attendance), the two resolved to hold a convention and form a society to advocate the rights of women when they returned home.[22]

Over the next several months Mr and Mrs Stanton travelled in France, Ireland, and Scotland, where they sailed on Loch Lomond, took numerous excursions on foot, and rode donkeys in the Grampian Hills. Against the advice of their host, they decided to climb Ben Nevis (the highest peak in the British Isles) without a guide. The harrowing adventure took them twelve hours; and they were greatly relieved when at twilight a guide met them and led them the rest of the way down. During these ventures, Mrs Stanton wore what she described as a 'short dress reaching just below the knee and a pair of long boots'.[23]

Residence in Boston upon their return brought the Stantons into contact with many of the leading reformers of the times. Elizabeth recalled often walking the two miles to Marlbourgh Chapel to hear Theodore Parker preach and attending lectures and events that kept her 'mental powers' at 'the highest tension'. Both intellectual milieu and physical comforts were considerably different when in the spring of 1846 the growing Stanton family moved to Seneca Falls, New York. Having temporarily left her children with her parents, the young mother turned to overseeing the repairs of the house on the outskirts of town in which they would live for the next sixteen years. Henry was frequently away; the family was growing; and Elizabeth ('a notable housekeeper and excellent cook')[24] was burdened with innumerable duties. She also was called upon to intercede when drunken husbands beat children and wives, and to minister to the sick. Such exhausting tasks left little time for the intellectual activities she so much enjoyed but gave her direct and graphic experience with the many difficulties that confronted women and the necessity of remedying these.

In early July 1848 Mrs Stanton was invited to a gathering at which Lucretia Mott, Mott's sister Martha C. Wright, and others who shared in various ways Stanton's sympathies were present. As Elisabeth Griffith and Alma Lutz have observed, all of the women present had children and were not 'embittered by hard experiences or filled with antagonisms toward men' as newspapers so often portrayed supporters of women's causes. Nonetheless, all 'felt keenly their inferior position before the law, in education, and in the thoughts of the world'. Led by Mrs Stanton, a decision was made to call a Woman's Rights Convention for 19–20 July 1848 at the Methodist Church in Seneca Falls 'to discuss the social, civil, and religious condition and rights of women'.[25]

At this now famous convention, the thirty-three-year-old Stanton invoked a fundamental tenet of the Declaration of Independence when she declared:

> We hold these truths to be self-evident; that all men *and women* are created equal; that they are endowed by their Creator with certain inalienable rights; that among these are life, liberty, and the pursuit of happiness; that to secure these rights governments are instituted, deriving their just powers from the consent of the governed.[26]

'The history of mankind', she continued, 'is the history of repeated injuries and usurpations on the part of man toward woman'. Of the eleven 'resolutions' that comprised the Seneca Falls 'Declaration of Sentiments' only number nine ('that it is the duty of the women of this country to secure the sacred right to the elective franchise') was not unanimously adopted. Husband Henry, who stood by Elizabeth in most matters, was among those who had advised against including such a radical statement. So had Lucretia Mott, who said: 'Oh, Lizzie, if thee demands that thee will make us look ridiculous. We must go slowly.' Stanton was undeterred! Published widely, the Declaration of Sentiments raised such public consternation and rebuke that many women and men who had endorsed it subsequently withdrew their support.[27]

Since the press and most journals were hostile to their cause, the women had to rely upon Horace Greeley's *New York Tribune*, abolitionist newspapers, and those that they themselves established. The first issue of *The Una*, published by Paulina Wright Davis, included an article entitled 'Woman as Physically Considered' in which the author declared: 'Our aim in these remarks is to come to the physical organization of the sexes, and to prove that woman is not man's inferior.' Although men might be physically stronger, they were not necessarily superior beings; and in some respects, the physical ability of women was greater.[28] These were views with which Elizabeth Cady Stanton thoroughly agreed. In an early issue of *The Lily* (writing under the pseudonym 'Sunflower') she began a discussion of the topic 'man's claim to physical superiority'. When women were allowed what society made possible for men, she insisted, there would be many great women 'for we have them here and now in the midst of the most depressing circumstances'. How could man's 'superiority' be fairly claimed until women had had a 'fair trial'?[29]

Reflecting the same sentiments to be found in Mary Wollstonecraft's *Vindication of the Rights of Woman* (1792), Stanton declared: 'We cannot say what the woman might be physically, if the girl were allowed all the freedom of the boy in romping, swimming, climbing, and playing hoop and ball ... Physically as well as intellectually, it is use that produces growth and development.'[30] In *The Una*, for which she also wrote, Stanton asserted that harmonious development of all the 'faculties', which needed daily exercise, was the source of the truest pleasure.[31]

What were the bases of Stanton's views regarding the importance of exercise and 'physical education'? Over and above her own early interest in simple games and outdoor activities – and her insistence that men and women had the right to achieve all of which they are capable – she surely derived some of her ideas from the various reform movements that swept the United States from the 1820s to the 1850s. While living in Boston, where her husband had established a law office in 1842, she had met Elizabeth Peabody and Bronson Alcott (both deeply committed to educational reform), Ralph Waldo Emerson (ideological leader of American Transcendentalism), and others who shared in various ways beliefs in human perfectibility. She also visited Brook Farm, one of several short-lived communitarian settlements that were organized in antebellum America. At Brook Farm enjoyment in out-of-door activities was deemed almost an imperative. Children were to be raised under the constant influence of wise elders and surrounded by intellectual endeavours, pure amusements, and strengthening and exhilarating games. Boys and girls boated on the Charles River; young men and women skated in winter and went sledding and coasting.[32]

She was familiar with the views of feminist writer Margaret Fuller, who was praised by the editors of *History of Woman Suffrage* (Stanton, Anthony, and Matilda Gage) as having had 'more influence on the thought of America' than any woman previous to her time.[33] (The first woman on the staff of *The New York Tribune* and editor of the Transcendentalist journal *The Dial*, Fuller drowned in a shipwreck in 1850.) Believing that her own 'bodily life' had been impaired by the ignorance of her parents, Fuller held that both body and soul must be 'freely developed' and that adults as well as children could benefit from exercise. She approved of what she saw as a growing attention to physical education in the United States and spoke favourably about Dr John Warren's *Physical Education and the Preservation of Health*.[34]

The British-born feminist Frances Wright, likewise, was honoured by the editors of *History of Woman Suffrage*, who credited her 'great educational work' as one of the 'three immediate causes that led to the demand for the equal political rights of women'.[35] Wright, who had been associated with the communitarian settlement at New Harmony, Indiana, called for the full development of all a woman's faculties – physical, mental, and moral. Although it was not necessary for them to emulate all men's activities, women should be taught at an early age to swim, excel in the race, and use 'every exercise which could impart vigor to their frames and independence to their minds'.[36]

Stanton surely knew of the struggles of Elizabeth Blackwell, who graduated in 1849 from the medical school in nearby Geneva, New York (the first American woman to accomplish this goal) in spite of the opposition of its all male faculty. In 1852, publisher George P. Putnam issued Blackwell's *The Laws of Life, With Special Reference to the Physical Education of Girls* in which she criticized the typical curriculum for its failure to attend to the child's physical training and called for the adoption of 'scientific gymnastics' and 'every kind of sport'. 'Education of the mind', Dr Blackwell declared, 'shall always be subordinate to our education of the body, until the body has completed its growth'. In 1869, when Stanton addressed the sixth annual commencement of the New York Medical College for Women, she stated: 'I had always hoped that, with the coming of woman into the profession of medicine, we should see a closer study and observance of the laws of life and health' – and was disappointed that this had not yet occurred.[37]

A firm believer in the importance of proper prenatal care, Stanton took mild exercise and moderated her various reform activities during her own pregnancies. Beginning with the birth of the first of her seven children she had rejected customary child-rearing practices, finding homeopathic ideas more sensible than those of 'regular' doctors.[38] To the consternation of the hired nurse she opened windows and followed recommendations of Andrew Combe, the Scottish physician whose *Principles of Physiology Applied to the Preservation of Health and the Improvement of Physical and Mental Education* was published in the United States in 1836. Following Combe's advice on 'Infancy', she rejected swaddling bandages and insisted on the value of proper clothing, proper diet, and pure air.[39] Infant and child care was one of the many topics about which she frequently spoke during her Lyceum lecture years.

If the adoption of proper clothing was a health issue for children, it was both a health issue and a political statement for females. Fashion – and decorum – dictated that women wear dresses with skirts that reached to the ground. Several layers of petticoats were the norm. From an early age girls (at least middle- and upper-class girls) were heavily corseted. The compression of vital organs and the skeletal deformities that 'tight lacing' caused resulted in a variety of health problems. Shortly after it began publication, *The Lily* began to advocate 'dress reform'.

In 1851, Elizabeth Smith Miller had come to Seneca Falls to visit her old playmate Elizabeth Cady Stanton. For some time Smith had been wearing a costume that consisted of a skirt that fell below the knees and full 'Turkish trousers'. According to Lutz, Miller (who had been brought up to 'romp and play like a boy') had been encouraged to adopt this form of dress by her father Gerrit Smith, 'who maintained that as long as women wore clothes which crippled and handicapped them physically, they would remain in a state of slavery'. A married women with children to care for – and with the support of her husband – Miller had designed a costume similar to that used by women in sanitoriums who were recuperating from 'tight-lacing' and lack of physical exercise.[40]

Often referred to as 'the Bloomer' (after Amelia Bloomer, owner and editor of *The Lily*, which advocated its use), the costume and the issue of 'dress reform' were taken up by several feminists. For the July 1851 *Lily* Stanton wrote:

> The reform in dress now contemplated, does not seem to strike at all minds with the seriousness and the importance it does to mine. A girl of sixteen, in full dress, has not one available limb or muscle in case she wished to escape from some wild animal, or thunder storm, leap a ditch or fence, walk a beam over a stream, or climb some steep ascent.[41]

Instead of the restrictive clothing that fashion dictated, Stanton wished to have a woman rely 'for support and comfort, strength and health, on her own God-given spine and ribs, and the free use of her lungs, her eyes and her powers of locomotion'. She took to wearing the costume, to the displeasure of residents of Seneca Falls. Although her husband made no objections, other members of her family did. On one occasion she reported that so attired she and Henry 'had danced till four o'clock ... . Everybody said I had looked well'.[42] The costume was used by skaters and given endorsement by a growing number of 'physical culturalists'.[43] (Drawings of women in Dioclesian Lewis's 'new gymnastics',[44] first published in an 1862 series of articles in Henry Barnard's *American Journal of Education*, clearly are wearing a version of the 'bloomer'.) As more women began to adopt the costume, the clergy invoked the Scriptures to condemn it and the general circulation press increased its denunciations. The costume caused so much ire that most women's rights advocates came to the conclusion that it was impeding their other efforts and gave up wearing it.

Mrs Stanton put into practice many of the ideas that she had regarding the importance of exercise. Aware that boys needed healthy diversions, she had swings, bars, and ladders put up in the grounds of her home and had the barn equipped with gymnastic apparatus for use on rainy days. So that her sons would not frequent the town's billiard establishment (where gambling and other vices might tempt them) she bought a table for the home. She organized a dancing school for the youth of Seneca Falls and fostered the creation of a boys' gymnasium. Since it was important that girls also 'grow up strong, well-developed, and free', she often marched a number of them to the gymnasium after school, where they were given the same exercises as the boys.[45]

Among the many subjects that continued to engage her active mind were coeducation and the liberalization of divorce laws. As Mary Wollstonecraft had been a half century earlier, Elizabeth Cady Stanton was a staunch advocate of educating the sexes together. (Paradoxically she sent her two daughters to all-female Vassar College rather than to one of the coeducational institutions that began to open after the Civil War.) When friend and co-labourer in the field of woman's rights, Susan B. Anthony, was asked to address the New York State Teachers' Association on the subject of educating the sexes together, she turned to Stanton for help in developing her speech. At the urging of Stanton, the following year Anthony offered a resolution that would have had all schools and colleges open their doors to women.[46]

In March 1860, Stanton had addressed the Judiciary Committee of the New York Legislature on another of her favorite topics – the extension of women's property rights. In April, she wrote to Anthony indicating that she had just finished a speech to be delivered at the forthcoming Woman's Rights Convention. Its subject was reform of divorce laws, a topic that would absorb an increasing amount of her attention. Not only must women have the opportunity to free themselves from brutal and drunken husbands, they had a right to dissolve a loveless union.[47] In editorials for *The Revolution*, a journal that she began with the abolitionist Parker Pillsbury in 1868, she regularly attacked existing divorce laws. This did not mean that Stanton took marriage lightly. Quite the contrary! She repeatedly insisted upon the importance of educating sons and daughters 'into the most exalted ideas of the sacredness of married life, and the responsibilities of parenthood'. What she objected to was that the marriage contract was a wholly unequal and unjust one as it robbed women of their rights as persons, their rights to their children, their property, their wages, and their 'life, liberty and the pursuit of happiness'.[48]

During the Civil War many individuals committed to advancing women's position in society turned their attention and support to other causes. Both Stanton and Anthony remained fully committed. In spring 1862, she and the children moved to New York City where Henry's new job had taken him. Fort Sumter had been fired upon the previous April and war was raging. She wrote to a cousin about her boys 'drilling every afternoon in the gymnasium' and her girls playing and skating outdoors. 'I place the gymnasium above the meeting house', she continued, and 'I have great respect for saints with strong bodies.'[49] It is probable that this last sentence was a reference to an article titled 'Saints and Their Bodies' that the *Atlantic Monthly* had published in 1858. Its author, Thomas Wentworth Higginson (a frequent writer on the benefits of physical activity and a supporter of expanded opportunities for women) criticized the limited attention that Americans gave to exercise, especially for girls. Commenting on contemporary practices, Higginson wrote:

> In female boarding-schools, teachers uniformly testify to the aversion of pupils to the prescribed walk. Give them a sled, or a pair of skates, or a row-boat, or put them on horseback, and they will protract the period of exercise till the teacher in turn grumbles.[50]

In 1866, the National Woman's Rights Convention (held in abeyance since 1860) was scheduled to coincide with the first meeting of the American Equal Rights Association. With the latter's support, the Fourteenth Amendment was ratified in July 1868. While this settled the status of citizenship (women were nowhere mentioned), it did not settle the matter of enfranchisement. Therefore, a Fifteenth Amendment was drafted. Stanton was incensed when she learned that this would give the vote to black *males* while all females would continue to be excluded. She and Anthony insisted that the wording be changed to include *women*.

At the 1869 meeting of the newly formed Woman Suffrage Association of America (held in Washington, DC), Stanton implored participants to demand a Sixteenth Amendment to enfranchise women. Grace Greenwood, a reporter for the *Philadelphia Press*, was laudatory about Stanton's speech, describing it as a model of composition – clear, compact, elegant, and logical. 'She makes her points with particular sharpness and certainty, and there is no denying or dodging her conclusions.'[51] Stanton then persuaded congressman George W. Julian to introduce such a bill, undertook a tour of several states in an effort to gain support for its passage, and proposed that petitions be carried to

Washington 'by young girls, twenty-one years of age – one from each state – strong, well-developed girls, with sensibly large waists'.[52]

Many abolitionists were alarmed that such efforts might adversely effect the Fifteenth Amendment, which still had to be ratified by the states. Intense debates ensued; and a schism developed among supporters of women's issues. In 1869, Stanton and Anthony founded the National Woman Suffrage Association (Stanton served as its president until 1890). A less radical separate organization (the American Woman Suffrage Association) also was formed.

In 1868, Elizabeth and the children had moved from New York to Tenafly, New Jersey. An opportunity to extend her message about various reforms – and also to earn money for the college education of her younger children – was afforded when in 1869 she became a registered lecturer with the New York Lyceum Bureau. Soon she was earning three to four thousand dollars annually. This new undertaking also provided a degree of independence that had been impossible when her children were young. The previous year she and Henry had mutually agreed to an informal separation. For the next 11 years she spent several months each year travelling to various parts of the United States lecturing on child rearing, property rights, divorce laws, coeducation, sanitary reform, suffrage, and much more.[53] As Banner has observed, this was 'a final step in her declaration of independence from her husband and from the strictures about woman's role that she had learned in her childhood'.[54]

A speaker much in demand, now over fifty years of age, Stanton travelled in all kinds of weather, often at night, usually alone but sometimes with her co-agitator Susan B. Anthony. Although she preferred good food and comfortable surroundings, she endured dingy and uncomfortable hotels and rough fare. At a time when women were expected to remain demurely still, she would walk up and down her rail car for exercise. She also travelled by a variety of horse-drawn conveyances. In California, she and Anthony sailed on San Francisco Bay and made a demanding trip to visit Yosemite Valley. According to her own description, the two decided to descend into the Valley riding 'astride' and had 'suits made for that purpose'. (Convention held that 'ladies' should ride side-saddle.) However, Stanton could not reach the stirrups of her ample steed and decided to walk. The descent was steep and difficult; and she arrived exhausted. A few days later the two visited the Calaveras Grove and rode horseback through a section of one of the fallen and decayed Sequoia trees.[55] During an especially severe Iowa winter, she travelled six hours by sleigh to deliver a lecture. Always immaculately dressed and coiffured, the poised and articulate mother of seven was well received. When the occasional male listener offered an insult her retort was so adroit that the audience usually turned upon him.[56]

In 1879, as women in larger numbers were entering higher education, historian Francis Parkman, arguing against suffrage, declared in the *North American Review* that 'a greater strength', firmer muscles, and 'sterner spirit' impelled men to action and war; while 'rounded outline and softer muscles of the physical frame' destined women for entirely different ends. The article engendered immediate responses from Stanton, Higginson, Lucy Stone, and others who wrote on 'The Other Side of the Woman Question'. Stanton retorted: 'The organism of woman is as complete as that of man.' Coeducation had proved that 'girls were equal to boys in every department of learning'. They now were physicians, lawyers, pastors, and 'laborers in many forms of industry'. Moreover, they could do equally good work in government if given the opportunity.[57]

Stanton continued to support herself by writing. In 1885, at the age of 70 and now quite corpulent, she delivered an address entitled 'The Pleasures of Age'. Returning to themes that she had sounded for more than 30 years, she insisted that those who had 'obeyed the physical laws will have sound bodies and not be racked by pain or disease'. 'Passive exercise' was now her enjoyment – such things as riding in sleighs and carriages and vicariously enjoying the waltz, quadrille, and Virginia reel. Those who had obeyed 'the laws of mind' and enriched their lives with a knowledge of art, science, and literature, she continued, would have 'resources to fill their own lives and make life profitable for others'.[58]

During the 1880s, Stanton spent a great deal of time with her married daughter Harriot in England and with her journalist son Theodore in Paris. While abroad she endeavoured to interest British and French women in establishing an international organization; and in 1888 the International Council of Women was formed. Her husband died in 1887; her remaining sister in 1891. When in 1890, the long separated National Woman Suffrage Association and American Woman Suffrage Association merged, she objected to the section of the proposed constitution that would allow men to hold office because of her commitment to women's self-reliance.

At the request of Anthony, Stanton was named president of the newly formed National American Woman Suffrage Association (NAWSA). In 1892, she resigned the presidency and never again attended any of the conventions. That year she delivered before the Judiciary Committee of the United States House of Representatives what she considered to be her most important speech: 'The Solitude of Self'. 'The Solitude of Self' stressed the absolute necessity of a 'woman's absolute self-reliance – physical, emotional, financial, political, intellectual and legal independence'. In the final analysis every individual must rely upon her or his resources. Women were more vulnerable, however, because custom and law prevented them from adequately preparing themselves for life's challenges:[59]

> The strongest reason for giving woman all the opportunities for higher education, for the full development of all her faculties, her forces of mind and body; for giving her the most enlarged freedom of thought and action ... is the solitude and personal responsibility of her own individual life.[60]

For a long time Stanton had been critical of the Church, which she believed degraded women, and of Biblical authority, which gave this sanction. In *The Woman's Bible* (which appeared in 1895) she provided commentaries on those portions in which women were cast as inferior beings, making such observations as: 'not one word is said giving man dominion over woman' (Genesis i, 26–28). *The Woman's Bible* elicited a storm of protests from clergy yet went to seven printings before the year was out. Younger suffragists were alarmed that criticisms it elicited might impair their other efforts, but Stanton remained undeterred. Whereas many of the younger group found her intransigent, Stanton found the younger leaders timid. She was, as several biographers have observed, 'a defiant old lady'.[61]

As she further aged, Stanton became increasingly obese and subject to various aliments. She visited the Dansville Sanatorium, where she underwent a regimen consisting of massage, electrical therapy, dietary therapy, and a various exercises of the 'Swedish movement cure'. Although she lost only five pounds, she said that she 'felt like a new being'.[62] During the 1890s, the 'bicycle craze' was sweeping the nation and women were taking to 'the wheel' in increasing numbers. This new activity, Stanton held, 'was a great blessing to our girls' because it compelled them to develop 'self-reliance' and cultivate their 'mechanical ingenuity' (they often had to repair their cycles). In 1896, she recorded in her diary that she had just finished for *The Wheelman* (which some years earlier had changed its name to *Outing*) an article dealing with such questions as: 'Should women ride the bicycle?' 'What should they wear?'[63]

By 1900, her eyesight was failing rapidly yet she continued to express her views on a range of topics. Her voluminous writings sometimes reflect inconsistent thought (what human beings do not!), but throughout her lifetime Elizabeth Cady Stanton remained constant in her belief that women have a right to develop all their powers and share equally in the benefits and responsibilities of life. In a tribute published in the *American Review of Reviews* shortly after her death, Ida Husted Harper wrote:

> Mrs Stanton was able to disarm every criticism made of the early advocates of woman's rights. She was a wife, mother, far from angular, beautiful in person, and exquisite in dress. Her voice was rich and musical, and the powerful philosophy of her arguments ... relieved by a fine humor and graceful wit ... conquered prejudice and captivated an audience ... . But it seemed as if no woman ever so deeply felt the disgrace of her legal and political condition ... certainly none ever so strongly expressed it by voice and pen.[64]

These sentiments were echoed by her granddaughter Nora Stanton Blatch, the first woman to graduate from Cornell University (1905) with a degree in civil engineering:

> [H]er dignity, humor, and unbounded health and energy carried her through an ocean of ... frustrations, prejudice, and intolerance ... .My memories of my Queenmother, as all us grandchildren called her, are of a delightful person to live with and play with.[65]

Following her death, Susan B. Anthony, Stanton's long-time friend and fellow labourer in the cause of women's rights, declared her to have been 'the central figure through two generations ... of women's evolution'. Every one of the 'privileges' that women now enjoyed had been 'demanded by her before the present generation was born'.[66]

NOTES

1. These words appear in an article that Stanton wrote (under the pseudonym 'Sunflower') for *The Lily* in April 1850.
2. After her husband's death Lawrence came east to study 'physical culture'. She subsequently became a professor of physical training at Columbia Teachers College. See L. Banner, *Elizabeth Cady Stanton: A Radical for Woman's Rights* (Boston, 1980), pp.170–71 (hereafter *Radical for Woman's Rights*); E. Griffith, *In Her Own Right: The Life of Elizabeth Cady Stanton* (New York, 1984), p.174 (hereafter *In Her Own Right*).
3. T. Stanton and H.S. Blatch (eds.), *Elizabeth Cady Stanton as Revealed in her Letters, Diary, and Reminiscences*, Vol.I (New York, 1922) p.368 (hereafter *Elizabeth Cady Stanton*, I.). According to Griffith, *In Her Own Right*, Stanton 'sent a similar appeal to Mrs Roosevelt', p.217. During the nineteenth century, the term 'woman's rights' – rather than the later 'women's rights' – was frequently used.
4. Reflecting upon her mother's career, Margaret Lawrence declared in 1920: 'Elizabeth Cady Stanton's demand from the first was these three little words: "votes for women".' Margaret Stanton Lawrence, letter to the editor of the *Indianapolis Star*, 12 November 1920.
5. *Radical for Woman's Rights*, p.69.
6. Ibid., p.72.
7. *In Her Own Right*, p.xiii; 'Elizabeth Cady Stanton Dies at Her Home', *New York Times*, 27 October 1902, 1. *The Times*, 28 October 1902, commented upon various aspects of her career and noted that at the time of her attempt to run for Congress in the 1860s Stanton had said: 'My creed is free speech, free press, free men, and free trade – the cardinal points of democracy', 8. As editor Nancy F. Cott observes in the introduction to 'Woman Suffrage' in *History of Women in the United States: Historical Articles on Women's Lives and Activities*, Vol. XIX, 2 (Munich, 1994) 'historians generally date the beginning of the woman suffrage movement from the 1848 Seneca Falls meeting'. p.xi.
8. *Elizabeth Cady Stanton*, Vol.I , p.xiii.
9. Ibid., p.xvii; E.C. Stanton, *Eighty Years and More: Reminiscences, 1815–97* (New York, 1898), pp.5–6, 27–28 (hereafter *Eighty Years and More*). This work is a somewhat modified version of Vol.I of *Elizabeth Cady Stanton*.
10. *Eighty Years and More*, p.33.
11. Ibid., pp.20–1.
12. *In Her Own Right*, pp.8–9.
13. *Eighty Years and More*, p.34.
14. *Radical for Woman's Rights*, p.7.
15. E. Flexner and E. Fitzpatrick, *Century of Struggle: The Woman's Rights Movement in the United States* (Cambridge, MA, 1975), p.67.
16. *Eighty Years and More*, p.48.
17. Before the Civil War, indeed before the 1880s, the term 'physiology' was far more likely to refer to 'health and hygiene' than to anything of a scientific nature. The literature dealing with various antebellum 'health reform' movements is now considerable. For a good account of women's participation in these matters, see M.H. Verbrugge, *Able-Bodied Womanhood: Personal Health and Social Change in Nineteenth-Century Boston* (New York, 1988).
18. *Elizabeth Cady Stanton*, I, pp.37–43; 'Mrs Stanton's School Days', *The Woman's Journal*, 25 June 1892, pp.208–9.
19. *Eighty Years and More*, pp.45–6.
20. For a sensitive account of this phase of Stanton's life, see A. Lutz, *Created Equal: A Biography of Elizabeth Cady Stanton, 1815–1902* (New York, 1940), pp.13–23 (hereafter *Created Equal*).
21. *Eighty Years and More*, pp.71–6.
22. Ibid., pp.76–91. Perhaps no other event in the eventful life of Elizabeth Cady Stanton has received more attention from historians that her attendance at the 1840 Convention.
23. Ibid., pp.100–3.
24. Ibid., pp.132–5; 'Elizabeth Cady Stanton: Some Reminiscences of Her Life in Seneca Falls by an Old Acquaintance', 18[??]. Seneca Falls Historical Society.
25. *Created Equal*, pp.44–54; *In Her Own Right*, pp.50–1.

26. E.C. Stanton, S.B. Anthony and M.J. Gage (eds.), *History of Woman Suffrage*, Vol. I (New York, 1881), p.70 (hereafter *Woman Suffrage*, I).

27. Ibid., pp.71–4; *Created Equal*, pp.44–54; Margaret Stanton Lawrence, letter to the editor of the *Indianapolis Star*, 12 November 1920. In this letter Lawrence recalled two incidents in particular. Apparently, Stanton once had asked Frederick Douglass what blacks most needed and Douglass had replied, the ballot, to which she responded: 'I see that the ballot is exactly what we women need'. On another occasion the famous orator Daniel O'Connell had replied to her inquiry regarding whether or not he would secure the Irish vote: 'No ... but when asking for anything always demand the utmost then you'll get something.'

28. *The Una* (1 February 1853), 8–9.

29. *The Lily* (1 February 1850), 12.

30. *The Lily* (1 April 1850), 31. On Wollstonecraft and other eighteenth-century women who advocated similar views, see R.J. Park, 'Concern for the Physical Education of the Female Sex from 1675 to 1800 in France, England, and Spain', *Research Quarterly*, XL (1974), 104–19.

31. *The Una* (September 1885), 140.

32. On Emerson, Margaret Fuller, and others, see M.V Allen, *The Achievement of Margaret Fuller* (University Park, PA, 1979); R.J. Park, 'The Attitudes of New England Transcendentalists toward Healthful Exercise, Active Recreations, and Care of the Body: 1830–1860', *Journal of Sport History*, VII (1977), 34–50. On Brook Farm and other groups, see R.J. Park, 'Harmony and Cooperation: Attitudes Toward Physical Education and Recreation in Utopian Social Thought and American Communitarian Settlements, 1825-1865', *Research Quarterly*, XLV (1974), 276–92.

33. *Woman Suffrage*, I, pp.801–02.

34. Margaret Fuller, *Woman in the Nineteenth Century and Kindred Papers Relating to The Sphere, Condition and Duties of Women*, A.R. Fuller (ed.) (Boston, 1860), p.96; J.C. Warren, *Physical Education and the Preservation of Health* (Boston, 1846).

35. *Woman Suffrage*, I, p.52.

36. See A.S. Rossi (ed.), *The Feminist Papers from Adams to Beauvoir* (New York, 1963), pp.105–7.

37. Elizabeth Blackwell, *The Laws of Life, With Special Reference to the Physical Education of Girls* (New York, 1852), p.34; E.C. Stanton, 'Commencement of the Medical College for Women', *The Revolution*, III (1869), 201.

38. On antebellum attitudes regarding health and exercise, see J.C. Whorton, *Crusaders for Fitness: The History of American Health Reformers* (Princeton, NJ, 1982); H. Green, *Fit for America: Health, Fitness, Sport and American Society* (New York, 1986); R.J. Park, 'Healthy, Moral, and Strong: Educational Views of Exercise and Athletics in Nineteenth Century America', in K. Grover (ed.), *Fitness in American Culture: Images of Health, Sport, and the Body, 1830–1940* (Amherst, MA, 1989), pp.121–68.

39. *Eighty Years and More*, pp.115–19.

40. *History of Woman Suffrage*, I, pp.127–8; *Created Equal* pp.63–70

41. 'Our Costume', *The Lily* (July 1851), 50.

42. *Created Equal*, p.69.

43. *Elizabeth Cady Stanton*, I, pp.170–4; D.C. Bloomer, *Life and Writings of Amelia Bloomer* (Boston, 1895), pp.65–81.

44. D. Lewis, *The New Gymnastics for Men, Women, and Children*, 7th edn (Boston, 1864).

45. *Created Equal*, p.100.

46. Ibid., pp.103–4.

47. Ibid., pp.111–18.

48. E.C. Stanton, 'Divorce Versus Domestic Warfare', *The Arena*, I (1890), p.563; E.C. Stanton, 'Women Their Own Emancipation', *The Woman's Journal* (25 August 1894), 1.

49. *In Her Own Right*, p.108; T. Stanton and H.S. Blatch (eds.), *Elizabeth Cady Stanton*, Vol.II (New York, 1922), p.91.

50. T.W. Higginson, 'Saints and Their Bodies', *Atlantic Monthly*, I (1858), 591.

51. Quoted in *Created Equal*, p.169.

52. *In Her Own Right*, pp.125–38; *Created Equal*, p.181.

53. *Created Equal*, pp.189–206.

54. *Radical for Woman's Rights*, p.111.

OLSON LIBRARY
NORTHERN MICHIGAN UNIVERSITY
MARQUETTE. MICHIGAN 49855

55. *Elizabeth Cady Stanton*, I, pp.241–6.
56. *Created Equal*, pp.189–206.
57. F .Parkman, 'The Woman Question', *North American Review* CXXIX (1879), 303-21; E.C. Stanton, 'The Other Side of the Woman Question', *North American Review*, CXXIX (1879), 432–39.
58. E.C. Stanton, 'The Pleasures of Age: An Address Delivered on her 70th Anniversary', Seneca Falls Historical Society.
59. *In Her Own Right*, pp.203–4.
60. E.C. Stanton, 'The Solitude of Self', in E.C. DuBois, *Elizabeth Cady Stanton/Susan B. Anthony: Correspondence, Writings, Speeches* (New York, 1981), p.247.
61. *In Her Own Right*, pp.191; 210–13.
62. *Eighty Years and More*, p.419.
63. Ibid., pp.456–57; *Elizabeth Cady Stanton*, II, pp.318–19. (It does not appear that these remarks were ever published.)
64. I.H. Harper, 'Elizabeth Cady Stanton', *American Review of Reviews*, XXVI (1902), 715.
65. N.S. Blatch, 'Life Sketch of Elizabeth Cady Stanton', Seneca Falls Historical Society.
66. S.B. Anthony, 'Woman's Half-Century of Evolution', *North American Review*, CLXXV (1902), 800.

2

A Martyr for Modernity:
Qiu Jin, Feminist, Warrior and
Revolutionary

FAN HONG and J.A. MANGAN

PROLOGUE

Warrior, 'maid-in-waiting' and victim – these are the three roles assigned to women in war. However, in the history of warfare, women warriors are in short supply, – the saints and sacrificial lambs predominate.[1] Those women who do choose to fight 'claim a place for themselves among those men who have achieved the respect of their fellow citizens for their willingness to risk their lives for the sake of their country or their ideals'.[2] This was certainly the claim of the Chinese patriot, warrior, educationalist, feminist and revolutionary, Qiu Jin, a woman who sought to project a masculine image in order to acquire independence, equality and power by transference. She created a dramatic visual language to make her political point and to establish her desired political identity. Her system of iconic signs was strongly masculine. She was her own visual propaganda, a feminist who rejected the feminine – the perceived source of inferiority, oppression and servitude. Her chosen self-image was direct, simple, clear. It was her statement of both desire and intent. To other radical women, it was an invitation and an incantation. On both levels it worked. To them she was a woman for her time: 'In a world of symbols defeat was ... transformed into triumph.'[3] This was precisely the fate of Qiu Jin.

In one recent study of women and war in the twentieth century,[4] it has been noted that women seemed to gain as individuals or as a group under the various wartime situations. Posthumously, if tragically, this was true of Qiu Jin in her brief declared war on Chinese feudalism. She sought martyrdom and through it she achieved immortality and the certainty that her message was not ignored.

SETTING THE SCENE

By the end of the nineteenth century Chinese radicals had begun to seek
a new image for Chinese women. Modern feminism found its first
Chinese exponents among those members of the educated urban élite
who were passionate about the future of their country. Many Chinese
radicals were ready to accept unreservedly the foreign claim that 'the
position of women was one of the dark blemishes in the social life of the
Chinese'.[5] These radicals devoted considerable energy to reform. The
traditional female image was now strongly challenged.[6] However,
Chinese sympathetic receptivity to Western images of women and any
impulse to redefine femininity depended less on the intrinsic moral
merits of those images than on China's humiliating and inferior
international position. Women's physical health accordingly became a
foremost concern and almost every reformer now stressed the need to
'unbind' the feet of Chinese women and advocated physical exercise for
women substantially if not completely to ensure *fit* mothers for a *fit*
nation which was able to resist imperialism in all its forms.[7] One indirect
and unsought consequence was that the bodies of women became the
battleground for redefining a fundamental human relationship, that of
woman and man. For conservatives, traditional sexual inequality was a
requisite barrier to improper egalitarianism,[8] while for liberals sexual
equality was a necessary requirement for proper egalitarianism.[9]

As mentioned above, what aided the reforming liberals in their
struggle for change was China's political feebleness and military
humiliation by the European powers in the second half of the nineteenth
century. China, claimed these liberals, needed healthy mothers to bear
healthy sons to preserve and promote the state. Women's traditional
bodies were described by liberals as 'political anomalies'. They required
reconstruction.[10] The general principle laid down for women's education
was 'to nurture women's moral restraint, to provide necessary
knowledge and skills, while paying attention to physical development'.[11]
Consequently, footbinding was widely and increasingly opposed.
Physical education was advocated to promote 'the regular growth of the
body and the smoothness of movement' of the four limbs. Health
measures such as sound diet, hygiene and physical exercise became
increasingly centred upon the functions of reproduction and child-
rearing.[12] However pressing the need for fit, healthy and strong mothers,
many male reformers opposed women's demands for *full* equality on the

grounds that women's physical nature, represented in general by her body but manifested in particular by her reproductive function, disqualified her from public life and thus from full participation in society. As the well-known reformer Liang Qichao[13] claimed, 'The equality of men and women meant not that women could do whatever men could, but that the different endowments of the sexes – modesty, gentleness, tenacity and patience on the part of women; boldness, strength, and grasp of general principle on the part of men – were to be equally respected. They made an equally important contribution to society.'[14] In short, for many progressive men, through their bodies women still represented and confirmed earlier social realities and ideals. The 'new woman' was to be 'a helpmate to her husband, a source of instruction for her sons; in her immediate surroundings, she would give ease to the family, and in a wider sphere she would improve the race'.[15] In other words, 'Traditional prejudices were not set aside but rather incorporated into the language of reform.'[16]

Although advocacy of the virtuous wife and healthy mother held the field among most radical men at the turn of the century, there was a growing number of educated women who were not satisfied with this narrow if improved perception of their role. Some were destined to attempt to play a crucial part in their country's future.[17] Qiu Jin, for one, who in the role of subversive physical educator, was executed in 1907 after leading an abortive anti-feudal rising in Zhejiang province, was a leading pioneer of Chinese women's emancipation. She can be seen as a striking period representative of feminism, radicalism and revolution.

QIU JIN'S EARLY LIFE IN HUNAN AND BEJING

Qiu Jin's family was a respectable gentry family from Shaoxing, a city of Zhejiang province. Several generations had served as officials of the Qing government. Her great-grandfather served as the county magistrate in various places in Zhejiang. Her grandfather was a senior official in Fujian province (Amoy). Her father served as a secretary in the governor's office in Taiwan and senior official in Fujian and Hunan provinces, respectively.[18]

Qiu Jin was born in 1877 in Fujian.[19] She moved with her father to Taiwan in 1891 when her father was invited by the governor of Taiwan, the reformer Shao Youlian,[20] to serve as his secretary. Two years later, when Shao Youlian became governor of Hunan, Qiu Jin and her father moved with him to Changsha, the capital of Hunan province.[21] From a very early age Qiu Jin moved with her grandfather and father from one place to another. This widened her vision, broadened her experience and made her different from many Chinese women of her time. Inspired by Western ideals and the associated change of the attitude towards women's education in the Late Qing dynasty, her family paid the same attention to their boys' *and* girls' education. Her father employed teachers to teach all his children at home. Qiu Jin thus received a good education along with her sister and brothers. She was 'a clever girl with a very good memory'[22] and the favoured daughter of the family. Her love of poetry was one of Qiu Jin's great passions. Her favourite poets were Du Pu and Xin Qiji, the famous patriotic poets of the Tang and Song Dynasties.[23] In 1887 when she was eleven years old Qiu Jin started to write poetry herself.[24] Through her poetry she earned the title of a 'talented girl'.[25] Her first patriotic poem was written in 1894 on the outbreak of war between Japan and China.[26] On her death she left more than 100 poems.[27] Many were patriotic. In general, Qiu Jin's upbringing was both extremely advantaged and unconventional. She was not encouraged to learn what was normally considered women's work, such as sewing and cooking. Instead, she learned to ride a horse and use a sword.[28] Her travels, education and upbringing turned her into a questioning, talented, unconventional and strong-willed young woman, accustomed to having her own way. (Figure 2.1.)

The turning point of her life was her marriage. In 1895 her father was appointed as a senior official of Xiangxiang county, Hunan province. The family therefore moved from Changsha to Xiangxiang. There Qiu's father became a friend of the wealthy merchant and philanthropist Wang Fuchen.[29] The Wang family was one of the richest families in the county. The two men arranged for Qiu Jin to marry Wang Fuchen's youngest son, Wang Zifang. In April 1896, when Qiu Jin was twenty, the wedding took place despite the fact that she was unhappy about it. She later wrote: 'The marriage was my father's wish, not mine.'[30]

Qiu Jin's marriage, by traditional standards, would have been considered a happy one. Although Wang's family was conservative there was no indication that she was mistreated or restricted. Wang himself had the reputation of a rich man with a kind heart.[31] Wang's family respected Qiu Jin, because she came from an educated middle class family. Her position in her husband's family was strengthened by the birth of a son in 1897.[32] Her relationship with her husband in the early

FIGURE 2.1

QIU JIN (1877–1907)

years was normal. Her husband, according to Qiu's daughter, was educated, pleasant and handsome, but not ambitious.[33] However, for Qiu Jin married life proved inhibiting and boring.[34]

While Qiu Jin was questioning conservative marriage, others were questioning conservative China. Many progressives appreciated that if China was to grow strong in order to catch up with and match the West, major changes to its political system and its culture, including the reform of moral, intellectual and physical institutions and the introduction of a new educational system, were essential. Influential Chinese intellectuals therefore now demanded radical reconstruction. In 1898 a movement, the Constitutional Movement (or the One Hundred Days Reform),[35] was launched with the aim of bringing Western democratic ideas and political practices to China. The Movement was led by Kang Youwei[36] and Liang Qichao and supported by the Emperor, Guangxu.[37] Among other things, the leaders of the Movement considered that Western military exercise and general physical exercise programmes were conducive to boosting their revolutionary ideas, which they saw as embodied, to some extent, in the energy, fitness, stamina, strength and self-reliance produced by such programmes. Kang Youwei wrote a memorandum to the Qing government recommending the abolition of traditional military training and examinations and the creation of Western style military schools throughout China for the new generation.[38] Thus, the idea of saving the country, in part by promoting Western patterns of physical exercise, was advocated. This became a major ambition of the reformers.

Hunan was one centre of the reform movement. Progressives dominated the provincial government. New schools were opened with a Western curriculum including modern physical exercise. New journals and newspapers were published to promote educational change. New societies were formed to discuss and to promote innovatory modern ideas. Anti-footbinding societies were founded to abolish the inhuman practice of 2,000 years.[39] In the implementation of the new radicalism, it was reported that 'Hunan was the most energetic province in the country'.[40] Qiu Jin found herself at the centre of reform and was certainly influenced by it. She read extensively and was attracted by the new ideas: eject the foreign powers and save the country through strength, science and democracy.

Although the Empress-dowager Cixi showed some sympathy for elements of Western modern culture and initially supported the Constitutional Movement, she would not permit the wholesale transformation of Chinese traditional culture and would not tolerate any significant transformation of the indigenous social and political systems. Hence, when she perceived that Western cultural influences had become a threat to the Chinese feudal legacy, she resorted to force to suppress the Movement. The leading reformers were arrested and killed, and the Emperor Guangxi was put under house arrest, and was later poisoned. The Constitutional Movement only lasted for 100 days. Cixi then supported the Boxer Rebellion, which started in 1898 as a movement to drive out the foreigners and to preserve the Qing dynasty.[41] In 1899, when the Boxers besieged the foreign legations in Beijing, Cixi rode the anti-foreign wave by declaring war upon the foreign powers. This untimely decision failed to gain the full support from the provincial governors of the South as well as the court. Hence, when in 1900 the Western allies (Britain, USA, Japan, Russian, Germany, France, Austria and Italy) sent an expeditionary force to Beijing to relieve the legations, the Qing government was unable to put up an effective resistance. The Boxer Rebellion collapsed. A harsh settlement was imposed by the imperial powers, including the payment of an indemnity and permanent stationing of foreign troops between Beijing and Tianjin.[42]

The crushing of the Constitutional Movement of 1898 was a disappointment to Qiu Jin, but the heroes, such as Tang Cichang and Sheng Jin, who died for the cause of reformation, became her inspirational icons.[43] The defeat by the Western allies aroused Qiu Jin's patriotic passion. She expressed it in verse. In one poem she wrote: 'I want to go to the battlefield to die for my country, but as a woman I have to stay at home.'[44] In another, she wrote: 'At this moment, even … a woman wants to leave her home to become a soldier.'[45]

By this time, Qiu Jin was a mother. Her second child, a girl, was born in August, 1901.[46] Then in October, her father died. At the beginning of 1902 Qiu's family turned to trade for a living and opened a local bank (qianzhuang), but it failed at the end of the year. Subsequently, Qiu's position in the Wang family deteriorated.

In the spring of 1903, Qiu's husband purchased a post in Beijing. She therefore moved to Beijing with her husband, mother-in-law and her two children.[47] She remained in Beijing until 1904 when she left for Japan. In the early 1900s Beijing was a congenial social milieu for reform-minded lower-grade metropolitan officials and their wives. The men were interested not only in the traditional pastimes of the privileged – lavish entertainment, art collecting, and gambling, but also in fashionable Western ideas and customs. Their wives, therefore, enjoyed considerable social freedom with little opposition from their husbands.[48] They formed a sisterhood, visiting each other, exchanging poems and discussing modern ideas. They enjoyed this intellectual and physical independence. Qiu Jin soon formed a very close relationship with a group of women who later provided important support when she left home. One of the them, Wu Ziying, the calligrapher, poetess and feminist, became her life-long friend.[49]

Qiu Jin's life in Beijing provoked in her a grave concern about China's future. She had been greatly distressed by the Sino-Japanese War in 1895 and the defeat by the allies in 1900 when she was in Hunan. However, it was the occupation of Beijing by Western troops and the sight of foreign soldiers walking on the streets of the city like masters that shocked her most and convinced her that China was on the brink of disaster. She was now of the view that all Chinese, men and women, should work for their country's salvation.

   Simultaneously with her growing anxieties over her country, during
1902 and 1903 several significant articles and works in translation
touching on the question of female emancipation became available in
China. In 1902 a hagiography of Mme Roland of the French Revolution
was published in which her 'many-sided talents ... her natural gifts for
leadership, her political intrigues, the pathos of her death, were vividly
set forth'.[50] Mme Roland passed into the hagiography of feminist and
revolutionary writers as an exemplar of the forceful and determined
woman patriot. Joan of Arc was similarly adulated. Her biography was
first published in serialized magazine form in 1900, and appeared in
book form in 1904. These Western heroines became role models to
forward-looking Chinese women. With their lives available in the
Chinese language and to a Chinese female audience, the scope of their
influence was marked. However, the most important stimulus for change
was the influence of those radical female students, inspired by
revolutionary idealism, who travelled with their male colleagues to Japan
– at that time in the throes of urgent Westernization.
   Japan attracted the close attention of the Chinese at the time. There
were three reasons for this: first, Japan's victory in 1895 provoked
Chinese envy and ambition. Second, the Japanese modern education
system attracted the admiration of the Chinese. Third, Japan was the
nearest and cheapest place to go for this 'Western learning'.[51] In
consequence, Japan became a favoured destination for Chinese
reformers. For the sake of the future of China, a large-scale migration of
students to Japan took place. It grew from 13 in 1896 to 13,000 in 1906.
It included female students.[52] It was in Japan, therefore, that many
Chinese men and women became acquainted with Western learning,
joined in debate on the future of China, set up revolutionary
organizations and published progressive journals and newspapers, for
example, *New People's Journal* (Xinmin congbao), *The Tide of Zhejiang*
(Zhejiang cao), *Hubei Students Journal* (Hubei xueshengjie) and *The
Journal of Jiangsu* (Jiansu).[53] In Beijing Qiu Jin read them and was
stimulated by them. She wrote to her sister in Hunan in 1902: 'There is
no old Confucian smell in *New People's Journal* (Xingmin congbao) ...
Women in Beijing all like to read it. It provides models for our women.'[54]
While stimulation was all around her, she was particularly fond of the
books about Western heroines. She wanted to follow in their footsteps
and devote her life to move the cause of revolution. In her intensity she
felt increasingly alone. She wrote a poem in July 1902 to express her

feeling: 'Although I am not a man, my heart is more progressive than any man. ... Ordinary people will not understand me. Where can I find people who know me?'[55] By the end of 1903 Qiu Jin felt an acute discontent with her Beijing friends and her family. She no longer found poetry and friendship a sufficient distraction. She no longer found her family life a sufficient outlet for her energy. At the same time her personal life was painful. Her husband had become more and more interested in gambling and prostitutes. Qiu Jin wrote to her brother in Hunan: 'Zifang's behaviour was worse than an animal's. ... He is dishonest, without emotion, gambles, visits prostitutes...'[56] Distressed by her powerlessness, humiliated by her situation and driven by her desire to save her country, in January 1904 she decided to join the radical students in Japan.

Her husband disagreed with her decision and refused to give any financial support. Qiu Jin sold her dowry, left her eight-year-old son with her mother-in-law in Hunan and her two-year-old daughter with her friend in Beijing, and set off for Japan in April 1904. Before she left her beloved country, she wrote a patriotic poem entitled 'The Song of the Sword':

> I look back at the capital Beijing several times,
> I see only the lost country and tears,
> I hear only sad songs,
> For the eight nation allies have invaded our lands.
>
> ...
>
> We Chinese must use the heaven and the earth as a stove,
> Use the sun and the moon as coal to
> make hundreds and thousands of swords,
> In order to drive the foreigners out of our land.
> We must revive our ancestor's glory
> And wash away the humiliation in our history.[57]

The swords she mentioned in this poem, or of which she wrote in other songs, and the one she carried and had herself photographed with later, were to her symbols of struggle and hope. On the ship to Japan Qiu Jin desolately summed up the twenty-six years of her life:

> Sun and moon have no light left, earth is dark;
> Our women's world is sunk so deep, who can help us?
> Jewellery sold to pay this trip across the seas,
> Cut off from my family I leave my native land.
> Unbinding my feet I clean out a thousand years of poison. With

heated heart arouse all women's spirits.
Alas, this delicate kerchief here
Is half stained with blood, and half with tears.[58]

Beneath this sadness was determination also expressed in verse: 'Do not say a woman cannot become a hero, I am now alone to go to Japan to search for the way to save China.'[59]

ARRIVAL IN JAPAN

Qiu Jin arrived in Japan in May 1904. She was resolute in her determination to make the most of her new freedom. From now on her life revolved around the three interlocking themes: education, feminism and revolution. In the autumn, she joined a revolutionary organization, the Society of Harmony (Sanhehui), which aimed to 'overthrow the Qing dynasty and establish a new China'.[60] At the same time she herself founded the Society of Public Speech (Yanshuo lianxihui). The society held a public meeting once a month to discuss current issues and to 'awaken people's consciousness'.[61] Qiu Jin was frequently a key speaker. Public speeches were not enough and Qiu Jin decided to publish a journal. She claimed: 'If we wanted a new society we must educate the ordinary people. We must publish newspapers and journals like the Westerners do. We must write in simple language so that women and children can read and understand it.'[62] Her journal, therefore, was named *Simple Language* (Bai Hua). The journal was published in September. Its aim was to advocate revolution, democracy and female emancipation. In the second issue of the journal Qiu Jin published an article entitled 'To the Two Hundred Million Chinese Women'. She wrote:

> We, the two hundred million women of China, are the most unfairly treated objects on the earth. ... Before many years have passed, without anyone bothering to ask if it's right or wrong, they take out a pair of snow-white bands and bind them around our feet, tightening them with strips of white cotton; even when we go to bed at night we are not allowed to loosen them the least bit, with the result that the flesh peels away and the bones buckle under. The sole purpose of all this is just to ensure that our relatives, friends, and neighbours will say: 'At the so-and-so's the girls have small feet'. Not only that, when it comes to the time to pick a son-

in-law, they rely on the advice of a couple of shameless matchmakers, caring only that the man's family has some money or influence. … When it is time to get married and move to the new house, they hire the bride a sedan chair all decked out with multicoloured embroidery, but sitting shut up inside it one can barely breathe.[63]

In this powerful essay Qiu Jin argued strongly that Chinese women should first release their bodies from the feudal tradition of footbinding and then free their minds to care about their country. Women should come out of their homes and participate in physical exercise. Exercise, she argued, develops women's determination, and kindles women's desire to contribute to the nation's well-being – positive contributions towards a new China. Finally, patriotism, she asserted, would eventually demand revolution, for only if China's rottenness, epitomized by the Qing dynasty, was dug out and only if China's ignorant populace was educated, would the country gain the qualities required to survive and then to flourish.[64]

Women were not excused from her criticisms. Qiu Jin blamed women themselves for their traditionally subservient position. Women had been forced to mutilate their bodies and hide themselves indoors. They had surrendered their rights and denied their abilities by acquiescing in an indoctrination that destroyed independence of thought and of action. Women, she demanded, should develop new mental and physical qualities in preparation for a new era.[65]

She certainly practised what she preached. In 1904 she enrolled in a Japanese language school in Surugadai in the Kanda area of Tokyo and later transferred to Shimoda's Vocational School. This school emphasized physical education and provided a one-year training course for teachers. Physical education was compulsory.[66] In 1905 Qiu Jin wrote to her brother: 'I am in the College. I am tough and healthy. I take part in gymnastics everyday to keep me fit.'[67] Furthermore, she was engaged in militant self re-education and reconstruction. Besides attending the physical education course in the school, she learnt sword fencing and archery at the Martial Arts Society in Tokyo, dressed in male clothing, carried a short sword, practised bomb-making and marksmanship and drank considerable quantities of wine.[68] This behaviour was closely tied to the image of a 'masculine heroine' protesting energetically against traditional restrictions, in love with physical power and attracted to playing a traditionally male role in the cause of female liberation. As Qiu Jin explained: 'My aim is to dress like a man! ... In China men are strong, and women are oppressed because they are supposed to be weak. I want somehow to have the mind of a man. If I first take on the appearance of a man, then I believe my mind too will eventually become like that of a man.'[69] She now gave herself a second name, Jin Xiong, which meant 'able to compete with men'. She also called herself 'Jianhu nuxia' which meant 'Knight-errant of Jian Lake' (the lake by her family home).

Feminism was not simply a gender issue for Qiu Jin. It was an integral part of any answer to the political problem to which she sought solutions. In October 1904 she and her friends reorganized the Humanitarian Society (Gongaihui).[70] The aim of this organization was to promote Chinese women's education and rights. It advocated that Chinese women should join the army and contribute to the cause of throwing out the Qing dynasty and saving China. In the winter of 1904 when she heard that in Hunan, her home town, the conservatives had decided to close down girls schools, she published 'A Letter to The First Girls' School in Hunan' in the *Women's World* (Nuzi shijie). In the letter she encouraged the girls to fight for their education and freedom:

> If we women want to be free from men's oppression we must be independent. To be independent we must have education and learn to make a living. ... If women can support themselves, they will be equal to men. The whole country would not have a wasted person. The country would be strong again. Women's education is very popular in Japan. If any of you want to come to study here I will help you.[71]

She not only encouraged girls and women in China to make trips abroad, but also persuaded women around her in Japan to fight for their independence. When the Editor of the journal of *Subao*, Cheng Fan came to Japan in 1905, he brought his daughter and two concubines with him. Qiu Jin encouraged the daughter to resist her father's arrangement to give her as a concubine to one of his friends, and also urged the two concubines to assert their independence by becoming students.[72]

In June 1905 Qiu Jin joined the Restoration Society (Guangfuhui), a well-known revolutionary party.[73] In July, in addition, she became one of the first female members of the new revolutionary party – Revolutionary Alliance (Tongmenghui) led by Sun Yat-sen.[74] Qiu Jin was elected the head of the Zhejiang (her home province) branch of the party.

On 6 October 1905 the Japanese Ministry of Education issued 'The Regulation for Chinese Students in Japan' which banned Chinese students' political activities, free speech, public meetings and the publication of radical journals and newspapers. The authorities now had the right to censor Chinese students' letters. Chinese students were obliged to obey the Qing government even when they were in Japan. Anyone who disobeyed the Regulation would be sent back to China.[75] The Regulation provoked an intense debate among some 8,000 Chinese students in Japan. Finally they divided into two groups. One opposed the Regulation and called for a strike. They demanded that the Japanese should abolish the Regulation, otherwise all Chinese students would go back to China. The other group argued that study was the priority. They prefer to reach a compromise with the Japanese, obey the Regulation and finish their studies in Japan.[76] On 12 November a radical student, Cheng Tianhua, committed suicide by jumping into the sea in protest against the Regulation. He left a poem and a letter to the board members of the Chinese Students Union in Japan. In the letter Cheng hoped that his suicide would shame those who wanted a compromise and inspire those who had the courage to return to China.[77] Qiu Jin was greatly upset by Cheng's death and she actively participated in the strike. She wrote to her brother:

> Recently we protested against the Regulation. If the Japanese government does not abolish it we will all go back to China. The ambassador to Japan has done nothing to help us. It seems that the Japanese will not change their mind. Our Union, therefore, has asked all Chinese students to take action. Up to now, some 2000 students have returned. I will be back soon.[78]

She went back to China at the beginning of December.

BACK TO CHINA

Qiu Jin arrived in Shanghai in the winter of 1905. After three years in Japan, she had progressed from housewife to revolutionary. She wrote a letter to her friend in Japan to express her determination:

> I am back home now. I will try my best to organise revolutionary activities to save our country, so that we are able to meet in our new country in the future. I do not know whether we will succeed, but I determine to devote my life to the Cause. From 1898 and the

failure of the Constitutional Movement, I have given my life to the cause of salvation. I will not regret it if I die. ... Restoration of China is urgent. There are so many men dead for it, but not a single woman. It is a shame. I will die for the country when it needs me.[79]

In the letter she named the heroes who died trying to assassinate high officials of the Qing government. Although unsuccessful, they had been convinced that the situation demanded their sacrifice.[80] Qiu Jin felt a similar allegiance to nationalist and republican causes. The self-sacrificing, sometimes superhuman, and often tragic militant hero was the model for her. She was always impressed by such famous nationalist figures as Joan of Arc, Napoleon, George Washington, Sophia Perovskaya (who helped assassinate Alexander II), and the nineteenth-century Polish patriots. She read Byron's poetry. She was also inspired by the Chinese heroic figures in Chinese popular literature, especially the women warriors. She was particularly drawn to heroines like Qing Liangyu[81] and Yangjia nujiang (the women in the Yang family)[82] who helped their husbands to try to save the country. She also referred to such semi-mythical figures as Hua Mulan,[83] who disguised as a man, served for years in the army in her father's stead. Qiu used the martial heroic ideal to open up new possibilities for herself as a woman, but she, in fact, divorced herself from the historical figures. The traditional heroines, like Qing Liangyu and the Yangjia nujiang went to the battlefield because all the male commanders had died. The semi-mythical figure Hua Mulan joined the army because of her filial piety (her father was ill). These women were wives and daughter first, and warriors second. For Qiu Jin, her moral commitment and emotional dedication were not to her family but to her country. When she went to Japan she abandoned her marriage and left her son and daughter behind. In Japan she wrote many letters and poems to her friends but none to her children. Although Qiu Jin's happy childhood memories kept her close to her mother and brother, she herself rejected the role of mother and wife. She wanted to be a man, wanted to be a hero who championed the crucial cause of republican revolution. In January 1906 she had herself photographed in male attire: dark three-piece suit, wing collar, soft cloth cap, walking shoes and cane. On the photograph she wrote a verse:

Who is this man staring at me?
It should be me.
I was born into the wrong sex.

...
You and I should have got together long ago,
and shared our feelings;
Looking out across these difficult times our
spirits garner strength.
When you see my friends from the old days
tell them I have scrubbed off all that old mud.[84]

However, since she was still a woman, she believed that through heroic deeds she might wash away the shame of her former subservience, demonstrate her patriotic fervour and illustrate her moral courage. Traditional and modern heroines inspired her to be one of the leaders shepherding the Chinese into the future.[85]

In 1905 Qiu Jin started to write a novel, *Stones of the Jing Wei Bird* (Jing Wei Shi). She completed three chapters in 1905, two chapters in 1906 and six chapters in 1907.[86] However, the book was never finished. Interestingly, it was semi-autobiographical. The main female character was called Huang Hanxiong. She was born into the gentry. She later rebelled against forced marriage, footbinding and seclusion. She was inspired by the most modern ideas of women's emancipation, fled her home and went to Japan. In Japan, she joined a revolutionary party and fought for freedom and salvation alongside male radicals. In the first chapter, Qiu Jin wrote: 'Only with the overthrow of the Qing dynasty, can the country be peaceful and prosperous, can men and women be equal. There is no difference between man and women in terms of human rights, therefore, they should devote their lives to the republican revolution together.'[87] The unfinished book reflected Qiu Jin's ideal of women's liberation – a blend of nationalism, feminism and political principle.

In February 1906 a member of the Restoration Society recommended Qiu Jin for a teaching post involving Japanese physical education and history in the Minde and Xunyang girls' schools in Nanxun.[88] The Principal of Xunyang Girls' School was Xu Zihua, a poetess and educationalist.[89] Qiu Jin and Xu Zihua became very close friends. In April, a conservative member of the board of the school accused Qiu Jin of teaching students revolutionary ideas and forced her to resign. In protest against the accusation Xu Zihua resigned, while Qiu Jin left the school for Shanghai and stayed with friends planning and preparing revolutionary activities. There she almost blew up her room experimenting with explosives.[90]

In October, Qiu Jin returned to her feminist interests. She told Xu Zihua: 'Women must get educated and strive for their own independence. They cannot just go on asking the men for everything. The young intellectuals are all chanting: "Revolution, Revolution", but I say the revolution will have to start in our homes, by achieving equal rights for women.'[91] She decided to publish a journal for women. In January 1907, with the aid and financial backing of Xu Zihua and others, the first issue of the *Chinese Women's Journal* (Zhongguo nubao) was published. Qiu Jin wrote the preface for the first number stating in it that the aim of the journal was to enlighten Chinese women and to promote women's liberation in China.[92] She also published an article entitled 'To My Sisters', in which she gave full and clear expression to her views on female emancipation. She attacked the traditional evil treatment of women involving footbinding, arranged marriage, enforced chastity, confinement and denial of education. To break free from this legacy of oppression Qiu Jin stressed that girls should seek a modern education so that they might earn a living, thereby winning the respect of their families, ensuring their independence, underlining their social importance and developing relationships beyond the home.[93] The journal stopped after two issues because of a shortage of funds. However, Qiu Jin had an opportunity to put her feminist ideals expressed cogently in it into practice when she became Principal of the Datong Normal College in Shaoxing, her home town, in February 1907.

DATONG NORMAL COLLEGE

Datong Normal College was founded in 1905 by Xu Zilin[94] and his comrades of the Restoration Society.[95] The purpose of the College was to train revolutionaries. There was a physical education institute attached to it which was to train revolutionary soldiers. Xu Zilin was a revolutionary and a founder of the Restoration Society. He came from the gentry. He was first a teacher at, and subsequently the Principal of Shaoxin School from 1901 to 1904. He set up Zhejiang Sports Society in the spring of 1905 and opened Datong Normal College in the autumn of the same year. At the beginning of 1907 he decided to go to Japan to learn military training methods for revolutionary purposes. He recommended Qiu Jin as his successor.

Qiu Jin inherited the fruits of a two-year effort by her friends but she extended their revolutionary endeavours beyond the college and used sports societies as locations for the preparation of violent revolutionary action. First, she reorganized the old sports society in Shaoxing and changed its name to the Datong Sports Society. Then she established a new sports society called North District Sports Society. She also tried to found a women's sports society but she failed due to the opposition of local conservatives and decided, therefore, to train women soldiers in the Datong Normal College.[96]

In her role as Principal of the College, Qiu Jin introduced her revolutionary ideas into her teaching, placing a great emphasis on military exercises such as fencing and riding. One of her students recalled: 'We spent most of the time at the college on physical and military training. Every morning we had three hours' military gymnastics class. In addition, every Monday, Wednesday and Friday we had one hour's athletics class.'[97] Another student recalled that Qiu Jin always wore men's clothes, rode horseback astride and insisted on her girls doing physical training. She herself rode, fenced and boxed well. A poem of the time expressed general admiration of her: 'A Heroine (Qiu Jin) is part of male society, her military spirit and physical ability are well-known in Zhejiang. She advocates physical exercise and nobody can compare with her. All admire her.'[98] Qiu Jin ensured that the women in her care were physically capable of taking a strong and active part in her revolutionary schemes. Her aim was nothing less than the development of Chinese women with active minds and bodies, an appreciation of China's crisis and an acceptance of their responsibility for solving it – if necessary, by force. Her poem 'Women's Rights' best expressed her emphatic opinions: 'Men and women are born equal. Why should we let men hold sway? We will rise and save ourselves, ridding the nation of all her shame.'[99] She had the resolve of a Joan of Arc and her concept of the relationship between women's freedom and revolution reflected an intense personal commitment that earned her an early death. She established a local reputation as a scholar and teacher, but also as a deviant and dangerous nonconformist. A woman in her position and with her views was certain to become an object of curiosity and ultimately fear and hatred among the traditionally minded. She was regarded as a dangerous example for girls in the city. Such was the hostility she inspired that on one occasion when Qiu Jin and her students came back from their physical training, she was attacked by reactionaries.[100]

Several months later, Xu Zilin came back from Japan. With his reputation as an educationalist and expert in military training, he was appointed by the Qing government as assistant principle in a police academy in Anqing, the capital city of Anhui province. Xu used the Academy as a training base for revolutionary forces right under the Qing government's nose. He, Qiu Jin and other leaders of the Restoration Society felt that if they sowed the seeds in two places – Anhui and Zhejiang – revolutionary flowers would soon bloom in these places. This would provide support for uprisings in Guangdong province led by Sun Yan-sen. The republican revolution would soon then spread to the whole country.[101]

They decided on simultaneous uprisings on 19 July 1907. Qiu Jin wrote the Announcement of the Uprising of the Restoration Army in which she claimed that the aim was to overthrow the Qing government and establish Republican revolutionary bases in the two provinces.[102] Qiu Jin also drew up elaborate plans for the military organization called the Restoration Army, down to the details of their uniforms and their flag – which she envisaged as a giant version of the ideograph for 'Han Chinese', in black, sewn onto a pure white ground. She also held a number of planning meetings, raised funds, contacted local secret society leaders and won their support, and tried to keep communications open by courier.[103] However, she was never able to reach out to the broader masses who might have supported a revolution. She had no experience of communication with ordinary peasants and urban workers and yet the province was ripe for political violence: a desperate peasantry had endured a succession of near-famine years, poor conditions in the province were exacerbated by the presence of thousands of refugees from beyond Zhejiang, and the famished townsmen of Shaoxing had rioted twice for food in 1907.[104] On 12 May Qiu Jin went to Hangzhou to raise funds for guns. She met Xu Zihua. Xu gave all her jewellery to Qiu Jin. Before her departure, the two women visited the tomb of the Song hero Yue Fei[105] on the bank of the West Lake (Xihu). They walked back and forth until dusk spread over the West Lake and the hills grew dim. Qiu Jin asked Xu Zihua to promise that if she died in the revolution, Xu would bury her beside the tomb of Yue Fei.[106]

The revolution did not go as planned. In Anqing, detailed plans for the armed revolt leaked out. The Governor of Anhui issued an order that all revolutionaries be seized. Pre-empting this situation, Xu Zilin therefore invited the Governor on 6 July to inspect a police drill at his academy. When the Governor arrived, Xu Zilin approached him, gave a military salute in the European manner and, drawing a revolver from his boot, fired at the Governor three times, inflicting mortal wounds. Xu

Zilin then cried out in a loud voice: 'I glory in belonging to the Revolutionary Party!' The Qing government army besieged the academy and finally captured him. He was led before the dying Governor and then before a tribunal, where he frankly declared his revolutionary ideals and ambitions. The Vice-Governor pronounced the death sentence: Xu's body should be opened, his living heart removed and offered to the dead Governor's memory.

Xu Zilin died on 6 July, but the news of his execution did not reach Qiu Jin until 9 July. In the meantime, the relationship between Xu Zilin and Qiu Jin was discovered by the Qing government and on 13 July Qiu Jin learned that government troops were coming to arrest her. The situation was hopeless but she was too involved to flee. With her students she resisted the soldiers in a brief battle and was captured. In her lesser role of physical educator, she was accused of anti-government activity.[107] After interrogation under torture she refused to confess. The conservatives of the city demanded: 'This kind of woman should be executed as soon as possible.'[108] The government also feared that Qiu Jin's comrades would soon start another rising to rescue her. They decided to kill her. In the early morning of 15 July 1907 Qiu Jin walked to the place of execution, the town centre of Shaoxing, in fetters and handcuffs. She was calm and unhurried. When she arrived she said to the executioner: 'Wait a minute, let me have a look and to see if my relatives and friends have come to say goodbye to me.' She looked around, but nobody was there. Her mother had died two years earlier, her brother and sister were in hiding from the Qing government and her friends did not expect that she was going to be executed so soon, for it was only two days since her arrest and they were still planning to rescue her. Qiu Jin then closed her eyes and said quietly: 'Now, I am ready.'[109] She was beheaded at the age of thirty. She was the first female to die for the cause of the republican revolution.

The main inspirations behind Qiu Jin's death were patriotism, emancipation and self-sacrifice. In the moments before her execution a Qing official asked her to write a confession. Instead, she wrote a final single line of verse, a sentence of seven characters containing her own surname Qiu, which in Chinese has the literal meaning of 'autumn', which is linked to rain and wind. Qiu Jin evoked the chill dampness of the autumn and expressed her sorrow for the unfinished revolution and her unfulfilled ambition as a woman led to the heights of revolutionary zeal: 'Autumn rain, autumn wind, they make one die of sorrow.'[110]

None dared to claim the body and it lay on the execution ground until a cleaning woman from Datong College wrapped Qiu's body in a straw mat. A charitable association provided a coffin and they buried her on a near-by hill. Four months later, in November, Qiu Jin's best friends Xu Zihua and Wu Zhiying moved Qiu Jin's coffin to Hangzhou, to the bank of the beautiful West Lake. There they built a new tomb for her.

RESURRECTION AND TRIUMPH

After her death the government closed all the sports societies in Zhejiang province. The term 'physical education' was banned. It now implied 'revolution'.[111] Throughout society anxiety spread. Conservatism was re-established with a vengeance. Young girls, who had given up footbinding, feared that they might be considered revolutionary and reverted to the practice. Girls were taken from school and their books were burned by the old people of the clan. Even Qiu Jin's tomb was destroyed by the government.[112]

However, all was not lost. The revolution to overthrow the Qing government and end the feudal social system, which had dominated China for thousands of years, finally triumphed in 1911. During the revolution Qiu Jin became an inspirational icon to militant girls and women. They either joined the revolutionary army or formed women's regiments. In Shanghai, Wu Mulan, one of Qiu Jin's students, organized the Women's Military Training Alliance and became its commander.[113] Interestingly but perhaps unsurprisingly, Zhejiang, where Qiu Jin had given her life, was an area in which women were most active in the revolution. According to a report in the *Min bao* (News of People), women, led by Lin Zhongxue, established Zhejiang Women's Military Regiment. In their Declaration, they claimed that they were following in Qiu Jin's footsteps and they were determined to fulfil her revolutionary aims and honour her sacrifice. Yun Weijun, a female physical education instructor, was the Commander of the Women's Zhejiang Northern Expeditionary 'Dare-to-Die' Regiment. In the fighting for Nanjing, her troops fought in the front line. People lauded her and she has been revered as a shining star in the history of the republican revolution ever since.[114] For many radical women in this period, Qiu Jin was clearly a model of female accomplishment and her spirit was frequently invoked during the 1911 Revolution.

In the summer of 1912, in Hangzhou, the new Republican government led by Sun Yat-sen held a funeral and built a new elaborate monument for Qiu Jin over her grave. On a new gravestone, was carved in Sun Yat-sen's handwriting style 'Long Live Heroine Qiu Jin'. More than ten thousand people attended the funeral. Nearby a Wind and Rain Pavilion was erected in memory of Qiu Jin's last verse. In Shanghai, Qiu Jin's comrades set up a girls' school named after her. In Shaoxing, at the fifth anniversary memorial service of Qiu Jin's execution, the members of the Restoration Society, decided to 'reinstate the sports society which was founded by Qiu Jin and establish Zhejiang Sports School in her memory'.[115] In 1930 the Restoration Society built the 'Qiu Jin Martyr Monument' at the place of execution in Shaoxing where the heroine gave her life. In 1981 a new even more elaborate monument for Qiu Jin was completed in Hangzhou (Figure 2.2). Sun Yat-sen's words were retained on the new tombstone.

FIGURE 2.2
QIU JIN'S MONUMENT BUILT IN 1981
HANGZHOU, ZHEJIANG PROVINCE, CHINA

Qiu Jin came to mean more than nostalgia. She came to symbolize the new woman of strong mind and strong body pledged to the strengthening of the nation through women's liberation. She proved a continuing inspiration to her sex. There had been little assertion and confrontation before 1900. Now girls and women, with strong bodies and minds, became one of the most important groups to gain prominence in China in its period of twentieth-century social revolution.

EPILOGUE

The story of Qiu Jin is the story of an icon at once central and at the same time marginal to tradition. She contradicted the most cherished customs of Confucian Chinese culture. She was a radical force who thrust her way to the centre of the concentric circles of customs surrounding this culture and was pushed back to the margins by the forces of conservatism. She challenged a long-established mythology of an exclusively masterful patriarchy – and created a counter myth of purposeful patriotic feminism. She was a counter-cultural icon who changed perceptions of Chinese femininity. She gave courage, confidence and purpose to those women who came after her and absorbed her ambitions for modern Chinese womanhood. For them she was a modern national heroine and a personification of a modern nation of equal men and women.

As a revolutionary militant she was a failure: as a revolutionary talisman she was a success. For the Chinese women of the 1911 Revolution hers was an exemplary emancipatory story: subscribe, struggle, sacrifice. Her heroism was firmly outside the historic patriarchal order. Her adulation is thus all the more remarkable because of the profound traditions she rejected, the controversial mannerisms she adopted, the uncompromising attitudes she embraced. She eschewed motherhood, abandoned marriage, dismissed femininity, and yet won acclaim in the most traditional of cultures.

Qiu Jin was admired, respected and emulated by radical Chinese women and men seeking a new society accommodating new women. Her modern feminism struggled to overcome an ancient patriarchy. Here was her appeal. She exuded no moral ambiguity. Consequently, if she was demonized by the conventional, she was deified by the radical – and inspired them as they contemplated and attempted to construct the future.

There is a point, of course, that should not be overlooked. Qiu Jin, in fact, is not divorced from modern culture and political iconography.

Qiu Jin is international in her posture. In the wake of the modern women's movement, women with guns have become a common feature of modern militarism.[116] The reason is obvious. The modern gun is effective whatever the physical strength of the user. Force, that potent means to power, is available to the gun user irrespective of age or sex – with a resulting 'crucial alteration in the sexual politics of violence'.[117]

The Woman with a Gun can now be emphatically heroic – without duplicity, without deceitfulness, without subterfuge. Moral ambiguity in action has been abandoned. She becomes an unambiguous potent force – an armed woman faces an armed man on equal terms – physically psychologically, morally. Equality offers the legal right and responsibility to kill in the name of patriotism. Modern culture has caught up with Qiu Jin.

It is important to recognize the link between the international Women's Movement, the Woman with a Gun and Qiu Jin: 'Women's claims to equal rights, public roles and political recognition all base themselves upon the fundamental claim for as much affectivity as men have traditionally possessed.'[118] In this setting, female political violence signifies equality in any action to bring about political change.

In China Qiu Jin is remembered, so is her poem:

> How many wise and heroic men were there
> In the dust and the dirt of the world?
> Famous heroines may be said to have risen
> Among moth-eyebrows only!
> Liangyu's deeds bring tears to the eyes,
> And Yu-ying's deserts make the blood boil.[119]
> The strokes of their swords
> Whistled like dragons
> And their sounds were followed by pain.
> The perfume of freedom burns our minds.
> When will the grief for our country be vented?
> I admonish you, my companions,
> Put all your strength into the fray!
> Fight, think of peace for this species,
> So that not they alone who wear nephrite belts
> May boast of abundance.
> Deformed feet, three inches long, are for so long!
> They should be abandoned!'[120]

NOTES

We wish to thank Professor Tan Hua of China South Normal University, Zhao Jianhua of Zhejiang University and Editor Yan Xuening of the People's Sports Press for providing source material for this article. We owe a debt of gratitude to the Universities' China Committee in London for its research grant to obtain material.

1. The terms are those of Nicole Ann Dombrowski, the editor of *Women and War in the Twentieth Century* (New York, 1999), p.2.
2. Ibid.
3. Mark Crocker, *Rivers of Blood, Rivers of Gold: Europe's Conflict with Tribal Peoples* (London, 1998), p.205. The statement is about General George Custer but applies equally to Qiu Jin.
4. Drombrowski, *Women and War in the Twentieth Century*, p.2.
5. Fu Jia, 'Chan Zhu Lun' (On Footbinding), *Wanguo gongbao* (International News) (August 1896), p.91. See also Fan Hong, *Footbinding, Feminism and Freedom: The Liberation of Women's Bodies in Modern China* (London, 1997), p.78.
6. The traditional womanhood was under the domination of the 'three obediences': father, husband and son, and it was enforced by chastity, prearranged marriage, concubinage, permanent widowhood, educational ignorance and footbinding.
7. Huan Zhexian, 'Hao xian gao shi' (The Bulletin on Footbinding), *Xiang bao* (Hunan News) (9 May 1898). See also Fan, *Footbinding*, p.78.
8. 'Na nu pindeng zhi yuanli' (The Theory of Sexual Equality), in *Qing yi bao quan bian* (The Complete Works of Newspapers of the Qing Dynasty), Vol.25 (Beijing, 1936). See also Fan, *Footbinding*, p.78.
9. See Jin Yi, *Nu Jie zhong* (Bell of Women), published by the Patriotic Girls School in Shanghai in August 1903. See also Fan, *Footbinding*, p.78.
10. Fan, *Footbinding*, p.79.
11. 'Xuebu zhouding nuzi xiaoxuetang zhangcheng' (Rules of the Ministry of Education for Girls' Elementary Schools), *Zhongguo xinnujie* (China's New Women), Vol.3 (April 1907), p.175.
12. Jia Hong, 'Ai nu jie' (For Women), *Nuzi shijie* (Women's World), no.8 (24 August 1908); Gao Yabin, 'Fei gang pian' (On Abolishing the Three Obediences), *Tianyi* (The Will of Heaven) (1907), pp.11–12. See also Fan, *Footbinding*, p.79.
13. Liang Qichao (1873–1923) was a well-known scholar and a leader of the One Hundred Days Reform Movement of 1898. Exiled to Japan after the conservative coup of 1898, he used his writing to raise support for the reformers' cause among overseas Chinese and foreign governments.
14. See J. Allen Young, 'The Difference Between Men and Women', translated into Chinese and published in Li Youning and Zhang Yufa (eds.), *Jiadai Zhongguo nu quan yundong shiliao* (Source Materials on the Feminist Movement in Modern China) (Taibei, 1975), pp.382–8. See also Fan Hong, *Footbinding*, p.80.
15. This view was advocated by Liao Qichao and several reformers at that time. See Liang Qichao, 'Chuang she nuxuetang qi' (Advocacy of Establishing Girls' Schools), *Shiwu bao* (Current Affairs), no.45 (15 November 1897); Zheng Guanyin, 'Zi yiyizi zhuren lun tan nuxuexiao shu' (On Jiyizi's Letter about Women's Education); Zheng Guanyin, *Shen shi weiyan* (My Opinion on the Current Issues) (Shanghai, 1900), Vol.2, pp.70–1.
16. Fan Hong, *Footbinding*, p.80.
17. Ibid., pp.67–8, 83–90.
18. Guo Yanli, *Qiu Jin nianpu* (A Chronicle of Qiu Jin's Life) (Jinan, 1983), pp.1–4.
19. There is some argument about Qiu Jin's birthday. Some said that she was born in 1875, some said that she was born in 1876 or 1877. According to Guo Yanli's thorough research Qiu Jin's birthday is 1877. This article adopts Guo's view. For details of the research of Qiu Jin's birthday, see Guo Yanli,*Qui Jin's Life*, pp.5–10.
20. Shao Youlian (1840–1901) was born in Yu Yao, Zhejiang province, and was a family friend of Qiu Jin's father. He became the governor of Taiwan in April 1891.
21. See Guo, *Qui Jin's Life*, pp.21–2.
22. Qiu Zhongzhang, 'Liu liu si cheng', *Dongnan ribao – Wuyue chuenqiu* (South-east Daily –

Zhejiang's Spring and Autumn) (1934). Qiu Zongzhang was Qiu Jin's half brother. He published this article recalling Qiu Jin's childhood.

23. Du Pu (712–770) was an influential patriotic poet of the Tang dynasty. Most of his poems are in *The Collections of Poems of Du Pu* (Du Gong Bu Ji). Xin Qiji (1140–1270), a famous patriotic general and poet of the Song dynasty. Most of his poems are in *The Collections of Poems of Xi Qiji* (Jia Xian changduan ju).

24. See Qiu Zongzhang, Spring and Autumn.

25. Tao Yudong, 'Qiu Jin yiwen' (The Story of Qiu Jin), *The Special Issue of the 20th Anniversary of Qiu Jin's Death in Hangzhou* (1927).

26. See Qiu Jin, 'Zhen Zheng Zhushi', Zhonghua shuju (ed.), *Qiu Jin Ji* (Shanghai, 1960), p.78 (hereafter, *Qiu Jin Ji*). In this poem Qiu Jin expressed her anxiety about the future of China.

27. See Guo, *Qui Jin's Life*, pp.173–5.

28. Qiu Gao, 'Qiu Jin Yishi' (The Story of Qiu Jin). The article is in Shaoxin Archives, Shaoxin, Zhejiang province, China.

29. Guo, *Qui Jin's Life*, p.24.

30. Feng Zhiyou, 'Jianhu nuxia Qiu Jin' (Jianhu Warrior Qiu Jin), Quoted in Guo, *Qui Jin's Life*, p.25.

31. Guo, *Qui Jin's Life*, pp.23–4; Qiu Canzhi, *Qiu Jin gemingzhuan* (Biography of Qiu Jin) (Taibei, 1984), pp.5–6.

32. Qiu Jin's son was Wang Yuante (1897–1955). He grew up with his grandmother. He later graduated from Chengfeng University and worked as a journalist and a middle school teacher. He remained in mainland China after 1949 and became Secretary of the Hunan Office for Research on Archives.

33. Qiu Canzhi, *Biography of Qiu Jin*, pp.6–7.

34. Ibid., pp.715–18.

35. The Reform Movement started on 11 June and ended on 21 September 1898. It only lasted about 100 days. So it was called 'the One Hundred Days Reform'. During this period Kang Youwei and his supporters influenced Emperor Guangxu to issue edicts on political and economic reform. It ended when Cixi staged a coup, imprisoning the Emperor and executing six leading reformers.

36. Kang Youwei (1858–1927) was a Confucian scholar, influential in late Qing reform movements. His plans for reform were supported by Emperor Guangxu in 'the One Hundred Days Reform' of 1898.

37. Guangxu (1871–1908) was chosen at the age of four by his aunt Cixi to be the ninth emperor of the Qing dynasty after the death of his cousin Emperor Tongzhi in 1875. Sympathetic to the appeals of reformers such as Kang Youwei, Guangxu helped launch the One Hundred Days Reform Movement in 1898, but was imprisoned by Cixi that same year for supposedly plotting to remove her from power.

38. Qiao Keqin and Guan Wenmin, *Zhongguo tiyu shixiangshi* (Chinese Sports Philosophy) (Nanzhou, 1993), pp.204–5.

39. See Charlton M. Lewis, *Prologue to the Chinese Revolution: The Transformation of Ideas and Institutions in Hunan Province, 1891–1907* (Cambridge, MA, 1976).

40. Fan Wenlan, *Zhongguo jindaishi* (The History of Modern China) (Beijing, 1955), p.301.

41. Jian Bozan (ed.), *Zhongguoshi gangyao* (The History of China) (Beijing, 1964), Vol.4, pp.81–92.

42. Ibid., pp.96–104.

43. Tang Cichang (1871–1900) was a famous reformer in Hunan. When the Reform Movement failed in 1898 he was exiled to Japan. Later he came back to China to organize the 'Independent Army'. Its aim was to 'defend China's rights and establish a new independent country'. His attempt failed and the conservatives killed him. Sheng Jin (1872–1903) was a progressive reformer in Hunan. When the Reform Movement failed in 1898 he was exiled to Japan. He came back to China in 1900 and joined Tang's Independent Army. After Tang's death he went to Beijing and became a journalist. After he revealed the Chinese and Russian secret treaty in a newspaper the Qing government arrested him and beat him to death.

44. See Qiu Jin 'Qiren you', quoted in Guo, *Qui Jin's Life*, p.30.

45. Qiu Jin, 'Gan Shi', *Qiu Jin Ji*, p.77.

46. Qiu Canzhi (1901–67) was Qiu Jin's daughter. When she was born she was called Wang Canzhi (Wang was her father's surname). Later she changed her surname to Qiu (her mother's surname). When Qiu Jin left her for Japan she was only 2 years old. She stayed in Beijing with her mother's friend. A few years later when she was very ill, her father took her to Hunan to live with her grandmother and brother. However, her grandmother disliked her and the little girl had a very hard time there. She became more and more like her mother when she grew up. She wrote poems and did physical exercise regularly. In 1927 she was invited to be the principal of Jin Xong School, which was named after her mother. When she was 17 years old she went to study as an aircraft engineer in the USA. After her graduation she was appointed professor at a Chinese university. After 1949 she went to Taiwan. She was Qiu Jin's biographer. For details about her, see Qiu Canzhi, *Biography of Qiu Jin*, pp.211–23; Wang (Qiu) Canzhi (ed.) *Qiu Jin nuxia yiji* (The Collections of Qiu Jin) (Shanghai, 1929), pp.96–7.
47. Qiu Jin's mother-in-law disliked living in Beijing, therefore in summer she went back to her home in Hunan with her favourite grandson. Qiu Jin's son virtually grew up with his grandmother.
48. M.B. Rankin, 'The Emergence of Women at the End of the Ch'ing: The Case of Ch'iu Chin', in M. Wolf and R. Witke (eds.), *Women in Chinese Society* (Stanford, 1975), pp.47–8.
49. Wu Zhiying (1867–1934) was a well known poetess, calligrapher and feminist. She was Qiu Jin's close friend. After Qiu Jin's death Wu and Xu Zihua, another friend of Qiu Jin, bought a piece of land on the bank of the West Lake and buried Qiu Jin. Wu also wrote the inscription on the memorial tablet in Qiu Jin's tomb. The Qing government accused her of being Qiu's revolutionary comrade and tried to arrest her. She was ill in a German hospital. According to law the Qing government did not have the right to arrest anybody in an area of foreign occupation. Therefore Wu escaped.
50. Reference to this book is made in T.C. Chu, 'Magazines for Chinese Women', The China Continuation Committee (ed.), *China Mission Year Book 1917* (Shanghai: The Christian Literature of China, 1927), p.454.
51. The fuller explanation of why the Chinese went to Japan to learn modernization is in Fan's book, *Footbinding*, pp.81–2.
52. Ji Yihui, 'Zhongguo nuzi liuxue Riben' (On Chinese Women Studying in Japan), *Dalu* (Journal of the Continent), 1 (1902). See also Fan, *Footbinding*, pp.82–3.
53. It was against the law of the Qing government to publish revolutionary journals and newspapers in China. Many overseas students therefore edited and published progressive journals and papers in Japan and then brought them back to China secretly.
54. Quoted in 'Yi Qiu Jin' (Remember Qiu Jin), *Hangzhou daxue xuebao* (The Journal of Hangzhou University), nos.1–2 (1979), p.154.
55. See Qiu Jin, 'Man Jian Hong: Xiaozu jinhua', *Qiu Jin Ji*, p.101.
56. Qiu Jin's letter to her brother is in *Qiu Jin Ji*, pp.35–6.
57. Qiu Jin, 'Baodao ge', *Qiu Jin Ji*, p.82.
58. Qiu Jin, 'You Hui', *Qiu Jin Ji*, p.87. The translation was adopted from Jonathan D. Spence, *The Search for Modern China* (London, 1990), p.52.
59. Qiu Jin, 'Riren Shijin jun shuohe jiyong yuanyun', *Qiu Jin Ji*, p.83.
60. Wang Shize, 'Huiyi Qiu Jin' (Recall the Life of Qiu Jin). The article is in Hunan Museum, Changsha, China.
61. Qiu Jin, 'Yanshao de haochu' (The Benefit of Learning to Speak in Front of the Public), *Qiu Jin Ji*, p.34.
62. Qiu Jin, 'Yanshuo de haochu', *Qiu Jin Ji*, p.34.
63. This article is in *Qiu Jin Ji*, pp.4–6.
64. Ibid.
65. Ibid.
66. Fan, *Footbinding*, pp.90–1.
67. See Guo, *Qiu Jin's Life*, p.64.
68. Bao Jialin, 'Qiu Jin yu Qingmo funu yundong' (Qiu Jin and the Women's Movement in the Late Qing period), Bao Jialin, *Zhongguo funushi lunji* (On the Women's Movement in China) (Taibei, 1988), pp.353–7; Chen Qubin, 'Jianhu nuxia Qiu Jin Zhuan' (Qiu Jin's Biography)

and Xu Zihua, 'Jianhu nuxia mubiao (Qiu Jin's Life), in Qiu Canzhi, *Selected Works of Qiu Jin*, p.9; Fan, *Footbinding*, p.91.

69. Quoted in Ono Kazuko, *Chinese Women in a Century of Revolution* (Stanford, 1989), p.60.
70. The Humanitarian Society was founded by a group of Chinese overseas female students in Japan on 8 April 1903 before Qiu Jin arrived. The 'Rules of the Humanitarian Society' was published in the journal *Jiangsu*, no.2 (27 May 1903). For reasons that are not clear the society ceased its activities some time later. When Qiu Jin arrived in Japan in 1904 she and her friend Chen Jiefen reorganized the society. For further details, see the report 'Gongaihui de shexin' (The Establishment of the Humanitarian Society), in *Jingzhong ribao*, 3 October 1904; and 'Gongaihui zhangcheng' (The Rules of the Humanitarian Society), *Jiangsu*, 2 (27 May 1903).
71. The letter is in *Qiu Jin Ji*, p.32.
72. Guo, *Qui Jin's Life*, pp.63–4.
73. A famous anti-Qing dynasty organization in the Late Qing period. Qiu Jin and Xu Zilin were its leaders.
74. An anti-Manchu organization led by Sun Yat-sen, the father of the Chinese republican revolution. It was reorganized in the 1920s and renamed as the Guomindang, the Nationalist Party.
75. He Xiangning, 'Wo de huiyi' (Autobiography of He Xiangnin), The Chinese People's Political Consultative Conference (CPPCC) (ed.), *Xinhai gemin huiyi lu* (Recollections of the 1911 Revolution) (Shanghai, 1961–64), Vol.1, p.18.
76. Sanetou Keisyu, *Cyugokujin Nippon-Ryugakushi* (The Chinese Overseas Students in Japan) (Kuroshio Syuppan, 1981), pp.47–473.
77. Cheng Tianhua (1875–1905) was an influential writer at the time. He advocated women's education, emancipation and republican revolution. His letter is to be found in *Cheng Tianhua Ji* (The Collected Works of Cheng Tianhua) (Hunan, 1958).
78. Qiu Jin, 'Zi Qiu Yuzhang shu' (Letters to Qiu Yuzhang (Qiu Jin's elder brother)), *Qiu Jin Ji*, p.45.
79. The letter is in *Qiu Jin Ji*, pp.46–7.
80. Ibid.
81. Qing Liangyu (1574 or 1584–1648) was born in Zhong county, Sichuan province. She was the wife of a Ming general. After her husband died, she sent troops under the command of her son and daughter-in-law Shen Yuying to aid the dynasty. When the Ming government collapsed, she managed to keep her base in Sichuan intact, and her family's position there was eventually recognized by the Qing government. See Feng Rekang, *Guren shenghuo jianyin* ('The Life of the Ancient Chinese) (Beijing, 1999), pp.278–9.
82. Yangjia nujiang: a dramatized story which was adapted from books *The Story of Yang Family* and *The History of the North Song Dynasty* published in the Ming period (1368–1643). The story described a group of women from General Yang's family during the North Song dynasty (969–1132). After the father and sons died, the mother and daughter-in-laws commanded Yang's army to aid the dynasty. They became in consequence women famed for their political and military exploits.
83. Hua Mulan's story came from a poem called The Poem of Mulan. It was published in the North Wei period (386–420) or Tang dynasty (618–960). The poem described a young woman who had no other choice but to replace her father in the army, because her father was ill. She wore men's clothes and fought at the front. When her sexual identity was discovered she left the army and became a woman again. The poem praised the girl's filial piety and her feminine quality. When she came back from the war the Emperor wanted to reward her. She said that she wanted to go home. When she returned home she took off her male clothes, put on her women's clothes and make-up. She was very happy to become a woman again. See Zhu Yian, *Nuwuo de yanjing* (The Eyes of Women) (Shanghai, 1999), pp.79–87.
84. The poem appears in *Qiu Jin Ji*, p.78.
85. See *Qiu Jin Ji*, pp.78–9.
86. This unfinished book is in *Qiu Jin Ji*, pp.121–66.
87. *Qiu Jin Ji*, p.121.
88. See Fan, *Footbinding*, p.93.
89. Xu Zihua was born in Shimen, Zhejiang province. She was famous for her poems. She met Qiu Jin in February 1906 when she was teaching at Nanxun Girls School in Zhejiang. Qiu Jin

went to see her and found her responsive, intelligent, sympathetic, and wholly delightful. For the next six months the two women worked together in close intimacy. Qiu Jin had at last found a 'zhiyin' (a true friend).

90. See *Qiu Jin Ji*, pp.12–13.
91. Wu Zhiyin, 'Ji Qiu Nuxia yishi' (Qiu Jin's Story), *Qiu Jin Ji*, pp.189–90.
92. The article is in *Qiu Jin Ji*, pp.12–3.
93. *Qiu Jin Ji*, pp.13–16.
94. Xu Zilin (1873–1907) was a revolutionary and a founder of the Restoration Society. He was a teacher and subsequently the Principal of Shaoxin School from 1901 to 1904. He set up Zhejiang Sports Society in spring 1905 and opened Datong Normal College in autumn the same year. His aim was to gather together and train a revolutionary force to overthrow the Qing dynasty.
95. Chinese Society of the History of Physical Education and Sport (CSHPES), *Zhongguo jindai tiyushi* (Modern Chinese Sports History) (Beijing, 1989), pp.91–2; Yao Tinhua, 'Datong xuetang kao' (Datong Normal College Textual Research), *Zhejiang tiyu shiliao* (The Historical Materials of Zhejiang Sports History), no.1 (1984), 23.
96. Zhu Fangdong, 'Jianpin Qiu Jin' (On Qiu Jin), CSHPES (ed.), *Tiyushi lunwenji* (Collected Works on Sports History) (Beijing, 1986), pp.51–2, 54–5; Zhu Zanqin, 'Datong shifan xuetang' (On Datong Normal College), CPPCC, Vol.4, p.145.
97. Ibid.
98. Quoted in Qiu Shixiong, 'Jiahu nuxia yu tiyu' (Qiu Jin and Exercise), *Tiyu bao* (Sports Daily) (10 March 1980).
99. Qiu Canzhi, *Selected Works of Qiu Jin*, pp.57–8; see also E. Croll, *Feminism and Socialism in China* (London, 1978), p.45; Fan, *Footbinding*, p.94.
100. Tao Chenzhang, 'Zhe an jilue' (The Record of the Zhejiang Uprising) (1910); see also *Zhejiang tiyu shiliao* (The Historical Materials of Zhejiang Sports History), no.1 (1984), 8–11.
101. Sun Yat-sen wrote: 'When I and the Revolutionary Alliance organized uprisings in Guangdong province, revolutionaries in other provinces were preparing rebellions to support us, such as Xu Zilin and Qiu Jin.' See *Sun Zhongsan xuanji* (The Collected Works of Sun Yan-sen) (Beijing, 1956), p.202.
102. *Qiu Jin Ji*, pp.21–2.
103. *Qiu Jin Ji*, pp.23–6.
104. Spence, *Search for Modern China*, p.60.
105. Yue Fei (1103–1142) was a famous patriotic general and national hero of the Song dynasty. He was executed by the conservative official Qin Kuai. Later people built his tomb on the bank of the beautiful West Lake in Hangzhou and made a statue of Qin Kuai kneeling before the tomb.
106. Chen Qubin, 'Xu Zhihua zhuan' (The Biography of Xu Zihua), *Nuzi shijie* (Women's World) no.1 (Jan. 1915).
107. The government was careful to avoid any mention of the fact that she was a college principal – a figure of authority.
108. Quoted in Hu Shun, *Cong yapian zhanzheng dao Wusi yundong* (From the Opium War to the 4 May Movement) (Shanghai, 1982), p.928.
109. See Guo, *Qui Jin's Life*, p.147.
110. Guo, *Qui Jin's Life*, pp.135–6.
111. Fan, *Footbinding*, p.94.
112. Guo, *Qui Jin's Life*, p.149.
113. Fan, *Footbinding*, p.96.
114. Ibid.
115. Ibid., p.95.
116. See Margarita Stocker, *Judith Sexual Warrior: Women and Power in Western Culture* (London, 1998), p.211.
117. Ibid., p.220.
118. Ibid.
119. Liangyu and Yu-yin were heroines in Chinese history. For details see note 81.
120. *Qiu Jin Ji*, p.110.

3

A Militant Madonna:
Charlotte Perkins Gilman, Feminism and
Physical Culture

PATRICIA VERTINSKY

INTRODUCTION

Charlotte Perkins Gilman was one of the 'new women' of the late nineteenth and early twentieth centuries – one of a growing number of women who struggled to extend the parameters of their physical abilities within a patriarchal tradition of female confinement and subordination. An exceptional woman of considerable talent, she became a major intellectual force in turn–of–the–century America. As a result of her prolific writing and lecturing on her theory of the evolution of gender relations and women's need to become socially useful in the larger world of production, she became known worldwide as a feminist theorist and iconoclastic social critic. 'Writer, philosopher, socialist and feminist, Gilman has come to stand for the potentialities of American womanhood.'[1]

Taken together, Gilman's actions and writings about female struggles for creative fulfilment and physical autonomy reflect her life-long preoccupation with physical fitness and good health practices and her desire for unrestricted physical mobility as a critical component of emancipated womanhood. Analyses of her feminist writings, fiction, poetry, diaries and autobiography all provide rich insights into her strivings for physical autonomy and intellectual freedom. Her autobiography gives us further access to the life of a remarkable and courageous woman. Indeed the emergence of Gilman as a 'new woman' can best be understood as her break from the accepted medical paradigm based on the Cartesian split of mind–body and her forging of a radically new mind–body concept as synergistic. Tragically, she was never able to achieve that liberation and finally ended her own life on 17 August 1935 as the ravages of breast cancer destroyed her future chances of physical emancipation. But her interest in physical fitness as a means to gain personal autonomy, and the emphasis she placed on physical mobility in her numerous fiction writings were direct and enduring comments on the barriers blocking women from physical emancipation in the real world.

Only recently have her literary works been recognized as having a significant meaning for feminists.[2] Relatively unexamined until the second wave of feminism in the twentieth century, the context and substance of her writings, especially *The Yellow Wallpaper* are now considered 'sites of historical struggles well worthy of investigation'.[3] In a wave of empathy for her struggles in the birth of the women's movement, and shortly before she, too, died from breast cancer, feminist historian Joan Kelly wrote in 1982:

> I can read, and do, Charlotte Perkins Gilman and feel my life connect with hers, my cause with hers. Hope I can contribute as she did; know I have, but now I want to do more. I want that suffering that we can control to stop, it outrages and tears at me, the cruel and stupid political world. And I want women's indignities to be ended – millennia long, borne with such endurance and grace. I want, what I really want, and now great pleasure comes through me: I want our day to come. I want women to take the lead. And I know, in the depth of my being, and in all my knowledge of history and humanity, I know women will struggle for a social order of peace, equality, joy. Women will make the world concern itself with children. Our problem is, how do we 'make' the world do that? Oh, I want an end to patriarchy! Passionately![4]

EARLY INFLUENCES – RELATIVES, TEACHERS, AND A DISASTROUS MARRIAGE

Charlotte Perkins Gilman was born in 1860 in Hartford, Connecticut, grand-niece to Catharine Beecher and Harriet Beecher Stowe, author of *Uncle Tom's Cabin*. She was heir, certainly, to the former's enthusiasm for purposive exercise and healthful physical education, though not to her conservative views on gender roles. Catharine Beecher was an early and influential leader in ante-bellum America to stress the value of female exercise through calisthenics and female gymnastics. Her book

Physiology and Calisthenics for Schools and Families (1856) popularized courses in hygiene and calisthenics in women's colleges and seminaries, but more broadly her mission was to re-emphasize the domestic role and responsibilities of women in a world seen to be in crisis from encroaching industrialization and urbanization.[5] Beecher's 'cult of domesticity' enjoined middle-class women to refit themselves for effective child-rearing and housekeeping, but it also had the unanticipated effect of propelling some of them into launching an assault on patriarchal traditions. 'By suggesting that women's bodies could be trained, Beecher empowered women to begin viewing their bodies as uniquely their own.'[6]

FIGURE 3.1
CHARLOTTE PERKINS GILMAN

Courtesy: Schlesinger Library, Radcliffe College.

FIGURE 3.2
CHARLOTTE PERKINS GILMAN IN 1898

Courtesy: Schlesinger Library, Radcliffe College.

Charlotte Perkins Gilman thus became one of a number of remarkable women to involve themselves in crusades to change the status of women by reclaiming their bodies through health and exercise, nurturing the first American feminist movement, fighting for better conditions for working women, and seeking entry into higher education and the professions. Her demands for purposive physical activity, her pursuit of physical and mental well-being and her desire to become a professional writer were expressions of the rising aspirations of women in the struggle for identity and equality that she shared with other feminists of the late nineteenth century. What is so interesting about Gilman's efforts, however, is that she claimed to have been fundamentally changed by her pursuit of health reform and her love of gymnastics, even while being treated by leading physicians of the day for depression and incipient insanity. Her imprisoning and infantilizing experiences with the medical profession profoundly affected her understandings of reality and the dangers to health of physical restraint, a forced docility and bondage to male authority.[7] To understand Gilman, therefore, it is necessary to examine the prevailing medical attitudes of her era towards female work, health and the mind–body relationship as well as the role that exercise played in that paradigm.

Gilman's dedication to physical fitness derived partly from her childhood feelings, intensified at adolescence, that she needed strength to cope with what she was already beginning to perceive as the female burden of economic dependence and confining domestic role. Abandoned by her father and suffocated by an emotionally controlling mother who was apparently unable to show her any affection, she led an unhappy and rootless childhood. Her family moved nineteen times during her first eighteen years. At age thirteen, and now living in Providence, Rhode Island, she was strongly influenced by two physicians who visited the private school she attended. Calisthenics, taught by an upright young Dr Brooks, strongly appealed to her love of movement. But it was Dr Studley, a young woman physician who gave a lecture to her school on hygiene who made, she said, 'an indelible impression on my earnest mind. Forthwith I took to dress reform, fresh air, cold baths, every kind of allowable physical exercise. To that one lecture is to be attributed the beginning of a life-long interest in physical culture.'[8] Certainly, from that moment, Gilman's growing and acknowledged desire for strength and independence compelled her to compensate for more formal education by learning to 'vault and jump … go up a knotted rope, walk on my hands under a ladder, kick as high as my head and revel in the flying rings'. 'Best of all,' Gilman reported, 'were the travelling rings, those widespaced, single ones, stirrup-handled that dangled in a line the length of the hall.' 'My health was splendid, I never tired … [I was] … as strong as a horse.' 'I could easily have been an acrobat,' she wrote later, 'having good nervous co-ordination, strength, courage and excellent balancing power.'[9]

As adolescent enthusiasm turned to adult preoccupations, Gilman increasingly began to realize how the locus of inequality lay in the relationship between the home and the workplace. Lacking guidance or much formal education, she could locate herself firmly in neither place, as she realized keenly only after having reluctantly embraced marriage and motherhood at the age of twenty-four. She quickly found herself unfit for, and unwilling to play the conventional role of wife and mother, 'indicting Victorian marriage and motherhood as maddening for women'.[10] She later reflected these views in her poetry.[11]

To The Young Wife

Are you content, you pretty three-years' wife?
Are you content and satisfied to live
On what your loving husband loves to give,
And give to him your life?

Are you content with work, – to toil alone
To clean things dirty and to soil things clean;
To be a kitchen-maid, be called a queen, –
Queen of a cook-stove throne?

Are you content to reign in that small space –
A wooden palace and a yard-fenced land –
With other queens abundant on each hand,
Each fastened in her place?

Are you quite convinced this is the way,
The only way a woman's duty lies –
Knowing all women so have shut their eyes?
Seeing the world today?

Have you no dream of life in fuller stove?
Of growing to be more than that you are?
Doing the things you now do better for?
Yet doing others – more?

As her marital relationship deteriorated, she became increasingly anxious about her physical and mental weakness and bouts of depression, and criticized her husband for pressing her into marriage without understanding her needs. 'Men are attracted by women's femininity and charm,' she wrote, 'but care not a whit for their real personalities and concerns.'[12] She was particularly concerned with a 'growing melancholia' involving 'every powerful mental sensation, shame, fear, remorse, a blind oppressive confusion, utter weakness, a steady brainache that fills the conscious mind with crowding images of distress', remembering 'every mistake and misdeed of a lifetime'. In her diary she blamed herself for her depression. 'You did it yourself! You had health and strength and hope and glorious work before you – and you threw it all away ... No good as a wife, no good as a mother, no good at anything. And you did it all yourself.'[13] When a therapeutic gymnastic programme failed to stave off her continuing bouts of mental depression, she was persuaded to enlist the help of society doctor, Dr S. Weir Mitchell.

DR S. WEIR MITCHELL AND THE LATE NINETEENTH-CENTURY MEDICAL ESTABLISHMENT

Dr S. Weir Mitchell was the most distinguished American neurologist of his time and became well known in the history of psychiatry for his 'rest cure', used both in its original form and with variations in the United States and abroad.[14] As a physician in Philadelphia he conformed to the mores of a highly conservative community, authoritarian in his approach to his patients, and dogmatic in his views about limiting the place and role of women in American society. His immediate diagnosis of Gilman's problem was neurasthenia, a disorder first articulated by neurologist George Beard as one 'characterized by attacks of absolute exhaustion, often accompanied by the feeling that the exhaustion is so extreme that one experiences a going-to-die feeling'.[15] Beard saw a significant correlation between the demands of modern social organization and nervous exhaustion, first among male intellectuals and business men and then among over-ambitious educated, urban, middle-class women.[16] Highly specialized in the treatment of female neurasthenics, whom he considered 'those sensitive creatures whose destiny if not handled properly was the shawl and sofa', Mitchell treated Gilman as a dominating and manipulative woman in need of a therapy which might return her to a state of compliance and acceptance with her marital and mothering obligations. Gilman accepted the treatment but later reflected upon his rapid diagnosis, and the inappropriateness and/or the failure of the rest cure as therapy:

> I went to him and took the rest cure; went with the utmost confidence, prefacing the visit with a long letter giving 'the history of the case' in a way a modern psychologist would have appreciated. Dr Mitchell only thought it proved self conceit. He had a prejudice against the Beechers. 'I've had two women of your blood here already' he told me scornfully. This eminent physician was well versed in two kinds of nervous prostration; that of the business man exhausted from too much work, and the society woman exhausted from too much play.[17]

In mapping out his cure for Gilman's nervous condition, Dr Mitchell closely reflected the attitudes of establishment male physicians of his era toward emancipating women. Late nineteenth-century medicine relied heavily on systems of gender differentiation. Fear of the effects upon health of female independence and competition, and the movement of nineteenth-century medicine toward somaticism inclined establishment physicians to concentrate upon the close supervision of female patients and the regulation of all aspects of their lives.[18] At that time, arguments about women's limited physical and mental capacity and the centrality of the reproductive process for understanding women's bodies increasingly defined medical views of women's health and the productive boundaries of their lives. Ostensibly basing their views on new scientific evidence, influential medical practitioners, many of whom were men, utilized pseudo-scientific theories about the effects of the reproductive life cycle upon women's physical capabilities in order to rationalize the life choices of middle-class women and define limits on their activities. The laws of nature were advanced as reason for this close regulation over the mental and physical efforts of women. Perceived as a discrete energy field, the body was believed to contain a specific amount of vital energy. If excess energy was used in one direction, less would be available for other needs. Hence energy had to be husbanded for the specific needs of mind and body, in the present as well as for the future. Influenced by social Darwinist views, those concerned about social progress underlined the crucial importance of motherhood to evolution and the need to focus limited female energy upon the reproductive rather than the intellectual development of women. Physicians and social theorists were easily convinced, therefore, that intellectual education, professional or indeed any 'non-feminine' kinds of activity would overtax women and rob them of energy required for maternity and wifehood.[19]

The tension between a medical paradigm which restricted physical mobility and non-domestic activity and the new momentum in women's search for self development was evident in claims of a disturbing increase in female ill health – especially nervous disorders. Confronted with what they perceived to be an epidemic of nervous ailments, male doctors, especially an articulate group of neurological specialists, pronounced neurasthenia and other 'female diseases' the result of the 'new woman's' indifference to her domestic role and her attempted incursion into the male's professional and public world.[20] New women, and nervous illness went together, they claimed, and neurologists readily fashioned treatments which were designed to ease the anxieties of female patients by defusing their ambitions and re-socializing them to their traditional sphere and its familiar obligations.[21] Neurasthenic women, said the doctors, were those who led faulty lives and must correct their lifestyles to regain their health at the domestic hearth.[22]

Carroll Smith-Rosenberg, Elaine Showalter, and other leading feminist historians suggest that Gilman, and others like her,[23] were attempting to escape from their traditional role of housewife and mother, and cope with the stress of real or perceived situational anxieties by adopting depressed or hysterical behaviour. They imagine that their miseries and crippling indecisiveness on entering womanhood were common among tens of thousands of women. It was as if they had come to the brink of adult life and then refused to go on.[24] Gilman herself commented on this in her poem 'Women Do Not Want It':

Women Do Not Want It

When the woman suffrage argument grew vigorous and wise,
And was not to be silenced by these aposite replies,
They turned their opposition into reasoning severe
Upon the limitations of our God-appointed sphere.

We were told of disabilities – a long array of these,
Till one would think that womanhood was merely a disease;
And 'the maternal sacrifice' was added to the plan
Of the various sacrifices we have always made – to man.[25]

THE REST CURE AND THE YELLOW WALLPAPER: IS THERE A DOCTOR IN THE TEXT?

Dr Mitchell's rest cure was based on the notion that neurotic phenomena had a somatic base (structural lesions in the brain cortex), such that one could heal the mind only by first restoring the body to health. The key to cure, and the basis of the rest treatment, therefore, lay in conserving energy through enforced rest, followed by the provision of a complete moral and physical re-education. Patients such as Gilman were asked to relinquish total control to the physician and concern themselves with nothing but following directions.[26] Once the doctor established control over the patient he began a treatment which consisted of complete rest, seclusion and excessive feeding. 'I do not permit the patient to sit up or to sew or write or read, or to use the hands in any active way except to clean the teeth,' said Mitchell.[27] After prolonged rest, the process of moral re-education began by focusing on how to keep personal feelings under control. The patient was to fight every desire to cry, or twitch or grow excited. She was to learn to stop sharing her feelings with others, and to carefully schedule every detail of her daily routine – 'a measured and tempered existence allowing no indulgences or excesses'.[28]

'We can speculate,' says Ellen L. Bassuk, 'that for some Victorian women the rest cure recapitulated elements of the patient's earlier conflicts with parents and later with husband and family, but within a safer context and with a more successful outcome. Not only did it offer an acceptable model for avoiding independent strivings and sexual expression, but it also reinforced the Victorian viewpoint about the inferiority of women, without undermining their self-esteem. Once cured, the Victorian woman could assume a pseudo-independent style of functioning at home.' Superficial adaptation, of course, was costly. 'It affirmed the success of Mitchell's moral re-education and the women's resignation to the limitations of a traditional domestic role.'[29]

For Gilman the rest cure was a conspicuous failure.[30] She was sent home with a prescription to concentrate upon living as domestic a life as possible. 'Have your child with you all the time … Lie down an hour after each meal. Have but two hours intellectual life a day. And never touch pen, brush, or pencil for as long as you live.'[31] She later reported in her autobiography that attempting to follow these prescriptions for some months brought her perilously close to losing her mind. Her solution was to escape her marriage and take up a writing career. 'It was not a choice,' she said later, 'between going and staying, but between going, sane, and staying, insane.'[32] Forty years later, she still believed she carried the effects of 'nerve bankruptcy' and humiliating weakness from that period of her life. But she felt that she had at least tried to convince Dr Weir Mitchell of the errors of his rest treatment by writing one of her best and most famous short stories, *The Yellow Wallpaper*, first published in the *New England Magazine* in 1892.[33]

The Yellow Wallpaper was read by contemporary readers and reviewers as a tale of incipient insanity, but it is seen today by feminist scholars largely as a depiction of the consciously and unconsciously designed male chauvinistic medical practices to which women were exposed. Gilman's 'haunting and passionate protest against the rest cure has become a modern feminist classic, a paradigmatic text for critics and historians looking at the relation between sex roles, madness and creativity'.[34] The story line of *The Yellow Wallpaper* is simple. The narrator, a writer, finds herself increasingly depressed. Her husband John, a physician, believes she needs complete rest and a cessation of her work (her writing) in order to recover. She is thus hustled off to a country house to a life of enforced idleness where she is consigned to an upstairs room, a former nursery, whose major features are peeling yellow wallpaper, bars on the windows and a bedstead nailed to the floor (a symbol perhaps of the state of childlikeness or mindless sexual object in which her husband would like to maintain her).

Trapped in this room, the writer begins to feel that the wallpaper is the only part of her life that she can control. 'I'm getting really fond of the room in spite of the wallpaper. Perhaps because of the wallpaper. It dwells on my mind so!'[35] She begins to see in it a movement and a purpose – and a woman trapped beneath the pattern. 'Behind that outside pattern the dim shapes get clearer every day ... It is like a woman stooping down and creeping about behind that pattern ... And she is all the time trying to climb through.'[36] Suddenly we are not sure which side of the paper the narrator is on. The rescue of the woman behind the wallpaper eventually becomes her main purpose. 'As soon as it was moonlight, and that poor thing began to crawl and shake the pattern, I got up and ran to help her. I pulled and she shook, I shook and she pulled and before morning we had peeled off yards of that paper.'[37] She finally realizes that the woman is in fact herself. 'I've got out at last,' said I, 'in spite of you ... and I've pulled off most of the paper so you can't put me back.' Thus, by identifying with the woman behind the wallpaper and helping her to escape, Gilman is seen to effect her own liberation from disease and find that she too has entered 'the open space of her own authority'.[38]

In her analysis of the story, B. Schöpp-Schilling suggests that the heroine of the story, after having been forbidden by her husband to exercise her creative powers in writing, defies him by turning to a different kind of paper, the hideous wallpaper with which he forces her to live. Through her exclusive preoccupation with its design, she descends into a kind of madness which ultimately allows her to creep triumphantly over her husband.[39] Thus the story becomes a parable of literary confinement with Gilman 'speaking her way out' through the wallpaper. S. Bordo views the hallucination that there is a woman trapped in the wallpaper of her bedroom struggling to get out as 'at once both a perfectly articulated expression of protest and a completely debilitating idée fixe that allows the woman character no distance on her situation, no freedom of thought, no chance of making any progress in leading the kind of active, creative life her body and soul crave'.[40] The story has became a narrative of a woman's growing complicity in her own destruction, where Gilman learns madness as masochistic self-assertion.[41] Jerome M. Schneck has a further explanation, noting that *The Yellow Wallpaper* incorporates a fascinating description of a variant of Capgras' syndrome, involving an hallucinatory autoscopic double.[42] 'One variant of Capgras' syndrome is the autoscopic type in which patients see doubles of themselves in persons or objects nearby.' One of the earliest descriptions of this phenomenon in a well-known work of fiction was Dostoyevsky's novel *The Double* about a clerk in government service haunted by just such an hallucinatory autoscopic double.[43] This was the case in Gilman's story, where her protagonist ultimately deteriorated into a paranoid psychosis after having confronted her double. Schneck explains that among the proposed psychodynamic theories of Capgras' syndrome is 'the ambivalence theory' – where the strong ambivalence of Gilman's patient heroine toward those significant to her (her husband/her doctor) leads to regression and inexorably to psychosis.[44]

There are feminist interpretations of Gilman's writings, and of the events of her life after her marriage, which view her near descent into madness, particularly as described in *The Yellow Wallpaper* as a subtle form of growth, 'a way to health and as a rejection of and escape from an insane society'.[45] By interpreting madness as a higher form of sanity one could read Gilman's story as a quest for her own identity. From this perspective, madness became her only freedom in an oppressive patriarchal social system which prevented women from functioning as full human beings. S.L. Post further suggests that while growing up feminine was certainly blocked and distorted by fearful demands of the times, the emergence of the creeping woman, given understanding, could be seen as the beginning of cure. What emerges, unfortunately, is a monster, twisted and stunted, a woman who can never come to full bloom, while John (the physician/husband), locked away in his own narrowness, never knows what he is missing.[46]

PHYSICAL CULTURE, AND THE LIBERATORY ASPECTS OF GILMAN'S WRITING CAREER

Moving west to Pasadena after her nervous breakdown and the failure of the rest cure, Gilman began her 'professional living' in a small cottage and wrote, 'in that first year of freedom, some thirty-three short articles, and twenty-three poems, besides ten more child-verses'.[47] Her life in California was, Lane notes, 'filled with confusion, compromises, ambivalences and other damages done to women who move from their assigned place'.[48] 'She was not an introspective person. The only deeply self-examining writing she ever did was the short story *The Yellow Wallpaper* – Gilman did not want anyone – a doctor, the public or even herself probably – to delve into her dark places.'[49]

Gilman did, however, develop a growing reputation as a writer and lecturer, publishing a cornucopia of fiction, poetry and reform tracts before her death in 1935.[50] It is within this abundant literature that we can follow Gilman's continued interest in physical culture and her avid promotion of healthful physical activity for women.

Central to all heroines in Gilman's writings was the recognition of the need to maintain health and strength through physical activity. Lifelong habits of physical culture seemed to be one clear way to remove the badge of female dependence. Claiming William Blaikie's *How to Get Strong and How to Stay So* as her bedside bible, her Atalanta guidebook for the coming race, her interest in physical fitness remained with her throughout her life.[51] Indeed, she was proud to report that she navigated the travelling rings, 'the whole row and back' at sixty-five while on a lecture tour.[52]

> Five little rules of health I devised: good air and plenty of it, good exercise and plenty of it, good food and plenty of it, good sleep and plenty of it, good clothing and as little as possible – the result of all this training was to establish a cheerful vigor that enjoyed walking about five miles a day, with working hours from six a.m. to ten p.m. except for meals … When asked, 'How do you do?' it was my custom to reply 'as well as a fish, as busy as a bee, as strong as a horse, as proud as peacock, as happy as a clam'.[53]

Gilman's first major study and most important work, *Women and Economics*[54] was 'a serious and sweeping analysis of the history, sociology and political economy of the female sex'.[55] In this influential treatise she brought together feminist and socialist views to define a humane social order supported by female health and strength, as 'the moving force in the reorganization of society'.[56] Her views on socialism and gender were strongly influenced by Edward Bellamy who, in *Looking Backward 2000–1887*[57] constructed a Utopian future devoid of poverty and injustice and dedicated to co-operation, industriousness and equality of the sexes. Public kitchens, dining rooms and nurseries relieved women from domestic activities and in the educational system particular prominence was accorded physical culture, games and athletics for boys and girls. In particular 'full play (was given) to the differences of sex rather than in seeking to obliterate them'.[58] Relieved from demands of an unnatural rivalry with men, women could develop their own latent talents as 'wardens of the world to come'.[59]

Gilman followed Bellamy's argument closely, envisaging communal kitchens, public nurseries and women's freedom from domestic tasks and the confinement of the home. In the Utopias that she constructed in her writings, her perfect environments were those where women could develop their own health and autonomy in places free from male habits of dominance and power. Thus in her three Utopian novels, *Moving the Mountain* (1911), *Herland* (1915) and *With Her in Ourland* (1916) the transition to socialism is achieved in societies where women have reclaimed leadership over education and the economy. In *Moving the Mountain*, men and women learn to live harmoniously together, while in *Herland* there were no men at all. (They had all been gradually killed off allowing a female community to flourish through a kind of virgin birth which only yielded girl children.) Her ideal women in her Utopia, *Herland* built spacious parks and gardens to encourage athletic development and tilled collective fields to produce nutritious food.[60] They were agile, strong and healthy in body and mind, and their organizational forms allowed them 'the life of comparative freedom and great activity that Gilman always yearned for'.[61] Indeed, her efforts to control her body were always maintained within her larger programme to control her life.[62]

In many respects, the characterization of Charlotte Perkins Gilman as a 'militant madonna' by an auditor at one of her public lectures was astute.[63] Gilman suffered throughout her life from her inability to reconcile her conformist tendencies toward the rigid and narrow maternal mould that had been created for Victorian middle-class women and her desire to transcend the limitations of female experience of the day. While rebelling against the constraints of an oppressive patriarchal system, she was no revolutionary. She never denied the differences between the sexes or denigrated the importance of women's traditional roles. Wifehood and motherhood, she wrote in 1923 'are the normal status of women and whatever is right in women's new position must not militate against these essentials'.[64] In her Utopia *Herland*, society was patterned after those principles which govern the home, 'like a pleasant family – an old, established, perfectly run country place'.[65] Here a supportive, secure, home-like environment encouraged the full development of each individual and the sentimentalization of motherhood without allowing a man on the scene to construct sexist power structures and use force to establish order. Charlotte Gilman's women were emancipated mothers, strong and healthy, and 'free from the rape of their minds as well as their bodies'.[66] But they were also mothers fulfilling their appointed role, dedicated to the highest ideals of duty to family and womanhood.

The significance of Gilman's feminist Utopian thinking, and her voluminous and influential fiction and non-fiction writings which spanned the decades between 1890 and 1930 lay in the clarity with which she exposed and described the disabilities imposed by society upon women and of their subsequent role on both sides of the Atlantic. 'It is not that women are really smaller-minded, more timid and vacillating,' she wrote in 1903, 'but that whosoever ... lives always in a small dark place [and], is always guarded, protected, directed and restrained, will become inevitably narrowed and weakened by it. The women is narrowed by the home and the man is narrowed by the woman.'[67]

The salvation of women, Gilman believed, lay in the 'joy and duty' of work.[68] 'What we have to do,' she explained, 'is to recognize the woman as a human being ... to learn how to reconcile happy work with a happy marriage' and 'to prove that a woman can love and work too.'[69] And, central to the promotion of meaningful work for women was their need and responsibility to pursue health and maintain physical fitness for both their benefit and 'the common good of all'.[70]

That her quest to achieve a sound mind in a sound body failed may have been due, in large part, to her inability to reconcile her conflicting desires for self-development and love in a patriarchal society. Though choosing love initially, she came to believe that she had bought dependence at the expense of self-expression. The misery and depression associated with the guilt she felt about her nonconformity paved her descent into mental illness, and despite her persistence in maintaining a well-trained physique she experienced bouts of uncontrollable mental depression for the rest of her life. She came to understand that a strong and healthy body was a necessary but not sufficient condition for mental health. 'You must understand', she once told an acquaintance before her death, that 'what ails me is a weak mind in a strong body'.[71]

Gilman's portrayal of female health and disease in the context of Victorian traditionalism and the importance which she attributed to physical fitness as a bulwark against the imprisoning sphere of home-making and child-rearing were important indicators of the new woman of the early twentieth century, yet the independent womanhood she espoused retained 'the crucial social and psychic trappings of the old'.[72] Certain sports, especially those involving the throwing of a ball, she conjectured would never appeal to women because they were 'only masculine, not human'.[73] Crucially, missing from *Herland* was competitive sport, dramatic literature and great science. Adventure and excitement were still the lot of men, and women, despite their health and strength, remained the tranquil and the nurturers. 'Women' in the feminist Utopia, 'for all their evident intellect ... were as calm as cows'.[74]

FEMINISM WINS:
EUTHENASIA AND REWRITING THE MEDICAL TEXT

In the end, however, Gilman died in a manner that testified to her continued struggle to make choices during her life and her determination not to allow the medical profession to control her passing. She discovered she had cancer of the breast in 1932. 'I had not the least objection to dying. But I did not propose to die of this,' she wrote, and 'promptly bought sufficient chloroform as a substitute.'[75] 'Refusing interventionist medical treatment, her death was of her choice, in the long run, though within the sharp limits set by her cancerous body. Still it was an act of will, of rationality, of affirmation. As she had lived in her life, so she used her death for its instructive value. She preferred, as she explained in the note she left behind, 'chloroform to cancer'.[76]

> No grief, pain, misfortune or broken heart is excuse for cutting off one's life while any power or service remains. But when all usefulness is over, when one is assured of unavoidable and imminent death, it is the simplest of human rights to choose a quick and easy death in place of a slow and horrible one.[77]

NOTES

1. C.R. Berkin, 'Private Woman, Public Woman. The Contradictions of Charlotte Perkins Gilman' in Carol Ruth Berkin and Mary B. Norton (eds.), *Women of America: A History* (Boston, MA, 1979), p.150.
2. Gary Scharnhorst, *Charlotte Perkins Gilman: A Bibliography* (New Jersey, 1985), p.vii. Gilman's works were 'virtually forgotten until 1971 when the Schlesinger Library at Radcliffe College acquired her papers, totalling 29 boxes of diaries, scrapbook, correspondence and clippings'.
3. Daniel Cotton, *Social Figures: George Eliot, Social History and Literary Representation* (Minneapolis, 1987), p.211.

4. Joan Kelly, *Women, History and Theory: The Essays of Joan Kelly* (Chicago, 1984), p.xv.
5. Jan Todd, *Physical Culture and the Body Beautiful. Purposive Exercise in the Lives of American Women, 1800–1875* (Georgia, 1998), pp.136–7.
6. Todd, *Physical Culture*, p.161.
7. Stephen L. Post, 'His and Hers: Mental Breakdown as depicted by Evelyn Waugh and Charlotte Perkins Gilman', *Literature and Medicine*, 9 (1990), 179.
8. Charlotte Perkins Gilman, *The Living of Charlotte Perkins Gilman: An Autobiography* (Wisconsin, 1935), p.29.
9. Ibid., p.71.
10. Ibid., p.xxiii.
11. Charlotte Perkins Gilman, *In This Our World* (Boston, 1899), pp.1–3, 6–7.
12. Patricia Vertinsky, 'Feminist Charlotte Perkins Gilman's Pursuit of Health and Physical Fitness as a Strategy for Emancipation', *Journal of Sport History*, 16 (1989), 24.
13. Gilman, *The Living*, pp.87, 90–1.
14. Jerome M. Schneck, *A History of Psychiatry* (Springfield, IL, 1960), p.81.
15. G.M. Beard, *A Practical Treatise on Nervous Exhaustion (Neurasthenia): Its Symptoms, Nature, Sequences, Treatment*, 2nd edn. (New York, 1880), p.66. Such a diagnosis some suggest, has now been replaced by the descriptor, chronic fatigue syndrome. S.E. Abbey and P.E. Garfinkel, 'Neurasthenia and Chronic Fatigue Syndrome: The Role of Culture in the Making of a Diagnosis', *American Journal of Psychiatry*, 128 (1991), pp.1638–46. Kleinman helpfully notes that neurasthenia can most fruitfully be conceptualized as illness experience. A. Kleinman, *Rethinking Psychiatry: From Cultural Category to Personal Experience* (New York, 1988).
16. Elaine Showalter, *The Female Malady* (New York, 1985).
17. Gilman, *The Living*, p.95.
18. Ellen L. Bassuk, 'The Rest Cure: Repetition or Resolution of Victorian Women's Conflict', *Poetics Today*, 6 (1985), 245–57.
19. For a fuller discussion, see Patricia Vertinsky, *The Eternally Wounded Woman: Doctors, Women and Exercise in the Late Nineteenth Century* (Manchester, 1990).
20. John S. Haller Jr, 'Neurasthenia: The Medical Profession and the "New Woman" of the Late Nineteenth Century', *New York State Journal of Medicine*, 71 (1971), 475.
21. Vertinsky, 'Feminist Charlotte Perkins Gilman's Pursuit of Health and Physical Fitness', 13.
22. G.M. Hammond, 'Nerves and the American Woman', *Harper's Bazaar*, no.40 (1906), 591; H.J. Hall, 'The Systematic Use of Work as a Remedy in Neurasthenia and Allied Conditions', *Boston Medical and Surgical Journal*, 152 (1905), 29.
23. For example, Jane Addams, Elizabeth Cady Stanton, Margaret Sanger, leading English abolitionist, Josephine Butler, and German suffragette, Hedwig Dohm.
24. Carroll Smith-Rosenberg, 'The Hysterical Woman: Sex Roles and Role Conflict in Nineteenth Century America', in *Disorderly Conduct: Visions of Gender in Victorian America* (New York, 1985), p.207. Elaine Showalter, *The Female Malady: Women, Madness and English Culture* (New York, 1985).
25. Gilman, *In This Our World*, p.155, verses 2 and 3.
26. H.J. Byford, *Manual of Gynecology*, 2nd edn. (Philadelphia, 1897), pp.180–5; Bassuk, 'The Rest Cure'.
27. S. Weir Mitchell, *Fat and Blood and How to Make Them*, 8th edn. (Philadelphia, 1900), p.66.
28. Bassuk, 'The Rest Cure', p.250.
29. Ibid., pp.255–6.
30. G.J. Barker-Benfield, 'Mother-Emancipator. The Meaning of Jane Addams "Sickness and Cure"', *Journal of Family History* (1979), 395–420.
31. Gilman, *The Living*, p.96.
32. Ibid., p.97.
33. Beate Schöpp-Schilling, 'The Yellow Wallpaper: A Rediscovered "Realistic Story"', *American Literary Realism*, 8 (1975), 284–6.
34. Showalter, *The Female Malady*, p.142.
35. C.P. Gilman, 'The Yellow Wallpaper', *The New England Magazine*, 5 (1892), 647–59. Published in book form in 1899 it was later included in William Dean Howells (ed.), *The Great Modern American Stories/An Anthropology* (New York, 1920), 320–37.
36. Gilman, 'The Yellow Wallpaper', pp.325, 330.
37. Ibid., p.332.

38. Vertinsky, *The Eternally Wounded Woman*, p.79.
39. Schöpp-Schilling, 'The Yellow Wallpaper: A Rediscovered "Realistic" Story', p.285.
40. Susan Bordo, 'Anorexia Nervosa: Psychopathology as the Crystallization of Culture', in Irene Diamond and Lee Quinby (eds.), *Feminism and Foucault. Reflections on Resistance* (Boston, 1988). pp.87–118.
41. Barbara Johnson, *The Feminist Difference. Literature, Psychoanalysis, Race and Gender* (Cambridge, 1998), p.27.
42. Schneck, *A History of Psychiatry*, pp.120–2.
43. Fyodor Dostoyevsky, *The Double* (1846) (London, 1972).
44. Jerome M. Schneck, 'S. Weir Mitchell, Charlotte Perkins Gilman's "The Yellow Wallpaper", and Capgras' Syndrome', *New York State Journal of Medicine* (1991), 445–9.
45. Jean E. Kennard, 'Convention Coverage or How to Read Your Own Life', *New Literary History*, 13 (1981), 76.
46. S.L. Post, 'His and Hers', 172–80.
47. Gilman, *The Living*, p.107.
48. Ann Lane, Foreword in *The Living*, p.xv.
49. Ibid., p.xvi.
50. Carl N. Degler, 'Charlotte Perkins Gilman on the Theory and Practice of Feminism', *American Quarterly*, VIII (1956), p.22, fn. 6.
51. Mary A. Hill, *Charlotte Perkins Gilman: The Making of a Radical Feminist, 1860–1896* (Philadelphia, 1980), p.65.
52. Gilman, *The Living*, p.67.
53. Ibid., pp.62–71.
54. Charlotte Perkins Gilman, *Women and Economics: A Study of the Economic Relation Between Men and Women as a Factor in Social Evolution*, 1898 (repr. New York, 1966).
55. Ann Lane, Introduction to Charlotte Perkins Gilman, *Herland: A Lost Utopian Novel* (New York, 1979), p.v.
56. Lane, *Herland*, p.x.
57. Edward Bellamy, *Looking Backward, 2000–1887* (Boston, 1888; New York, 1996).
58. Bellamy, *Looking Backward*, p.126.
59. Ibid., p.131.
60. Rosalind Rosenburg, *Beyond Separate Spheres: Intellectual Roots of Modern Feminism* (New Haven, CT, 1982), p.58; Charlotte Perkins Gilman, *Herland: A Lost Feminist Utopian Novel* (New York, 1979 (1915).
61. Hill, *Radical Feminist*, p.101.
62. Mary A. Hill, Charlotte Perkins Gilman, 'A Feminist's Struggle with Womanhood', *Massachusetts Review*, 21 (1980), 504.
63. Carl N. Degler, Introduction in Charlotte Perkins Gilman, *Women and Economics*, p.xvii.
64. Charlotte Perkins Gilman, 'The New Generation of Women', *Current History* (1923), 1735.
65. Gilman, *Herland*, p.238.
66. Carol Pearson, 'Coming Home: Four Feminist Utopians and Patriarchal Experience', in Marlene S. Barr (ed.), *Future Females: A Critical Anthology* (Bowling Green, OH, 1981), p.64.
67. Charlotte Perkins Gilman, *The Home, Its Work and Influence* (New York, 1910, first publ. 1903) p.129.
68. Charlotte Perkins Gilman, *Human Work* (New York, 1904), p.182.
69. 'The Single Woman's Problem', *American Magazine* (1906), 428; Letter from Charlotte Stetson (Gilman) to Houghton Gilman, 26 July 1899.
70. Gilman, *Women and Economics*, p.313.
71. Gilman, *The Living*, p.103.
72. Berkin, *Women of America*, p.167.
73. Charlotte Perkins Gilman, *The Man-Made World of Our Androcentric Culture* (New York, 1911), pp.114.
74. Lane, *Herland*, p.22.
75. Gilman, *The Living*, p.333.
76. Ann J. Lane, 'The Fictional World of Charlotte Perkins Gilman', *The CPG Reader*, 1980, p.ix.
77. Gilman, *The Living*, p.334.

A Lifetime of Campaigning:
Ettie Rout, Emancipationist beyond the Pale

JANE TOLERTON

In the southern New Zealand city of Christchurch in 1904, 16 women posed for a photograph which would be called: 'Christchurch School of Physical Culture: Group of Non-Corset Women'. At the back, tallest and leanest, is Ettie Rout. Twenty years later, living in London, she would publish her book for women, *Sex and Exercise*, a title which sums up just two of her campaigns in a life of campaigning on women's health issues. (Figure 4.1.)

At the time the photograph was taken she was already known around town for her unorthodox dress and progressive views. She regarded herself as 'peculiar enough to be as God Almighty intended [women] to be – the equals of men, physically and mentally'.[1] When people looked for a word to describe her, the one they came up with first was 'energy': 'stupendous energy', 'superhuman energy', 'as full of energy as a dynamo' are descriptions of a woman about whom little has been written.

She was born in 1877 in Australia's southern state of Tasmania to a Congregationalist family. Although Ettie Annie was a twin, with Nellie Frances, she was treated as and acted like the eldest of the family of three girls and, like many eldest daughters in all-girl families, took the role of an eldest son. When, as a young woman, she wrote a tale of childhood in which the characters were drawn from life to the point of being given their real names, she characterized herself as a tough tomboy, full of both brains and brawn. The self-confidence, the sheer energy, the cheeky, teasing attitude to those in authority, the enthusiastic display of having done her homework, the sense of acting in the interests of those less capable (her sisters, portrayed as prissy) and of patiently carrying out a game plan supervised by herself and ruined by idiots were all characteristic of the adult Rout as well as the one in the story.[2]

Courtesy: Canterbury Museum, Christchurch, New Zealand.

Her father was an ironmonger who took his family from Tasmania to New Zealand in 1885, setting up business in the capital, Wellington. Genial William John Rout was a tinkerer. He invented a coffee percolator, which he patented, but his plumber's business went bankrupt. This put an end to his daughter's education. She had gained a scholarship to the girls' high school, with primary school marks well ahead of the competition at her own school. But she was forced to give it up when the family moved to a provincial town, probably to stay with a relative in the wake of the bankruptcy.

Several years later, in the mid-1890s, they arrived in Christchurch where Rout attended the first commercial college in the country, Gilby's College, learning shorthand and typing, and teaching both. On her extraordinarily fast shorthand typing skills, and a big black bike she rode around the streets, on which she collected and delivered work, she built a highly successful business as a public typist.

In 1902 she was one of the first batch of government-appointed shorthand writers to work in the courts and on commissions of inquiry. She made a point of typing into the early morning hours so as to get transcripts of the previous day's evidence before a judge next day. This gave her a rare insight into parts of society usually hidden from middle-class women. Super-intelligent, she read voraciously and wrote articles for the local liberal paper, the *Lyttelton Times*. She was well known for the collection of 'advanced' books she kept in her office.

Only the advanced went to the Christchurch School of Physical Culture, begun by Irishman Fred Hornibrook who had arrived in New Zealand in 1900 having studied in Britain with strongman Eugen Sandow. The narrow-minded stayed away and talked about how the physical culturists went into the showers and cold plunge baths in the nude. Rout taught the children's class there on Saturday mornings and sent her young women apprentices.

Hornibrook declared that Rout was the only woman he had ever met who came up to the Venus de Milo standard of physique. To the people around her she seemed Amazonian – not only for her renowned energy, or because she was probably the fittest woman they had ever encountered, but because her shape was 'peculiar' to use her word. She did not 'go in' in the middle like the majority of women, wearers of the fashionable S-bend corset. Neither did the Venus de Milo – which was Fred's point.

She also dressed differently, wearing men's overcoats and having suits made up by a men's tailor, with long loose jackets and skirts in plain colours. When not on assignments she sometimes wore the cream pullover of the physical culture class with a calf-length skirt and men's laced-up boots. Christchurch had been the centre of the rational dress movement during the 1890s when the city had a Rational Dress Association but few women had actually worn the knickerbockers it had argued for. Rout did, but found public response was too extreme for comfortable city wear; she did wear them hiking at the weekends. Whilst most women wore huge shoulder-spanning hats, she was conspicuous by wearing either no hat or a small, neat, man's one. And she was one of the few women who cut off her hair before the First World War (Figure 4.2).

Her manner too was 'peculiar' for a woman. There was no lack of feminists in New Zealand – where the vote had been won easily and early in 1893, as a result of strong argument and good organization with massive nationwide petitions making it clear what women wanted. But they were generally careful to seem harmlessly womanly. Rout was direct and straightforward to the point of seeming brusque. Throughout her life she had few female friends. As a man who had known her when she was a young reporter wrote perceptively in the *Sydney Bulletin* obituary

FIGURE 4.2

FIRST WORLD WAR PASSPORT PHOTOGRAPH OF ETTIE ROUT

after her death, 'She had the respect and admiration of every man who ever tried a mental tussle with her, but she would have been better liked if she hadn't had such contempt for all the little shams and humbugs that make life bearable.'[3] Note that he says every 'man'; she had few women friends then or later. Another wrote of that time that she seemed 'a lonely figure, sexless, without emotion, having a cold cleverness, an impersonal contempt for correct opinion ... a sexless person, male in mind and manner'.[4] Rout, in turn, thought other women were kept from being like herself by having had their minds 'warped and stunted' by 'countless conventions' and their bodies by 'ridiculous and restrictive dress you couldn't work in if you tried'.[5]

As a successful career woman she championed the right of women to enter the workforce on the same basis as men. 'What a man says she can't do, let her try and find out she can.'[6] She entered public health campaigns often acting as a backroom organizer for progressive pro-regulation doctors who were therefore, if not her friends, then certainly colleagues in the fight against regulation-resistant businessmen for things like provision of seating for female shop assistants and better ventilation for workplaces.

She got involved in the labour movement in 1907 when she was taken on to provide a transcript of an investigation into farm labourers' conditions for the conciliation board appointed under New Zealand's arbitration system of solving labour disputes. Although the board had both employer and employee representatives, she did not charge the union, making up the difference by charging the employers double. She was made an honorary member of the Shearers' Union and was the founding editor of its newspaper, a job she did gratis. However, when the shearers joined the Federation of Labour it took the paper as its own and she lost her position as editor.

In the years that followed, Rout did a turnaround in her views on the position of women. She had once attacked 'the now quite stupid assumption that there is only one kind of woman – the mother of the race'.[7] Now, having read the works of Swedish feminist Ellen Key she took on the concept of 'universal motherhood'. The 'mother of the race' need not be a biological mother but was a woman who did social work for the good of humanity. Rout took this role for herself and it fuelled her campaigning for the rest of her life. She also followed Key in taking a position against the 'social purity' style of feminism.

When the First World War broke out in 1914, New Zealand men raced to join up for what they saw as a government-funded adventure on the other side of the world. Women were called upon to support the war effort by giving up their sons and husbands and forming committees to provide 'necessities' and 'luxuries' for the troops, knitting and sewing and packing food treats.

In the spirit of the 'universal mother' Rout believed New Zealand women should go with the men to look after them. She set up the New Zealand Volunteer Sisterhood and called for women between 30 and 50 to go to Egypt, where the troops were then based, during the Gallipoli campaign, and do whatever work was needed. When she began this work, in July 1915, the government was not even allowing nurses to go overseas. In spite of government disapproval, which some commentators felt was so strong as to be a 'prohibition' on their going, Rout took several dozen women to Egypt at the end of 1915. They worked in hospitals and canteens. (Figure 4.3.)

When, after the Gallipoli campaign, most of the New Zealand troops left for France, Rout stayed on and set up canteens in the desert for the mounted troops in the Sinai–Palestine campaign. In what she saw as 'a civilising and socialising centre' to redress the balance of the

FIGURE 4.3

THE VOLUNTEER SISTERHOOD, WITH ETTIE ROUT, HATLESS, IN THE CENTRE

Courtesy: Earle Andrew Collection, Alexander Turnbull Library, Wellington, New Zealand.

dehumanizing military machine, she made huge vats of fruit salad (aware of the need for fresh food and vitamins) when the men lived on 'bully beef and biscuits'.[8] She sent for sports equipment from New Zealand to provide facilities for rest and recreation. 'I don't know why we don't look after our menfolk better,' she wrote to the general's wife who helped fund her endeavours. 'I suppose it is because there are not enough women connected with the commissariat department of military work. The human care of men, sick and well, has been our job for millions and millions of years ...'[9] For this work Rout was mentioned in dispatches, and in the Australian official history of the war. She also became sick, contracting malaria which recurred throughout her life.

On arriving in Egypt in early 1916 she had become aware that venereal disease was one of the biggest social and medical problems of the war. In that pre-penicillin time, she knew syphilis and gonorrhoea would cause massive health problems post-war. Syphilis was a killer disease and caused infertility in women as did the less dangerous gonorrhoea. About 20 per cent of the New Zealand Expeditionary Force would get one of these diseases during the war. In trying to cope with the problem, the army was not allowed to move beyond 'moral prophylaxis' – pleading by chaplains and lectures by medical officers – to 'physical prophylaxis' like condoms. Rout knew where she stood from the beginning – clearly on the side of physical prophylaxis, in favour of prophylactic kits and properly inspected brothels as well as straightforward sex education so men knew about the risks they were taking. She also knew that this would be anathema to the women of New Zealand and would be seen as trying to 'make vice safe'. Her response was: 'I see no reason why it should be left dangerous.'[10] 'All I want to do with regard to venereal disease is adopt the ordinary methods we apply to other diseases.'[11] 'The question at root seems simple to decide. Is sexual relationship a necessity for the troops or is it not? The troops have certainly decided, Yes. Then our duty is to make that relationship accessible and harmless. Why get into moral tangles?'[12]

In her first month in Cairo, before turning to her canteen work, Rout had done her research in the brothel district and interviewed the army's chief medical officer about what he was doing. He was shocked. She was horrified about his unwillingness to do anything. She typed up the interview and sent it to the Minister of Defence. She had taken her typewriter and cyclostyling machine with her to war.

On a short visit to London in early 1917, she realized that the venereal disease rate had not dropped as the authorities had thought it would with men going on leave to Britain, still regarded as 'Home' by the colonials. In May she moved to London and began what we would now call her 'safe sex' campaign in earnest. She visited the major experts in the field and put together the most comprehensive and convenient prophylactic kit in existence. It contained Condys Crystals (potassium permanganate), a disinfectant for washing with, condoms (much thicker than the modern variety), even though she knew many men would not use them, and calomel ointment, for smearing on the genital area before sex, which is what she put her faith in. When the army refused to adopt the kits, sticking to its 'moral prophylaxis' alone policy, she set up a 'medical club' near the New Zealand Convalescent Hospital in Hornchurch and started handing them out to soldiers. It was Rout's publicity on the problem back home that changed the policy to include 'physical prophylaxis'. She wrote a letter which was printed in the New Zealand *Times* in October 1917 outlining the problem and her solution and making it clear she was already giving soldiers kits. A deputation of women visited the Prime Minister, asking him to get Rout away from the troops. He could not do that, but he could have Cabinet ban mention of her in the New Zealand press under the War Regulations, which he did.

At the same time, however, the newspaper article sparked the adoption of the kit. The Defence Minister told the force's commander in England to do whatever he thought necessary. They were not only adopted officially but were handed out on a free and compulsory basis. Men going on leave had to take one. Rout's long-time friend, Fred Hornibrook, who had been working as a masseur on hospital ships, was appointed official prophylaxis lecturer. Rout had been working on schemes where Hornibrook could combine his physical culture skills with prophylaxis in a gymnasium-cum-prophylactic centre, but had not been able to achieve this.

In 1918 Rout moved on to the other plank in her campaign, safe brothels. As these would be against the law in England, she moved to Paris, where she found a madame who would allow her to supervise her brothel and make sure it was run on 'safe sex' lines. She had cards printed up which said Madame Yvonne's maison 'makes safe and suitable provision for the sexual needs of the troops'.[13] She stood on the platform of the Gare du Nord as the troop trains rolled in from the front with soldiers on leave, rounded up the New Zealanders, introduced herself, gave each one her trademark kiss on the cheek, checked that they had their kits and handed out her cards (Figure 4.4). She ran what amounted to a complete social and sexual welfare service for New Zealand troops, finding accommodation, nursing the sick, interceding with authorities, giving advice, making up baskets of food for the return journey. She stayed in Paris after the Armistice but in mid-1919 she toured the camps in England where New Zealand soldiers were waiting for ships home. One later wrote: 'Some [soldiers] threw [her] nervous and unaccustomed salutes, which they would have denied to brigadiers. What meant more were the smiles that went with them, the way in which unemotional (and often self-conscious) men called to her and went up to make themselves known.' When he spoke with her he found she was 'very frank about what she had done and the price she had to pay and was still to pay. Nor did she boast of sacrifice, nor expect credit or mercy.' She mocked the 'curdled Christianity' of some New Zealanders. 'As for herself, she had never thought of being afraid.' Whether or not he knew of her 'universal mother' concept, he concluded, 'She had

FIGURE 4.4
ETTIE ROUT SURROUNDED BY SOLDIERS, PARIS, AUGUST 1918

Courtesy: New Zealand National Archives.

become the mother. A mother wise and wistful of many reckless sons, full of pity for the worst of them, and ready to comfort all who might suffer.'[14] She could be spotted, that summer on Salisbury Plain, sitting on the grass, deep in conversation with individual soldiers. Today we would call it counselling. The topic was often what to say to wives and girlfriends. Her advice was that honesty was the best policy, rather than endangering their health.

At the end of the summer, Rout returned, with Hornibrook, to France and ran an American Red Cross station in the ruined Somme town of Villers Brettoneux where she fed 200 children a hot midday meal, also operating the depot as a canteen for all comers, including the British graves detachments still working along what had been the Western front. For this and her work in Paris she was awarded the Reconnaissance Française medal by the French. But her own government ignored her. She became *persona non grata* in her homeland. The ban on information was kept up informally by newspapers after the war was over. When the official history was written she was not in it, not even for the socially-condoned Volunteer Sisterhood work. The Australian official histories mentioned her several times, for her prophylactic as well as canteen, work. New Zealand soldiers wanted to give her some sort of award for service and collected £100. But they did not publicize this. Those who had benefited most from her work had the most reason to keep quiet about it.

Rout and Hornibrook moved to London in 1920, and married. Why marry, at the age of 43, when they had spent so many years together unmarried? Possibly because Hornibrook was about to set up as a physiotherapist and wanted the respectability that went with marriage. For Rout marriage was even more a professional prerequisite. She was about to begin her publishing career, writing about issues only married women were supposed to know about. She made a point of saying she drew on her experience as a reporter, a social worker, and a married woman, in arguing for venereal disease prophylaxis and birth control, into which field she moved in the 1920s. She gave evidence before the Joint Select Committee on the Criminal Law Amendment Bill[15] in October 1920, telling the committee 'you want everything' in combating venereal disease – including prophylactic kits and controlled brothels. This was a long way wide of the mark of acceptability in England, but Rout was used to that. As part of her continuing campaign, she published a account of her work in Paris. The title, 'Two years in Paris', shows Rout was much more a campaigner than an historian, as she was in Paris for only about a year.[16] And it was more an argument for prophylaxis in post-war Britain than a record of her time in Paris. Although it is the most autobiographical thing she wrote, there are no interesting details of anything but the campaign or thoughts on anything but the war on venereal disease.

Rout's most useful champion among the doctors who approved of her work was Sir William Arbuthnot Lane, who wrote the forewords to her books. 'Her superhuman energy and indomitable perseverance enabled her to perform, in the most efficient manner possible, a work which few women would care to handle, and of which but an infinitesimally small number are capable,' he wrote.[17] Sir William suggested Rout help Marie Stopes with her book on venereal disease – a cause Stopes was entering with the air of a grande dame lending her name, having become famous with *Married Love* in 1918. Rout provided Stopes with research material – books and bundles of wartime correspondence – and read over the resulting manuscript, adding her suggestions. Stopes said she could use one or two of them, but her moral code was much stricter than Rout's. She was opposed to sex before marriage, for example. It ended in a fight with Stopes telling Rout, 'You are so much in the subject that you do not realise what an electrifying thing my book is',[18] and Rout telling Stopes, 'it is disinterested field-workers that are wanted not museum Hypathias or Prophetesses. You can write well, talk well, and I believe you could work well – if you would empty out the rubbishy emotionalism, the superstition, the vanity and egoism with which you becloud and degrade your work.'[19]

As with the venereal disease campaign, Rout brought to birth control an intense practicality. In 1922 she hosted a meeting in her own sitting room. The invited men were to come up with a chemical formula which could be put into a soluble and effervescent suppository for women and kill not only venereal disease microbes, but also sperm. She tried out a large number of different formulae for the prophylactic-contraceptive suppository on herself and her friends and finally found one that would foam. She decided to market this, but under the 1917 Venereal Disease Act, though the tablets could be sold, they could only be sold without instructions. Even chemists were not allowed to tell women at the point of sale what they were for. So Rout wrote her book *Safe Marriage – a return to sanity*, giving the formulation and instructions. If it had reflected Rout's real views, the book's title would have been 'safe sex', a phrase that was still six decades away. *Safe Marriage* was a play on the accusation she had heard so often – that she was trying to 'make vice safe'. It was marriage that was unsafe in a social climate in which people did not protect themselves from venereal disease, she contended. 'At present marriage is easily the most dangerous of all our social institutions', she wrote.[20] A survey had just established that 75 per cent of married women who had syphilis had been infected by their husbands, 86 per cent of them within the first year of marriage.

Safe Marriage, the first of six books Rout wrote between 1922 and 1925, told women it was their duty to understand the processes involved in sex and take responsibility for protecting themselves from the possible consequences. 'A woman's body is her own, and she will never be really free until she knows how to look after it properly,' she wrote in *Safe Marriage*.

> If she is fit to vote, fit to pay taxes, fit to hold her own estate under the Married Women's Property Act, why should she not learn to exercise intelligent and responsible control over her own self? Why do so many women *allow* themselves to be impregnated and

infected against their own will? Because they do not understand
the construction and function of their own bodies. When they do
understand this, they will guard their own health as carefully as
they guard their reputation.[21]

Women could gain absolute control over their reproductive lives, she
said, by spending a bit of time and money, much less than they spent on
the care of their teeth. They were advised to equip themselves with a
'sexual toilet outfit' – enamel bidet, soluble suppositories, suitable
syringe and properly fitted diaphragm (known as a rubber pessary or
Dutch cap) which, used with a spermicide, was Rout's favoured birth
control method.

    Along with the practical instructions went the philosophy. She
redefined chastity as 'happy healthy sexual intercourse between a man
and a woman who love one another; and unchastity is sexual intercourse
between a man and a woman who do not love one another. No sexual
intercourse at all is neither chastity nor unchastity; it is the negation of
both, and it ends in extinction.'[22] She also redefined vice and sin. 'For a
healthy woman to give herself sexually to a healthy man without Love –
that is Vice. For her to refuse herself to a man when there is mutual love
and desire – that is Sin. Vice is something which harms only Ourselves:
Sin is something which harms Society. To quench Love is to damp –
perhaps to extinguish – Life itself.'[23] Removing the fear of pregnancy
and of disease would destroy the prevailing system of morality, she
argued. As things stood, legality had been substituted for morality. Legal
monogamic indissoluble marriage deprived people of love-life while 'the
claims of sex-love should be paramount'.[24] She wanted a new system of
morality whose object would be personal happiness and a healthy race.
Its pivot would be 'the fastidiously selective passionate love of a free
womanhood'.[25] The 'fastidiously sexual selection by woman of the finest
men for the fathers of her children' was 'the greatest dynamic force on
earth'; it could be released if contraception and prophylaxis were 'rightly
used and rightly understood', she wrote. Legal marriage had abolished
sexual selection and therefore got in the way of evolution towards 'higher
types'. 'Private property in women and children is the real object of legal
monogamic marriage,' she said. Women and children had to be
maintained by society, economically independent of individual men.
'Until women are economically independent, free to exercise sexual
selection in accordance with their own sense of natural chastity, the race

cannot and will not evolve.'[26] Such support for women would also put an end to prostitution. But what if three or four women chose the same man to father their children? No problem. 'Many women wd. select the same man & the human race wd. begin again to evolve & our present civilisation wd vanish,' she wrote to her friend H.G. Wells who, as he was the advanced thinker of the day was bound not to baulk at it the way most Englishmen would have.[27] She did not make this point so clearly in her writings for the public, but it was implied. She could not understand the conservatism of the population on birth control. 'A society which is wilfully slaying soldiers by the million, and negligently destroying coal miners, lead painters and other artisans, and then objecting to birth control as 'murder' is surely straining at the gnat and swallowing the camel.'[28]

She loved to throw about the Biblical quotations learnt in her youth, before she became a Freethinker and left the Congregationalism of her family behind, and use slang, particularly soldiers' slang when writing about the war. Her style was modernly straightforward, fitting somewhere between Marie Stopes' euphoric, mystical approach to sex and the arid descriptions of the sexologists. She put her emphasis on simple human psychology – what people could do without embarrassing themselves and others. 'I want people to have more sexual intercourse and have it safely and happily: there is no need to make unpleasantness the price of safety,' she told H.G. Wells.[29] And in a lecture to members of the National Secular Society, published in the society's *New Generation* magazine under the title 'Freethought and Sex' she said the great 'blunder' of Christian ethics was the assumption that morality was founded on the suppression of sexual appetite, rather than its expression. 'We all want to be happy and none of us can be so very happy for so very long. Why strive to take the shine out of things so relentlessly?'[30]

Published by Heinemann, endorsed by the Society for the Prevention of Venereal Disease and launched by the helpful Sir William in May 1922, *Safe Marriage* quickly went into multiple editions. In the fourth, Rout was announcing a whole range of contraceptive/prophylactic medications and devices she had made up under the brand name Proseldis, including calomel cleansing cream, cocoa butter suppositories, a chinosol–calomel effervescent suppository and a diaphragm. She answered readers' questions in appendices which grew with each new edition. The book received endorsements from Havelock Ellis and

Edward Carpenter, and excellent reviews. Sir James Barr said that if the Liverpool City Council gave out 100,000 free copies it would soon be able to reduce its medical staff by half. H.G. Wells said he wished everyone could have a copy to read before turning twenty-one. But the New Zealand government, true to form in its dealings with Rout, banned the book. Interestingly, once again, as with her war work, she was a catalyst for a change in the system. The Solicitor General agreed to use a censor to make the decision on what publications were indecent, and a censorship appeal board was set up to advise the government. *Safe Marriage*, however, remained banned. Rout pointed out that while birth control information was banned, an abnormally high number of New Zealand women were dying as a result of septicaemia after abortions or attempted abortions. In fact the problem was so bad the government was to set up a commission of inquiry into abortion in 1936.

Rout played a major role in the last big birth control trial in Britain. This took place in 1923 after copies of *Family Limitation*, by the American birth control campaigner Margaret Sanger were seized when Guy Aldred and Rose Witcop, who were selling them in Britain, had failed to make a purchaser – a plain-clothes police inspector – swear he was over twenty-one and would keep it away from unmarried people under that age. Rout had met Sanger in London in 1920; on the same visit the American had become H.G. Wells' lover. Rout persuaded Aldred and Witcop to let her manage their defence for the trial, extracting from them a promise that they would accept her advice. In return she would give evidence for them. She believed this was a test case for birth control and wanted activists in the cause to fight the case strongly because as she saw it the principle of freedom of speech in writing about sex in practical terms was at stake. She roped in Wells, and using his money, engaged a lawyer whom she provided with books, speech notes and lists of witnesses, including her prominent medical friends – and herself. She also typed out all the witnesses' evidence for him. When the case went to court in January 1923, he argued that the book was not obscene, that it had been written by a woman of refinement and education and that the ideas it advocated could be found in many medical books. The magistrate held that the pamphlet was not obscene in itself, but that its publication had been indiscriminate and he ordered it to be destroyed. Rout regarded this as a 'half-victory'. In the spirit of solidarity, she sent a copy of *Safe Marriage* to the Director of Public Prosecutions and invited him to take action on that too as it was indiscriminately sold by shopkeepers. An appeal was lodged, but Rout had a lesser role in that case. Dora Russell is usually credited with having organized the appeal, it is her name which is associated with the entire case, while Rout has gone uncredited. In fact, the appeal was less successful. This time the judge disallowed would-be witnesses like Rout and Wells, on the grounds that they were not doctors, and decided the pamphlet *was* obscene.

Rout cultivated her friendship with Wells as he was the foremost spokesman of his time for a change in sexual attitudes, one of the most prominent writers, and someone who had access to money – if not his own, other people's. Rout always had some scheme she wanted him to find someone to fund. In 1922 it was a publicity bureau to sell books on prophylaxis and contraception; two years later a shop selling equipment for both. Later she asked Wells to help her establish a 'Marriage Training Centre' which would provide medical help with 'all matters relating to married life … Please remember this when you meet anybody who does not quite know what to do with some surplus money.'[31] There is no evidence that any of these schemes got off the ground.

Rout's interest in the body was holistic, going beyond the intense interest in sexual health which opponents saw as an obsession, to the 'physical culture' she had embraced in her early twenties. She and Hornibrook were in the vanguard of the 'keep fit' movement which hit Britain in the late 1920s. Rout lectured for the Health and Strength League, encouraging women and girls to join. Hornibrook was still the strong man; he broke the British professional weight-lifting record in a pub in Buckingham Palace Road on his birthday in 1922. Professionally, he now set up as a physiotherapist and became famous – famous enough to be hailed as 'unquestionably the world's best known physiotherapist' in an obituary after his death in 1965.[32]

His clients included Wells, Arnold Bennett, Somerset Maugham and Aldous Huxley who mentioned him in a novel as one of the greatest of modern prophets. He invented a new exercise system which he published in his book *The Culture of the Abdomen*, which told readers how they could keep in trim in their own bedrooms in 'rather less than seven minutes a day' by strengthening the abdominal wall.[33] The book went into eighteen editions. It was given a publicity boost by humorist A.P. Herbert who wrote a piece for *Punch* about a Mr Mafferty who, on a sea cruise, refused to join in physical pursuits because he was already exercising while in his deck chair. Herbert did the exercises himself for the rest of his life.

In 1924 Rout told Wells she wanted to write another small work on 'practical sex ... Really it is shameful that something which is so necessary to health and happiness & quite indispensable to creative work should be persistently denied & muddled – it is so stupid – & so cruel.'[34] *Sex and Exercise: a study of the sex function in women and its relation to exercise* set out to explain to women in simple terms how their bodies worked. Young women, married and unmarried, were 'almost incredibly ignorant' about their bodies, Rout noted in the book.

> Thus the physical basis of marriage is genuinely beyond her comprehension and outside her efficient management and control. In anticipation she regards marriage as a social companionship and a gallant adventure in housekeeping, differing in no vital manner from friendship, excepting, of course, that babies come – just how or why, she does not exactly know ... Soon after marriage however she realises that happiness – and even fidelity – are dependent much more on the personal efficiency of marital intercourse than on the technical control of fertility. There are no English books on this aspect of life – books free from hectic emotionalism, mercenary quackery, and cold-blooded materialism.[35]

Women who knew little about sex had bad sex, leading to nervousness, ill-health, irritability, disgust and frigidity, she said. This artificial frigidity, where there should have been 'the natural warm-heartedness of youth' ruined many marriages.[36] *Sex and Exercise* was, in some respects, a female version of *The Culture of the Abdomen*; it had a set of exercises at the back based on the same principles (Figure 4.5). But the element that dominated the book was Rout's message to the women of the civilized world: that they must, for the sake of their health and the benefit of their sexuality, 'go native'. 'Native' was a category into which Rout threw all the world's people except what she called 'the white races'. 'Natives' did not do exercises. They danced instead. And they danced with their bodies, not solely with their feet, like Europeans. As a result they did not suffer from constipation and had better sex lives, between which there was a direct correlation. Combating constipation was an important side effect of the exercises. Constipation was a cause of frigidity, Rout held; when the bowel was overloaded with 'waste putrefactive matter' normal sexual desire was replaced by abnormal sexual disgust.

When Twenties Britain was in the grip of dance mania Rout and Hornibrook entered that arena too. At one end of the dance spectrum

FIGURE 4.5

ETTIE ROUT POSING IN A SWIMMING COSTUME BEFORE THE FIRST WORLD
WAR. THE PHOTOGRAPH WAS THE FRONTISPIECE IN *SEX AND EXERCISE*

Courtesy: Auckland Public Library, New Zealand, photograph
collection.

were the tea dances and night clubs, foxtrots and Charlestons; at the
other were the likes of Isadora Duncan and Margaret Morris. But
further out on a limb were Rout and Hornibrook. Not so far out,
however, that they were considered merely exercise instructors; when
Health for All listed the pioneers in the regeneration of the dancing
tradition, it included not only Duncan and Morris but Hornibrook and
Rout. At invitation-only exhibitions in luxurious West End drawing
rooms, Rout explained the utilitarian nature of the 'native dance' and the
virtue of 'muscle rhythm versus muscle jerk'. Native dances, she said,
were really all a matter of body tensing and relaxing, the object being the
'rhythmic rotation and churning of the abdomen and its contents'.[37]
Then Hornibrook would slip off his dressing gown and, naked apart
from a pair of black tights, performed a variety of 'native dances' – from
a Hawaiian 'vibration dance' to a strenuous Maori 'paddle dance'. The

Maori danced, Rout explained, in an ordered sequence: vibration exercises to loosen up the body, breathing exercises, body movements centred in the abdomen, and finally vibration exercises to ensure complete relaxation. Hohepa Te Rake, a Maori elder from New Zealand, did the dances at some of these events. Among the guests at one in 1930 was Professor Julian Huxley, along with old faithfuls like Sir William Arbuthnot Lane, and H.G. Wells, who was the only layman among a group of physicians and surgeons at a dance display two years later.

The 1924 British Empire Exhibition at Wembley may have rekindled the interest Rout and Hornibrook had both shown twenty years previously at the Christchurch Exhibition when both had posed for photographs with the Fijian contingent who wore native dress. Rout had borrowed some items to have her photograph taken in male Fijian garb, probably with no thought of the cultural insensitivity that would be obvious now. During the British Empire Exhibition Rout had attended a private dance meeting and seen the various nationalities go through their paces, finding that 'the rigid, unblinking, unwavering attention each native gave to the dances of the others was a revelation'. When the topic of cinema films 'suitable for native populations' came before the 1930 Colonial Office Conference, she wrote to *The Times* suggesting 'accurate screen records of suitable dances ... would not only prove very attractive to natives but they would be of great value ethnologically'.[38]

She spent much of 1925 in the British Museum studying 'native life'. She blamed nineteenth-century missionaries for not having recorded the information she now wanted, accusing them of having 'frittered away ... priceless opportunities' for gathering knowledge, but excusing them because 'Had they recorded the facts of primitive savage life calmly and accurately, their supporters at home would instantly have cut off contributions.'[39] She urged a full investigation into the practices of 'native' life and called on doctors and scientists to sift the evidence collected in the past, and co-ordinate and index it. They must do this, she said, 'with at least as much skill as we display in our courts when dealing with matters of far less importance to humanity', bringing to the work the attitude of 'the patient, sympathetic students – not the arrogant, callous tourist'.[40]

Rout and Hornibrook went on a research trip to Tunisia and Algeria where they spent time studying 'native dances'. But Rout's main contribution to the research effort was her book *Maori Symbolism: being an account of the origin, migration and culture of the New Zealand Maori as recorded in certain sacred legends.* She stressed that the book was a report that she 'a New Zealand law court reporter' had made from the evidence provided to her by the 'witness', Hohepa Te Rake who had left New Zealand as part of the Pioneer (Maori) Battalion during the First World War and had married an English schoolteacher he had met on leave. A magnetic personality, he was renowned as a great practitioner of the haka (the warlike dance which can be seen internationally today whenever New Zealand's All Black rugby team play) and as an orator. He had a great sense of humour, and many felt he had brought this to bear on Rout because her book was a better description of her own idea of a Utopian society than it was of Maori society. In this society, ruled by eugenics, a couple's first sexual union took place at a ritual ceremony, race health tutors taught young men about sex and the healthiest men were kept out of battle so as to be preserved for breeding. Some felt Rout had been hoaxed as Margaret Mead was later believed to have been by the young Samoan women she quizzed about their sex lives. The book did get some things obliquely right (the equal value and complementary functions of women's and men's roles, for example) and covered some ground that was later fought over, including the idea that the Maoris' ancestors journeyed from South America, which formed the basis of Thor Heyerdahl's work. But if Rout had done the patient fieldwork she asked others to do she would have written a different book.

The following year she put one part of her own personal eugenics code into practice when she practised euthanasia on an old friend from Christchurch days – Professor Alexander Bickerton who had been living in London since before the war. Rout and Bickerton had a pact that when the pain of his cancer outweighed the joy of his life she would inject him. She did, with a mixture of morphine and heroin.

The same year as *Maori Symbolism* was published, Rout also put out a health food handbook entitled *Native Diet* and aimed at healthy bowel movements. The 'native diet' was based on fresh vegetables cooked in a minimum of water, root vegetables, fruit, herbs and plenty of what we now call 'fibre'. She stressed the virtues of soy bean products and advised cutting out red meat, drinking herbal beers instead of coffee and tea and using stone ground wholemeal rather than white flour. Rout had moved into the food field that year, becoming a foundation member, with 25 others, of the New Health Society, the first organized body dealing with social medicine. Dedicated to the proposition that 'prevention is better than cure', it aimed to educate the public on the need for good food, fresh air, sunshine and exercise. In 1927 Rout took charge of the wholemeal section of the society's stall at the Ideal Home Exhibition where she confirmed her suspicion that the public was not ready for full-scale wholemeal bread, but must be weaned off white bread. Once again she took to her typewriter in an effort to put things right. Her book *Whole-meal: with practical recipes*, showing women how they could use wholemeal in their own home baking, was published by Heinemann Medical Books in 1927. She announced to a friend that she had been taken on as adviser to a biscuit firm and was developing new recipes. Although no record can be found of which firm it was and whether any biscuits resulted, she often recommended Peek Frean's Vita-Weat. In letters to *The Times* she complained that Britain imported 'foreign food' when it should be eating its own and its empire's products. Britons should eat porridge made from their own wheat rather than importing American breakfast foods, for example. She wanted to see the unemployed given agricultural training in residential farm schools made from largely idle country estates. Her vision was of a vegetarian Britain based on tubers grown in terraced gardens which would make the country healthier, reverse the import-export balance in the right direction, and keep her free from susceptibility to siege. (She would not live long enough to see 'Dig for Victory' campaigns during the Second World War, but that is what she had in mind.)

She was still developing exercises, concentrating in the late 1920s on exercises for pregnancy and menstruation. She taught these new exercises to a qualified maternity nurse, but she wanted to teach them to the whole of the nursing profession. Her publishing career was still going strong. *Sex and Exercise* was reissued in abbreviated form as *Exercises for Women* and received recommendations from doctors. *Safe Marriage* was reissued as *Practical Birth Control* in 1927, selling out by early the next year. She wrote a series of articles for the *Daily Herald* called 'Dancing in the Sand', which gave exercise and diet advice for women on their summer holidays. Convincing women that becoming a mother did not mean the end of health and beauty was, for a while, her new campaign. She taught women exercises she had worked out to help them regain their figures after childbirth. She advocated 'la danse du ventre' – rotating the abdomen (Figure 4.6). Then she moved on to what she called 'sexual efficiency exercises'. She wrote to Wells in 1930 that she had started work on a new book dealing with 'the physical actions of marriage with suitable exercises to strengthen the muscles involved' and

FIGURE 4.6

BELLY DANCE FROM *EXERCISES FOR WOMEN*

Fig. 12.   Fig. 13.
DANSE DU VENTRE.

that she was basing the exercises in it on 'sex dances'. 'I stand with one foot on a hot brick and the other on a sheet of thin ice, so progress is rather slow.'[41] The resulting book was *Restoration Exercises for Women*, published in 1931 in Britain, and in 1934 in America as *Stand Up and Slim Down*.

Rout, whose early books were published under her own name, was now increasingly using 'Hornibrook'. The pair were often referred to as 'the Hornibrooks'. She talked in terms of 'we' when she spoke of getting lots of new women 'patients'. Rout went to New York in 1935 to publicize their work. She was reported there by journalist Mary Margaret McBride:

Mrs Ettie Hornibrook who has brought to American women all the way from New Zealand jungles certain graphic lessons in how to prevent that middle-aged spread, is 58 and doesn't care who knows it. She is just as upright and supple today as she was at 28 and weighs what she did then too – 130 pounds. ...To regenerate the middle-aged woman so that she will feel better, look better, do finer work and be surer of holding her husband is the energetic Mrs Hornibrook's mission in life. And all of it, she says, can be accomplished if only a woman will devote a few minutes a day to body movements copied from the native dances of Maori, Polynesian, Burmese and Sudanese women.[42]

While in America Rout criticized publicly the birth control movement there, particularly its lack of field work, thereby earning the enmity of Margaret Sanger who pointed out that there were 160 clinics and begged her to visit her and see for herself rather than staying in New York and making 'silly remarks about a campaign about which you know nothing'.[43] Rout had always alienated people, but letters from Sanger at this period make it sound as if she had become irrationally extreme. When Rout continued to argue the point with Sanger, Sanger scrawled a note to her secretary on the bottom of one of Rout's letters, 'Rose: This woman is a pest!' After another exchange of letters she wrote a final one:

> Dear Sadistic Ettie ... If you think you have 'cornered the market' on modernity, you should 'listen in' to some of the opinions people have expressed as to *your* ideas, speech, manners, exercises, to say nothing of your arrogance and conceit. Ever since I saw you in New York I have been hearing directly and indirectly from friends who have come across you lately. In nearly every case some mention has been made that you have gone 'sour'; that they recognise an embitterment that comes of disappointment; a peeved petulance which accompanies a thwarted egotism ... When jealousy and bitterness eat itself into the vanity of a peeved woman, she sounds 'dotty' ... Let us save stamps and time and discontinue this correspondence.[44]

By the time Rout returned to London several months later, Hornibrook had taken up with the woman he would marry after Rout's death. Several informants have said that Rout became addicted to some drug around this time, although perhaps this was a story put about by Hornibrook to explain what he must have partly viewed as his defection from the campaigning duo. Whatever the explanation, Rout left England in 1936.

She returned to New Zealand, was generally spurned and sailed for Rarotonga in the Cook Islands shortly afterwards. That September she died of a self-administered overdose of quinine, which she had taken during the recurring malaria attacks since her time in Egypt. In *Maori Symbolism*, she had written of 'the Peaceful Death' of the Maori, which meant euthanasia. She had helped Professor Bickerton with his death; now it seems she organized her own.

When the Press Association sent out an obituary, printed in a number of newspapers, it called her 'one of the best known of New Zealand women'. It did not spell out what she was well-known for, but implied it was for her shorthand and typing speed as a reporter at official enquiries.[45] In Britain the obituary published in the *New Generation* and the *Freethinker* was more fulsome, proclaiming that 'The world of fearless thinkers and speakers is the poorer by her death.'[46]

H.G. Wells called Rout 'that unforgettable heroine' in his novel *You Can't Be Too Careful*, published five years after her death.[47] But she had already been forgotten, particularly in her own country, because she had been suppressed during her lifetime. The lack of recognition, indeed an informal ban in the media, continued afterwards. She had no champions as other feminists had – women friends to write about them near the end of their lives and afterwards. Hornibrook had the opportunity but did not take it. He wrote two autobiographical books. In the first, published before Rout's death, in 1935, he made much reference to 'my wife' and her campaign, without ever mentioning her name; in the second he took her campaign for his own, referring to 'we' but not making it clear who but himself was included in the plural. The fact that she was difficult to get on with, that she gave her all to her campaigns and did not spend any time mollifying others or seeking approval worked against her when it came to posterity.

When a television docu-drama series entitled 'Pioneer Women' was made in the early 1980s, the Rout episode was put on half an hour later than the rest, which necessitated its being shown on another channel. In spite of an award-winning biography appearing in 1992, general knowledge about Rout and her activities seems to be lacking. In a listing of top New Zealanders of the century in the *New Zealand Listener* recently, her name was spelt incorrectly and the Second, instead of the First, World War, given as the time of her campaign.

Rout's work might have seemed irrelevant in the post-Second World War period, with penicillin appearing to be a 'magic bullet' in dealing with the traditional venereal diseases. But with the advent of AIDS in the early 1980s, her contribution snaps into focus as the same ideological ground has been fought over. She emerges as someone who not only risked her life and her reputation on behalf of men who denied her and women who were vehemently opposed to her, but as someone who presaged many of the ideas which people live by today. She went through many of the movements of the twentieth century – from socialism to safe sex. Her problem was that she went through them before most other people, but also that she went through them with an energy and a vehemence that was extraordinary. The world she wanted – one in which women practised safe sex and birth control, married for love rather than as a career choice, had easy access to divorce, could choose a partner just to have children with because his genes were what she wanted, understood the value of vegetables and could choose wholemeal over white flour, did pelvic floor exercises after childbirth, danced with their whole bodies not just their feet and exercised that way – is what we have now if we want it. Not only that, but today with more emphasis on exercise, diet (and safe sex) than ever before, most of it is the virtuous way. (Imagine how gratifying all the mechanisms and procedures for strengthening the 'abs' – abdominal muscles – would have been for Hornibrook and Rout). In her own lifetime, however, she found that, as she remarked to Wells, 'It's a mixed blessing to be born too soon.' Pushing the 1990s concept of 'safe sex' in the teens of that century spelt doom for her. It meant she became persona *non grata* in her own hypocritical country, which adopted her work and banned her at the same time.

NOTES

1. *Lyttelton Times*, 13 June 1904.
2. E. Rout, 'A Knight of the Bath', *New Zealand Illustrated Magazine*, X (1903), 225–7.
3. *The Bulletin*, 14 October 1936, 14.
4. G. Turner, 'Ettie Rout, friend of soldiers', *The Triad*, 10 March 1920, 35–7.
5. *Lyttelton Times*, 13 June 1904.
6. *The Press*, 2 July 1904.
7. Ibid., 13 June 1904.
8. Rout to Sir Thomas Mackenzie, 7 May 1917, New Zealand National Archives (NZNA), WA 10/3/2 ZMR 1/1/40.
9. Quoted in *Canterbury Times*, 22 November 1916, 67.
10. Rout to Lady Godley, 7 May 1917, NZNA WA 10/3/2 ZMR 1/1/40.
11. Rout to Sir Archdall Reid, 18 July 1917, NZNA WA 10/3/2 ZMR 1/1/40.
12. Rout to Col. Samuel, 26 August 1917, NZNA AD 24/46.
13. An example of this card is held in the Australian War Memorial, Canberra, Bean 3DRL 6673.
14. G. Turner, 'Ettie Rout, friend of soldiers', *The Triad*, 10 March 1920, 35–7.

15. Report of the Joint Select Committee on the Criminal Law Amendment Bill, October 1920, p.92.
16. E. Rout, *Two Years in Paris* (London, 1923).
17. Quoted in E. Rout, *Safe Marriage: a Return to Sanity* (London, 1922), p.vii.
18. Stopes to Rout, 8 July 1920, Stopes Papers, ADD 58540, British Museum.
19. Rout to Stopes, 24 May 1922.
20. *Safe Marriage*, p.17.
21. Ibid., p.17.
22. Ibid., p.30.
23. *Two Years in Paris*, p.7.
24. E. Rout, *The Morality of Birth Control* (London 1925), p.29.
25. Ibid., p.29.
26. *The Morality of Birth Control*, pp 30–1
27. Rout to Wells, 28 June 1924, Alexander Turnbull Library, Ms. 1690.
28. *The Morality of Birth Control*, p.78.
29. Rout to Wells, 28 June 1924.
30. E. Rout, 'Freethought and Sex', *New Generation*, 342.
31. Rout to Wells, 10 April 1931.
32. *Evening Post*, Wellington, 24 April 1965.
33. F. Hornibrook, *The Culture of the Abdomen* (London, 1924), p.5
34 Rout to Wells, 13 June 1924.
35. E. Rout, *Sex and Exercise* (London, 1925), pp.2–3.
36. Ibid., p.13.
37. E. Rout, *Health and Efficiency* (1927), p.614.
38. *The Times*, 27 June 1930, 10.
39. *Sex and Exercise*, p.62.
40. Ibid., pp.72–3.
41. Rout to Wells, 24 September 1930.
42. The *Washington Daily News*, 21 February 1935.
43. Margaret Sanger to Rout, 13 April 1935, Sanger Papers, Sophia Smith Collection, Smith College, Massachusetts, USA.
44. Sanger to Rout, 13 May 1935.
45. *Evening Post*, 19 September 1936, 11.
46. *New Generation*, October 1936, 118 and *Freethinker*, 27 September 1936, 621.
46. Rout to Wells, 30 December 1922.
47. H.G. Wells, *You Can't Be Too Careful* (London, 1941), p.116.

5

Breaking Bounds:
Alice Profé, Radical and Emancipationist

GERTRUD PFISTER

In the first third of the twentieth century there began in many respects a process of 'women's liberation' in Germany. Women were admitted to universities and the professions; they were granted the right to vote; and in everyday life outmoded notions of 'propriety and decorum' began increasingly to lose their significance. This 'women's emancipation' was accompanied by liberation of women's bodies: corsets were discarded and carried off to the museum while short hair and short skirts became fashionable. However, such 'liberation' from external constraints had its price; this was a growing internalization of ideals and disciplining of the body such as ever stricter norms of weight and size. New means of public transport as well as sporting activities like hiking and cycling allowed women greater freedom of movement; and sport, with its new credo of performance and competition, revolutionized ideas about the 'weaker sex'. Nevertheless, even in the 1920s resistance to women's sport had still not died out; on the contrary, using a great variety of moral, medical and aesthetic arguments, its opponents attempted to bar women from competitive sport and restrict them to their 'natural vocation' as wives and mothers.

Women challenged these views and attitudes in varying ways. There were sportswomen like the alpine skier Christl Cranz, the athlete Gisela Mauermayer and the pilot Elli Beinhorn, who through their sporting achievements invalidated the myth of the 'weaker sex'; there were officials like the president of the International Federation of Women's Sport, Alice Milliat, who fought for the unconditional integration of women into the world of sport, and there were, finally, scientists and academics, especially doctors, who sought to refute arguments and dispel doubts about women's sport. There was also a woman who was active in all three of these areas, a woman who practised sport herself, who as an administrator sat on committees and who as a doctor also fought for the liberation of the female body. This was Alice Profé, who was firmly convinced that women were the 'stronger sex' and that all that had to be done (especially by men) for this strength to manifest itself was to get rid of prejudice and remove restrictions.

ASSEMBLING THE MOSAIC

Many years ago, while I was collecting material on the subject of 'Girls and Women in Sport' I came across a number of articles by Alice Profé which immediately caught my attention. Although some of them had been written before the First World War, they struck me as still being highly relevant. What was so relevant about them was, firstly, Profé's fight against prejudice, discrimination and excessive tutelage by men; secondly, her striving to make the entire spectrum of sport and sporting activities accessible to women; and finally, her demands for equality and power for girls and women in sport. In spite of her sharp criticism of the prevailing conditions, her articles were never moralizing in tone and were always written in a lively and vivid style. On quite a few occasions I caught myself smiling with amusement, above all when Profé set upon her detractors' arguments with a scathing phrase or with subtle irony.

Who was this woman who spent her life advocating and promoting physical exercise for girls and women? After discovering the articles by Alice Profé I began to gather all the information on her that I could find. Again and again her name appeared in documents as a speaker at conferences, as the author of academic essays, as a committee member or as a school doctor. I combed through school yearbooks and medical registers as well as Berlin address books and all kinds of journals. One lead which proved especially fruitful was provided by a medical historian who had compiled material on German women doctors.[1] Through her I was able to get in touch with relatives of Alice Profé, who were also kind enough to place documents at my disposal. Furthermore, I succeeded in tracing a number of former pupils of Augusta School who were still able to remember their school doctor, Alice Profé. From these small pieces the mosaic of the life and work of Alice Profé can be reconstructed only fragmentarily. However, in spite of all the gaps, the image that unfolds is that of an inspirationalist who could still provide a model for girls and women in sport.

A DAUGHTER OF THE BOURGEOISIE BECOMES A DOCTOR: THE FIRST YEARS

Born in 1867 in Kletzko, a town in the then Prussian province of Posen (now Poznan, Poland), Alice Profé was the 11th of 14 children. Her father, Heinrich Eduard Profé, worked in the town as *Königlicher Distrikts-Commissarius* (Royal District Commissioner) but on his retirement in 1877 the family moved to Berlin.

Alice Profé enjoyed an excellent education for those times. At first she had a private tutor but later attended various girls' high schools in Berlin. (These were known in Germany as *höhere Mädchenschulen*. They provided private secondary education for daughters of affluent families.) In Prussia, however, before 1900 girls were not given the opportunity of taking the school leaving/university entrance examination and so were not admitted to higher education and thus to the professions. One of the few occupations that were open to girls from the bourgeoisie was that of a teacher, trained not at university but at the *höhere Mädchenschulen*. In 1887 Alice Profé took the exam which qualified her to teach at *mittlere* and *höhere Mädchenschulen*, i.e. the schools for the daughters of the privileged classes. Her report attested to her 'extensive knowledge, her teaching skills and an engaging and friendly way with children with which she easily wins their hearts'.[2]

For several years she worked as a teacher. What is rather unusual is the fact that she spent some time working in her chosen occupation in England. In an article for the journal *Körper und Geist* (Body and Mind) she recalled the time she spent there:

> I still have fond memories of the happy girls I saw on the playing fields in England. As a teacher, I used to accompany the girls of a large boarding-school on to the playing-field. From the pavilion the girls fetched sticks, balls and bats for hockey and cricket; the teams divided and the game began with eagerness and enthusiasm.[3]

In spite of these pleasurable experiences Alice Profé does not seem to have found teaching a totally rewarding vocation. She wanted more.[4] From 1891 to 1894 she worked as secretary to 'Herr v. K., former ambassador to Rome'[5] – but this too did not appear to be the career she was looking for. Her true wish was to become a doctor but this wish was not easily fulfilled since Alice Profé did not possess the formal requirements to study medicine. Moreover, in Prussia the universities remained inaccessible for women until 1908. In other parts of Germany the universities opened their doors to female students somewhat earlier, but even so the opposition of professors hostile to women students often made study impossible. What is more, an impressive body of resistance had formed against admitting women to the study of medicine. The advocates of this policy campaigned against potential female rivals (in a hitherto all-male profession) with a broad array of arguments. It was above all the myth of the weak female, along with her alleged proneness to indisposition and irritation which made women unsuited to academic professions.[6] A good impression of the arguments put forward against women's university study at the end of the nineteenth century is conveyed by a collection of essays edited by Arthur Kirchhoff, in which 'eminent university professors' were able to give vent to their hostile attitude towards women's ambitions. With few exceptions the authors, especially those representing the medical profession, took the view that menstruation, pregnancy and menopause totally disqualified women from taking up such a responsible profession as that of doctor.[7] It was against such prejudice and such obstacles that Alice Profé constantly had to fight. But there were other obstacles. She told one of her pupils about the harassment which female students faced and the tricks used by German professors in order to try to prevent women from studying: 'One professor thought up something special: he used to stop lecturing whenever there was a woman among his students. Another would carry on with his lectures, but wouldn't examine the students. One university would carry out examinations, but wouldn't let the female students sit them.'[8]

Since the only solution for women with aspirations for a career as a doctor was to study in Switzerland, Alice Profé also set off for the 'promised land' of women's university studies. From 1894 she followed a course of natural science in Geneva, where she received her *baccalauréat* in 1896.[9] She then studied in Zurich and Berne, taking the Swiss university entrance exam in Zurich. In 1900 she moved to Strasbourg and continued her studies there, spending one semester at Freiburg. In 1902 she qualified as a doctor in Strasbourg.[10] This was followed by work on a doctorate thesis on the subject of 'Brain herniation arising from the surgical treatment of brain tumours'. She gained her doctorate in 1903. In spite of all the hard work and the difficulties she encountered Profé later reckoned her university days in Switzerland among the most enjoyable of her whole life.[11] Also contributing to her happy memories of this period was undoubtedly her passion for the mountains.

After gaining her doctorate Alice Profé settled in Berlin in 1905, becoming one of the first women doctors to practise there. She practised medicine in Berlin until her death in 1946 and her name appears in Berlin medical registers variously as a paediatrician, a general practitioner and a doctor of sports medicine.

COMMITMENT TO WOMEN'S GYMNASTICS AND SPORT

Alice Profé spent her whole life fighting actively – in later years in leading positions in various associations and committees – for the interests of girls and women. Before the First World War, for example, she was a member of the executive committee of the Berlin branch of an association called Frauenbildung – Frauenstudium (Women's education – Women's study') which belonged to the radical wing of the bourgeois women's liberation movement and which fought, among other things, for women's political rights. She was also a member of the working committee of the Fortschrittliche Volkspartei (Progressive People's Party) founded in 1910, which set up the committee to prepare for a conference of Liberal Women. In addition, she was an active member of a society called Hospital of Women Doctors (a registered charity) as well as belonging to other doctors' organizations such as the Society of Internal Medicine and Paediatrics from 1905, and the German Society for Health and Hygiene at School from 1909.[12]

HEALTH AND HYGIENE AT SCHOOL

Alice Profé's work in school health and hygiene became so well known that within a short time of her qualifying as a doctor the publishing company of Schall und Rentel invited her to 'write an understandable set of guidelines on personal health care'.[13] In 1906 she published a manual on health matters, written in uncomplicated language and intended as a textbook for schoolchildren. Teaching health and hygiene was also one of her tasks at Augusta School, where she worked as a doctor from 1906 onwards. From 1925 to 1926 her official status was that of an *Anstaltsärztin* (doctor to this institution). In 1931/32 she was honoured for 25 years' service at the school.[14] Her interest in the subject led her to take part in various international conferences on school health and hygiene, for example in Nuremberg (1904), London (1907) and Paris (1910). Her report on the conference in Paris reveals her disappointment about the passivity of the participants but her enthusiasm for the 'rare and enchanting beauty of the city'.[15]

GIRLS' GYMNASTICS AND WOMEN'S SPORT

The emphasis of Alice Profé's activities lay on physical exercise for girls and women. The first articles she wrote on girls' gymnastics appeared as early as 1906 in the journal *Körper und Geist* and in the following years she regularly contributed her views, expressing critical comments, voicing demands as well as penning articles intended to give women encouragement and to dispel their fears.

At the turn of the century Alice Profé was not alone in criticizing the artificiality and the ineffectiveness of gymnastics lessons; the supporters of the Spielbewegung (games movement), too, were strong advocates of the reform of physical education. Partly out of their concern for the nation's fitness and its ability to defend itself, however, the games movement, whose initiatives were co-ordinated by the Central Committee for People's and Youth Games, founded in 1891, put most of their energy into promoting physical exercise for young men. Then, in 1912, with 'strong offspring can only be born of strong mothers' as its motto, a Committee for Women's Physical Fitness was set up with six men and five women as its members. Alice Profé was appointed its deputy chairwoman and from 1915 to 1916 its chairwoman.[16] At its first meeting this 'women's committee', as it was known, passed a declaration containing seven guiding principles for the furthering of gymnastics and sport for girls and women.[17]

She was not only concerned with female fitness but also with female equality. At the 8th Congress of the Central Committee for People's and Youth Games, Alice Profé gave a lecture on the 'physical exercise of our women' in which she demanded the equality of women and men in sport.[18] After the First World War Alice Profé kept up her efforts to improve the situation of girls and women in sport. She published articles, gave talks and ran courses, and continued to belong to various committees. In this way she was able to express her – still quite revolutionary – views at the major and pioneering women's sports conferences of the 1920s, for example at the Conference on the Physical Education of German Women, organized in 1925 by the Deutsche

Turnerschaft (German Gymnasts' Association), and in 1929 in Berlin at the Conference on Women's Gymnastics and Sport, at which she gave a widely acknowledged and frequently quoted lecture.[19]

Of particular importance in her work was her participation in the controversial discussions which took place in the field of medicine since the various medical arguments played a significant role in the discourse on women's sport. The 1920s saw the first tentative steps towards the professionalization of sports medicine, initiated and co-ordinated by the German Physicians' Association for the Advancement of Physical Exercise (DÄB). One of the measures taken by the DÄB was to establish a qualification for doctors of sports medicine, acquired by attending courses on theory as well as practical gymnastic exercises.[20] Alice Profé not only acquired the 'authorization to practise sports medicine' but also ran courses on women's sport in these training courses for doctors of sports medicine.[21] However, it has not yet been established whether Profé worked for the Sports Medical Advice Centre for Girls and Women set up in Berlin by the Association of German Women Physicians.[22]

Like many other organizations, the DÄB (apparently at the instigation of the Association of German Women Physicians, founded in 1924) established a Women's Committee, of which Alice Profé was also a member.[23] Among other things, the committee fought for the introduction of physical education for girls attending *Berufsschulen* (schools preparing older pupils for a vocation). The Women's Committee also tried to obtain a seat and voting rights – and thus more influence – on the DÄB's executive committee, but this attempt failed.[24] Consequently, the Association of German Women Physicians demanded that a woman doctor – the Association suggested Alice Profé – take part at the meetings and working sessions of the executive committee in an advisory capacity.[25] Profé was also a member of the Committee on Physical Exercise of the Association of German Women Physicians.[26] Then in 1927 the Deutscher Reichsausschuß für Leibesübungen (Committee of the German Reich on Physical Exercise), the umbrella organization of the bourgeois sports movement in Germany, also established a Women's Committee. Twelve women were appointed members of its leading body, the so-called Working Committee, among them Alice Profé.[27]

Besides her professional work as a doctor and her activities on numerous committees, Profé also ran various training courses at such institutions as the German College of Physical Exercise in Berlin. The main subject she taught was women's sport.[28]

FROM LEISURE ROWING TO SPORTS CONTESTS

Alice Profé, however, was no zealous remote functionary without contact with the grass roots; on the contrary, she fought for her ideals at an intensely personal level and always with concrete aims. As already mentioned, she was employed as school doctor at the state grammar school for girls, Augusta School, and not only taught there but also took her pupils swimming, skating and hiking.[29] A former pupil stressed in the address she gave at Profé's cremation service that Alice Profé wished to open the girls' eyes to the beauty of the world.[30] It was thanks to her personal endeavours that the school's girls' rowing club was able to develop considerably and in the 1930/31 school year she was made an honorary member of the club.[31] In rowing circles women were viewed with great scepticism, especially when they were not willing to limit themselves to stylistic or leisure rowing. In the 1920s stylistic rowing (in which the correct style of the rowers counted and not the speed of the boat) was favoured in women's rowing contests since competing for metres or seconds was felt to be 'unfeminine' and a risk to women's health. Alice Profé belonged to those who, like some women of the German Ladies' Rowing Association, campaigned vigorously for the participation of women in speed rowing.[32]

In many respects Alice Profé's initiatives corresponded with those of the International Federation of Women's Sport, which was founded in Paris in 1921 and whose activities focused on women's athletics. After the refusal of the IOC and the International Athletic Association to allow women to take part in the track-and-field events of the Olympic Games, the International Federation of Women's Sport organized Women's Olympic Games which took place in Paris (1922), Gothenburg (1926), Prague (1930) and London (1934). The programme of these Women's Games included numerous events which the IOC had refused to allow in the 'official' Olympic Games: this meant, for example, that women athletes could now take part in such activities considered 'unfeminine' as shot-putting or the 800 metres as well as games such as team handball. In the 1930 Women's Games in Prague a German team took part for the first time.[33] Accompanying the team as a coach was Alice Profé, and this team was to take first place in the nations' ranking.[34] In *Start und Ziel* (Start and Finish), an athletics magazine, Profé wrote an article on her 'Prague

Reflections', in which she began by emphasizing that the women's contests had gone off with neither dramatic collapses nor 'bouts of fainting or cramp'. Here, she was alluding to the newspaper reports of the women's 800 metres at the 1928 Olympics in Amsterdam. When several of the runners sank to the ground exhausted on reaching the finish, sports officials as well as the public regarded this as proof that women were quite unsuited to both strength and endurance contests. As a consequence, the 800 metres was excluded from the women's Olympic programme. In her 'Prague Reflections' Profé was pleased to be able to point out that the 'horror stories' that had been spread about women's competitions, 'unfortunately by doctors, too, and even by sports physicians', were based on male preconceptions and mere assumptions. In Prague, at any rate, first-aid workers had nothing to do. And since she stayed at the same hotel as many of the German competitors, Profé was able to report from first-hand experience on the congenial mood, the dances in the evening and the 'atmosphere of excellent health, both in body and in mind' that prevailed among the German team. Her impressions of the demonstrations and competitions in Prague contained two main messages: first of all, taking the 700 Sokol gymnasts as an example, she made it clear that this form of physical training ('exercises of the legs, arms and trunk with sometimes graceful arching and posing, accompanied by the symbolic throwing of flowers, and alternating with the old familiar jerking and stretching'), aiming as it did at disciplining the body and mind, was both out of date and out of keeping with women's needs. Secondly, she stressed the value of sporting contests as these could contribute towards developing personality and forming character. She viewed the Prague Games as proof that, in accordance with the needs of the times, young women had developed a preparedness to act, a will to work hard and a sense of adventure. And it was only through sport that these needs could really be satisfied; only through sport was it possible to acquire the necessary fighting spirit. 'Life is a struggle. One has to fight to overcome obstinacy, lethargy and narrow-mindedness. Nothing is of value just because it was of value yesterday or the day before. Let youth find its own new ideals, let young people live their own lives, whatever the risks.'[35]

FIGHTING THE MYTH OF FEMALE WEAKNESS

The views and utterances of Alice Profé[36] can only be judged in the light of the attitudes of mainstream medicine, which on the whole accepted and even propagated the myth of the weak female. Many doctors' thoughts on the subject of women's sport were concentrated on a woman's ability to have children: 'With regard to adult women, all physical exercise must be considered from the point of view of reproduction', wrote for example a senior consultant by the name of Küstner at the Women's Clinic of Leipzig University Hospital in 1931.[37] There were several medical theories about the 'adverse' effects of sport on childbirth. Influential figures in the medical profession, such as the director of the Women's Clinic in Leipzig, Hugo Sellheim, were of the opinion that sporting activity caused the womb to dislodge, the muscles of the pelvis to tighten, or the pelvis to narrow, thus impairing women's ability to give birth. Furthermore, doctors warned women against wasting their (limited supply of) energy, which they should save for their one important task (or duty) in life – bearing and raising children. Moreover, sporting activity in general was claimed to make women athletes more masculine, leading to the sexes growing more alike and thus representing an attack on the gender and social orders. Women's competitive sport, therefore, along with many types of sport and forms of exercise, were sharply criticized in many quarters and sometimes vigorously rejected.[38]

Alice Profé challenged these unproven assertions, just as she fought against all attempts by men to speak for women or limit their activities. Since she was not a scientist undertaking empirical research but a general practitioner, her observations were based on available studies, which she repeatedly cited, although she frequently interpreted them differently from mainstream doctors. In many of her articles she proved to be a mediator between research and practical medicine and her analyses were addressed not only to the authorities and politicians, and teachers and sports officials but also to the women directly affected. They are written in concrete and comprehensible language, and often spiced with a dash of irony, which makes them a pleasure to read.

Alice Profé's most important message was that girls and women should decide for themselves how far they wanted to go and what they wanted to achieve. She was clearly against women overstepping their limits but she also believed that it was enough to listen to one's body in order to find the right balance of athletic or sporting activity.[39] 'Girls and women should not seek to achieve the best performance of any other girls or women or men, but only their own personal best performance. This, at least, is how they should be trained.'[40] Further, Profé demanded that 'exercises should correspond to the strength and not the gender of the person doing them'.[41]

Profé had no objections to 'unfeminine' types of sport and also recommended heavy, muscle-building exercises as well as those requiring stamina. There was no proof at all, according to Profé, that middle- and long-distance running had deleterious effects on women's health, as was so often claimed.[42]

THE FIGHT AGAINST OBSTACLES

As Alice Profé pointed out with admirable clarity at the Congress of the Central Committee of People's and Youth Games in 1912, the obstacles facing women in sport did not in her view result from the physical and mental characteristics or disposition of the female sex but rather from the preconceptions and disadvantages with which girls and women were faced. And she was able to provide an impressive array of evidence in support of her assertions, ranging from the opening times of public baths to the inadequate amount of physical education at school and to the lack of public funding for youth work among girls and young women.[43] What angered her especially was the fact that the funding earmarked by the Prussian authorities for youth work in 1911 was to go exclusively to male institutions. 'I stand here and ask myself: what is worse – the ruthlessness or the short-sightedness? ... It is a good thing that they don't already start with the babies and demand mothers' milk only for the boys.'[44]

In lectures and articles she emphasized, moreover, that 'female weakness' was caused by a great number of interdependent factors such as education and upbringing, unnatural beauty ideals, the neglect of the body and even restrictive clothes. In addition, striving to 'nurture grace and feminine charm' in girls' gymnastics, selecting exercises because of their elegant movements and avoiding any exertion whatsoever was useless and dangerous:

> But in girls' gymnastics it isn't enough for the intricate steps to be practised separately, one by one. No, no. What an infinite abundance of enchanting patterns of movement is created by the transition from one step to the other, by the combination of steps with waving, bending and inclining arms, or with clapping the hands on the first, second or third beat. ... No, it isn't captivating.

But the body and mind of the gymnast feel like captives when the command is given: Apparatus gymnastics to music is another of the wonderful 'highlights' of girls' gymnastics. ... Girls' gymnastics, as it is today, has scarcely any advantage whatever for the organs of a child's body. ... Indeed, it puts a strain on the brain owing to the great amount of attention and memory that is required, so that it does not relax the mind but burdens it with new exertion.[45]

This passage is quoted to show what girls' physical education consisted of in those days and why, again and again, it was so sharply criticized by Profé. In place of this pointless 'playing around', she called for gymnastics 'which demand physical exertion, set difficult tasks and is thus rewarding for both the body and the mind'.[46]

EQUALITY OF THE SEXES

Strength and stamina can only be increased through the adjustment of the body to growing demands made on it: 'Exercise strengthens and develops the organs of the body; inactivity makes them waste away. This is a law of nature, universally valid.'[47] This law, of course, is still valid today! Accordingly, Profé demanded that the sexes be treated equally in respect of physical training with the following argument:

There is no female muscle, specially built and with specific female functions, that reacts in a particular, female way to the exertions of physical exercise. There is no special female blood, and no female breathing which makes women especially suited to sprightly exercises. There is no scientific proof for these assertions. Just as women eat no differently than men in order to grow strong and healthy, they also need no different kind of physical exercise to keep fit.[48]

Profé rejected all the arguments put forward by doctors, especially gynaecologists, to legitimize the exclusion of the 'weaker sex' from not only competitive sport but even various types of sport. Her response, for example, to the warning that sudden, jolting movements might lead to a dislodging of the womb was that this organ was 'well enough suspended' in the pelvis and so small that it could not be harmed by any of the physical exercises known to her.[49] And, in the highly controversial question of what women should and should not do during menstruation, her standpoint was quite unequivocal: girls and women should decide themselves how much exertion their bodies were capable of. 'The most harmful thing to do,' she wrote, 'is certainly to sit around for hours on end.'[50]

In spite of all this, Alice Profé did not deny that there were differences between the sexes; on the contrary, she believed that these were among the 'most wonderful provisions of nature'. But over and over again she pointed out that 'real femininity, i.e. everything that nature plants in women's bodies' cannot be harmed by 'external activity'. At the Congress of Traditional and Youth Games in 1912 she ended her lecture with the following warning: 'Too many people think they know what femininity is … Femininity is as deeply rooted in women's natures as masculinity is in men's; and men will always go wrong as long as they try to explain to women what femininity is.'[52] Profé also took the revolutionary view that in consultations on 'women's issues' women should be heard as experts. There is no need to add that such demands were not put into practice neither in the gymnastics and sports movement nor in society as a whole.

Her fundamental criticism of the aims and the contents of 'feminine' gymnastics – the low standards set, the unnatural, 'mannered' forms of movement and overdone femininity – forms a kind of motif that threads its way through her publications, which always contained the message that 'women's inferiority' was not only unnatural but also a perversion of nature.

REFORMS

The Women's Gymnastics and Sports Conference organized by the Berlin Women's Gymnastics and Sports Associations in 1929 was reported on extensively in the sports press. In a lecture she gave at this conference on the subject of the 'Physical Training of Young Women' Alice Profé again spoke out against the prevailing doctrine, which continued to stress the difference between the sexes. In particular, she pointed out that many of the myths surrounding the weak female should have long ago been dispatched to the realm of fiction and fantasy. In order to illustrate what she meant, she gave the example of doctors having to 'search desperately' if they wanted to show their students a case of female anaemia.[53] To counter these attitudes, she demanded a varied programme of girls' gymnastics at school, with exercises on apparatus, sports training to increase strength and stamina, physical contact games and contests. In the dispute over the 'right' kind of physical exercise for girls and women she took up a clear position against 'modern expressive gymnastics' and in favour of traditional, exercise-type gymnastics and sport. She was also against introducing one of the rival systems of gymnastics into schools since in her view these led to unnatural movements and posing among girls.

A further recurring topic of her lectures and articles was the reform of gym and sports dress. She categorically rejected the corset and advocated gym trousers right from her earliest contributions. She loathed any kind of prudery, moreover. In 1926 the Bavarian education ministry had prohibited the participation of girls at public gymnastic displays on moral grounds. In the magazine 'Physical Exercises' Profé spoke out against this ban, which she found inappropriate and out of keeping with the times. 'The more liberal fashion of women's dress has led to the fact that the natural forms of the legs of both men and women can be seen up to the knees (and even above) without decency and morality having gone to rack and ruin.'[54] According to Profé, the clothing worn for gymnastics had to be functional and hygienic and not hinder the gymnast even in the freest of movements: 'And this leads us not to indecency and vulgarity but to the realization that morals here again – as so often in the past – have adapted to the changing times and that "decent" is now what – through inexperience and obscure anxieties – used to be called "indecent".'[55]

THE LAST ESSAY

To my knowledge, Alice Profé's last essay appeared in *Deutsches Fiauentum und Leibesübungen* (German Women and Physical Exercise) edited by Warninghoff and Güssow. Whereas several of the contributions published in the collection had quite obviously been infected by National Socialist ideology on women and their place in society, Alice Profé had neither altered her views in any way nor adapted her manner of expressing them to the new regime. Although there were frequent demands for 'appropriate physical exercise particular to the female sex,' Profé remained adamant: 'There are no physical exercises,' she wrote, 'which must be generally prohibited for women on health grounds'.[56] She continued to follow her motto 'If you can do it, do it', justifying her now more than ever revolutionary views with the laws of physiology: 'It is nature's wish that the organs receive the 'optimum stimulus' in order to develop fully.' Nor did she conceal her scorn for the 'faint-hearted' or the 'scaremongers'. Dislodging the abdominal organs, the 'musculature of the taut fibres' and in general the dangers of sport for female health were in her view completely and utterly unproved, such assertions not only testifying to a lack of scientific logic but also contradicting all common sense.

Although Profé always laid great stress on the importance of physical exercise for health in her articles, she considered the recreational aspect, the relaxation and fun of sporting activities, just as valuable. In a brief essay for the *Reichsbahn-Turn-und Sportzeitung* (German National Railways' Gymnastics and Sports Paper) in 1929 she related an encounter with an elderly married couple on the ice in winter. After many years the couple had got out their old skates again because 'they hoped to have a good time'. For Profé it was a positive sign that the lady had not thought she had to legitimize her physical activity with grounds of health and hygiene.[57]

ENCOUNTERS, CONTROVERSIES AND ACCOMPLISHMENTS

What kind of reception did Alice Profé's lectures and articles have among the public in general and among women in particular? I have not been able to find very much to allow me to answer this question. In his history of physical exercise Edmund Neuendorff described her in the following terms. 'She was a splendid person, noble-minded, kind-hearted and womanly, with a deep understanding for the well-being and the woes of others; she was of great intellect and had a strong will to help where help was needed.'[58] During an interview Els Schröder, the first woman to become responsible for womens' gymnastics in the German Gymnasts' Association, also touched upon the subject of Alice Profé.[59] Schröder told me that she had been impressed by her lectures. She could still remember very clearly, she said, Profé's remarks on physical exercise and menstruation, and the encouragement she had given her audience to pay heed to their own bodies and pursue their sporting activities if they felt like it. Replying to objections that it was unhygienic for women to go swimming during their period, she declared that 'those few drops of blood' were no problem at all. Els Schröder felt confirmed in her belief that there was nothing to stop her from carrying on her training sessions when she was having her period. A number of former pupils of Augusta

FIGURE 5.1

DR ALICE PROFÉ

School recall Alice Profé as a very popular teacher and as a woman who although quite old (in the 1930s she was over 60 years of age) still seemed to them to be full of life and energy. She gave the pupils the impression that they were being taken seriously and that they could always talk to her about personal things.[60] I was able to trace four living relatives of Alice Profé, three of whom had not known her, however. Only Hanfried Profé recalled that Alice Profé, his father's cousin, had often visited his family. He had always thought of her as a kind relative, with a strong personality, and as a person who always stood up for others.[61]

Alice Profé wasn't afraid to swim against the current with her views and her comments. The writer of an obituary summed up her intellectual integrity in the following terms: 'Never did you alter your opinions for the sake of material gain, for the sake of a title or for the sake of promotion.'[62] Reading through Profé's essays, I am inclined to agree with this judgement. Profé's views met with opposition from many teachers, officials and politicians, especially those she crossed swords with, and she was never one to try and avoid offending the authorities or experts, if necessary attacking them vigorously. In her lecture to the Women's Gymnastics and Sports Conference in 1929, for example, she criticized the guidelines issued in 1926 on girls' gymnastics in secondary schools for possessing neither a 'clear spirit of objectivity' nor the will to 'show each individual pupil the way to achieving the maximum of health, strength, courage and self-confidence they are capable of'. It is no surprise to learn that the delegates representing the authorities at the conference vehemently rejected Profé's arguments. Agreement with her views was more to be found among the gymnastics instructors and doctors present.[63] The 'opinion that in physical exercise the same exertions can be demanded of the female body as those demanded of the male body'[64] was shared by neither the biologist E. Matthias nor the gynaecologist W. Wiegels, who accused Profé of 'serious errors' which might 'easily cause confusion among gym instructors, especially in a lecture given by a doctor'.[65] They failed, however, to offer any proof for their assertions.

Little is known about her life in the Third Reich, as already mentioned; Alice Profé it seems was not prepared to alter her views to conform with Nazi ideology. In his address to those present at Profé's cremation Hans Kollwitz drew attention to the fact that she bitterly and earnestly complained about the inhumanity of the National Socialist regime. From that period of German history I came across a detail from which it might be possible to infer something about her political convictions. For many years she was the doctor of Marie-Elisabeth Lüders, a member of the German parliament for the German Democratic Party. When Lüders was arrested by the Gestapo in 1937 and incarcerated, Profé petitioned for, and succeeded in obtaining certain improvements in the conditions of Lüder's imprisonment.[66]

In summary, at a time when women were regarded as the 'second sex', Alice Profé's goals were controversial – goals which she summed up in the following words: '"Make the train longer, and you make the wings shorter." I appeal to the strong and the happy: please help to make sure that a separate form of women's gymnastics does not become yet another train behind the robes of women striving against inhibitions and for freedom and self-reliance.'[67]

PRIVATE LIFE

From 1909 to 1946 Alice Profé lived in the Charlottenburg district of Berlin at Savignyplatz 3, the address of both her surgery and her private rooms. In the early years she lived with her mother, who died quite suddenly in 1914. She then 'lived in a common household and in cordial friendship' with Gertrud Seidel, who looked after the housekeeping. Sharing a home with a female relative or friend was not only a widespread phenomenon among activists of the women's liberation movement but also a form of household recommended for single women by guidebooks on morals and social conventions.[68] Gertrud Seidel and Alice Profé had much in common: both were very fond of literature and walking in the mountains. In his commemorative address Hans Kollwitz mentioned that he had met them in the Engadin in 1930 – 'two ladies, one older and white-haired and the other younger, both jauntily dressed in hiking gear'. Their close attachment lasted until Alice Profé died in 1946. Profé left her friend Gertrud Seidel all her possessions, including a small house on the Baltic coast.

Although little is known about Alice Profé's private life, it is reasonable to infer that sporting activities made up part of it. That she was a keen mountain hiker, undertaking tours in the highest altitudes, is not only known from Hans Kollwitz but also from one of her essays in which she described ice-skating on Lake Wannsee in Berlin. In a lecture she gave in 1912 she also talked about her 'own experience in a women's gymnastics club'.[69] We know, furthermore, that Profé used to row, and in many articles she mentions that she went on trips and hikes with her pupils. She was active well into old age. She still kept her surgery hours until shortly before her death at the age of 79.

Alice Profé died on 9 August 1946 after a short illness; she was cremated on 12 August 1946. Hans Kollwitz gave one of the two commemorative addresses. The other was given by a former pupil who called Alice Profé her second mother. In her address the pupil quoted the following poem, which Alice Profé had marked in a book – a poem that testifies to her and warmth and humanity.

Und ich denke so glühend, wie andere beten
An all jene Helden, die göttlichen, milden,
Die an der Spitze der menschlichen Gilde
Führend hintreten.
Funkelnden Regenbogen gleich
Stehen wir über dem armen Reich
Von Neiden und Hassen.

And I reflect so passionately, like others pray,

On all those heroes, the divine and benevolent,
Who at the head of the human guild
Take their place as leaders.
Like sparkling rainbows
We stand above the poor world
Of envy and hate.

NOTES

I would like to thank Eva Brinkschulte for her kind help. I was able to obtain a great deal of biographical information from documentation at the Institute of Medical History, compiled and supervised by Johanna Bleker.

1. Women Doctors under the Kaiser. Documents held at the Institute of Medical History.
2. Commemorative address by Marg. Munzel; material provided by Eva Brinkschulte.
3. A. Profé, 'Unser Mädchenturnen', *Körper und Geist*, 14 (1906), 409.
4. Obituary written by Munzel 1946.
5. A. Profé, 'Über die bei operativer Behandlung von Hirntumoren auftretenden Hirnhernien', dissertation (Stuttgart, 1903), curriculum vitae attached to thesis.
6. See B. Ziegeler, *Weibliche Ärzte und Krankenkassen: Anfänge ärztlicher Berufstätigkeit von Frauen in Berlin 1893–1935* (Weinheim, 1993).
7. A. Kirchhoff, *Akademische Frauen* (Berlin, 1897).
8. Munzel, 1946.
9. According to the c.v. attached to Profé's thesis. The baccalauréat, the lowest academic grade, is not conferred in Germany.
10. According to the c.v. attached to Profé's thesis.
11. Munzel, 1946.
12. Documentation on women doctors; Eva Brinkschulte.
13. A. Profé, *Lehrbuch der Gesundheitspflege* (Berlin, 1906), p.1.
14. Schuljahresbericht (school annual reports) 1925/26, 1930/31. The reports are kept in the archives of the Berlin Institute of Teacher In-service Training (BIL).
15. A. Profé, 'Vom internationalen Kongreß für Schulhygiene in Paris', *Körper und Geist*, 19 (1911), 230.
16. *Monatsschrift für das Turnwesen* (Gymnastics Monthly Magazine), 31 (1912), 466–7. On the composition of the central committee, see C. Schröder, 'Die Rolle des Zentralausschusses für Volks- und Jugendspiele (1891–1922) als 'Führerorganisation' auf dem Gebiete der Körperkultur' (Ph.D. thesis, Leipzig, 1967), supplementary volume. I am grateful to Eerke Hamer for bringing this to my attention.
17. *Körperkultur* (Physical Culture), 7 (1912), 202.
18. A. Profé, 'Die Ertüchtigung unserer Frauen', *Körper und Geist*, 21 (1913 a), 193–205. See also A. Profé, 'Unsinn im Mädchenturnen', *Körper und Geist*, 16 (1908), 72–7.
19. *Deutsche Turnzeitung* (German Gymnasts' Newsletter), 70 (1925), 229; *Frauen-Turn- und Sporttagung zu Berlin 12 bis 15 Juni 1929* (Conference on Women's Gymnastics and Sport in Berlin, 12–15 June, Berlin 1929). Reports on this conference are to be found in many magazines; they invariably contain references to Alice Profé.
20. It is so far not clear when she obtained this qualification. However, her name is to be found on the list of doctors of sports medicine published in October 1931. See *Der Sportarzt* (The Sports Physician), 7 (1931), 7. The requirements for obtaining this qualification are printed in *Der Sportarzt*, 4 (1928), 7.
21. Such a course was held at the German Stadium in Berlin in 1928; *Der Sportarzt*, 4 (1928), 13.
22. The head of the Advice Centre was Frau Moses-Rothstein; *Der Sportarzt*, 5 (1929), 6.
23. *Der Sportarzt*, 6 (1930); 7 (1931), nos. 17/18, 10; nos. 19/20, 10. This contained a report on the

committee's re-election. On the Association of German Women Physicians; see Eckelmann, 1992.

24. *Der Sportarzt*, 5 (1929), 6, 4.
25. *Die Ärztin*, 5 (1929), 8, 163. In the following years there was co-operation between the women's committee of the DÄB and the Committee on Physical Exercise of the Association of German Women Physicians.
26. *Die Ärztin*, 7 (1931), 41–2.
27. National Committee on Physical Exercise: Report of Activities 1927–28. Berlin 1928, p.40.
28. See, for example, *Die Ärztin*, 5 (1929), 80.
29. See Profé, 'Ertüchtigung', 204 ; A. Profé, 'Soll auch die Frau turnen und Sport treiben?' in C. Diem, H. Sippel and F. Breithaupt (eds.), *Stadion. Das Buch vom Sport und Turnen, Gymnastik und Spiel* (Berlin, 1928), p.99.
30. See Munzel, 1946.
31. *Schuljahresbericht*, 1930/31.
32. *Wassersport* (Water Sports), 47 (1929), 121.
33. See G. Pfister, 'Der Internationale Frauensportverband und die Olympischen Frauenspiele', *Jahrbuch des Sportmuseum* (Berlin, 1999).
34. A. Profé, 'Prager Gedanken', *Start und Ziel*, 6 (1930), 303–5.
35. Ibid., 305.
36. See A. Profé, 'Unsinn im Mädchenturnen', *Körper und Geist*, 16 (1908), 72–7; 21 (1913), 193–205; 'Ertüchtigung', 193–205.
37. H. Küstner, 'Frau und Sport', *Medizinische Welt* (1931), 791.
38. For a summary, see G. Pfister, 'The Medical Discourse on Female Physical Culture in Germany in the 19th and Early 20th Centuries', *Journal of Sport History*, 17 (1990), 183–99.
39. See, for example, A. Profé, '*Neuzeitliche Betrachtungen über die Leibesübungen der Frauen*', *Reichsbahn- Turn- und Sportzeitung* (1929), 132–4 (Carl-Diem-Archiv Mappe 471).
40. Profé, 'Soll auch die Frau', p.99.
41. Ibid., p.97.
42. Ibid., p.99.
43. See all the articles by Profé published before the First World War.
44. Profé, 'Ertüchtigung', 200; 'Unsinn', 72–7.
45. Profé, 'Unsinn', 76.
46. Ibid.
47. Profé, 'Unser Mädchenturnen', 408.
48. Profé, 'Soll auch die Frau', 100.
49. Profé, 'Ertüchtigung', 198; 'Soll auch die Frau', 101.
50. Profé, 'Soll auch die Frau, p.101.
51. A. Profé, 'Die körperliche Ausbildung der weiblichen Jugend', in *Frauenturn- und Sporttagung* (Berlin, 1929), p.7.
52. Profé, 'Ertüchtigung', 205.
53. Profé, 'körperliche Ausbildung', 8.
54. A. Profé, 'Zwei 'Kulturdokumente' aus Bayern', *Die Leibesübungen* (1926), 537.
55. Ibid.
56. A. Profé, 'Was die Hygiene zu den Leibesübungen sagt', in H. Warninghoff (ed.), *Deutsches Frauentum und Leibesübungen* (Berlin, 1936), p.41.
57. Profé, 'Neuzeitliche', 132–4.
58. Neuendorff, *Geschichte der neueren deutschen Leibesübung vom Beginn des 18. Jahrhunderts bis zur Gegenwart. Bd. IV.* (Berlin s.a.), pp.408–9; Michaelis, a woman doctor, called Profé a 'pioneer fighting for girls' gymnastics'; see *Die Ärztin* 5 (1929), 162.
59. Interview with Els Schröder by the author on 12 December 1991 in her Munich flat.
60. Telephone conversation with M.S. on 8 July 1997. The class M.S. was in took the German equivalent of 'A' levels (i.e. school-leaving/university entrance exams) in 1939.
61. Conversation with Hanfried Profé on 1 June 1997.
62. Copy from Hanfried Profé.
63. *Frauen-Turn-und Sporttagung zu Berlin 12. bis 15. Juni 1929* (Conference on Women's Gymnastics and Sport in Berlin, 12–15 June 1929) (Berlin, 1929).

64. E. Matthias, *Die Frau, ihr Körper und dessen Pflege durch die Gymnastik* (Berlin/Zürich, 1929), p.41.
65. W. Wiegels, 'Entwicklung von Sport und Leibesübung der Frau', *Zentralblatt für Gynäkologie* 50 (1926), 1840.
66. M.-L. Lüders, *Fürchte Dich nicht. Persönliches und Politisches aus mehr als 80 Jahren* (Köln/Opladen, 1963), p.131.
67. Quoted in G. Pfister (ed.), *Frau und Sport. Frühe Texte* (Frankfurt, 1980).
68. See, for example, A. Schaser, 'Helene Lange', in H. Huisbergen (ed.), *Stadtbild und Frauenleben. Berlin im Spiegel von 16 Frauenporträts* (Berlin, 1997), pp.175–201.
69. Profé, 'Ertüchtigung', 197.

6

At the Heart of a New Profession: Margaret Stansfeld, a Radical English Educationalist

RICHARD SMART

What is it that gives Margaret Stansfeld the claim to be considered one of the most significant contributors in England to the expansion of women's opportunities to enjoy sport and exercise? Firstly, and most obviously, she was the founder of one of the first and foremost of the women's physical training colleges, and its principal for over 40 years. She was both at the start and at the heart of a new profession, that of the female physical education teacher, a profession which was unusual in that it was not one dominated by men. Women like Stansfeld created, established and developed something new – a distinctively female tradition, in which men played little or no part.[1] She had the opportunity, which she grasped with enormous relish, to exert influence directly over 1200 young women, her students. They were trained to the highest standards, which they passed on as 'games mistresses' to generations of largely middle-class schoolgirls. It was, in turn, through the influence of such teachers, that generations of girls first gained their experience of a variety of forms of physical activity, and this mediation informed their attitudes to their own bodies as they grew up. Secondly, Stansfeld promoted the acceptance of physical activities for young women, both in challenging contemporary concerns about the problematic nature of vigorous exercise for women; and by promoting the academic and professional credentials of physical education, through the influence she exerted as a founder member of the Ling Association, from 1900, and more especially by persuading the University of London to offer a Diploma in Physical Education in 1935. Thirdly, she encouraged the spread of physical activities, for social reasons to working-class girls and women, including both exercise and leisure pursuits.

Nonetheless, Stansfeld was not an originator – she did not herself introduce new ideas in physical education; furthermore, she was conservative. She was not a supporter of the movement in education towards liberalism and child centredness – indeed, she remained a classic Victorian headmistress figure right through to the 1940s, autocratic and at times austere. She was no feminist – she did not support the women's movement in its aims to increase the independence and sexual freedom of women in the twentieth century; she disapproved of the expression of emotion and feeling in gymnastics – 'we are not theatricals', she once affirmed. This essay seeks to demonstrate that Stansfeld's major achievement was in her ability to reconcile the seemingly incompatible, and from this to create not merely a compromise, but an outcome which combined the best of each of the elements; and thus to gain that respect from a largely male-dominated society for the cause of increasing women's participation in sport, exercise and leisure activities crucial for its success.

The first example of the inherent contradictions in Stansfeld's life and career was one of social class: she who spent her long professional life in the company of the prosperous middle classes was born into a working-class family. Her father, James, was a master baker,[2] and so occupationally in the higher rank of the working classes, as a skilled artisan. Margaret was born on 20 March 1860, the third child, in a small house in Church Street, Edmonton. Within the next fifteen years the family moved three times, settling in Islington by the early 1870s.[3] By this time, there were seven children and, with only one wage to support them, money must have been short. Margaret and her elder sister Janet went to a local Board School, Bath Street, in Finsbury, in 1873, where they were to stay until 1885, during which time they grew up from their mid teens to their mid-twenties, passing through the stages of pupil, pupil teacher, assistant teacher and certificated teacher. The experience of these early years must have played a significant part subsequently in forming Margaret's attitude towards her profession.

Bath Street was a typical London Board School, situated between the City Road and Old Street, one of the poorest areas of London. Overcrowding was a serious problem, and staffing was a further one: inspectors commented in May 1873 that 'attainment is extremely low'.[4] When in 1874 Janet Stansfeld became apprenticed as a pupil teacher in the Infants' Department, to be followed by Margaret in July of the following year, they were beginning their careers in a school which placed very heavy demands on them, but which was showing signs of improvement, so that by 1879 Inspectors described Bath Street as

> a very good school, conducted in an excellent spirit ... bearing in mind the quality and quantity of the work done ... and the exceeding inconvenience of the premises ... with a staff of teachers numerically weak in comparison with that in other Schools of inferior merit, very high praise is due here. In the Girls' School especially the Teachers are decidedly overworked.[5]

There were at this time 310 girls and only six staff, a ratio of over 50:1, assisted by the pupil teachers.

Margaret soon proved herself as a pupil teacher. After her first year she obtained an 'excellent' grade,[6] and it is perhaps not surprising that three years later the work of her class (Girls, Standard I) was also adjudged 'excellent' in Drill.[7] Pupil teachers like Margaret Stansfeld were concerned not only with the problems of managing and teaching children in these difficult circumstances, but also with the responsibilities of their own studies, preparing each year for their own examinations and, at the age of eighteen, for the Queen's Scholarship. Academically, Margaret was a satisfactory but not an outstanding student,[8] and when in 1878 she took the Queen's Scholarship, she did not pass sufficiently well to gain one of the coveted places at college. Perhaps she was adversely affected by the death of her father in the previous year, at the early age of fifty, after a long illness, during which the financial straits which the family must have suffered would have weighed heavily on her mind.

Nonetheless, Margaret, like her elder sister, stayed at Bath Street with a welcome rise in salary to £50 per annum, working as an ex-pupil teacher. As such, she was assigned, with another ex-pupil teacher, to take responsibility for a class in the Girls' Department of no less than 129 children aged eight to nine,[9] while at the same time continuing her own studies, now working as an external student towards the same certificate examinations which were taken by students from training colleges. This was a difficult and demanding exercise, as external students were in a sense part time students who had to compete with full time students. Though failing some aspects of the course,[10] Margaret was successful in gaining a 2nd Class Certificate in December 1881,[11] an excellent achievement, in view of the low pass rate achieved by external candidates nationally.

Margaret continued both in her post, completing her two years of probationary service in 1883, and in her studies, now taking courses at Birkbeck College leading to the Department of Science and Art examinations in Advanced Sciences in 1884 and 1885, probably in biology and physiology.[12] There she would have mixed with a wider circle of students, and been taught by distinguished academics – T.H. Huxley, for example, was the Professor of Biology[13] – until, in the summer of 1885, both the sisters left Bath Street after ten years of apprenticeship. Margaret was now a certificated teacher, earning £98 per annum, ranked as the third in the girls' department, which comprised eight teachers. She had become experienced in teaching and managing a very large number of difficult children in the classroom, and accustomed to a life of hard work, in which teaching and studying had always gone hand in hand, and in which progress was monitored annually, with rewards or penalties dependent on the level of success or failure, both in the classroom and in the examination room. She had also begun her life's work of training students, since from 1883 she would have been responsible for one or more pupil teachers.

Life at home must also have been hard, and Margaret must have felt the responsibility which this placed upon her as a teenager: even the meagre income of a pupil teacher was a vital component in the family's struggle for survival. Margaret's failure to achieve a place at a training college must have been a disappointment, but in the long run it might have been the crucial determinant in her career – for if she had gone away to receive the traditional two-year training of an elementary school teacher she might never have come into contact with the new developments in physical education in schools which were being sponsored by the London School Board, and her career might have taken a very different turn. The inspiration for Margaret was the work of a Swedish gymnast, Martina Bergman who, in the same month that Margaret took her examination for the Teachers' Certificate (December 1881), was appointed by the Board to the post of Superintendent of Physical Education in Girls' Schools.[14]

The London School Board's interest in developing physical education in its schools had begun in the 1870s, though limitations of space, staffing and large class sizes restricted what was possible to 'physical training, exercise and drill'.[15] Exercises in which the whole class took part as one were not simply the only practicable form of physical training in promoting fitness, but they also inculcated discipline and obedience to authority. Both of these attributes were as important for girls as for boys, and in one of its women members, Mrs Alice Westlake, the Board had a firm advocate for including girls in its provision. Mrs Westlake was a supporter of what she saw as a vastly superior scheme of physical exercises based on scientific principles which enabled the whole body to be exercised, and could be developed in a progressive way, and at various levels, suitable for both sexes and all ages. The system, inspired by a Swedish gymnast, Per Henrik Ling, was known as 'Swedish gymnastics' and it was to dominate the world of women's physical education for half a century. It was this method which it was Mrs Westlake's intention to promote in the girls' departments of the Board Schools.

Ling's interest was in gymnastics as a field for remedial treatment of bad posture and physical disorders, stressing the therapeutic value of the exercises, and linking physical education with the study of anatomy, physiology and hygiene. It was Ling's son Hjalmar who organized his father's work and tabulated it, so that in one gymnastic lesson the whole body could be exercised, and it was possible to assign the different exercises to students of different ages and levels of ability, girls as well as boys. Ling junior also devised apparatus suitable for the use of large numbers of students at any one time. Some of Ling's students brought the new 'Swedish gymnastics' to England, but it was not widely popular at first, although it had some distinguished supporters, among them the great public health reformer, Edwin Chadwick. In 1860 Chadwick commented that:

> in Sweden a special system of school gymnastics for females, formed by a celebrated medical professor of the name of Ling, has been long introduced ... In England, mothers of the middle and higher classes take their daughters into the towns to receive dancing lessons. In Sweden, mothers of the same class take their daughters into Stockholm to receive gymnastic training ...[16]

Chadwick's criticism of the provision for middle-class girls of opportunities for physical exercise ran counter to the prevailing concept of the need for such girls to learn to be ladies. The differences between the sexes was absolute. Whereas for boys, strenuous participation in games and athletics was an essential part of developing manliness, for their sisters, physical activities, except of the most genteel nature, were inappropriate. Apart from dancing classes, opportunities for girls were limited to organized walks, two by two, crocodile fashion; demure games, such as croquet; and callisthenics, a form of physical exercise consisting of rhythmical movements using rings and wands, usually accompanied at the piano, and designed to improve the figure and promote deportment.

The appointment by the Board in 1879 of Fr. Lofving, as the first Superintendent of Physical Education in Girls' Schools and then her replacement in December 1881 by Martina Bergman[17] (after her marriage known as Mme Bergman-Osterberg), marks the real beginning of the renaissance in women's physical education in Britain. Mme Osterberg, a graduate of Ling's Institute in Stockholm, certainly made her mark in the six years during which she worked for the London Board. She gave classes for three nights a week to women teachers (one per school was obliged to attend), many of them qualifying for the certificate. Eighty had qualified when she began, and over 700 by 1887, so that almost every Board School had a qualified teacher on the staff of its girls' department.

But she was not satisfied with this stage. She found that the officials of the Board were obsessed with bureaucracy and restricted her freedom to develop as she wished. More important, she did not feel that she could achieve her vision with the poor and physically puny youngsters from the working classes in London. Osterberg did not accept that Ling's exercises, or any remedial work, could remedy the serious problems resulting from malnutrition, neglect and dreadful living conditions – 'unless the conditions could be changed, no radical improvement could be effected'. And so, in 1885 Mme Osterberg set up her own private college, the Hampstead Gymnasium, with four students, a counterpart to the Stockholm Institute where she had herself studied. The college was successful from the start – there was no shortage of applicants and in 1887 she felt confident enough to resign her post with the School Board.

It was the appointment of Mme Osterberg in 1881 as adviser in girls' physical education to the London School Board which provided Margaret Stansfeld with the opportunity to begin her life's work, when she joined Osterberg's classes as the representative from the Bath Street Board School. This took place in 1882 or 1883, during the two years after Stansfeld had gained her certificate and before the two years in which she studied for the Advanced Science certificates of the Department of Education and Science. When Osterberg founded her college in

Hampstead, Stansfeld was invited to join, occupying a role somewhat similar to that of a pupil teacher in the maintained sector, both teaching and studying, completing her course in one year only, the first of the many students at Dartford to do so. Although Stansfeld began her lecturing career as Mme Osterberg was furthering hers, by making the same move from the maintained to the private sector,[18] the younger woman was never to lose contact with her roots in the elementary schools.

Stansfeld now needed other employment, and for the next twenty years this was to be rooted firmly in the middle-class sector. She began by joining her older sister, Janet, at the Dame Alice Owen School in Islington in 1886, and in the following year started at Bedford High School. It is not clear what were the reasons for persuading Stansfeld to make the all-important decision to go to Bedford. She needed more work and wanted to further the cause, and the High School provided her with opportunities for both. Bedford was within easy travelling distance of London, and the town's reputation as a centre of educational excellence must have been known to her. In addition to the two new girls' schools, there was also the Froebel Training College – all three were only five years old. The close links that existed between Swedish gymnastics and the kindergarten may have drawn her – both were innovative approaches to education, both were based on a philosophy, claiming 'scientific' basis for a closely worked-out system. Gymnastics in a Froebel school or college meant Swedish gymnastics – it was the Froebelians who had been among the first to support its introduction.

However this may be, physical training in 1887 at the High School in Bedford was not of the reformed kind. The girls had drill with a man instructor, there was a shed for a gymnasium, with very little equipment, and only the gravel playground for games where 'hockey was played with ash sticks and a string-covered ball'.[19] By 1900 Stansfeld's advocacy had helped in the decision to purchase a school field – where it is at present, between Beverley Crescent and the railway line – and cricket, tennis, hockey and lacrosse made their appearance. An old student of hers, Freda Young, describes one of her gym lessons at the High School in 1900, capturing the magnetism of her personality.

> How vividly I can see her as I did at my first gymnastic lesson – her raven black hair, her energy, her slim body, and her wonderful voice. I had no idea what it was all about. I was abnormally shy, I had never been to school before, and when my form responded

with alacrity to the familiar command, 'In two lines, fall in', I could only creep to the back of the class; then, with a freezing, stunning fear I saw what might happen. Regardless of nothing but self-preservation, I inserted myself half-way up the line, a scuffle ensued. Miss Stansfeld glued us to rigidity with her eye. What on earth was I doing and why? I made no reply. Then she said with a smile of such understanding kindness, 'Afraid the worm might turn, are you? Well, stay where you are.' One new girl realized she had found a friend.[20]

Stansfeld spent some seventeen years teaching in a variety of schools and colleges – from as far west as Shrewsbury (the High School) to Cambridge (Homerton), from Islington (Dame Alice Owen's School) to Leicester – but her base was increasingly Bedford, where she came to live in the early 1890s. The idea of starting her own training college must have derived from several sources: the example of Osterberg at Dartford, and of a later student of Osterberg, Rhoda Anstey, who founded the college named after her in 1897; the satisfaction of her work with students in training at the Bedford Froebel College, of her private students, and the encouragement of those who admired her work. These certainly included Miss Armstrong, the Headmistress of Dame Alice Owen's School, who tried to persuade her to open a Physical Training College in North London, using Owen's as a training school. The idea of settling down and concentrating her energies in one place must have been attractive, after all the moves of her early years, followed by the travelling involved in teaching in schools such a distance apart.

Bedford it was to be. The town had a high reputation as an education town, with its four public schools, two of them for girls, its large middle-class population, and its proximity to Oxford, Cambridge and London. And Stansfeld had already built up a reputation, and recruitment of students would be assisted by her contacts in the area. Nonetheless, she must have felt apprehensive on the September morning in 1903 when she met the first set of students at the house she bought to be a college, a large Victorian villa in Lansdowne Road, Wylam Lodge (Figure 6.1). One of them recollects that 'she talked to us of our responsibility – if we failed, College would fail; its reputation depended on our attitude and loyalty'.[21] It did not take long for Miss Stansfeld to gain confidence; recruitment was sound and two more houses were acquired by 1905. By 1914, when war came, there was a fourth house and almost 40 students.

FIGURE 6.1
WYLAM LODGE 1905

The background of 'Stan's stues', throughout the first fifty years, was overwhelmingly middle class. Girls were eager to come to Bedford from some of the 'best' schools in the country, both Girls' Public Day School Trust schools and boarding schools, among them Wycombe Abbey, and particularly, Cheltenham Ladies' College. Bedford had the reputation of being snobbish. One old student recalls, from 1927, a member of staff asking her from which school she came, and on her replying 'Henrietta Barnet', responded sarcastically 'Dr Barnardo's, did you say?'[22]

It was all a far cry from Bath Street Board School. But Stansfeld would never have made such a remark – quite the reverse. In fact, from the earliest years, Bedford students were unusual in that they taught not only in the two Harpur Trust middle–class girls' schools but also in all the elementary ones, particularly Ampthill Road. What to Stansfeld must have seemed a small school after ten years at Bath Street must have appeared to her middle-class students noisy, crowded and somewhat threatening. 'Then you did feel a pioneer, then your training showed up, and your personality! Those miraculous people who could keep order in a class of large, unruly boys ... Those large classes of keen to bursting small girls!'[23] The Borough of Bedford was clearly grateful for the invigorating input of confident, enthusiastic, lively young women into its schools. In 1923 the Higher Education Sub-Committee expressed their 'appreciation of the splendid work done in the Borough Elementary Schools by Miss Stansfeld, her Staff, and the Students of the Physical Training College'.[24]

The extent of this contribution was spelled out by Stansfeld herself, never one to let an opportunity for good publicity to pass her by, in the same year, in response to a Board of Education Circular suggesting that LEAs should appoint Organisers for Physical Education.[25] Stansfeld replied to the Board, pointing out that Bedford was exceptionally fortunate in having a Physical Education college in the town which met all requirements, that virtually every school had instruction in PE from college students, some having college lecturers attached to their staff. She stated that all students taught throughout their three years' training except for the first term, that during their second term they taught part of a primary school class, and this was extended so that during the third year a student would teach as many as 12 lessons a week and also take part in games coaching and umpiring (Figure 6.2). As no class was to be left without a teacher, this meant that another student would have to cover, and would cycle from one side of the town to the other in order to do so. She also pointed out that the PE organizer for Nottingham had 90 schools in her care, and saw each one every two years, whereas in college there were five lecturers who continually supervised the work of the students in school.[26]

Stansfeld's letter rapidly had its effect – only eight days later she was appointed the Physical Education organizer for Bedford. As if to demonstrate her new role, and that of the college, a display was mounted in July in the Corn Exchange. It was on a vast scale and included 360 children of all ages, boys and girls from the elementary as well as the Harpur Trust schools, together with 40 senior and 20 second year students. The display consisted of running, jumping, skipping and games by the children and by the students a demonstration of a gymnastic table and some vaulting.[27] Displays and demonstrations by the college students were a regular feature, not just in Bedford, but all over

FIGURE 6.2
STUDENTS WORKING WITH CHILDREN IN 1933

FIGURE 6.3
WEMBLEY FESTIVAL OF YOUTH 1937

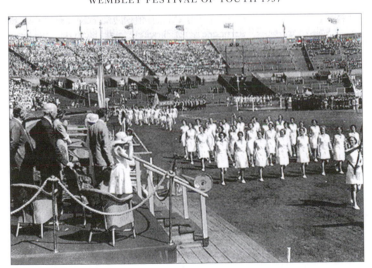

the country, the highlight probably being the college's appearance in 1937 at the Festival of Youth in Wembley Stadium where 350 students from from Bedford and other leading specialist colleges (Anstey, Chelsea and Dartford) mounted a gymnastic display planned and presented, not by Stansfeld, but by one of her old students, Cicely Read, then the college's vice-principal. The Festival was attended by the new King George VI and Queen Elizabeth, and two more of Stansfeld's distinguished old students had the honour of being presented to Their Majesties at the end: Phyllis Colson and Phyllis Spafford (Figure 6.3).

The work of these two encapsulated the new approach to physical education in a much broader field, that of the promotion of recreational activities for all, children and adults of all ages and social classes. Colson, while working with Spafford for the National Council of Girls' Clubs organizing physical education, was struck by the poor provision of recreational facilities for young people. Her 'great idea' was to create an organization which would co-ordinate the activities of all groups and individuals willing to provide them. The result was the establishment of the Central Council of Recreative Physical Training in 1935, now the Central Council for Physical Recreation. Like so many good ideas, it was amazing that no one had thought of it before, and it immediately captured support and interest. The Keep Fit movement was the best known aspect of the Council's work, and Phyllis Colson herself returned to Bedford in 1936 to launch it in the town in the company of the Mayor of Bedford and of her old principal, aged seventy-six, who announced that classes would be started for women and girls 'from fifteen to ninety years of age' (laughter).[28]

Another much appreciated link with the town was the remedial work undertaken by students. The college itself ran a clinic four times a week in which free treatment was given by students under staff supervision to any child recommended by his or her GP. In the course of the academic year 1927/28, some 3207 such treatments had been performed and an additional 3921 treatments had been carried out in the Outpatients Department at the County Hospital, where Senior Students attended five times a week. After another display in 1928, given to the Rotary Club, the Mayor congratulated the college, praising the excellent work it was doing in educating teachers and commenting that 'those interested in elementary schools and the members of the Education Committee had a very real knowledge of the work done at the College, and highly appreciated it.'[29] Bedford students had a much closer and more regular contact with the world outside the middle-class sector than those of most of the other PE colleges, and it is to Stansfeld's early experience of London's elementary schools that this must be attributed.

Middle-class parents were clearly prepared to accept that their daughters would spend some of their time teaching in elementary schools, in order to broaden their experience, even if they would expect them to spend their professional lives, if they did not marry, in the sort of schools they had themselves attended. Their attitude to the prospect of their daughters spending two years or more studying and practising PT was more problematic, both with regard to the status of the subject and of the games mistress in the school staff-room, and because of the possible damage that strenuous and frequent physical activity might result in. Stansfeld rejected both of these damaging prejudices. The question of the academic standing of the subject was the harder of the two to challenge; indeed, in some quarters it still exists. The first steps to remedy this were taken in 1900, when she and other former students of Bergman-Osterberg founded the Ling Association as a professional organisation of women physical education specialists, with the aim of raising the status of the profession and so encouraging girls and women to participate in sport and exercise.[30]

Stansfeld was fully involved with the Association from its inception in 1899, being elected to its first committee, and for nineteen years (1901–20) serving consecutively as its Vice-President and then President. She was keenly involved in most of its activities, becoming Secretary of the Book Club, assisting with the drawing up of syllabuses for an Elementary Certificate in 1901, and then acting as Examiner for this and for the more advanced Diploma.[31] During the first World War, Stansfeld represented the physical training colleges and the Ling Association as a member of the Central Council set up by the War Office for the purpose of regulating the supply of massage personnel for the use of the War Office and the Ministry of Pensions. After the war, Stansfeld was involved with the move to add a third year to the course in order to be able to seek recognition from the Board of Education. The third year allowed more scope for academic development, but it did not seem to lighten the heavy work load and the mad rush from one activity to the next, nor was it sufficient to gain recognition, the problem being the low level of academic entrance qualifications achieved by many students at the time.

The three-year course was welcomed by most students. The post-war mood was much more amenable to middle-class women training for a profession, and the imbalance between the numbers of young men and the larger numbers of young women resulting from the tragic level of war deaths, meant that marriage was not a possibility for many of them. They would need a career, and from 1917 applications soared. By 1931 there were nine houses, over 120 students and 14 resident staff; in 1911, there had been 33 students in three houses with five resident staff.

The extra year enabled Bedford students to take a series of specialized examinations in the medical and therapeutic aspects of their subject, the 'Conjoint' Examination of the Chartered Society of Massage and Medical Gymnastics, the Royal Sanitary Institute examination in School Hygiene, and to obtain certificates in First Aid and Home Nursing from the St John's Ambulance Association. If they were successful in all these, passed their own internal examinations and practical tests in gymnastics and games, then they would be awarded the BPTC Diploma and be entitled and justly proud to wear the college badge – 'the thrill of having the Badge pinned on one's new tunic and then exit through the front door of "No. 37"'![32]

Worthy though this collection of certificates was, it did not have the stamp of academic credibility, which could only be gained from a university. An important step forward was taken in 1928 when a deputation from the leading women's PE colleges visited London University to lay before the Senate their request that they should offer a Diploma in the Theory and Practice of Physical Education. It took four years for agreement to be reached, and another three before Bedford was able to apply for recognition. And so in 1935 two inspectors visited the college to judge the standards in two areas, science and practical work (including gym, games, dancing and teaching). Not surprisingly, they were impressed.

> The whole college is admirably organised. The students are delightfully housed, and there is no doubt that they have the opportunity of securing a first class all-round training ... The fact that during their three years they receive training in gymnastics from no less than three different lecturers is in itself good ... The important point to be stressed ... is the very satisfactory amount of teaching practice and games coaching which every student has during her career at college ... every type of school in Bedford is staffed by students or members of staff from the ... college ... I was struck by the general atmosphere – an atmosphere of goodwill;

keen co-operation and of vital interest in the work of the college ... such an atmosphere cannot but help to foster willing response and that loyalty which is the backbone of every good college.[33]

The college was accepted in May 1935, and students with a School Certificate were able to sit the London University examination and obtain a Diploma from then on. The achievement of academic recognition and approval by one of the country's great universities, together with the addition of the college to the list of the Board of Education's 'recognized institutions', was clearly an important success for the college and for the cause to which Stansfeld had devoted her life, though it was not a degree, and Bedford students had to wait another forty years before that was achieved.

But it was perhaps the controversy over the effects upon young women of frequent participation in strenuous physical activities which proved, for a while, the hardest example of prejudice for Stansfeld to overcome, even though time has proved the fears voiced over a period of half a century completely unfounded. The controversy began in the time of Stansfeld's childhood. At first, the debate centred on the potentially damaging effects of the developing opportunities in the education of middle-class girls and young women in schools (such as those in which Stansfeld was teaching in the 1890s) and in the universities. How much more powerful did the arguments seem to some when, from the 1880s, they began to be directed not at women blue-stockings, but at women who were athletes and games players! In 1899 it was, somewhat ironically, a woman doctor, Arabella Kenealy, LRCP, who sparked off a new phase with her article entitled 'Woman as an Athlete',[34] in which she depicted an example of the 'New Woman', who spends much of her time bicycling, playing tennis and hockey, instead of engaging in the typically feminine pursuits of the traditional middle-class young woman (whom she personifies as 'Clara'), providing comfort and sympathy for her parents, nursing the sick and sewing ribbons on hats. Dr Kenealy drew on the current concern about eugenics, in suggesting that too much muscular development tended to de-sex 'Clara' and her kind, so that she began to display masculine traits – 'her voice is louder, her tones are assertive ... that blemish of modern woman'.[35] The suggestion in this article that masculine women tend towards 'unnatural' sexual orientation is strengthened in Dr Kenealy's later book, called unequivocally *Feminism and Sex-Extinction*, published in 1920.

'Attachments between women and women are strengthening and intensifying, absorbing the emotion and devotion normally bestowed on members of the opposite sex.'[36]

Of greater concern at the turn of the century was that of the quality of the race, first identified by Francis Galton, and debated by the eugenicists. Kenealy was not alone in believing that 'the stock' would suffer, not only because muscular women would have fewer offspring, but also because the children they did have would be inferior specimens – 'puny, ... spectacled, knock-kneed'.[37] These unsubstantiated assertions were damaging to the cause of women's increasing involvement in sport and exercise, and Stansfeld played her part in refuting them. In 1908, she assisted Galton by providing him with statistical evidence relating to the physical characteristics of her students. After the war, the issue arose again, against a background of a falling birth rate caused by the massacre of young men, which prompted Kenealy's book in 1920, together with further attacks from a headmistress and a doctor in *The Lancet*. The theme this time centred on amenorrhea, or the cessation of menstruation, which rendered the womb temporarily or permanently barren. Stansfeld once again countered what she described as 'the many vague statements with no shred of evidence to bolster them' with detailed evidence derived not only from her own Bedford students, but from a questionnaire sent to all old students who had children, and presented the results at a meeting of the Medical Officers of Schools Association on 'Games for Girls' in 1921, which was printed in *The Lancet*.[38]

Stansfeld stated that the students coming to Bedford were, at age eighteen, among the best games players in their schools, yet rejection on grounds of physical unfitness was 'the very rarest thing', and that although at college they increased their physical work about ten times, their health remained extremely good. From a sample of 100 students, she had investigated the effect of such an athletic life on menstruation: 64 reported no pain; 26 recorded slight pain, but of these, 20 said that training lessened the pain; and ten said that the pain was rather bad, though of these three noted that this only occurred in the holidays. Stansfeld also investigated the effect of games on maternity, and received answers to her questionnaire from 34 old students. They reported no unusual problems with their pregnancies or their labour, and in every case 'the weight and general health of the babies left nothing to be desired'. Her evidence must have inspired confidence in the assembled medical men and women as in the subsequent questions she was addressed as 'Dr' Stansfeld.[39] Although this argument has by now been won, there remains a debate concerning the possibility of women being able to compete on the same terms as men. Some suggest that women's sporting achievements have been retarded more by the myth of their relative physical frailties than by the realities of the physical differences between the sexes, while others consider that the differences in strength are so marked that women will never be able to achieve this in any sport where strength and stamina are crucial.[40]

Stansfeld's struggle to gain acceptance for the concept of physical training as an appropriate career for middle-class girls was waged not only in the public arena and sporadically, at appropriate times, but was also centred closer to home, within the college at Lansdowne Road and continuously. Students were expected to behave in a ladylike manner, both in public and in private. In public, even when walking the distance of 30 yards from No.29 to No.37, students were obliged to wear a long skirt, down to the ankles, a hat, with a hat band in the college colours of blue and yellow, gloves and a coat. (Figure 6.4) 'In our day, legs were indecent things to show … Our trouble was: shall I put the skirt on over my tunic and spoil the pleats, or do I put it under my tunic and look a sight?'[41]

FIGURE 6.4

MARGARET STANSFELD (CENTRE) AND TWO STUDENTS

Such concessions to middle-class mores were not permitted to damage the quality of the students' practical work. Here, the question of clothing was significant, and Stansfeld did not compromise. The struggle was not an easy one. Osterberg had introduced the gym tunic as early as 1884 when, in a display in a London Board School, to which Stansfeld may well have contributed, the girls wore 'blue serge tunics and knickerbockers'.[42] When Stansfeld began teaching at Bedford High School, in 1887, the custom had been that the girls wore their ordinary clothes, long dresses and tightly corseted. Parents had to be won round to accept the idea of their daughters wearing a gym tunic which, in the context of the period, was provocatively revealing – Victorian males allegedly got excited over the sight of an ankle, quite apart from a knee. Such was the strength of feeling that even eleven years later, and despite Stansfeld's not inconsiderable best efforts, there were still two families who would not accept the tunic. As she put it, 'these two families my utmost powers have failed to persuade to get costumes. These exceptions are my failures ... '[43] Stansfeld did not fail at Lansdowne Road. The gym tunic itself was navy blue, knee length, with three pleats, and tied with a girdle at the waist. This was worn with a white blouse, yellow silk tie, thick blue woollen knickers and black woollen stockings (Figure 6.5). All of these were worn for gymnastics and for dancing, though further concessions to freedom were made when Greek dance, associated with the work of the flamboyant Isadora Duncan, was introduced to Bedford in 1914. Now students danced barefoot and barelegged with tunics or dresses of flowing material.

Stansfeld's acceptance of such an un-Victorian costume and of the work of such a very un-Stansfeld like woman, the exotic and unconventional figure of Isadora Duncan, illustrates well her approach to change – conservative, and no originator, but prepared to consider new ideas and to support the development of a broader, more liberal approach to the study and teaching of gymnastics and dance, incorporating ideas from outside the familiar ground of Ling. In the late 1940s and early 1950s Ling was to be displaced by Laban, and Swedish gymnastics was consigned to the footnotes of history, but the seeds had been sown by women such as Duncan. Her achievement was 'to liberate movement from the formalities of classical ballet'.[44] Bedford students, when first introduced to Duncan's Greek dance, were amazed to find that they were expected to dance barefoot, and when Freda Colwill, a recent ex-student, joined the staff in 1916 as dancing specialist, she lost

FIGURE 6.5

THE SECOND SET OF STUDENTS 1904–5 WITH STAFF,
MARGARET STANSFELD CENTRE

Staff wore gym tunics and ties identical to those of their students, emphasizing the college's
unity of purpose. Although quite formal, as a uniform, the display of women's legs, even
encased in black woollen stockings, was not acceptable outside the confines of the college
buildings.

no time in going one step further – persuading Miss Stansfeld that
dancing in heavy serge tunics was not in the spirit of the thing and that
crêpe de chine was more appropriate.

The world of gymnastics was changing, too. At Bedford in the
Holiday Week of 1920 a new gymnastics teacher replaced Miss
Stansfeld, who had given up her gymnastics teaching both at the college
and at the High School at the end of the war – she was sixty years old,
after all! Miss Cicely Read's classes were different, and met with a mixed
reception. They 'were entirely on the new system of relaxed movements,
and were most interesting', even though many complained after them
that they felt they had done no work.[45] The 'new system' was the work
of the Finnish gymnast Elli Bjorksten. In essence, it liberated the study
from the rigidity and limitations of Ling's system. Movements could be
executed in rhythm, using music, and replacing static positions and
tension with more freedom and relaxation. Changes in gymnastics
resulted, not in the abandonment of Ling, but in the addition to his
scheme of elements which were lacking in the original. It was not to be
Bjorksten's relaxed gymnastics which removed Ling from the timetable,
but developments in the world of dance, which succeeded in
bringing the two disciplines, which were at first disparate, together
as 'movement'.

The apostle of the art of movement was Rudolf Laban, and his work was brought to Bedford, probably earlier than anywhere else in the country, through the interest and support of Margaret Stansfeld. Perhaps surprisingly, in view of her conservativism in some respects, she offered a year's secondment to Freda Colwill to study with one of Laban's pupils in Vienna, and then a few years later, a similar secondment to Miss Colwill's successor, Joan Goodrich, to go to Dresden to study with Mary Wigman, one of his most famous pupils. Laban was a character as exotic as Isadora Duncan had been. He was involved with eurhythmics and ballet and attracted the avant-garde artists and dancers as he began to develop his concept of 'Central European Dance' in Italy, Switzerland and Germany in the first decades of the century. The essence of it was that it was absolute and abstract, like music, not attempting necessarily to illustrate anything, but essentially expressive. It was not elitist – participants had no need to be slim or balletic, because the purpose was not artistic perfection, but 'the beneficial effect of the creative activity of dancing on the personality of the pupil', as Laban put it.[46] Much of the benefit of its development of personal and social awareness was derived from the interaction of individuals within a group situation, in which together they would improvise and create.

In 1938 Laban himself came to England. He found some of his pupils, notably Lisa Ullmann, already established over here (Miss Ullmann at Dartington). He found some of his pupils' pupils teaching students (notably Joan Goodrich at Bedford). He found some of their pupils beginning to take modern dance into schools. He found others writing about it (e.g. Diana Jordan, ex-Bedford student, who wrote the first book in England on movement education, published in the year of his arrival in this country).[47] The success of modern dance in the following decade owed not a little to the influence of Margaret Stansfeld, her staff and students. These were significant changes, and Bedford PTC played a leading role in their development.

But for the majority of students it was a feature of the college which did not change which both attracted them to it in the first place and gave them their greatest satisfaction as students – i.e. the college's success on the games field. The reputation of BPTC here was daunting. Every year, in six main sports (lacrosse, hockey, netball, cricket, tennis and swimming) hardly a match was lost. In 1934, for example, 102 matches were played in the six sports involving 26 teams – only six were lost.

Many students, particularly in hockey and lacrosse, were at international level or would go on to play at this level as Old Students – in 1934, for example, there were three internationals for hockey and 15 for lacrosse. The success of BPTC certainly owes much to this. Even the most chauvinistic opponents of women's increasing role in society must have respected such outstanding results, in games which were not exclusively female ones, such as hockey, tennis and cricket.

But the success of the college, the increasing acceptance of women's right to participate in sport and physical recreations, and the reputation of Stansfeld, rests not so much on any of the above, as it does on the impact that her students made on the hundreds of schools in which they became games mistresses, and on the hundreds of thousands of their pupils. There is no doubt that Bedford-trained students were very much in demand. 'Headmistresses all over England consulted her, or came to Bedford to study the field. Job advertisements between the wars might specify "Bedford or Dartford-trained". They were, as the father of one girl put it, "the Oxford and Cambridge of PT colleges", and from the mid-1920s to the mid-1930s it could be said that Bedford was top.'[48]

There is no doubt, either, that it was the influence of Stansfeld which was the vital driving force from the establishment of the college in 1903 until her retirement in 1945, at the age of 85, even though she had ceased to teach students after about 1920. She was in the tradition of the great headmistresses (Miss Buss and Miss Beale, who Cupid's darts did not feel)[49] and the heads of the women's colleges, such as Emily Davies at Girton – autocratic and charismatic.[50] There were no committees and the minimum of paper work – a disadvantage to historians if to no-one else. She controlled everything. The college belonged to her not just financially (at least until 1930, when it became a limited company) but professionally and emotionally. Starting from 1906, nearly all the staff were her ex-students who, when the summons came to return to Bedford, were thrilled to be asked. For Freda Colwill in 1913 'it was the greatest honour in the world ... I thought, well I must do it, if Miss Stansfeld really wants me ... I felt I owed her an enormous debt for what she'd given me at college'.[51] Staff were controlled as closely as students – there was no private life for either. Freda Colwill had to ask Stansfeld for permission to attend a Cambridge May Ball; permission was given reluctantly – 'Yes, as long as your work doesn't suffer.'[52] Students were not even permitted to choose their first teaching posts: when Stansfeld had decided which one the student should apply for, her form was checked and she appeared before the principal to be vetted in the clothes which she proposed to wear for the interview. And, as has already been indicated in the case of Freda Colwill, Stansfeld's interest continued, either to command a return to Bedford or to suggest a move to a more senior post.

The strength of the tie between ex-students and College symbolized by Stansfeld was particularly illustrated by their loyalty to the Old Students' Association, still flourishing (2000) half a century after Stansfeld's death. Virtually all students joined it when they had qualified and it boasted over 1,000 members in the 1940s. Year by year Old Students returned to Lansdowne for a week in the summer, meeting old friends, reminiscing about the past, comparing notes about their own schools and pupils, working at gymnastics and dance, learning about the latest developments in physiotherapy, rejoicing in the successes of present students, and renewing the bonding process which had begun so strongly in their own days as students. Year by year, the renewal of shared experience reinforced the effectiveness of the networking process, and in a sense completed the circle, for they would recommend their best games players to apply to Bedford.

When such students came to Bedford for their interview, they must have been better prepared for the sarcasm and ridicule which formed one side of the process of cutting students down to size. 'Coming from Cheltenham, I don't think I doubted she'd accept me.'[53] Those from less eminent schools found their initiation difficult. Girls who had been 'captain of everything' at school found themselves struggling. 'I get to Bedford, and up against girls who had been coached by first rate staff – games coaches – I was nowhere. And I was pulled up time and again, and humiliated and made to take a free hit again and again and again, and muffed it worse and worse and worse! It was very public the humiliation.'[54] The selection process was not over, for students were on trial for the first term, and every year a proportion, often as high as 25 per cent, were asked to leave.

Those who survived the filtering process were subjected to a daily timetable which would leave modern students speechless. The day, which sometimes began before breakfast, continued with gymnastics, lectures and teaching practice in the morning, games in the afternoon and more lectures and private study in the evening. Hard work was compounded by constant criticism – students were never praised. The process was similar to that adopted in the armed forces, one of empowerment, where the subject is first ground down by exhaustion and humiliation until he or she is deemed psychologically fit to begin the process of being built up again, to emerge stronger, more confident and more determined than before. Bedford was not unusual in the rigour of this training. Hard work and constant criticism were the practice in the other women's PT colleges, such as Chelsea, Dartford or Anstey.

What was distinctive about Bedford was the combination of the Spartan atmosphere with the familial one. In the years before 1914, BPTC was small and domestic in scale. First year students, the Juniors, never more than 20 in number, lived at 29 Lansdowne with Elizabeth Roberts, and then moved to 37 with Miss Stansfeld as Seniors. Size made a family atmosphere possible, but not inevitable. The women's colleges at the universities did not adopt it. When Emily Davies had established the college at Hitchin in the 1860s, later to become Girton, with fewer students than at Lansdowne, she deliberately rejected the family model in favour of 'that of a society, not a family ... Our college is not a place for young girls, any more than the other colleges are for young boys. It is a place for women.'[55] But Emily Davies was determined to demonstrate that women were men's equal, and so chose to adopt the male model of the men's college as it already existed. Stansfeld's concept was based on a different experience – of a profession which was not dependent on male role models. The female tradition created in England by Mme Osterberg and continued and strengthened by Stansfeld demanded something more in tune with matriarchal rather than patriarchal values.

A further reason for the adoption of the family rather than the collegiate model must have been Stansfeld's personal experience of her own large and close family, which she had helped to support financially from a young age as a pupil teacher, and from which she had derived strength, particularly from her mother. In college, she herself was the mother figure. Sometimes it was that of a caring mother, balancing the demands of family and career. On Wednesdays she was away from Bedford, teaching in London. Freda Young, one of the first set of students, who had also been a pupil of Miss Stansfeld's at the High School, recollects that

> one day, as she was running downstairs to the horse-drawn cab that was to take her to the London and North-Western Station, she heard a student sneeze. Later in the day, Miss Roberts received a

telegram, 'Get Freda hot – signed Cinnamon'. Always, when she had been away, and frequently other evenings, she would come to our rooms and discuss the events of the day, help where help was needed, and perhaps clear up some misfortune which had befallen us, as it invariably did if she were away.[56]

Sunday, as in the domestic model, was a family day.

> After breakfast … we could borrow books from the drawing-room, and in the evening we had the pleasantest hour of the week, when Miss Stansfeld read to us; this custom died out as College got larger, but another delightful custom lingered on – that of going to the drawing-room for coffee after dinner, when staff and students and later old students could meet informally.[57]

Students who survived the experience never forgot it. The strength and confidence it inspired in them were a vital ingredient in the success of Bedford Old Students as games mistresses; like their college experience, they were both tough and tender, not an inappropriate combination for a twentieth-century woman. They played a large part in the genesis of the 'games mistress' in girls' boarding and day schools, a woman who although without the high academic standing of most of her colleagues, often exerted a much stronger influence in the school. She taught almost all the girls; she was closer to them, in a more informal way, in the changing rooms, in the coach travelling to matches, as the 'health mistress', and often through her role as organizer for speech days and the like. Their worth was recognized by pupils as well as by staff;

> Thinking back to my own schooldays at Clapham High School, I realize the confidence we had in the sense of justice and fair play of the Gymnastic Mistresses, who came to us then from Bedford Physical Training College. I can recall many incidents in our school life that impressed this upon us, and the enjoyment we had in trying to live up to the standards they put before us.[58]

They were able to empower their pupils in a similar way to that in which their training had empowered them. They were confident: as one recollects, 'it suddenly came over me – the power of the eye – I could have done anything I wanted with those girls!'[59] But confidence was tempered with humility (as Stansfeld told her students, 'a true teacher must be imbued with the will to serve')[60] and with humanity – as one ex-student said of her pupils, 'I think they liked us and thought we were human. At least we knew every one of them ... as people.'[61]

Yet Stansfeld's students, although of outstanding quality, were not unique: those of the other women's PT (now increasingly known as 'Physical Education') colleges had passed through similar experiences. In 1942 the University of London submitted evidence to the McNair Committee (which was drawing up a Report, *Teachers and Youth Leaders*, published in 1944) in which the contribution of all these colleges was warmly acclaimed. 'The women trained in these Colleges are responsible, directly or indirectly, for most of the physical education of women and girls in this country.'[62] The gymnastic lesson in girls' secondary schools was praised as giving 'not only physical vigour and poise, but also mental balance and serenity ... grace and alertness become in varying degrees the attributes of all who share in this all-important physical side of the school's work, and regular exercise in the open air brings health even to those whose natural inclinations have not been towards health-giving activities'.[63] The McNair Report in 1944 recognized the joint achievement of all six of the private women's colleges in producing specialist PE teachers who 'take an important part in the life of the school ... Head Mistresses have spoken highly of their widespread influence and responsibility.'[64] It was recognized that there was nothing comparable in the field of men's PE training and that the 'advance in physical education is owing largely to the pioneer "private" effort of the founders of the Women's Physical Education Colleges'.[65]

How does Stansfeld's contribution compare with that of those other 'pioneers'? Hers was not the first college: Bergman-Osterberg's Dartford has that honour. Nor was she the originator of the curriculum adopted by the specialist colleges; the combination of gymnastics, dance, games and what is now known as physiotherapy. This is once again the legacy of Madame. But Stansfeld outlasted her mentor by over 30 years (Madame died in 1915). Her career spanned the whole of the golden age of the women's specialist colleges, right from the beginning, with Madame's classes under the aegis of the London School Board in the early 1880s, to the 1940s, when all the colleges struggled financially – a period of over 60 years. It was only four months after Stansfeld's death in 1951 that the decision was made which led to the transformation of Bedford College into a maintained college under the control of Bedfordshire County Council, and all the other five colleges were to lose their independent status within a few years. Stansfeld was responsible for training over 1200 students, Begmann–Osterberg about 500.[66] Stansfeld was also much more flexible than her mentor, who refused to associate herself with the Ling Association, on the grounds that if membership were opened to all fully trained gymnastics teachers it would dissipate the standards she felt were only to be achieved by her own students, and resented the foundation of both Anstey and Bedford as rivals to Dartford, a limiting policy which if adopted would have slowed the progress of the movement. Stansfeld's work compares favourably with that of the other 'second generation' of college founders in terms of length of service alone. Ill health forced the retirement of Rhoda Anstey – who was, like Stansfeld, a pupil of Madame's at Dartford in 1918 – after only just over twenty years, while Dorette Wilkie, the founder of Chelsea in 1898, remained at its head until 1929, just over thirty years.

The pivot of the whole process was Stansfeld herself – autocratic, austere, but an inspirational teacher – feared and loved in equal proportions. Students who succeeded were empowered – 'She prepared us for LIFE!' – and it is through their work that her own life was fully rewarded. Some were figures of national importance. Phyllis Colson, was the originator and director of the Central Council of Physical Recreation. Marion Squire was Principal of Anstey College from 1927 to 1954.[67] Some outstanding teachers brought the newest innovations into schools (for example, Elizabeth Swallow was the first to introduce Laban into a school – QES, Mansfield – in 1939), many became trainers themselves. Hundreds of others, less well known, in schools all over Britain and abroad, gave their pupils pride in themselves, not only through the experience of games, gymnastics and dance, but through moral example – 'fair play'.

Stansfeld was successful because in developing such a strong and genuine female tradition she did not alienate a male-dominated society. She achieved this partly by insisting on acceptably 'ladylike' behaviour in conventional social situations, and by bringing the college and its students into the public arena, through displays of gymnastics, through the use of elementary schools for part of the student teaching experience, through the running of a physiotherapy clinic at the college where treatment was given free of charge, and through the use of students in the outpatients ward of the local hospital. She herself was PE organizer for Bedford from 1923. But she was not afraid to fight against prejudice which was demonstrably based on false premises, for example, medical opposition to women taking part in strenuous physical exercise,

FIGURE 6.6

A GROUP OF SWEDISH GYMNASTS VISITING THE COLLEGE IN 1948, WITH
MARGARET STANSFELD, AGED 88,
AND HER SUCCESSOR, CICELY READ (FAR RIGHT)

or to insist on appropriate clothing for physical activities, however indecorous some might have considered it.

Her indomitable spirit was always in evidence, even at the end of her life – she returned to the office of Principal for a few months in 1948 aged eighty-eight, three years before her death, after the unexpected death of her successor (Figure 6.6). It was this strength of will and character above all else which empowered her students as women and as teachers, and which enabled them in their turn to empower their own pupils. Stansfeld was justifiably recognized in her time as a pioneer in the advancement of women's PE. She was awarded the OBE in 1939, and was the first Englishwoman to be awarded the Swedish 'Grand-titre honorifique de la Fédération Internationale de Gymnastique Ling'. She was the last survivor of the originators of women's PE, and the most influential. It was said of Bergman-Osterberg, but is more applicable to Stansfeld, that 'the liberation of women's bodily powers, which we owe largely to her influence, has a direct association with the present manifestation of women's capacity and energy in the general work of the world'.[68] It is ironic that the rise of feminism in the second half of the century coincided with the dissipation of the female tradition,

FIGURE 6.7

MEN AND WOMEN STUDENTS IN 1999

The female tradition as Stansfeld knew it is dead, but these women students and their young women pupils will enjoy far more opportunities for participation in sport and exercise then did their predecessors. It is unlikely that they appreciate the importance of the contribution made to this by the woman whose portrait (LHS) gazes down on them.

epitomized by Stansfeld, as physical education for women, developed by women, in the first half of the century increasingly came to be controlled by men in the second half. It is perhaps the ultimate demonstration of the success of Stansfeld's work that, despite this, at the beginning of the twenty-first century women are free to participate in and enjoy sport and exercise in a way that would have seemed impossible at the beginning of the twentieth (Figure 6.7).

NOTES

I would like to thank my colleague Dr Kelvin Street for sharing with me some of the results of his research while he was in the final stages of writing up his Ph.D. thesis, a reference to which is to be found in the Select Bibliography. The ideas which arose from our discussions helped me in preparing this chapter rather more than they did Kelvin in the completion of his thesis. I congratulate him on the award of his doctorate. I would also like to thank the Bedford Physical Education Old Students' Association for allowing me to use some of the excellent and evocative photographs which form a part of the important archive at Lansdowne, still the base of physical education at Bedford; and I am grateful to Christopher Smart for the expertise with which he has managed to enhance their quality in the process of digitizing them for use in this chapter.

1. See Sheila Fletcher, *Women First: the Female Tradition in English Physical Education, 1880–1980* (London, 1984), Introduction and *passim*.

2. His marriage certificate describes him as a baker, the birth certificates of his children as 'master baker'.
3. Information derived from a combination of birth certificates, James' death certificate and the census returns for 1881.
4. London School Board (hereafter LSB), Minutes, 14 May 1873.
5. Ibid., September 1879.
6. LSB, Inspector's Report, 9 September 1875 (LCC/EO/PS/12/B18/2).
7. Ibid., 4 December 1878 (LCC/EO/PS/12/B18/4).
8. LSB, Minutes, August 1876.
9. Ibid., September 1878.
10. Ibid., December 1878.
11. Ibid., March 1882. Margaret's sister Janet only achieved a 3rd Class Certificate.
12. Ibid., March 1883.
13. Department of Science and Art, *Reports*, 1884.
14. LSB, Minutes, 5 December 1881.
15. Ibid., 1 February 1871.
16. National Association for the Promotion of Social Science, *Transactions* (1860), 594.
17. LSB, Minutes, 15 December 1881.
18. *Margaret Stansfeld*, a booklet published by the College to mark her death in 1951.
19. Ibid., p.10.
20. Ibid, pp.10–11.
21. Ibid.
22. Interview, 1980, Jean Lindsay (1927–30). Interviews with Old Students form a valuable source of evidence. The first date is that of the interview, the second dates, in brackets, the years during which the interviewee spent as a student at Bedford.
23. Interview, 1943, D. P.Payne (1903–5).
24. Borough of Bedford, Sub–Committee on Higher Education, 13 February 1923.
25. Board of Education, Circular 1291 (1923).
26. I am grateful to the work of an Old Student for this information – Jeanette E.M. Ferrier, a Special Study in Education, 'The Development of Physical Education Training for Women, with particular reference to the Bedford College of Physical Education', 57–8.
27. From an article in the *Bedford Record*, 12 June 1928, 'Bedford Physical Training College: its Work Described and its Methods Demonstrated'.
28. *The Bedfordshire Times and Independent*, 10 July 1936.
29. *The Bedford Record*, ibid.
30. Jonathan May, *Madame Bergman-Osterberg* (London, 1969), p.77.
31. Yvonne Moore, 'A Brief Outline of Some Activities of the Ling Physical Education Association', *Journal of Physical Education*, XLI (1949), 31–43.
32. Cited in Fletcher, p.68.
33. Report of Inspectors (Professor W. Cullis and Miss A. Ash) from the University of London's Extension and Tutorial Classes Council, University Extension Committee, 18 March 1935.
34. *The Nineteenth Century*, XLV (April 1899).
35. Ibid.
36. Arabella Kenealy, *Feminism and Sex-Extinction* (London, 1920), p.259.
37. Arabella Kenealy, 'Woman as an Athlete', *The Nineteenth Century*, XLV (April 1899).
38. *The Lancet*, 29 October 1921, 903–4.
39. Ibid., 904.
40. Professor Ellis Cashmore (Staffordshire University) has recently advocated the former view. 'It is ... possible that, if medical knowledge about women was more enlightened and women had been allowed to compete openly, that in all sports that demand skill as opposed to pure brawn – and, weight lifting apart, it is difficult to think of many exceptions – women might have been competing at levels comparable with their male counterparts.' *British Journal of Sports Medicine*, 33 (April 1999), 76–7. This interpretation is challenged by many contemporary sportswomen, e.g. Kate Howey (judo) and Rachel Heyhoe-Flint (cricket): see *The Times*, 31 March 1999, 13.
41. Interview, 1943, B.H. Haldane (1906–8).

42. *Daily News*, July 1884.
43. Dartford College Archives C15/3.
44. Fletcher, p.92.
45. Bedford Physical Training College Students' Association, *Report (1920–21)*, p.10.
46. Rudolf Laban, *Modern Educational Dance* (London, 1948), p.11.
47. Diana Jordan, *The Dance as Education* (London, 1938).
48. Fletcher, p.69.
49. The Misses Buss and Beale were the archetypes of the Victorian spinster Headmistress. Frances Mary Buss founded the North London Collegiate School for Ladies in Camden Town in 1850, Dorothea Beale was Headmistress of Cheltenham Ladies College from 1858 until her death in 1906. Their lack of interest in matters conjugal is best remembered in the anonymous contemporary jingle:

> Miss Buss and Miss Beale
> Cupid's darts do not feel.
> How different from us,
> Miss Beale and Miss Buss.

50. Like the above, Miss Davies was a pioneer figure in the development of female education. She is best known as the founder of the first women's college at a unversity in Britain – Girton College, Cambridge – in 1873.
51. Interview, 1980, Freda Colwill.
52. Fletcher, p.71.
53. Interview, 1980, Joan Goodrich (1922–25).
54. Interview, 1980, Jean Lindsay (1927–30).
55. Cited in Fletcher, p.57.
56. *Margaret Stansfeld*, p.12.
57. Ibid., p.13.
58. Miss Moller, Principal, Lady Mabel College, *The Leaflet*, 54 (Jan.–Feb. 1953).
59. Interview, 1980, Margaret Boyd (1932–35).
60. Cited by Phyllis Colson, 'College Tradition', Report of Old Students' Day, Diamond Jublilee, 1963.
61. Interview, 1981, Holly Graham (1929–32).
62. University of London, University Extension and Tutorial Classes Council, Advisory Committee on Diploma in Theory and Practice of Physical Education, Evidence to McNair Committee, 1942, later published as *Memorandum on Physical Education* (28 January 1944), p.5.
63. Ibid., p.2.
64. *Teachers and Youth Leaders* (The McNair Report) (1944), p.161.
65. University of London, *Memorandum on Physical Education*, p.5.
66. May, p.126 and Bedford Physical Training College Old Students' Association, *Report* (1945), p.15.
67. Colin Crunden, *A History of Anstey College of Physical Education 1897–1972* (Anstey College of Physical Education, 1974).
68. H. Greene, 'Madame Bergman Osterberg – An Appreciation', *Report of the Trustees, 1915–17*, Dartford College Archives.

7

Alexandrine Gibb:
In 'No Man's Land of Sport'

M. ANN HALL

Alexandrine Gibb has probably had as much to do with the tremendous development of girls' sport in Canada as any other individual in the country. She is a dark young lady with beautiful brown eyes, who went to Havergal and subsequently refused to bob her great mass of hair until her friends had given up hope of inducing her to do so. Then she bobbed it.[1]

In 1928, the date of the above quotation in the title, Alexandrine Gibb was in her mid-30s. She had already distinguished herself as an athlete, a pioneering leader and administrator of women's sport, manager of several international athletic teams, and was about to embark on her primary career as Canada's most pre-eminent woman sports journalist of this era. Yet, she has been almost forgotten by today's sports world, and certainly by the newspaper, the *Toronto Star*, where she worked for thirty years. Although this is her story, it is also an account of the early days of organizing women's sport in Canada, especially in the 1920s and 1930s, when Gibb and her contemporaries were major players.

EARLY YEARS

Under a large tombstone in St James Cemetery in Toronto, marked 'Sparks' on one side and 'Gibb' on the other, rest 18 people, among them Alexandrine Gibb. She was born in Toronto in 1891 to John and Sarah (Sparks) Gibb, the fourth child of six, although her two oldest siblings lived no longer than a year.[2] Her mother was the daughter of Captain James Sparks, best known as one of the early Great Lakes captains, from whom Sarah Sparks inherited a love of boats and the outdoors. Growing up in the 1870s, she was often spotted rowing a heavy craft down the Don River or out across the bay to Toronto Island. In winter, she would don skates and glide up and down the river and around the bay, much to the disapproval of local residents. At seventeen she married John Gibb, twelve years older, and thereafter devoted herself to a growing family. Alexandrine Gibb's father owned and operated a dairy on Broadview Avenue, and both parents were active members of Queen East Presbyterian church.[3]

As the century ended, Alexandrine attended Morse Street School, and later she went to Havergal College, a private girls' school founded in 1894, located then at 354 Jarvis Street in Toronto. At that time, Havergal was the most athletically advanced of the Ontario private schools for girls. In 1902, with the arrival of a games mistress trained at the famous Sargent School of Physical Education in Boston, the Havergal gymnasium was equipped with parallel bars, ladders, and a box horse for gymnastics. Introduced soon after were Swedish-style gymnastics comprising remedial and aesthetically pleasing exercises designed to promote harmonious bodily development. The proper gymnasium costume consisted of long black stockings, a knee-length, full-skirted tunic with a long-sleeved middy blouse top and loose-fitting roped belt.[4] Sports and games were also important in the daily life at Havergal with board courts being erected first for tennis and basketball. Cricket was also popular, encouraged and instructed by the English Cambridge graduates whom the headmistress hired as teachers. Ice hockey in the winter, golf and track in the spring were also favoured, and by 1905 an Athletic Association had been formed to bring the various sports clubs together under one organization. Construction began in 1902 for an addition to the school including a larger gymnasium and something quite unusual for schools at that time, a swimming bath, which opened in 1906. By 1909, matches against other private schools in Toronto – Branksome Hall, St Hilda's, University College, St Margaret's, and Bishop Strachan – were hotly but politely contested since it was forbidden by the Havergal headmistress to cheer for your own team: 'Let the other school clap, and you clap them.'[5] We can only assume that Gibb benefited from Havergal's positive sports environment because there is no record of her involvement in any of its athletic teams.[6]

After Havergal, Gibb joined the ranks of the many young, single women who left the surrounding farms or the drudgery of domestic service and entered Toronto's paid labour force prior to the First World War. They were the country's first working girls, 'the pioneer urbanites in an era when less than one-quarter of Canadians lived in large towns or cities', who took up jobs in Toronto's expanding, industrial economy.[7] Gibb went to work as a secretary, possibly for the realty firm of Gibson Brothers, and later for a Toronto mining broker: 'She is the kind of girl that a busy man likes to have for a secretary ... quite capable of bullying a fellow into keeping his appointments.'[8] Toronto's single, wage-earning women of this era were no longer confined to the home or the farm, and like others, Gibb was free to do as she pleased outside working hours. She chose to continue her involvement in sports, especially basketball, in Toronto's newly organized women's league.

Prior to the onset of the war in 1914, women's sport in Canada had taken hold on both a recreational and competitive basis. Very little of this sport was run and controlled by women, but the war brought about some change. Although major tournaments were cancelled and Dominion and provincial championships postponed, women often competed in local and club tournaments in order to raise funds for the Red Cross, prisoners of war, or the war effort in general. Within the private sports clubs, their participation increased often to support patriotic causes, and with the men away they took on more organizational responsibility, which would reap benefits for them when the war ended. Alexandrine Gibb most likely continued to work as a secretary during the duration of the war, and according to one source, she was engaged to marry Lieutenant Harry Dibble, a Canadian infantryman killed in action in France in August 1918.[9]

Now in her late twenties, Gibb became more focused on the organization, administration, and promotion of women's sport especially in Toronto, but also in Ontario. In 1919 she helped organize the Ontario Ladies' Basketball Association, and a year or so later she became a founding member of the Toronto Ladies Athletic Club, and its first president. Her philosophy, 'girls' sport run by girls', was uncompromising, and put into practice through the Toronto Ladies club, an exclusively women's organization with teams in several sports (basketball, softball, track and field) all coached and managed by women.[10] It never sought commercial sponsorship for its teams, and maintained a summer cottage in Etobicoke for its members. In 1922, with the formation of the Canadian Amateur Basketball Association, Gibb was elected second vice-president, the only woman on the executive. In 1925 she became president of the Ontario Ladies' Basketball Association. Outside of work, her life revolved around sport both as an organizer and as an active participant. In summer she was prominent on the tennis courts, and an active member of the Cedar Brook Golf Club, where she sat on the ladies' committee. In winter she continued to play basketball for the Toronto Ladies (the 'Maple Leafs'), Eastern Canadian champions from 1922 to 1924. The team travelled by train to Edmonton in September 1923 to challenge Percy Page's Edmonton Commercial Graduates for the Underwood Trophy, donated by the Underwood Typewriter Company to encourage basketball among girls' teams particularly in Canada and the United States. Resplendent in their twenty-four pleated orange and black bloomers, the Maple Leafs were roundly defeated by the Edmonton Grads. They played them again the following spring when they returned for the Dominion championships, and again were trounced, even though this time they brought their coach and more players.[11] Gibb continued to play left guard for the team until at least 1925.[12]

Just when Gibb aspired to be a sports journalist is not known. One source suggests that she began writing short articles for a publication called *Toronto World* just after the First World War.[13] She is also suppose to have written articles for one of the Toronto dailies, the *Evening Telegram*, around the same time. In 1924, when she travelled to Edmonton to play basketball, articles about the team note that she is a 'newspaper writer' and 'literary light'.[14] It has not been possible to locate any of these early publications, and the first article found with her byline was written on 26 September 1925 for the *Toronto Daily Star* about plans to form the Women's Amateur Athletic Union of Canada. Gibb was among the many aspiring women journalists in Canada in the early 1920s brought on to the major dailies for on-the-job training, sometimes without pay. Women readers, although still interested in recipes and the latest fashion trends, also wished to be informed about current political and social issues within Canada and elsewhere. One entirely new area for women writers was the sports page.[15]

FIRST INTERNATIONAL EXPERIENCE

Gibb first came to public attention in the summer of 1925, when she was asked by the Amateur Athletic Union of Canada (AAU of C) to conduct selection trials for a Canadian women's team invited, all expenses paid, to compete in an international track and field meeting in England. Until then the AAU of C had paid no attention to women, and did not accept female registrations because most of the male ruling elite argued that highly competitive or physically demanding sports were unsuitable for girls and women. The most they had done was to set up a national committee on women's athletics. With both the International Olympic Committee (IOC) and the powerful International Amateur Athletic Federation (IAAF) opposed to including women's track and field events in the summer Olympics, Canada's governing body took a 'do nothing' position. That was the case until 1922 when French sportswoman Alice Milliat, and her newly formed Fédération sportive féminine internationale (FSFI), organized a spectacular international track and field event in Paris and called it the *Olympiques Féminines*. The IAAF finally took notice and asked its member nations to take charge of women's track and field in their respective countries. With no official body for women's track and field in Canada, the AAU had two options – one was to encourage women to form their own association to control the sport – the other was to take control themselves. At that point they chose the latter course. Canadian women did not compete in these first women's world track and field meetings because the AAU had little interest in promoting the sport for women even though Canada was formally admitted to the FSFI at its third congress in Paris in 1924.[16] By 1925 even male sportswriters in Canada recognized the potential: 'The point is that Canadian girls, as never before, and in ever-increasing numbers, are storing up health, discipline, self-control and a fine spirit of sportsmanship on the playing fields of the Dominion, and that the performances of many closely approximate those of the world's women leaders in track events.'[17]

Gibb's appointment to select and manage the team invited to the international meeting at Stamford Bridge in London was controversial. Apparently the Ontario Branch of the AAU of C had initially received the invitation and immediately appointed Walter Knox of Orillia as manager and coach because of his experience with the men's team at the 1912 and 1920 Olympics, even though the invitation specified that the expenses of ten girls and two 'lady assistants' would be paid.[18] The national AAU stepped in and confirmed Gibb's appointment stating that she was a 'tireless and conscientious worker in the interests of women athletes'.[19] However, this left Gibb precisely one week to organize the selection trials to be held at the University of Toronto stadium on 11 July since they were to sail for England on 17 July. Naturally there was consternation in the press that athletes from outside Ontario would be unable to compete, which in the end was true. Five athletes from Toronto, three from Hamilton, and one each from Montreal and St Catherines made the team with two reserves from Toronto. The two best sprinters in Canada, Rosa Grosse and Fanny 'Bobbie' Rosenfeld, did not try out for the team because they were previously committed to the Ontario track and field championships later in August.

Undeterred, Gibb and her athletes left Canada as scheduled under the watchful eye of chaperone Mrs Gordon Finlay, sister-in-law to the AAU of C president. Gibb dutifully reported that the girls trained each day in the ship's well-equipped gymnasium and by walking around the decks. After dinner they were allowed to dance until 10 o'clock as long as they were in bed soon after. 'What makes me so glad,' she enthused, 'is that everyone seems surprised at the high type of girl we have with us.'[20] On arrival in London, the Canadians received last minute coaching from British coaches Frederick Webster and Sam Mussabini (the personal coach of Harold Abrahams, immortalized in the film *Chariots of Fire*), both strong supporters of women's athletics. Although they finished third overall behind Great Britain and Czechoslovakia in the nine events, Webster commented on their remarkable improvement in the space of a week, and that 'they spared no pains to put themselves right'.[21]

This first international trip had been very instructive for Alexandrine Gibb. She had observed the female-controlled British Women's Amateur Athletic Association first hand, and become friends with one of its founders, Sophie Elliott-Lynn (Lady Heath), an all-round international athlete who competed in the javelin at the triangular meeting in London. In fact, the two of them planned to write a book about women's athletics. Gibb was delighted and impressed by how seriously she and her athletes had been treated in England.

WOMEN'S SPORT RUN BY WOMEN

When Gibb returned to Canada, she immediately set out to establish a Women's Amateur Athletic Union affiliated with the AAU of C. She was determined that women should run their own sports, that girls should be coached by women, and although men were encouraged as advisors, they must stay in the background. Along with other prominent women's sport leaders in Toronto, Gibb wanted to create a national organization with branches in all provinces to administer and control girls and women's sports. They formed the Canadian Ladies Athletic Club, which would provide opportunities in baseball, ice hockey, softball, and track and field across the country, and at the same time provide the structure for a national governing body should the AAU oppose it.[22] Gibb became its first president.

At its annual meeting on 11 September 1925 the AAU of C approved the formation of a 'women's branch', called the Women's Amateur Athletic Union of Canada, which would be governed entirely by women, but would 'retain the advice and counsel' of the AAU's all-male women's committee. Janet Allen, President of the Ontario Ladies' Hockey Association was elected 'provisional president', and Marie Parks, who taught physical education at the University of Toronto, 'provisional secretary', with a temporary committee, which included Gibb, instructed to draft a constitution.[23] In one of her first articles for the *Toronto Daily Star*, Gibb took stock of the situation across the country, suggesting that the best way to proceed would be to organize branches in each province. Ontario, she admitted, was in the best position with a number of already existing women's sport organizations including those for basketball, ice hockey and softball. Quebec (and by this she meant English Montreal) was active in basketball, ice hockey, and swimming; there was little activity in the Maritimes; whereas in the west, Alberta was strong in ice hockey and basketball (the Edmonton Grads were well on their way to fame); British Columbia and Manitoba were 'being organized', but she made no mention of Saskatchewan.[24] She also made it clear that since women had not had the same executive experience as men, they should welcome their advice and guidance. Some years later, after a majority of women were elected to a local softball executive and the men running the league threatened to walk out, Gibb wrote:

> Men are very useful. They can help with advice and many men have done just that. Men have had years and years of experience in sport organizations and the girls have only been in the game for the past ten years. So we have lots to learn, girls. But we want a chance to learn it. If we can look after our own affairs we too will gain experience and be experts. If we keep asking the men to take all the responsible offices we will always be in the background. Don't misunderstand me in this struggle for the right of girls to sit on their own executives. Keep the men with you if you can, but impress on the men the importance of learning how these things should be done.[25]

The Women's Amateur Athletic Federation of Canada (WAAF of C) was officially formed at its first convention in Montreal, on 7 December 1926. Affiliated branches had been established in Ontario, Quebec, and the Maritimes, and the number of athletes registered in the Federation was approximately 1200 although most of these were from the Ontario Ladies Softball Association. The convention was attended by representatives from the newly formed branches, other women's organizations, interested women athletes and physical educators, and not surprisingly, a large number of men, including executive members of the AAU and the Canadian Olympic Committee. A photo in a Montreal newspaper shows almost 40 women and some 10 men. Strange as it may seem to us now, it was important that the 'ladies' receive the men's blessing in their new venture, although I doubt if many were prepared for the paternalistic remarks of John DeGruchy of the AAU who:

> expressed his personal gratification and delight at the way the ladies had thrown themselves into the work of the organization. He was amazed at the energy they had shown and wished to congratulate them upon their business-like methods....He wished to emphasize, however, that in all these athletics for women, the womanly side must not be lost sight of, and that the women themselves must always keep in mind that the important thing is not so much athletics for women as that they are the mothers of the coming nation.[26]

WRITING A DAILY SPORTS COLUMN

Nineteen twenty-eight was a banner year for Alexandrine Gibb. In May she began writing her women's sports column on a regular basis for the *Toronto Daily Star*; she was manager of the highly successful women's track and field team at the Amsterdam Olympics; and in November, she was elected President of the WAAF of C. Her two careers, one as sportswriter and the other as sports executive, now merged because she had a powerful platform from which to express her views, and to affect change. 'No Man's Land of Sport: News and Views of Feminine Activities' appeared six days a week in the *Toronto Daily Star*, an influential Toronto paper, which still exists today.[27] Her column appeared prominently on the *Star*'s sports pages, often alongside 'With Pick and Shovel' written by sports editor Lou Marsh, her respected and adored 'chief'. It was not unusual in those days for sport reporters to be actively engaged in the organizations they covered. Lou Marsh 'moonlighted' as a hockey referee who wrote about the games he officiated; Henry Roxborough published many articles about amateur sport for *MacLean's* and other magazines while active on the AAU's publicity committee; and W.A. Hewitt edited the *Toronto Star*'s sports page and at the same time ran amateur hockey.[28]

Among the women sports writers of this era, each one was either an active or former athlete, and many were directly involved in the organizations about which they wrote, mostly with great enthusiasm but sometimes critically, and in Gibb's case with acerbic wit. She wrote her column for twelve years beginning in May 1928 and ending in November 1940. Her contemporaries, Myrtle Cook and Fanny 'Bobbie' Rosenfeld, international athletes she knew well, were actively engaged in a variety of women's sport associations from the early 1920s. Cook began her career as a sportswriter with the *Montreal Star* in 1929, writing her column 'In the Women's Sportlight' for over forty years. In the early 1930s, Rosenfeld wrote briefly for the *Toronto Star Weekly* and the *Montreal Daily Herald* before settling in at the *Globe & Mail*, where her column, 'Feminine Sports Reel', appeared from 1937 until 1958. Phyllis Griffiths, whom Gibb knew from her basketball days, was already employed with the *Toronto Telegram* while active in playing and organizing many sports. She began writing her column, 'The Girl and the Game', in 1928, almost at the same time as Gibb started hers, and it continued until 1942. Further west, Patricia Page Hollingsworth, whose father Percy Page coached the Edmonton Grads, wrote briefly for the *Edmonton Journal* between 1935 and 1940. She used her column, 'Feminine Flashes', to bolster publicity for the Grads when interest in the team waned (they folded in 1940 after more than twenty years). Lillian 'Jimmy' Coo, daughter of the news editor of the *Winnipeg Free Press*, although an athlete and volunteer administrator in her own right, wrote 'Cherchez la Femme' briefly before and after the Second World War (1937–42, 1946–7). On the west coast, the *Vancouver Sun* employed Ann Stott between 1939 and 1941, and Ruth Wilson during 1943–5 to write a column about 'Femmes in Sport' (later 'Femmes and Foibles in Sport'). It was Gibb, however, who led the way, being the first to parlay her experience as a sport administrator into her position at the *Star* as a daily sports columnist.[29] She set the example for the others to follow, becoming what later commentators called the 'dean of women sportswriters'.[30]

Through her column, Gibb dispensed information, promoted all varieties of women's sport (basketball and softball were among her favourites), commented on the issues of the day, and made clear her philosophy concerning, for example, amateurism, opportunities for 'working girls', gender equity, health concerns, and 'mannish' women athletes. She gave her readers, 'girls' as she called them, essential information, helpful advice, and occasionally a swift, symbolic kick if someone did something not to her liking. 'Plain foolishness' was her favourite reproach to athletes like the Supremes softball pitcher who pitched two games on the same night at Sunnyside in Toronto, or to the swimmer who competed in the Dominion championships 'against doctors' orders while suffering from a severe cold in her back'.[31] She was constantly answering reader inquiries about women's sporting activities, and as the years went by, she became an indispensable, almost encyclopaedic, source of information:

> All in one day I have been asked to give information about the following. Where is there a ladies' billiard parlor in Toronto? Where can a novice learn to figure-skate? How much do the skates cost? Does it take long?… How do you start a ping-pong club in a small community? What is the exact height and what are the exact dimensions of the table, and so on![32]

She also provided news about league openings (especially softball), game schedules, and club activities (her beloved Toronto Ladies' Athletic Club for example). Her column contained public service announcements like those for out-of-town athletes wishing to try out for a local club or, more important, looking for a job. She kept track of former well known athletes by announcing engagements, marriages, births, and, when she didn't have anything concrete to announce along marital lines, hinted at an imminent 'sport romance'. She said virtually nothing about herself, except occasionally to mention her dog 'Hoot', a winter holiday in warmer climes, or to thank concerned readers when she was ill and away from her column.

What Gibb did make clear was her opinion on important issues and her general philosophy towards women's sport. Like most sport administrators of her day, she was a staunch believer in amateurism and the 'amateur code', which prevented anyone from profiting financially either from playing or teaching sport.[33] Amateurs and professionals must never mix, and Gibb was ever vigilant in reporting even a hint that some athletes might be receiving 'gifts' for their services, especially during the Depression years. 'When I played basketball we would have fainted away if any gift of $40 had been presented. When you go through your sport life buying your own uniform, shoes and sport socks, this money, ... is quite a jump to make in one hop.'[34] On the other hand, she understood that commercial or industrial sport was the only opportunity for the thousands of 'girls' who worked in the factories, shops, and downtown businesses to play sport at all. 'The girls lure the commercial firms into supporting them, so they can play ball under proper circumstances, be properly clad with clothing and have bats and balls and fun.'[35] These same working girls, members of the many softball, basketball, hockey, and track and field clubs, were the backbone of the WAAF of C, which is why Gibb lobbied constantly on their behalf whether it was for facilities, playing times, and even jobs from the same commercial firms who sponsored the teams. She also worked to ensure that top-level athletes, who again were primarily young working women, were able to train and compete even though they held down jobs. For those who could afford to belong to tennis and golf clubs (like Gibb herself), she frequently made a plea from the 'business woman's point of view' for the same playing opportunities given men. Although Gibb would never have labelled herself a 'feminist', her philosophy towards gender equity was very much what today we would describe as 'liberal' feminism, with its primary focus on ensuring girls and women equal access to sport and recreation opportunities long available to boys and men.

Gibb's views were progressive in some areas, but her notions of femininity and athleticism fitted the prevailing attitudes of the time. She was forever reminding readers about the beauty of Canadian women athletes with comments like she is a 'looker' or a 'fair-haired beauty', and at the same time, she was caustically critical of 'mannish women athletes' especially when the Canadian 'dainty girl runners' had to compete against them. Tall and muscular athletes like the ('six-foot mannish in appearance girl runner from Missouri') Helen Stephens, or the ('huge and husky, deep-voiced') Polish-American Stanislawa Walasiewicz (Stella Walsh), all came in for particular censure, to say nothing of the women who had competed as females and were now ostensibly male. 'I'd like to see a special 100 metres at the Olympic Games. In it I would put Stella Walsh, Helen Stephens, a couple of special German contestants, at least two English girls, and one or two other Europeans. Canada would

not be entered.'[36] After the British Empire Games and the Women's
World Games in London in 1934, Gibb called for physical examinations
of all athletes wishing to compete as female. 'I had a dressing room full
of Canadian girls weeping because they had to toe the mark against girls
who shaved and spoke in mannish tones!'[37]

Whether or not it was true, Gibb was convinced that every
international team she managed, beginning with the first one in 1925,
was the most feminine team that ever stepped on the cinder paths. She
was incensed when Andy Lytle (sports editor at the *Vancouver Sun* and
eventually at the *Toronto Star*) called women athletes 'leathery-limbed,
flat-chested girls'. She and other women sportswriters mounted a
spirited defence of female athleticism in their columns, also sending out
through Canadian Press a photo of comely Olive Hinder from the Laurel
Ladies' Athletic Club, a 'blue-eyed, lissom girl whose fair hair hangs in
soft ringlets to her shoulder'.[38] Gibb's main defence against attacks on
women athletes was to point to their obvious beauty, and to implore the
'girls' to conduct themselves with the appropriate feminine decorum.
She wanted them well dressed, well behaved, and well spoken, and she
was intolerant of anything less. Following a fracas in a basketball game
in Montreal, she admonished: 'Girls will learn some of these days that if
they desire to continue in sports they must learn to control their
tempers. Mere men can get away with a fistic argument in a game, but
let a feminine fist fly or a hair pulling argument start, and it's all wrong.
Curb your tempers girls or go back to knitting.'[39]

WOMEN'S SPORT POLITICS

Gibb also kept her readers informed about much of the political
infighting in women's sport, particularly as it affected the Women's
Amateur Athletic Federation of Canada, which she had helped to create
and in which she continued to play a major leadership role.[40] She was
elected first Vice-President at its second annual meeting in Toronto in
November 1927, and at the same time was secretary to the Ontario
Branch of the Federation. In May 1928, following a recommendation
from the WAAF of C to the Canadian Olympic Committee, Gibb was
appointed manager of the Canadian women's Olympic team, the first
one to compete in the newly approved IOC track events that summer in
Amsterdam. The six-women team, dubbed the 'Matchless Six' (Figure
7.1) by the Canadian press, performed brilliantly by winning a gold in

the high jump, silver in the 100 metres, and another gold in the 4 x 100 metre relay race.[41] Gibb, however, was furious when Dr A.S. Lamb, President of the AAU of C and overall manager of the Canadian team, refused to allow an official protest over the results of the 100 metres. In an impossibly close race, Gibb and others were convinced that Canadian Fanny Rosenfeld had won over the American, Betty Robinson. She was even more incensed when Lamb, without consulting her or anyone else from the WAAF of C, voted against women competing in any further Olympics. In an article she wrote later for a national magazine, she attempted to rationalize his actions by lashing out at the negative attitude towards women athletes in Montreal:

> Dr Lamb comes from Montreal. In Montreal, competitive athletics for women are practically a minus quantity. This biggest city of Canada never had an outstanding woman athlete in track and field. It did not have a single representative at the final Olympic trials in Halifax. Undoubtedly, this was due to the objection that exists in Montreal against competitive sports for women. Every other eastern province was well represented but Quebec was simply out in the cold.[42]

In his defence, Lamb pointed to the 'many glaring inaccuracies and untruths' in the press reports including those of Gibb, although in retrospect, he admitted that it would have been wise to have consulted both Gibb and Marie Parkes in the matter of future participation by women at the IOC Olympics.[43]

Gibb was elected President of the WAAF of C at their third annual meeting in November 1928. Shortly after, along with other members of the executive she represented the Federation at the annual AAU of C meetings, where the WAAF of C was given complete control over Canadian women's sports both nationally and internationally. She held the presidency for two years until 1930, when Toronto softball organizer Mabel Ray unexpectedly took over even though it was due to move west to Victoria Sallis of Vancouver. Unfortunately Ray, who was also president of the Ontario Branch of the Federation and the Toronto Women's Softball Association, became embroiled in a nasty softball dispute – she was found to have mismanaged TWSA funds – which meant she should be disciplined by the very associations over which she presided. 'The situation is decidedly awkward,' commented Phyllis Griffiths in her *Toronto Telegram* sports column.[44] Ray refused to back

FIGURE 7.1
GIBB (TOP RIGHT) AND THE MATCHLESS SIX AT THE
1928 SUMMER OLYMPICS

Courtesy: National Archives of Canada, PA 151001.

down, but in November 1931 she was ousted as head of the WAAF of C and Gibb again took over the presidency for one year, allowing them, as one member put it, to come through a distressing year 'with their colors flying so high'.[45]

At the 1932 annual WAAF of C meeting in Winnipeg, Gibb was asked to remain president for another year, but she refused, partly due to a motion put forward by the Quebec (i.e. Montreal) branch that would make sportswriters ineligible for office in the Federation. They would also be compelled to sever all association with sports while employed as journalists. Defenders of the new clause argued that sportswriters could not be loyal to the Federation while at the same time expressing their views in public, nor should the press have access to the organization's private affairs.[46] Even though the motion was defeated 22 to 8 (the latter from Quebec and British Columbia), it must have given Gibb pause for thought about her continued role in the organization. The vast distances separating Federation leaders, and a lack of money especially in the

Depression years, led to serious regional conflicts most particularly between western and eastern Canada. Since she no longer had an official position, Gibb was often outspoken about the organization in her daily column, referring to it as the 'Waaflets'.

By spring 1934 relations between Gibb and the Federation were such that 'scrappy' secretary Ann Clark announced that both Gibb and Fanny Rosenfeld were no longer 'persona grata' in the organization.[47] The two had been appointed manager and coach respectively of the Canadian women's team competing in the British Empire Games in London that year, but the organizing committee had neglected to consult the Federation. Clark charged that Gibb no longer had any connection with the Federation, and furthermore could not fulfil her roles as reporter and manager at the same time, despite the fact that Gibb had done this on several occasions before. At the time Gibb was in hospital recovering from an operation; however, the AAU affirmed the appointments, and the two went to the Games as scheduled that summer in England.

By now, Gibb was assistant sports editor at the *Toronto Star*, and probably the most well known women's sports advocate in Canada. When she was appointed to the Ontario Athletic Commission in September 1934, the first woman then or since, her boss at the *Star*, sports editor Lou Marsh, wrote:

> Miss Gibb knows sport better than any other woman in the country and as well as any other man whose name was mentioned in the tentative line-ups of the new commission. Her experience as a writer of sport on this paper has taken her into all branches of sport, both amateur and professional, and she has an intimate knowledge of the politics and intrigues of both brands of sporting activity. Her executive ability has been frequently recognized by her appointment to important positions in connection with Olympiads and other forms of international sport, and also by her selection to represent Canada on bodies which govern amateur sport for the entire world.[48]

Gibb was particularly proud when the Ontario Athletic Commission agreed to supply free medical examinations for all girl athletes in the province, the first time, she noted in her column, 'the O.A.C. has never officially recognized that we have in Ontario a steadily growing band of feminine athletes who are in active competition in many sports'.[49] As Gibb took up new challenges, she became increasingly cynical about the

WAAF of C, frequently berating the leadership or dissuading them from an unpopular decision through her column. In exasperation, she wrote: 'No wonder men laugh at women's meetings and associations. This splitting of hairs and ridiculous rulings make men feel that women don't know what it is all about.'[50] She had stopped writing about them altogether by the time her column ended in 1940. Sadly, the Second World War took its toll, money became even more scarce as did the women leaders, so that in 1953 a decision was taken, accepted by some and resented by many, to amalgamate the Federation with the men's AAU of C.

INTERNATIONAL TRAVELS AND THE WAR

In 1935, Gibb was sent by her newspaper on a trip to the Soviet Union and through several Mediterranean countries to write a special series, and as a result she was gone from her regular column for five months (Figure 7.2). The left-wing Workers Sport Association of Canada, affiliated with the Young Communist League, announced that it would send a group of Canadian athletes and coaches to the Soviet Union for competition, and also to visit sports schools, factory fitness programmes, and Young Pioneer summer camps.[51] The *Toronto Star* was sufficiently interested to send Gibb on an extended tour of the Soviet Union, to cover the 'woman's angle'. She travelled throughout the summer and her series appeared in the autumn, but was written as if she were still on tour.[52] In Russia, where she spent forty days, she travelled south from Leningrad through Moscow and Kiev towards the Black Sea and then into Persia (Iran), and home via Turkey, Greece, Yugoslavia, and northern Europe. Although her focus was occasionally women or sport, she wrote mostly about daily life in the Soviet Union. Gibb was certainly not a Communist sympathizer (she openly supported the Liberal party), and she was indifferent to the 'rabid Communists' who decried living conditions among the Canadian poor, when in her view they lived much better than a good many people in Russia. Nonetheless, she was impressed by what she saw in the Soviet Union, and reminded readers how life had improved for so many since the revolution. She was 'astounded and thrilled' when she observed over 100,000 athletes marching before Stalin in Moscow, but at the same time warned that these same athletes, the 'stalwart big-busted girls who carry themselves with head erect and shoulders back', were preparing for both labour and

FIGURE 7.2

READY FOR HER TRIP TO THE MIDDLE EAST IN 1935

Courtesy: Toronto Star.

FIGURE 7.3

IRAN, SUMMER OF 1935

Courtesy: Toronto Star.

defence. Women, she admitted, seemed to have more equality in Russia. They were everywhere in employment, although she had reservations about what they had gained. 'I saw women doing much too heavy work for their physique', and she was 'appalled' by the working conditions among women in a tractor and automobile plant. Wary about the 'propaganda' spread by her guides, Gibb was realistic about what she had observed, stating that 'Red Russia' was by 'no means the heaven the Soviets picture it to other countries'. After the solemnity of the Soviet Union ('I have come out of the tunnel into the bright sunlight'), her reports from Persia, the 'storied land of romance', were quite a contrast (Figure 7.3). On one occasion she described how she bribed a policeman with two bottles of vodka to catch a glimpse of the Shah.

After her exotic adventures Gibb returned to the daily grind of writing her sports column. In 1936 she was again appointed manager of the Olympic women's track and field team competing that summer in Berlin, but did not make the trip due to her mother's illness. Her discussion of the Olympics and reports of the progress of the Canadian team lacked the first-hand experience of her articles from the 1928 Olympics and her daily, detailed reports from Los Angeles in 1932.

On 26 November 1940 Gibb writes in her column: 'So long until the summertime. Keep your chin up but not out. I'll be seeing you.' She explains that she has been given the responsibility of editing the *Star*'s section on Women's War Work – 'C'est la guerre! C'est la vie and au revoir to sports!'(Figure 7.4) What Gibb did not reveal was that she had been unwillingly removed from her column by the *Star*'s sports editor, Fred Jackson, primarily at the request of Andy Lytle, her old nemesis, who soon succeeded Jackson as sports editor.[53] She and Lytle detested each other, and Lytle made it clear in his own column that he had little empathy with amateur sport. After former sports editor Lou Marsh's early death in 1936, Gibb no longer had the support she needed, and she became something of an outcast in the sports department, although a more respected 'member of the gang' in the newsroom. She never did return to her daily sports column. The paper tried to maintain news of 'Feminine Sports' by having someone else write a 'No Man's Land of Sport' column, but by 1944 it too had disappeared.

The war went on much longer than anyone, including Gibb, predicted and she toiled on the women's war work column, writing about their efforts to sew and mend uniforms, operate canteens and 'hostess houses' for the troops, and the like. It is difficult to tell whether or not

FIGURE 7.4

PHOTO HEADED HER NEWSPAPER COLUMN IN THE 1930s

Courtesy: Toronto Star.

FIGURE 7.5

GIBB IN 1951

Courtesy: Toronto Star.

she liked this new role at the paper; she probably had little choice. After the war, Gibb mainly wrote features at the *Toronto Star* although it becomes increasingly difficult to find her byline. In 1951 she was part of the press corps that accompanied Princess Elizabeth and the Duke of Edinburgh on a royal tour throughout Canada. Gibb may well have enjoyed this experience, but her articles in the *Toronto Star* about what the Princess wore or how many fish Philip caught were a sad reminder, to this observer, that Gibb no longer was writing about the things that mattered most to her (Figure 7.5).[54] In 1954, however, Gibb was primarily responsible for persuading Canadian marathon swimmer Marilyn Bell, who at the time was comparatively unknown, to challenge the American Florence Chadwick in her attempt to swim Lake Ontario. The *Star* agreed to sponsor Marilyn and another Canadian swimmer, Winnie Roach Lueszler. Only the sixteen-year-old Marilyn made it across that cold, dark night in September. Gibb, along with thirty other *Star* reporters and photographers covered the event, as well as the ensuing mania over Canada's newest sweetheart heroine, and she was later singled out and thanked by Bell and her coach Gus Ryder.[55] By 1956 Gibb was writing a new column for her paper containing news items and gossip of local interest called 'Have You Heard', which was to be her last.[56] She died of a heart attack after a brief illness at the age of sixty-six on 15 December 1958.

A GOOD REPORTER

'Gibby was a mean bitch, which made her a good reporter', according to former *Toronto Star* sports editor Milt Dunnell.[57] As a young reporter in the early 1940s, he had worked with Gibb at the paper, and thought her 'one of the best reporters on the news side', but 'a lousy writer'. Trent Frayne, who at the same time was just beginning his career at the *Globe & Mail*, remembers Gibb as a 'powerful' woman, and physically a 'good size' (she was in fact about 5ft 5in).[58] According to both men, she was not 'beautiful', but there was nothing particularly unattractive about her. 'Essentially feminine' and 'a most likeable person' commented Elmer Ferguson, sports editor of the *Montreal Star* with whom Gibb had clashed many times, in his tribute to her when she died.[59] Dunnell also mentioned that she was 'full chested' with a history of low cut dresses and blouses leading to allegations among the men at the *Star* that she used her bosom to good advantage.

Lotta Demsey, who joined the *Star* just before Gibb's death in 1958, wrote a moving tribute to the woman she had known more by reputation than personally. 'I watched Alexandrine Gibb at first when she came sailing into my prairie town. I envied her ease and comfortable rapport with any manner and matter of folk; traits not characteristic of those of eastern stock, born and bred in Toronto.'[60] She was, according to Dempsey, 'a name to be respected mightily', and one that struck 'terror into the hearts of the less gifted, less dedicated, on any assignment'. Gibb may not have been the best of writers, but there was never 'so experienced and perceptive a student of the human drama'. 'I have seen her,' continued Dempsey, 'at flood, fire, shipwreck, and other calamity, looking as weary and unremitting as the men and women caught up in the chaos. In a way she was; living it with them, step by gruelling step.'

There seem to be two views of Alexandrine Gibb, both probably a little true, but neither entirely accurate. She was breezy, assertive, even formidable, and would probably do just about anything to get a story. Milt Dunnell told me how she scooped everyone in reporting the suicide of a former Toronto Chief of Police. Gibb was actually in Hyde Park on the day it happened (in the summer of 1958), but the police had cordoned off the park and would not let anyone out. Of course when Gibb went to phone her story to the paper, the police stopped her but she immediately threw, in Dunnell's words, a 'wing ding' – screaming, yelling, and much carrying on – to which the police responded with 'get that bitch out of here'. Gibb got her story before anyone else.

Honesty and compassion were the other side of Gibb, as well as a sense that what she said and did mattered. She frequently asked her readers for donations to help women athletes travel to the Olympics or other international meetings, and she promoted the numerous benefit games held to raise money for an injured player or athlete travel. She attended these games or events herself, and reported on the funds raised the following day. One time, she 'adopted' an elderly pair of women who were in need of housing, furnishings, and general assistance, all of which she obtained through pleas in her column. Gibb loved being a reporter, and with enormous energy and zest she gave all she had to make her paper, the *Toronto Star*, the best. 'Alex', wrote Lotta Dempsey, 'belonged to the paper and the paper belonged to Alex'.

Alexandrine Gibb worked tirelessly and long for the benefit of women's sport in Canada. Through her newspaper column in the important organizing decades of the 1920s and 1930s, she spoke her mind, and was always uncompromising about what she believed in and what in her view was right for women athletes. She won the respect and admiration of her many readers and of those who worked with her in the women's sport organizations of which she was a part. It is a shame that she has been so easily forgotten.

NOTES

I am grateful to the Social Science and Humanities Research Council of Canada for research monies to undertake an ambitious historical study, still in progress, of women's sport in Canada. For this particular essay, I also thank Bruce Kidd, Joyce Sowby, and Jane Haslett for their advice and assistance, as well as several former graduate students at the University of Alberta who helped with the research. I am also grateful to the *Toronto Star* for providing access to photos of Alexandrine Gibb.

1. 'Leader in Girls' Sport Movement', *Toronto Star Weekly*, 31 March 1928.
2. Most sources place Gibb's birth date as 1892, but the tombstone clearly shows 1891. Her siblings were: Sarah (1895–95), John (1887–87), Gordon (1889–1951), Robert (1897–1968), and Henrietta (1899–1977). Buried in St. James cemetery in the Gibb/Sparks plot, among others, are the four children of Capt. James Sparks and Ann Johnston (Gibb's grandparents), Gibb's parents and their children, and Harold Anderson, husband of Henrietta Gibb.
3. 'Mrs. John Gibb Passes Lifelong Ward 1 Resident', *Toronto Daily Star*, 17 December 1936, 1, 3. John Gibb's occupation was determined by an entry in the 1919 *Toronto City Directory* (Vol. XLIV, Might Directory Limited). He died in 1920.
4. See P. Olafson, *Sport, Physical Education and the Ideal Girl in Selected Ontario Denominational Schools, 1870–1930* (Master's thesis, University of Windsor, 1990), pp.123–32; M. Byers, *Havergal: Celebrating a Century 1894–1994* (Toronto, 1994), pp.39–40.
5. Byers, *Havergal*, p.46.
6. Although the fact that Gibb went to Havergal is mentioned in many sources, and she herself claimed this to be true, it cannot be positively confirmed. I do not know when exactly she attended the school, nor does her name appear on the Havergal 'Old Girls' list of graduating students. It is possible that Gibb attended Havergal, but did not actually graduate. According to Havergal records, an 'Alexina Gibb' graduated in 1908, which could be Alexandrine since she would have been 16 or 17 at the time. What is more curious is that a thorough search of *Ludemus*, the school magazine, between 1901 and 1915 turned up no mention or photos of Alexandrine Gibb. Nonetheless, based mostly on Gibb's own claim, I assume she attended Havergal at some point prior to 1910.
7. C. Strange, *Toronto's Girl Problem: The Perils and Pleasures of the City, 1880–1930* (Toronto, 1995).
8. 'Leader in Girls' Sport Movement'; 'Top News, Sports Reporter for the Star, Alexandrine Gibb Dies', *Toronto Daily Star*, 16 December 1958, 5.
9. 'Lost Good Friend in Alex – Frost', *Toronto Daily Star*, 16 December 1958, 5; Commonwealth War Graves Commission (http://yard.ccta.gov.uk/cwgc/register.nsf).
10. 'Leader in Girls' Sport Movement'; B. Kidd, *The Struggle for Canadian Sport* (Toronto, 1996), p.109. The actual founding date of the Toronto Ladies Athletic Club is either 1920 or 1921. Although Gibb referred to the TLAC several times over the years in her sports column, she was inconsistent as to its founding date.
11. The best accounts of these games are in the *Edmonton Bulletin* (Sept. 1923 and April 1924).
12. Gibb's name appears on the player list of a game reported in the *Toronto Star* on 2 April 1925. In her 'No Man's Land of Sport' column in the *Toronto Star* on 20 October 1934 (p.13), she says that she 'turned my own Toronto uniform back' in 1925.
13. The source is Bruce Kidd both in personal communication, and in his doctoral dissertation: 'Improvers, Feminists, Capitalists and Socialists: Shaping Canadian Sport in the 1920s and

1930s', (University of Toronto, 1990), 205. However, a survey of *Toronto World*, which began publication in 1880 and ceased in 1921, produced virtually nothing on women's sport, let alone anything by Gibb.

14. 'Ontario Basketball Champions', *Edmonton Bulletin*, 12 April 1924, 4 and D. White, 'Sport is My Subject', *Edmonton Bulletin*, 21 April 1924, 4.

15. K. Rex, *No Daughter of Mine: The Women and History of the Canadian Women's Press Club 1904–1971* (Toronto, 1995).

16. Kidd, *The Struggle for Canadian Sport*, especially Chapters 2 and 3. See also F.A.M. Webster, *Athletics of Today for Women: History, Development and Training* (London, 1930) and G. Pallett, *Women's Athletics* (London, 1955) for detailed descriptions, including competitors, times, records, and photographs of these early international track and field meetings.

17. N.R. Raine, 'Girls invade track and diamond', *MacLean's Magazine*, 15 August 1925, 12–14.

18. 'Confirms Appointment of Miss "Alex" Gibb', *Globe & Mail*, 9 July 1925, 7.

19. *Globe & Mail*, 4 July 1925, 11.

20. A. Gibb, 'Canadian Girls Trained Faithfully', *Toronto Daily Star*, 4 August 1925, 10 (Note that this article appeared *after* the competition had taken place.)

21. Webster, p.53. The members of the Canadian team were: Clara Ballard, Grace Conacher, Hazel Conacher, Myrtle Cook, Josie Dyment, Kathleen Flanagan, Jean Godson, Velma Springstead, Mollie Trinnell, and Gertrude Woods.

22. Kidd, *The Struggle for Canadian Sport*, p.116.

23. 'Women's A.A.U. of C. Organized by Women', *Toronto Daily Star*, 11 September 1925, 79.

24. A. Gibb, 'Plans Outlined for Women's A.A.U. of C.', *Toronto Daily Star*, 26 September 1925, 105.

25. A. Gibb, 'No Man's Land of Sport', 1 May 1937, 17

26. 'Women's Athletic Federation Elects Its New Officers', *Montreal Daily Star*, 8 December 1926.

27. Since Gibb averaged 25 columns a month written between 8 May 1928 and 26 Nov. 1940, and taking account of the periods when she was travelling, on holidays, or ill, I estimate that she published between 3,300 and 3,400 columns. My content analysis is based on a reading of over 600 columns (May of each year, plus one other month per year for 13 years), about 17 per cent of the total. During this period, Gibb also wrote the occasional article for the *Toronto Star Weekly*, national magazines such as *MacLean's*, as well as additional articles on women's sport for the *Star*.

28. Kidd, *The Struggle for Canadian Sport*, p.263.

29. Kidd maintains that Mabel Ray, a contemporary of Gibb, who was very involved in organizing softball in Toronto, was the first to submit articles to the Toronto dailies in the mid-1920s. I believe this is true, but I have been unable to locate any articles with Ray's byline.

30. S.F. Wise and D. Fisher, *Canada's Sporting Heroes* (Don Mills, 1974), p.311.

31. 'No Man's Land of Sport', 21 July 1930, 8; 29 April 1939, 16.

32. 'No Man's Land of Sport', 24 November 1934, 11.

33. 'Constitution and Track & Field Rules & Regulations of the Women's Amateur Athletic Federation of Canada,' Revised January 1938 (National Archives of Canada, MG 30 C 164, Vol. 35, File 16). The WAAF of C amateur code was virtually identical to that of the AAU of C, which had not changed much since its creation in 1919. The WAAF of C constitution also laid out the many grounds for reinstatement (for example, physical educators and directors were regarded as 'non-competing amateurs' and would be eligible for their amateur card two years after they stopped teaching).

34. 'No Man's Land of Sport', 8 May 1940, 14.

35. 'No Man's Land of Sport', 6 May 1939, 14.

36. 'No Man's Land of Sport', 30 May 1936, 13. The athletes mentioned by Gibb who had changed their sex were Zdenka Koubkova (Zdenka Koubka) of Czechoslovakia, who in 1934 held the world record for the 800m; Mary Edith Louise Weston (Mark Weston), an international shotputter from England; and Sophia Smetkowna of Poland. When Stella Walsh died in 1980, it was discovered that she suffered from mosaicism, a condition producing an unusual chromosomal pattern and ambiguous genitalia.

37. Ibid.

38. 'No Man's Land of Sport', 25 and 26 January 1933, 10. See also A. Lytle, 'Sport Rays',

Vancouver Sun, 20 and 26 January 1933, 12; A. Lytle, 'Girls Shouldn't Do It', *Chatelaine*, (May 1933), 12–13.

39. 'No Man's Land of Sport', 3 February 1932, 13.

40. The best secondary sources of historical information about the WAAF of C are by Bruce Kidd. See his dissertation, 'Improvers, Feminists, Capitalists and Socialists' (especially Chapter 4), and his book, *The Struggle for Canadian Sport* (Chapter 3), which is a more popularized version of his dissertation. Unfortunately, according to Kidd, few WAAF of C records remain because they were either destroyed or stolen. We have both relied on the numerous press reports for our accounts. In this regard, Alex Gibb wrote extensively about the Federation in her columns as did the other women sports writers of the time.

41. For more information about the 'Matchless Six', see R. Hotchkiss, '"The Matchless Six" Canadian Women at the Olympics, 1928', *The Beaver*, 73 (1993), 23–42; D. Ransom, '"The Saskatoon Lily": A Biography of Ethel Catherwood', *Saskatchewan History*, 41 (1988), 81–98.

42. A. Gibb, 'Canada at the Olympics', *MacLean's Magazine*, 1 October 1928, 49.

43. A.S. Lamb, Report to the Amateur Athletic Union of Canada, December 1928 (National Archives of Canada, MG 30 C 164 Vol. 19 File 7).

44. P. Griffiths, 'The Girl and the Game,' 18 February 1931, 21

45. 'W.A.A.F. of C. Rejects Motion That Would Bar Sports Writers', *Winnipeg Free Press*, 28 November 1928, 15.

46. Ibid.

47. P. Griffiths, 'The Girl and the Game,' 9 May 1934, 23; 'Claim Insult to W.A.A.F. By Organizer' *Edmonton Journal*, 9 May 1934, 16.

48. L. Marsh, 'With Pick and Shovel', *Toronto Daily Star*, 8 September 1934, 10. For a history of the Ontario Athletic Commission, see B. Kidd, 'Making the Pros Pay for Amateur Sports: The Ontario Athletic Commission, 1920-1947', *Ontario History*, 87(2), 1995, 105–28.

49. 'No Man's Land of Sport', *Toronto Daily Star*, 9 Oct 1934, 11; 'O.A.C. Will Safeguard Feminine Athletics', *Toronto Daily Star*, 9 October 1934, 10.

50. 'No Man's Land of Sport', *Toronto Daily Star*, 30 October 1934, 12.

51. Kidd, *The Struggle for Canadian Sport*, p.176.

52. The articles, 35 in total, appeared from 9 September until 22 October 1935. They were usually on the front page of the paper and continued on an inside page, sometimes accompanied by an appropriate photo.

53. Author's interview with long-time *Toronto Star* sports reporter Milt Dunnell, 22 May 1998. Trent Frayne, another long-time Toronto sportswriter, confirmed that Lytle was a 'terrible man' and that the sports staff at the *Star* were 'terrified' of him (author's interview, 22 May 1998).

54. See, for example, A. Gibb, 'In Pencil Slim Skirt With an Inverted Pleat the Princess Arrives', *Toronto Daily Star*, 9 October 1951, 29, 54; 'Philip Catches 8 Grilse, Princess No Angler', *Toronto Daily Star*, 25 October 1951, 1.

55. Letter to H.C. Hindmarsh, president of the *Toronto Star*, reprinted in the *Toronto Star*, 15 September 1954, 3; 'Thanks for Star Backing that Made Swim Possible Voiced by Marilyn, Ryder', *Toronto Star*, 16 September 1954, 1, 20.

56. 'Newswoman Alex Gibb Dead at 66', *Toronto Telegram*, 16 December1958. However, a search of issues of the *Toronto Star* between 1956 and 1958 did not turn up any evidence of the column.

57. Author's interview with Milt Dunnell, 22 May 1998.

58. Author's interview with Trent Frayne, 22 May 1998.

59. E. Ferguson, 'The Gist and Jest of It', *Montreal Star*, 18 December 1958, 64.

60. L. Dempsey, 'Spirit of Alex Will Live On', *Toronto Daily Star*, 18 December 1958, 38.

8

A Glittering Icon of Fascist Femininity: Trebisonda 'Ondina' Valla

GIGLIOLA GORI

During the two decades of Fascism, the icon of the New Italian Man was Mussolini himself, an unequivocal inspirational model of virility for other men. In contrast, women had contradictory models of femininity, derived from tradition, religion and politics in a country with aspirations to modernity, secularization and imperialism. The model of the prolific mother was imposed from on high as the most suitable symbol of the new Italian woman. However, in spite of Fascist intent, the athlete Trebisonda 'Ondina' Valla – a woman of the people – became both a symbol and a myth and came to inspire Italian women.

Trebisonda Valla, who later came to be known by her nickname, 'Ondina', was born on 20 May 1916, in Bologna, as the last child and only female of five children.[1] Her family lived in a small village close to the city, but soon moved to the centre of Bologna, a modern and well-organized northern city. Her father was a blacksmith and her mother a housewife. Like most mothers of the time, Valla's mother preferred to stay at home and send her daughter or maid to do the shopping. At that time in Italy, female 'seclusion' permeated society due to the typical Italian husband's jealousy and the matter of a correct 'image'. Women did not like to go out and carry heavy parcels, or show themselves in public when not perfectly dressed, especially in little villages where most women spent their spare time watching the people from their windows. Furthermore, shopping, and indeed washing and shoe polishing, were considered improper work even for lower middle-class women like Valla's mother. Fortunately she could avail herself of an obedient daughter and a part-time maid, who helped her to look after the five men of the family.

When Valla was only three years old, she was sent to do the shopping for the first time. In the following years she walked to her primary school – a distance of some 500m – on her own. She was quite an energetic, independent little girl who loved physical activity and playing various children's games. Her tall, strong brothers also enjoyed physical activities and were particularly talented high-jumpers. However, after their schooldays they no longer trained or competed. In contrast, Valla began a brilliant career in athletics in 1927 which continued until 1943.

In 1927, when Valla was eleven years old, a Captain Costa, secretary of the Fascist Party in Bologna who tested schoolchildren for competitive athletic ability, was impressed by the young girl. Valla was tall, thin and timid. Her initial tests in jumping were unimpressive but Costa believed in her possible talent since she was the sister of good jumpers. Consequently, she was trained in high-jumping for about a month by a primary school teacher, a Mr Formigini, and won first place in the Bologna schools' championships with a jump of 1.10m. In the following year she could jump 1.25m easily, and was enrolled in the Bologna Sportiva Association. There she met both her strongest rival, Claudia Testoni, who became one of her best friends, and a good coach, a Mr Gaspar from Hungary, who usually trained the female athletes about three times a week. In 1929, in Bologna, Valla competed in an important international athletics meeting against French, British, Polish and Czechoslovak athletes. She was the youngest of the Italians and although she wore simple gym shoes instead of special jumping shoes, she won fifth place in both the high and the long jump.

In time, and with intensive training, Trebisonda became both tall and strong and took up various sporting activities including shot put, 100m and 80m hurdles, basketball, fencing, swimming and skating. In 1930, when she was only fourteen years old, the 'phenomenon', Trebisonda Valla, won recognition during a meeting at Naples against Belgium. She was the youngest in the Italian team and, although she did not win the 80m hurdles, at least one member of the press was rather impressed by the young athlete. There, during a boat excursion for the team and the press, one journalist declared that the name Trebisonda was too long and 'heavy' for such a slim, graceful adolescent, and proposed a more suitable nickname, 'Ondina' which literally means 'small wave'. 'Ondina' was appropriate because it captured the smooth style of her hurdling, just like a regular wave motion. With this nickname Ondina, Trebisonda Valla became a popular and successful athlete first in Italy and then throughout the world.

In 1930, as the holder of Italian records in both the 80m hurdles and high jump at Florence (Figures 8.1, 8.2), Valla was officially chosen to

FIGURE 8.1

VALLA AT THE 1930 NATIONAL CHAMPIONSHIPS IN FLORENCE

FIGURE 8.2

ONDINA VALLA (FOURTH FROM RIGHT) WITH MEMBERS OF THE NATIONAL
ATHLETICS TEAM IN FLORENCE, 1930

represent Italy at the Women's World Games in Prague. She later recalled that she endured a horrible trip by train for about thirty-six hours, sitting in a cheap, uncomfortable, second class carriage, and in Prague suffered poor accommodation and meals. In contrast, first class travel tickets, accommodation and subsistence were reserved for Italian male athletes as a matter of course.[2]

At this time, few female athletes who competed at international level challenged the widespread, narrow-minded patriarchal views of Italians, and were not supported financially or otherwise,[3] owing to the fact that sport was considered the pre-eminent expression of the strength and virility of the Italian male. Competitive sport for females was both criticized and undervalued, although a number of nonconformist women were obtaining good results in more than one sport.[4] Female athletes were given official uniforms and good quality shoes, but only for athletics events. They had to be returned after the competition![5] Gender discrimination was common at this time, not least in sport. Fascism emphasized male physical activity through its national organizations, in which men were strongly encouraged to enrol. In contrast, women were admitted later into sport and only allowed a considerably reduced programme. For example, boys practised organized physical education and sport in Opera Nazionale Balilla (National Balilla Group) ONB from 1926, but girls only from 1929; male university students could continue in sports through the Gruppi Universitari Fascisti (University Fascist Groups) GUF, from 1927, but female students could not enrol until 1931; male workers became members of Opera Nazionale Dopolavoro (National After-Hours Group) OND, from 1926, but female workers only in 1937; the male Academy for training physical education teachers was founded in 1927, but the one for female teachers only opened in 1932!

At the beginning of Valla's career, most travelling expenses were paid by her father. Her father and her brothers were pleasingly, and perhaps surprisingly, her strongest supporters. Her mother, however, discouraged her, saying she was not a little girl anymore, implying, of course, that women should not participate in sport. In line with expectations of the time, Ondina's mother preferred her daughter to be safe at home waiting for a good husband. But Valla, who greatly enjoyed athletics, continued to train with determination despite the personal sacrifices.

FIGURE 8.3

ONDINA IN THE HIGH JUMP, 1934

Unfortunately, Valla and the other members of the Italian female team could not go to Los Angeles for the Olympic Games of 1932, owing to firm opposition from Pope Pius XI. However, in 1933 Valla gained international recognition at the University World Games in Paris.[6] There, she won the 100m, 80m hurdles and 4 x 100m relay. A French journalist, deeply impressed by this seventeen-year-old girl, called Valla 'the little Italian wonder' (Figure 8.3). There was more to come. The most celebrated of Valla's victories was obtained at the Berlin Olympics of 1936, when she came first and equalled the world record in the 80m hurdles (11.6 seconds). Although Italian male athletes had been well trained and strongly supported by the party and the press as potential winners, the *only* gold medal in athletics was won by a young girl. Very little had been written about the seven female athletes Italy sent to Berlin, but they won the 80m hurdles and gained fourth place in both the 80m hurdles and the 4 x 100m relay. Their reward was to read their names printed in block letters in the pages of national Italian newspapers and specialist sports magazines.[7] After the amazing success of the female Italian athletes in Berlin, Mussolini declared that a number of select sportswomen could contribute to the strong image of Fascists as athletes and could serve to spread this image around the world. However, the rest of Italian womanhood was to restrict itself to basic physical activities thus preserving its female grace and modesty.

When Valla arrived back from Berlin, at Bologna railway station, she was received like a film star by the local authorities and excited fans. She confessed that she was greatly surprised, as she was not accustomed to such acclaim which was only normally paid to Italian sportsmen. Later, together with the Italian team, she was congratulated by Mussolini himself in Rome, and received the Gold Medal for Sports Achievement from his hands. Furthermore, during a special hearing in the Vatican, His Holiness shook hands with her and congratulated her as well. The Olympic victory had ensured a magical response. It had opened a breach in the masculine wall earlier erected against women's physical emancipation and Valla was pushed through it by *both* the most powerful figures of authority in Italy – the Duce and the Pope.

Many hundreds of letters, flowers, suitors, invitations, interviews, photographic sessions, and even the offer to be a film star, now considerably changed the hitherto simple life of Valla. Her success as the first female Olympic gold medallist in Italian history gave her prestige, money, a job in Bologna and, last but not least, a wealthy physician as a husband. Her fantastic performance in Berlin, and national records in high jump (5 times), long jump (1), pentathlon (1), 100m (2), and 80m hurdles (6),[8] made her an inspirational icon for Italian young women. She had at least reduced a feminine inferiority complex that had its origins in both the paternalistic tradition of the past and the new Fascist ideology.

REGRESSION

Although all Italians suffered from the policies of Fascism, there is evidence that women of all classes, especially in the poorest section of the population, had to adapt themselves to Mussolini's will and put aside most of their emancipatory aspirations. Fascinated by the charming Duce, on behalf of the Fascist cause, most Italian women tried to fashion their lives according to his demands. Female emancipatory trends in the twentieth century were inexorably weakened by Fascist masculinity, which affirmed that women were different from, and inferior to men.

Of course, this was a long-established view, but ironically it was not supported initially by Fascism, which in its pioneering years (1919–25) appeared as a modern, innovative and revolutionary movement dismissive of gender discrimination. At first, women were convinced that Fascism would fight for their rights, but in later years, after the regime was firmly established, the question of female emancipation was set aside in favour of a masculine hegemony based on a traditional paternalism that had been passed down through the ages.

Responding to the pressure of the powerful Catholic Church, which supported female modesty and maternity and in response to various economic problems demanding a high birth rate, Fascism abandoned support for the model of the modern working woman of its earlier years. Discouraging work outside the home, the regime aimed at restricting women to the home. In spite of sacrifices for the Fatherland, in and after the First World War, women were required to bear numerous children and limit themselves to housework. Apart from childbirth and child care, women were not considered important, and their political and social involvement was restricted to female Catholic associations and those organizations strictly controlled by the Fascist Party. Within this framework, women's physical education, athletics and other sports were considered a state affair, a means to strengthen the body and spirit of young Italian women for motherhood and population demands, according to the contemporary eugenic theories and expansionist plans, of the regime.

Two factors, in particular, contributed to the exclusion of women from sport in the 1930s: the opposition of the Church to female sport, as demeaning to women and Church, together with the belief that the unsatisfactory demographic increase – a thorn in Mussolini's flesh – was probably due to women's involvement in sport. This theory found reinforcement in the fact that eminent physicians of the time found few sports suitable for women. These factors together restricted the involvement of women in most sports. The result was that female athletes could not participate in the outstanding achievement of the 1932 Olympics of Los Angeles in which Italy gained second place after the USA. Nevertheless, from the mid-1930s more and more women took up sport and followed the example of 'professional' sportswomen who successfully competed in international meetings. Such was the impact of the Valla myth. Her success, and that of others, produced ambivalence in Fascist circles.

The inbalance was also created by other factors. Victory in the war against Ethiopia (1935–36) and the foundation of the Italian Empire, the alliance with Germany, the war in Spain and finally the Second World War, increasingly produced the militarization of both sexes. Sport physicians now encouraged women to be more active and dynamic. Women were mobilized alongside men in parades, galas and sporting displays. After years of quiescent sacrifice due to insistent patriotic propaganda, women even participated actively in the various wars. After the fall of Fascism in 1943, and the subsequent civil war which occurred at this time, many young women reached northern Italy, which was still held by Mussolini, and enrolled in the Fascist army as volunteers. There, they fought bravely alongside the soldiers of the new Repubblica Sociale Italiana of Salò. On the other hand, numerous women joined and supported the partisan groups of different persuasions, who were fighting against the Nazis and Fascists for the liberation of the country. Clearly during the fascist era the role of women had widened and some women had become more self-assertive, ready to leave home and family to fight for their ideological beliefs. Valla played her part in changing attitudes.

FEMMINISMO LATINO

In Italy, the end of the First World War was a dangerous period which could easily have led to civil war. It was a time characterized by social and economic problems, violence, individualism and fragmentation. During this period, the European feminist movement was admired by Italian women, but in general it was not considered a movement which would completely suit the Latin temperament. Latin women had to pursue their own way by adhering to *femminismo latino* based on a strong sense of maternity and sacrifice, an ideology which it was said could unify all women.[9]

At the same time, the battle for universal suffrage and other civil rights was occurring and this battle involved many movements of different political persuasions. Among them, the rising Fascist movement was considered to be one of the most effective, capable of rapidly assuring a new and modern order in tumultuous circumstances, with the result that at the beginning of the second decade of the century, a number of men and a few women joined the Fascist movement. In 1919, in the San Sepolcro Square in Milan, Mussolini and groups such as nationalists, socialists, futurists, republicans, and 'Arditi',[10] founded the movement Fasci di Combattimento (Fascis of Combat). Nine women were among them.

In the following years leading up to the famous 'march to Rome' of 1922, which brought Mussolini to power, several hundred women enrolled in the Fascist movement.[11] For instance, in the years between 1920 and 1922 there were 200 female Fascists in Brescia, 28 in Verona, 100 in Florence.[12] Mostly, these were eccentric and exceptional women interested in nationalist and/or socialist ideologies and politics, who believed in the ideas of modernity and emancipation that Mussolini and his followers were spreading all over the country. The first progressive Fascist programme of June 1919, for example, had declared support not only for full freedom for citizens in general, but also for the specific right of 'integral' suffrage for women. Believing in a new order, these women embraced the 'virile' and aggressive model of a new order previously proposed by futurism,[13] and participated in violent actions against their opponents in conjunction with male Fascist squads. For example, during the Venice Gymnastics Contest in 1919, a number of female athletes and their Fascist friends had a fight with a group of so-called 'cowards',[14] and in 1920 a certain Cesarina Bresciani accompanied her brother and other young Fascists in the bloody assault on the Verona Town Hall.[15]

Initially, Fascism was promoted both by aristocratic and middle-class women. Some, like the futurists Eva Kuhn Amendola and Elda Norchi, the famous socialist Margherita Sarfatti, and the journalist Elisa Majer Rizzioli were important.[16] The latter founded a new body in Milan in 1921, the Fasci Femminili (Feminine Fascis) to fight to affirm Fascist ideals and to increase Fascist power in the region alongside the masculine Fascis of Combat. The Roman Feminine Fascis was founded in 1921. About 20 Roman women of the group were very soon involved in dangerous scuffles with anti-Fascists.[17] They supported the 'march to Rome' by organizing a number of first aid centres in the capital, in case of a counter-attack by the Italian army. These Roman women had to leave their families, at least temporarily, to spend time working for the cause. One of the youngest, Piera Fondelli, wrote in her diary of the spirit that permeated those days:

> I was away from home for four days and nights. We used to sleep in the armchairs for a few hours in some hotels where we were in charge of organizing the first aid centres. Naturally the owners of the hotels were enrolled in the Fascist party. I kept in touch with my mother by telephone. We could not believe that the country, the

king, the army, the authorities, in brief Italy as a whole, would
surrender to us – a handful of men and a very small percentage of
women.[18]

All women who joined the Fascist cause saw themselves as modern and
emancipated, but in truth they still represented a bourgeois model
formulated by men many years before. Their rights, needs and
aspirations were unappreciated by men. The traditional feminine spirit
of sacrifice was simply utilized on behalf of the Fascist cause. In
previous decades the tradition insisted on women being healthy mothers
of numerous children for the glory of the Fatherland. Women had to
leave work and politics to the men. Certainly, the 'cause' required
women to fight and sacrifice once more alongside men, but the 'cause'
consisted in consolidating the glory of Mussolini and his virile and
misogynous ideology. Nothing had changed.

The Duce did not believe in, and therefore did not support, women
in politics. On 27 December 1921 his daily newspaper *Il Popolo d'Italia*
declared: 'The women's Fascist Groups will devote themselves to
propaganda, charity, welfare and other duties, ... all political action led
by the Fascis of Combat is banned'. It can be argued that Mussolini's
policy concerning women's rights evolved. Early in his political life he
was a socialist with moderate sympathy for feminism. (He later
abandoned this position.) In an interview published in the *Petit Parisien*
of 11 November 1922, Mussolini declared that he was in favour of
universal suffrage for men, but not for women, because women
invariably voted for men![19] During the Fascist women's congress held in
Padova in 1920, however, Mussolini had said: 'The Fascists do not
belong to the crowd of the vain and sceptics who want to undervalue
woman's social and political importance. Who cares about voting? You
will vote!'[20] Moreover, at the congress held in Rome on 14 May 1923, and
organized by the International Pro-suffrage Alliance, Mussolini
affirmed:

> Given Italian public opinion and the trend of our political
> development, the concession of the women's vote finds no
> opposition in any party. As far as the government is concerned, I
> feel I am entitled to declare that, apart from unforeseen
> circumstances, the Fascist government supports the right to vote
> for various groups of women ...[21]

This right was then enacted in law, but by the end of 1925 was replaced by Mussolini's new 'extraordinary laws' which lasted up to the fall of Fascism, in 1943.

It is clear that during the early years of Fascism a number of aristocratic and middle-class women put their hope in Mussolini. Even the conservative Catholic women thought that Fascism would help women's emancipation by promoting female employment. The Catholic magazine *La donna italiana* argued in 1924:

> The right to work is a holy human prerogative which has been sanctioned by religion, won through titanic battles, and fully granted by common conscience, nowadays. We should not stop claiming that not only men, but also women should have to earn their bread by the sweat of their brow, and protection and respect should be paid to those women who leave their quiet homes and enter the wild forest of the world.[22]

However, Mussolini's attitude concerning women's rights, which in the beginning had been supportive, became totally anti-feminist once power had been obtained. Nobody then could really plead the female cause.

In summary, during the early Fascist years only very few courageous women tried to oppose the Fascist misogynistic trend and supported the anti-Fascist cause,[23] whereas a number of women joined Fascist groups with optimistic enthusiasm and faith. The rest of the female population regarded Fascism with little hope or quiet resignation. Thus, in the first half of the 1920s, when the Fascists were fighting to assert themselves, the existing women's movements which were opposed to Fascism were too weak, divided and disorganized to be capable of developing their objectives while, on the other hand, those self-confident and aggressive Fascist women who had fought alongside Fascist men were now viewed by them as possible homosexuals, or dangerous in terms of political control. They were put aside without ceremony.

The case of one patriot, Ines Donati, is illuminating. She supported the Fascist cause with daring and courage and during the early days of Fascism she was celebrated as a heroine, but later her image was buried as ill-suited to represent the submissive woman of that period. Only in the second half of the 1930s was she celebrated again as an example of the faithful Fascist woman, when imperialist ambitions and general militarization made her acceptable again.[24]

In sport, female emancipation was permitted up to the late 1920s. In 1919, 10,000 women competed at the Venice Gymnastics Contest; in 1921 women participated in 'male' sports – shooting, javelin, and the shot put – at an exhibition in Rome. In 1923 the Federazione Italiana d'Atletica Femminile (Italian Federation of Female Athletics) was founded in Milan. This federation organized important national and international women's competitions, but step by step it had to give up its independence. After 1928 competitive women's sport was firmly controlled by the 'fascistized' Comitato Olimpico Nazionale Italiano (Italian National Olympic Committee) CONI, and the task of organizing leisure and educational physical activities was given to state bodies led by men who, in line with Fascist policy, discriminated more and more against women's sport.

FASCIST IDEAL WOMAN

During the Fascist era a model of the new woman was propagated in Italy alongside a model of the new man embodied by Mussolini himself. As mentioned earlier, in contrast to the brutal clarity of the image of the new man, the image of the new woman was unclear and what is more, no woman was so versatile, nor had enough charisma and power, to be able to embody it convincingly. The ideal female model supported by the regime was far removed from both the modern female models of the first quarter of the twentieth century – emancipated working women, and bellicose, Fascist women. The Fascist model woman reproduced an age-old image. In spite of a veneer of modernity, she had to be a daughter, a wife and a mother for life.

Women who persisted in claiming their rights were accused of being *démodé,* were accorded the contemporary negative image of the English suffragettes and ridiculed and depicted as 'emaciated and bespectacled old maids'.[25] Furthermore, the traditional themes of Italian women's modesty and spirit of sacrifice were exalted through both insistent Fascist propaganda and the consistent paternalism of the Catholic Church. In the first half of the century the new woman had to combine contrasting and even antithetical values, where respect for tradition meant spirituality and submissiveness, while modernity meant blatant physicality and confident self-assertion.

For his ideal Fascist woman Mussolini drew for inspiration on his mother, Rosa Maltoni, whose culture (she was a primary school teacher), religious spirit, firmness, exemplary life and early death left an indelible mark on the Duce. In his autobiography Mussolini wrote: 'My greatest love was for my mother. She was so quiet, so tender and yet so strong.'[26] Rosa Maltoni incarnated the typical 'Italian Mother' of the nineteenth century, namely the firm Roman Matron and Holy Madonna, respectively representing Latin and Catholic cultural models. Propaganda presented Rosa Maltoni's image as reincarnated in the Duce's wife Rachele, a silent, tolerant partner and prolific mother, and in his preferred daughter, Edda, who had a vivacious and passionate nature like her grandmother. The new generation was inspired by the sophisticated Edda, a seemingly acceptable modern and emancipated girl – she enjoyed sports, travel, cars, and even trousers – but, on the other hand, she was still respectful of traditional values as illustrated by the fact that during her lifetime she was generally reputed to have been an obedient daughter, a good wife and a tender mother.

Italian women were urged by the regime to reject the charming female image of modern literature and American films, the beautiful blond girl of slender body and free-and-easy manners, successfully involved in work and love affairs. The regime promoted the 'Latin model' – the robust rural woman whose broad hips and round bosom, it was suggested, favoured maternity.[27] A mother and wet-nurse, Antonietta Girolamo, became popular among Italians as the producer of about 2.5 litres of maternal milk daily![28]

Certainly the Latin new woman had to be healthy in body and spirit. By participating in basic physical education at school and taking some athletic exercise in the open air, it was argued, she would become sufficiently strong to bear numerous children for the Fatherland, and provide energetic support to men organized for war. But the competitiveness and muscularity of sportswomen were seen as inappropriate to Latin femininity and grace, and dangerous to traditional masculine hegemony.

MATERNITY

As previously suggested, Mussolini's position regarding women's rights, which had been ambiguous during the early years of government, became clearly anti-feminist from the second half of the 1920s, when the Fascist regime was fully established. Socialist and communist movements – which involved a number of women – were abolished in

Italy between 1925 and 1926, and only women's associations connected with Fascism or Catholicism were supported or tolerated.

On the occasion of the 'Speech of Ascension' of 26 May 1927, in an address to the Chamber of Deputies, the Duce clearly revealed his 'macho' inclination by announcing: 'A special Tribunal which is functioning perfectly without problems. It will improve further especially if the female element, that brings to serious things, the signs of frivolity, is excluded from it.' In the same speech, which was entitled *The fascist regime for the greatness of the fatherland*, Mussolini emphasized demographic power as crucial to the increase of the economic and moral power of a nation and affirmed that through this power the destiny of the Italian race would be assured.

Mussolini was convinced that 'size was power' at home and abroad.[29] He wanted a large Italian population and he intended to emulate the most powerful European nations by establishing colonies. There, the dream of giving a job to every citizen and civilizing the uncivilized under the Fascist flag, would be realized. As a consequence, it became necessary for the new Italian man to marry early and become the father of numerous children, while the new woman had to bring up children and be a good housewife. Work was considered a man's affair. A new organization to protect maternity and the health of children, Opera Nazionale per la Maternità ed Infanzia (National Maternity and Infancy Welfare Body), ONMI, was founded in 1925, special additional taxes discouraging celibacy were raised by law in 1926, and a number of laws discouraging or limiting female work were enacted in the years following.[30] Under a law of 14 June 1928, all families with six children and more received financial assistance from the state and were not required to pay annual taxes. This notwithstanding, the low salaries of most fathers of a family compelled them to control childbirth and send women to work. In 1931 approximately half of all Italian families lived on two incomes.[31]

A new penal code, progressively elaborated by Alfredo Rocco from 1926 to 1931, emphasized a still extant gender discrimination and even included legislation concerning the morality of families. As a consequence, the so-called 'honour crime' (Art. 587) permitted fathers, brothers and husbands to kill their daughters, sisters and wives respectively, with impunity, to protect their honour. This code, mostly pursuing the same principles of the old Pisanelli Family Codex of 1861, considered men's rights superior in the family and society. In addition, abortion was punished as a very serious crime (it was defined a crime against the race!) in order to protect the demographic policy of the time, and the family, a private institution, became increasingly public property.

From 1933 a special day was dedicated to maternity and infancy, so as to properly celebrate the most prolific Italian mothers. It was decided that the right day was 24 December, just before Christmas, to emphasize that to be a mother was both a civic duty to ensure the greatness of the Fatherland and a religious mission comparable with that of the Holy Madonna.[32]

Many women of good social standing and true faith were involved in this policy of maternity, and voluntarily spent their time visiting children and mothers of the poorest families, to whom they not only took food and clothing but gave sound advice on domestic matters. These families were also supported by ONMI and other Fascist associations and Catholic charitable bodies. Mussolini himself and his hierarchy, gave poor children gifts such as toys, during the famous ceremony called Befana fascista (Fascist Epiphany), which, by being held all over the country, constituted an effective tool of propaganda.

In spite of this, and although in perfect accord with the 1930 encyclical *Casti Connuby* of Pope Pius XI, which opposed any kind of birth control, the demographic plan to increase the Italian population was not successful. Statistics reveal that in Italy as a whole the birth rate was 29.9 in the years 1921–25; 27.1 in 1926–30; 24 in 1931–35; 23.4 in 1936–40; and 19.9 in 1941–45.[33] Statistics, of course, differed from region to region. The most prolific families lived in the south, where the traditional rural economy still needed many children for labour-intensive agriculture and infant mortality was high due to malnutrition and poor hygiene. In the northern and central regions of Italy industrialization had resulted in many people leaving the countryside and swelling the number of urban unemployed. During this time, only aristocratic and the middle-class families had an acceptable standard of life. Wishing both to give their children a comfortable childhood and a good education, and to maintain a satisfactory life style, these families limited their families.[34]

In brief, while activities supported by ONMI were efficacious in terms of hygiene and prevention of illnesses, especially through the work of sports physicians and health resorts,[35] on the whole the demographic campaign was not effective. Over and above the world economic crisis of 1929, this campaign was mostly hindered by an uneven national economy, in which low salaries and unemployment were widespread. This not only discouraged couples from increasing their families, but also encouraged women to accept any kind of job, even for a miserable wage, and to 'knock on different doors' – be they Fascist, religious, or private – asking for help. Mussolini attempted to oppose the trend towards limiting the family and denied that Italian women were discriminated against and submitted to men. With persuasive eloquence, the Duce often encouraged women to be fecund openly demonstrating his personal admiration for 'Latin femininity' in his speeches by saying for instance:

> The Italian woman has the great privilege of not having sacrificed her perfect femininity to any idol of the time. To speak about 'submission' to man is an absurdity, as well as to speak about an old-fashioned mentality. The Italian woman is a mother pre-eminently: instinctively she is reluctant to accept [women's] masculinization from overseas, which estranges women from their biological mission, which is the higher spiritual mission as well: to continue the race and therefore history through issue.[36]

IMPERIALISM

Mussolini had to adjust his low opinion of women when his foreign policy became more aggressive and his dream of re-establishing the Roman Empire became in part a reality. By the end of 1935, while men were fighting in Ethiopia, women were mobilized in a campaign for Italian economic self-sufficiency, in order to limit the influence of harsh sanctions by the League of Nations. Italian women, from Queen Elena to the poorest mother, generously answered the call and by way of a supreme gesture presented the Fatherland with their gold wedding rings. In addition, they revealed a special talent in substituting foreign with national surrogate goods and food and, what is more, displayed an unexpected determination in adapting themselves to new and hard sacrifices. Maternity aside, finally they felt they could actively participate in the foundation of a glorious Fascist empire.

On 7 May 1936, following the colonial forays in Africa, the victorious Mussolini spoke to the crowd from the famous balcony of the 'Venetian

Palace' in Rome. Popular support for Fascism had reached its apex, and Italians were completely fascinated by the Duce. During that speech he found appropriate words to congratulate the nation's women:

> The victory of our troops in Eastern Africa is also due to you, women of Rome and Italy. Fascist Italy ... had given you a delicate and decisive task: to make a fort of any Italian family so as to resist sanctions. You, Women, accomplished this task. The Fatherland offers you its gratitude.[37]

Women's voluntary charity work increasingly became service to the state and the existing female Fascist organizations grew considerably. Statistics reveal that from 1934 to 1937 the membership of the Donne Fasciste (Fascist Women) and Massaie Rurali (Rural Housewives) doubled,[38] and a new body, Giovani Fasciste (Young Fascists), was founded in 1935 for 18–21 year old young women. The ONB which oversaw the moral and physical education of Italian youth from 6 to 18 years old, had already reached its goal in 1934, when the number of female members was double that of 1931.[39] On the other hand, the percentage of female workers decreased from 32.5 per cent in 1921 to 24.0 per cent in 1936.[40]

To set sport and Valla within this political context it should be noted that from 1937 onwards, all sporting organizations involving students and workers were absorbed into a strongly militarized organization, Gioventù Italiana del Littorio (Italian Youth of Littorio) GIL. Female enrolment and sports competitions, thanks in part to Valla's impressive successes, increased – at least until 1941.[41] As previously noted, Valla had become an influential mythical figure, a glittering Italian icon, an inspiration for a number of young women and, what is more, this new iconic figure was not imposed by Fascism but was the spontaneous outcome of a talented ordinary girl who, in spite of old-fashioned attitudes that hindered female emancipation, had built an astonishing career as a *prima donna*. The positive influence of Valla upon young women is not only indicated by an increasing number of 'professional' sportswomen whose activities increasingly interested the national press, but also by an increase in amateur sportswomen who lived in the provinces and competed in a variety of sports, and who were supported by their local press.

By way of example, in Pesaro, a quiet, little town in central Italy, women's sport has been practised since 1934, but developed considerably after 1937. In the local pages of daily newspapers, a number of girls competed regularly in athletics, gymnastics, swimming, fencing, skating, target-shooting, archery, tennis and basketball. Even regional and national championships were held in Pesaro. Indeed, a local 'Ondina', Rina Serafini, became famous by winning first place in the long jump at the 'Littoriali' GUF Championship of Milan in 1939, and also competed in swimming and basketball until 1943.[42]

PROGRESS

Did Valla's mythical performances really change the opinions of the general public and the medical experts of Italy concerning women's competitive sport? In the first half of the 1930s, the sport medicine controversy over female sport demonstrated that generally physicians were too protective of women.[43] Female sport was considered a peculiar and delicate subject deserving of special attention and a protective spirit so as to preserve traditional maternity, modesty and femininity. The problem had been debated within the medical profession but had not involved the common people very much. However, parents were aware of both possible 'dangers' of sporting activity and the intransigent hostility of the Church with regard to female sport. Among many hostile actions, there is the letter, sent by the Pope to the Vicar Cardinal, opposing a women's gymnastics competition to be held in Rome,[44] the severe censure of Fascist eugenics and sexual education by Sant'Uffizio (the Holy Office)[45] and numerous moralistic articles such as the one published in *L'Osservatore Romano*.[46] As regards the general public, it is suggested that they were little concerned with media controversies or moral dangers. The attitude was simply sensual. Spectators watched women's sports more to admire the competitors' bodies than to appreciate their good form in the purely sporting sense.

In summary, even if some eminent physicians came out openly in favour of moderate female sporting activity,[47] in the mid-1930s they had little influence over a conservative country. Fascism, supporting the eugenic theory of race, discriminated against women and exaggeratedly protected maternity according to one very influential endocrinologist, Nicola Pende.[48] Fascist theory and thus the regime considered women as the products and prisoners of their reproductive organs.

Mussolini and his hierarchy were convinced of the intellectual and physical inferiority of females and believed that sport did not favour maternity, despite the fact that many physicians had demonstrated that such a belief was simply a prejudice. As mentioned earlier, the regime therefore reduced female sport until it became more and more a marginal activity. Girls had to do moderate, unexciting general gymnastics, led by conformist physical education female teachers in which perfect and simultaneous execution of the exercises counted more than technical content. In the 1930s the main objective of the regime was to forge new and strong soldiers by means of general sport, and healthy mothers by means of basic physical education. The regime concentrated on eugenic, aesthetic, and moral female achievements, such as providing strong and healthy children to please Fascism; grace and beauty to please men; modesty and composure to please the Catholic Church. This is clear from an Article 4 of the ONB Norms for Small Italians and Young Italians:

> Female physical education has to focus on increasing the endurance of the body, and on increasing the aesthetic conformation of small and young girls, whilst every competitive, or even athletic, form is to be excluded, as well as any professional tendency which is not suitable to the female disposition of the female body.[49]

At the same time, very talented young girls, such as Valla, were trained for competition against the rest of the advanced foreign countries. For this élite group, coaches were chosen from the most experienced, and generally were men from abroad, such as a Mr Gaspar from Hungary and a Mr Combstock from the USA, both of whom were Valla's trainers. After the fabulous Valla's Olympic victory, and the superb performance of the female athletic team at the Berlin Olympics, the competitive Fascist state began to consider women's sport as an important way of displaying to the world the fact that Italian women, as a whole, were neither inferior to or nor weaker than foreign women. Then in a dramatic volte-face, in the face of modern scientific evidence, the regime realised that women's sport could improve the quality and number of their children.

On the back of the good results of Italian female athletes at the 1930 World Games in Prague, the 1933 World Games in Paris, and the 1936 Olympics in Berlin, in the late 1930s women's involvement in sport became a subject of careful scientific investigation and consequent popularization. In a book published in 1940, the distinguished physician

Giuseppe Poggi-Longostrevi presented scientific data collected on the occasion of the Games at Prague, to convince the public that female athleticism was healthy and safe, even during the delicate period of menstruation.[50] Notwithstanding, female sport still roused conservative suspicions of possible dangers to health, maternity and 'virilization' of women, among the public at large.

Despite this, Italian women became increasingly aware of the possibility of emancipation through sport. After her gold medal at Berlin, Valla declared to the Italian press that she dedicated her victory to both the fatherland and the achievements of female Italian sport. But success did not mean it was all plain sailing for sportswomen in general and Valla in particular. Famous Italian sportswomen of that time were reassuringly depicted by the press as examples of modesty, femininity and filial love, so as to reassure anxious parents,[51] but it was also rumoured that Valla was sexually interested in her female companions.[52] However, when she became a mother, the news was trumpeted as an evident demonstration that sporting competition and maternity were not incompatible. Photographs of the child and his happy mother were issued to end false and malicious gossip over Valla's sexual inclinations.

In conclusion, by the end of the 1930s, after years of research, speeches, papers and successful examples, both modern sport physicians and sportswomen had convincingly demonstrated that femininity and sport and eugenics and demography were not antithetical but could jointly contribute to the political cause of developing the new Italian race, according to Mussolini's will. The question remains as to whether, as a whole, women's sport was a Fascist problem or success. Would the Party and the Church have judged, and the physicians have written about, women and sport in the same way outside a Fascist nation? It is possible. The same arguments for and against women's sport, for instance, can be found at the time in democratic England and the United States. In the final analysis it is therefore difficult to be precise about the extent to which Italian Fascism influenced the emancipation of modern women through sport.

Nevertheless, as noted above, Valla was a political instrument of Fascist purpose. As a by-product of this state of affairs she was a political icon who became a gender icon. In both roles she became a symbol of national self-congratulation but also of confrontation, contradiction and paradox. She redefined Fascist womanhood in Mussolini's pursuit of political international ambitions – the projection of the Fascist

Superman *and* Superwoman. Ordinary Fascist women, however, lacking supreme athletic potential, remained the prisoners of conventional gender ideology.

But Valla was more than a political instrument and icon. The value of Valla was that she encouraged the young among these ordinary women to attempt to force open the bars of their cages, and at the same time forced the Fascist ideologues to reconsider and reconstruct Fascist principles albeit in the interest of Fascist political publicity. In the long run all Italian women benefited.

NOTES

Thanks are extended to Dr S. Bandy for initial editorial assistance and in particular to Professor J.A. Mangan for further editorial assistance with both textual and analytical aspects of the essay.

1. Biographical data on Trebisonda Valla are taken from: A. Giovannini, 'La gara di Ondina Valla campione olimpionica vista e raccontata da lei!' (The Olympic Champion Ondina Valla Describes and Comments on her Race), *Lo sport fascista*, IX (1936), 17–9; 'Primato olimpionico delle atlete azzurre' (Olympic Record for Italian Female Athletes), *Tutti gli Sports*, XIII (1936), 5; R. Dotti, 'La quercia di Ondina Valla' (Ondina Valla's Oak), *Stadio*, 24 October 1958, 6; S. Artom and A.R. Calabrò, *Sorelle d'Italia – Quattordici Signore raccontano la loro (e nostra) Storia* (Milan, 1989), pp.271–85; F. Dominici, 'Gli intramontabili – Ondina Valla. Oro a Berlino negli 80 ostacoli primatista nel lungo e nell'alto. La regina con le ali' (Ondina Valla. Gold at Berlin in the 80m Hurdles, Record in High and Long Jump. The Winged Queen), *Corriere dello Sport-Stadio*, 1 April 1989, 1–3; Panathlon International Club Valdarno Inferiore (ed.), *Proceedings of the National Prize 'L'atleta nella Storia' 1988 Ondina Valla, Montecatini Terme, 22 October 1989* (hereafter '*L'atleta nella storia*') (Montecatini, 1989), pp.1–32; O. Valla, 'Ondina Valla', *Ternisport* (no date), 5. In addition, there is a recorded interview of 8 May 1994, that Trebisonda Valla granted to Gigliola Gori in L'Aquila (hereafter G. Gori, *Interview 1994*), and some articles in daily newspapers of 1936 which will be quoted from time to time.
2. V. De Grazia, *Le donne nel regime fascista* (Venice, 1993), p.293.
3. Artom and Calabrò, p.275.
4. At least the pilot Carina Massone Negrone, the skier Celina Seghi, and the skaters Adriana Rianda and Ada Spoto, should be cited for their world records.
5. G. Gori, *Interview*, 1994.
6. She was registered as a University student, but in truth this was not accurate because she stopped studying before University.
7. In August of 1936 a daily newspaper headlined: 'Un'altra luminosa giornata azzurra allo Stadio Olimpico. Ondina Valla vince la semifinale 80m. ostacoli migliorando il primato mondiale' (A new bright day in the Olympic Stadium. Ondina Valla wins the semi-final 80m hurdles bettering the world record), *La Gazzetta dello* Sport, 6 Aug; 'Il tricolore sventola nel cielo di Berlino. La giornata trionfale dei nostri azzurri. La Valla negli 80 metri con ostacoli e Gaudini nel fioretto campioni olimpionici' (The Italian flag is waving in the sky of Berlin. The triumphant day for our athletes. Valla in the 80m hurdles and Gaudini in fencing are Olympic champions), *Il Popolo D'Italia* of 7 Aug'; 'Il tricolore d'Italia sul più alto pennone dello Stadio per la vittoria di Ondina Valla negli 80 m. ostac'. (The Italian flag is flying from the highest pennant of the Stadium for Ondina Valla's victory in the 80m hurdles), *La Gazzetta dello Sport*, 7 August. Also specialist sport magazines wrote articles with such titles as: 'Primato olimpico delle atlete azzurre' (Olympic victory for Italian female athletes), *Tutti gli Sports*, XIII (1936), 5; 'La gara di Ondina Valla campione olimpionica vista e raccontata da lei!'(The Olympic champion Ondina Valla describes and comments on her race), *Lo sport fascista*, IX (1936), 17.

8. See A.M.O.V.A. (ed.), *Medaglie d'oro al valore atletico 1934–1985* (Rome, 1987), p.1061.
9. Matilde Serao, who was one of the most famous female writers, supported this ideology in *Parla una donna. Diario femminile di guerra, maggio 1915 marzo 1916* (Milan, 1916). On the peculiarity of Italian feminism see G. Parla, *L'avventurosa storia del femminismo* (Milan, 1976), *passim*, and M. De Giorgio, *Le italiane dall'Unità ad oggi* (Rome-Bari, 1993), pp.508–11.
10. The 'Arditi' were volunteer assault soldiers of the First World War, famous for being very courageous and pitiless.
11. De Grazia, p.9.
12. R. Lazzero, *Il Partito Nazionale Fascista* (Milan, 1985), *passim*. In general, on the Fascist female movement of the first years, see D. Detragiache, 'Il fascismo femminile da San Sepolcro all'affare Matteotti, 1919–1924' (Feminine Fascism from the Holy Sepulchre to Matteotti's Affair, 1919–1924), *Storia contemporanea*, XIV (1983), 211–51.
13. See G. Gori, 'Supermanism and Culture of the Body in Italy: The Case of Futurism', *The International Journal of the History of Sport*, XVI (1999), 159–64.
14. RADA (pseudonymous), 'Una pagina d'italianità sportiva' (A Page of Sporting Italianity), *Lo sport fascista*, I (1931), 39–40.
15. S. Bertoldi, *Camicia nera* (Milan, 1994), pp.111–12.
16. Margherita Sarfatti and Elisa Majer Rizzioli were fascinated by Mussolini's strong personality so much so that they were faithful to him even when they fell into disfavour in the following years. De Grazia, pp.57–61.
17. During a patriotic and Fascist celebration at Saint Lawrence Square of Rome, hidden opponents started shooting at the crowd, but these courageous women did not panic and helped the wounded. See L. Garibaldi, *Le soldatesse di Mussolini* (Milan, 1997), p.34.
18. Ibid., pp.34–5.
19. G. Mattazzi (ed.), *Benito Mussolini-Breviario* (Milan, 1997), p.148.
20. See the journal *La Provincia di Padova*, 1–2 June 1923.
21. Mattazzi, pp.150–1.
22. I. Montesi Festa, 'La Donna italiana' (The Italian Woman), *La Donna italiana*, I (1924), 6.
23. On anti-Fascism see: *Enciclopedia dell'antifascismo e della Resistenza* (Milan, 1968–89); F. Colombo and V. Feltri, *Fascismo, antifascismo* (Milan, 1994); G. De Luna, *Donne in oggetto. L'antifascismo nella società italiana (1922–1939)* (Turin, 1995).
24. On Ines Donati's story see: E. Carreras, 'Ricordi di Ines Donati' (Ines Donati's Memories), *Lavoro e famiglia*, I (1938), 4; I. Rinaldi, 'Ines Donati. Realtà e mito di una 'eroina' fascista' (Ines Donati. Reality and Myth of a Fascist 'Heroine'), *Quaderni di resistenza 'Marche'* (1987), 48–89; De Grazia, pp.59–60.
25. E. Scaramuzza, 'Professioni intellettuali e fascismo. L'ambivalenza dell'Alleanza muliebre culturale italiana' (Intellectual Professions and Fascism. The Ambivalence of the Italian Cultural Feminine Alliance), *Italia contemporanea*, 151 (1983), 121.
26. B. Mussolini, *My autobiography* (written by Arnaldo Mussolini and edited by Richard Washburn Child) (New York, 1928). On the relationship between Mussolini and his mother see also: L. Passerini, *Mussolini immaginario* (Rome-Bari, 1991), pp.90–3.
27. In 1928, the most prolific Italian families (about one million and a half) were investigated by a group of researchers on their morphologic characteristics. The result of this study, co-ordinated by Corrado Gini of the Central Institute of Statistics, demonstrated that short women with broad hips were the most prolific. De Grazia, p.79.
28. L. Gianfranceschi, 'Un'italiana fra i semidei ariani' (A Female Italian among Aryan Demigods), *'L'atleta nella storia'*, p.29.
29. E. and D. Susmell (eds.), *B. Mussolini, Opera Omnia* (Florence, 1951–1980) XXII, p.360.
30. For example, see the Royal Decree 9 December 1926, that did not allow female teachers to participate in contests for teaching Letters, Greek, Latin, History and Philosophy anymore; the Royal Decree of 20 January 1927, where female salary was reduced to half of that given to men; the Law Dispositions of 1928, that discouraged female students to continue their studies at secondary and University levels by doubling their taxes; the Law-Decree of 28 November 1933, where female employment in the state administration was limited considerably. It was said women could not easily reconcile work and maternal duties!
31. De Grazia, p.125.

32. Ibid., pp.107–11.

33. SVIMEZ (ed.), *Un secolo di statistiche italiane Nord e Sud, 1861–1961* (Rome, 1961), p.79.

34. On number of children in different social classes during fascism see M. Livi Bacci, *A History of Italian Fertility during the Last Two Centuries* (Princeton, 1972), pp.176–273.

35. On sport medicine see G. Gori, 'Sport medicine and female athleticism in the years of the Fascist regime' (hereafter 'Sport medicine'), in T. Terret (ed.), *Sport and Health in History, Proceedings of the 4th ISHPES Congress, Lyon, 16–22 July 1997* (Sankt Augustin, 1999), pp.192–201. On health resorts G. Gori, 'Health Resorts for Girls: a Healthy Way to their Physical and Political Education in the Fascist Regime' (unpublished paper presented at the International Pre-Olympic Scientific Congress of Dallas, July 1996).

36. This is part of the interview Mussolini granted the journalist Bodil Borge Ciccarella in November 1934. See Mattazzi, p.149.

37. Mattazzi, pp.152–3.

38. ISTAT (ed.), *Compendio statistico* (Rome, 1938), p.16.

39. On female physical education and sporting organization during the years of fascism see G. Gori, 'Female sport in Italy: A controversial symbol of the Fascist ideology', in F. van der Merwe (ed.), *Sport as Symbol, Symbols in Sport, Proceedings of the 3rd ISHPES Congress, Cape Town, 1995* (Sankt Augustin, 1996), pp.71–80.

40. G. Parla, *L'avventurosa storia del femminismo* (Milan, 1976), p.96.

41. In 1936, 9819 female sporting contests were counted in Italy, according to GIL (ed.), *P.N.F. Annuario sportivo dei giovani fascisti e delle giovani fasciste – A. XV* (Varese, 1938), n. p.; in 1941, 253, 459 contests were held in the territory, according to GIL (ed.), *P.N.F. Annuario sportivo generale – A. XIX* (Bergamo, 1942), p.7.

42. For example see the local pages of the daily *Il Resto del Carlino* of 27 February 1937; 19 September 1937; 19 March 1938; 13 August 1938; 23 November 1938; 30 May 1939; 1 May 1940; 11 September 1940; 4 October 1940; 23 September 1941; 9 September 1942; 13 April 1943; 29 June 1943, where amateur sportswomen's competitions are reported.

43. Gori, 'Sport medicine', *passim.*

44. Pio XI, 'Lettera al Cardinale Vicario', *Civiltà Cattolica*, 2 (1928), 367–372.

45. That censure was pronounced on 21 March 1931.

46. P.B., 'La donna e l'atletismo', *L'Osservatore Romano*, 16 May 1934.

47. Gori, 'Sport medicine', pp.193–6.

48. N. Pende, *Bonifica umana razionale e biologia politica* (Bologna, 1933), pp.97–137.

49. ONB (ed.), *Norme programmatiche e regolamentari per le organizzazioni delle 'piccole e giovani italiane'* (Rome, n. d.), p.6.

50. G. Poggi-Longostrevi, *Medicina sportiva* (Milan, 1940), pp.99–113.

51. A journalist concluded his article on Ondina Valla with: 'And Ondina Valla, Olympic Champion, now runs away, as it is just 7.45 p.m. In spite of any victory, Father Valla does not allow her out after 8 o'clock!' See Giovannini, 19.

52. Artom and Calabrò, p.279.

9

Ignoring Taboos:
Maria Lenk, Latin American Inspirationalist

SEBASTIÃO VOTRE and LUDMILA MOURÃO

INTRODUCTION

In sport, over the years, Brazilian women have earned the title of icons of feminine emancipation. In particular, Maria Ester Bueno, displaying a superb technique, won several Wimbledon championships, until she was known as 'the Wimbledon Queen'. Drawing the world's attention not only to tennis but to fashion, she surprised and delighted the public with her short skirts, which excited the world of sport, and are still in vogue today. At a time when the swimmer Violeta Coelho Neto wore a 'modest' swimming costume, Maria Lenk with her daring and low-cut swimsuits, and Yara Vaz, wearing bikinis on the southern coast on Rio de Janeiro beaches, were also breaking new ground by ignoring cultural taboos not only in sport but in their everyday lives. The feminine priorities in those days confirmed what A. Prost and G. Vincent would assert in the 1990s: 'Care of one's body is not only legitimate. To a woman, being beautiful becomes a true obligation.'[1]

Here the aim is to present, and comment on, some of the revolutionary arguments provided by the swimmer Maria Lenk,[2] concerning the role of women in competitive sporting events.[2] Lenk is widely recognized as an exceptional athlete who participated in Brazilian women's sport from approximately 1930 to 1950. Her star is not yet diminished. As a swimmer she still sets world records at the age of eighty-six. Sporting achievements, associated with this super champion, greatly impress professional swimmers and startle researchers due to her persistence over the years devoted to sport.[3]

This chapter provides a comprehensive description of the practices and examples[4] which allowed the dynamic trajectory of this extraordinary sportswoman, both in Brazilian and Latin American society in the first half of this century. It is a compilation of facts and interpretations which demonstrate Lenk's remarkable record in athletic activities. But perhaps even more to the point, the chapter points up issues which, to a substantial degree, map out the course of women's sport in the period of Lenk's involvement. Key questions may be asked about the social opportunities in the first half of the century in Brazil and South America, available to women to practice sport in their everyday lives. What moments favoured and advanced the participation of women in sport in Brazilian, American and international communities? What social representations, coming from different Brazilian social communities, and relating to women's athletic activities, prevailed at that time? To what extent did they subsequently change? Above all, what is the relationship of these social representations to the evolving representation of the female body?

SPORT FOR MEN

In the major Brazilian cities, the sports introduced by immigrants at the end of the nineteenth century were gradually incorporated into the everyday life of the élite, or rather, into the daily activity of the men of the elite.[5] Women were mostly excluded from this process. An image of athletic masculinity evolved in response. The dandy became the athlete.[6] In contrast, the middle-class Brazilian woman remained an outcast in the world of sport. She played a supporting role. She was not yet an active agent of her own history. The family, in particular, discouraged or prevented women from participating in sport, since this was regarded as a clearly masculine activity.[7] It was considered natural for men to think about, to talk about, to practise and to enjoy sport, while women's appropriate response was to watch – admiring and applauding.[8] At the very most, it was a time of subtle female adjustment, with no breach of taboos, no great change in both practice and representation.[9] The 1920s, a time of more rupture than adjustment, deeply marked the political, economical and cultural life of the nation, with crucial episodes and events such as the foundation of the Brazilian Communist Party,[10] the Week of Modern Art,[11] the Coluna Prestes,[12] the coffee crisis[13] *and* the women's suffrage movement.[14] This era of transition culminated in the consolidation of the national state, the 1930s revolution and Getúlio Vargas' ascent to power, which brought an end to the Old Republic.[15]

On the international scene, from the end of the nineteenth to the beginning of the twentieth century, the impact of social reforms –

brought about, to a certain extent, by the feminist movements,[16] and reinforced by industrialization,[17] brought about a reduction in women's subordination and dependence, and their social role, once passive in nature, became increasingly more active.[18] This state of affairs gradually influenced their everyday lives, and increasingly ensured their presence in the world of sport.[19] Women first took part in the modern Olympic Games in 1900 in Paris. However, it was not until 1932, in Los Angeles, that the first Brazilian and South American woman, Maria Lenk, competed.[20] South America lagged behind developments in North America and Europe.[21] For quite a long time, the number of Brazilian women taking part in the Olympic Games remained unchanged. Swimming was the sport that offered women most opportunity and eventually led to an increase in the number of female Brazilian competitors.[22]

The International Swimming Federation was the first international organization officially to include women's swimming competitions in the Olympic programme of 1912. This decision resulted in the opening of doors to the formal participation of women. Other international sporting organizations soon followed suit. Despite the initiative of the International Swimming Federation, the provision of support and incentives as well as the legitimization of women's participation in the Olympic Games, the flow of women into Olympic sports remained sluggish. This slow entry into the sporting arena by women was greatly influenced by strong social representations, made by society in general, which saw them as essentially procreators. It was a self-fulfilling set of imperatives:[23] women were procreators, procreators were women.[24]

The arguments that circulated, spread over a considerable time[25] and certainly consolidated in the twentieth century,[26] were hard to combat. Nevertheless, the incursions of women into sport had an impact. Participation increased. Expectations changed. Images were reconstructed. In the vanguard of change were iconic individuals who defied convention, resisted stereotyping, demanded and acted out change.[27] In this threatening context, new 'scientific' arguments were elaborated by men, to add to the traditional ones in order to keep women out of sport.

Many authors, such as J. Ezagui (1944), M. Mayne (1944), W. Areno (1945), S. Guérios (1948), I.P. Marinho (1956), E.M. Rezende (1978), and E. Romero (1997), drew on a long-standing myth of femininity, and advised women against sporting activities that required or developed muscular strength.[28] This negative representation of muscular strength, as part and parcel of women's athletic activity, is illustrated by J. Ramos,[29] when he maintains that all muscular strength exercises should be avoided, since a woman's physical build was not made for fighting but rather for procreation.[30] In 'Educação física feminina, rápido esboço sobre processos educacionais', mentioned in T. Azevedo's dissertation, one comment by Ramos really sums up neatly the views of most authors of the time, namely that female movement must reflect grace, beauty, flexibility, rhythm and the female mentality.[31]

Such views were an attempt to set down norms of behaviour, regulate action and determine women's progress in athletic activities, precisely at a time when Brazilian women were participating in growing numbers, and indeed, flourishing in the field of sport. In short, there was both continuity and change in women's circumstances in Brazil. In São Paulo, in 1930, the first women's basketball championship was held under the same rules as applied to men's basketball.[32] It was a milestone in that it transgressed traditional boundaries, asserted female freedom, denied history and set down new guidelines for female involvement in modern sport.

Nevertheless, in general both social representations and associated sporting activities aimed at producing acceptable female body shapes, and meeting the body shape demands of motherhood incorporated into the Decree 3.199, of 1941, which lasted in effect, until 1975. Section 54 of the Decree read: 'women will not be allowed to practise sports that are incompatible with their natural condition'. As late as 1965, the Conselho Nacional dos Desportos (National Sports Council) established rules for feminine participation in sport and dictated that the practice of 'fights' of any nature, soccer, indoor soccer, beach soccer, polo, weightlifting and baseball would not be allowed.[33]

All then was in harmony with restrictions on the emancipation of women's sport typical of the 1950s and earlier in Europe. Restrictions on women had been imposed earlier, of course, by Coubertin. In this tradition, the press, following A. DeFranz,[34] was biased against women in track and field events, for example, in the 1928 Olympic Games held in Amsterdam. In those games, there was a clearly stereotyped representation of the feminine role, which was supported by current 'scientific' arguments. J. Túnis, a writer of the period, described the women's 800 metres as follows: 'Eleven unfortunate women ran in that competition, five of whom abandoned the race before the end, and five others fainted right after reaching the finish line'.[35] Yet the photographs and cinematic images, in addition to official Olympic reveal that the runners were nine in number, and that all nine runners completed the race! Doubtless, after such a demanding event, the competitors were exhausted, but no one fainted, as was reported by J. Túnis. His distortions and those of other journalists are evidence of a wilful masculine sexist mentality, pervasive in the period.[36]

The attitudes of, and reports from, the media certainly contributed to regression in the progress towards feminine emancipation. For thirty-two years, for example, women were denied participation in distances above 200 metres.[37] The image projected of 'the frail sex' created a reality based on false premises. And from this creation, it is a simple matter to comprehend the barriers to women's advancement in relation to men, in track and field events.[38]

According to T. Azevedo,[39] most authorities between 1937 and 1987 regarded women as 'the frail sex', unable to endure sporting activities of medium and long duration, and in consequence, these authorities devised restrictions and even prohibitions involving women and these activities. Interestingly, these authorities provided no supporting evidence for their confident assertions.[40]

Despite evidence of little difference in some, and no difference in other performances of men and women, the expectations and tasks attributed to women, of course, have been different from those attributed to men in the past and more recently throughout the nineteenth and twentieth centuries. Women's performance in specific areas of responsibility, in large part, moulded women, across the world, and *naturalized* female behaviour and attitude in Brazilian society – conditioning attitudes to women's performance in and success at modern sport. Negative stereotypes, discrimination and inhibitions dominated perceptions.[41] W. Areno[42] argued over a long period that long and triple jumps should not be performed by women. These activities could cause damage to the ovary and even its dislocation.[43] Such 'arguments'[44] were made in the face of evidence that the uterus, and other organs involved in reproduction, are well protected against external impact.[45] Lesions, in fact, are more common among men than women. The probability of a female athlete suffering accidents such as traumatic impact or lesions is less than that of a male athlete.[46]

SPORT FOR WOMEN – THE CONTRIBUTION OF MARIA LENK

In this normative and restrictive atmosphere, in Brazil in the 1930s some bold young women, of pioneering spirit, started to organize in Rio de Janeiro, the first swimming, volleyball and basketball state championships, and created women's sporting associations in various clubs.[47] Among these young women was Maria Lenk. In 1932, Lenk, at the age of 17, was included for the first time in a Brazilian delegation to the Olympic Games. The famous swimmer Piedade Coutinho, a contemporary of Lenk, recalls the importance of that inclusion:

> There were many taboos in those days. A woman was a housewife, first and foremost, with children, and could not easily and comfortably participate in sport. It was difficult. We served as a new role model for Brazilian women and for their children. At the same time women strengthened their bodies and improved their health.[48]

In 1936 Olympic Games in Berlin, there were 49 countries and more than 4000 athletes, including 328 women, a record in women's participation.[49] In the Brazilian delegation of 72 athletes, there were two iconic women: Maria Lenk[50] and Piedade Coutinho.

From 1937 on, with the inauguration of Estado Novo,[51] the Brazilian government used sport to compose a nationalist profile. The high point of this political strategy was the creation of the National Sports Council. In 1941, the Brazilian victory at the South American Women's Swimming Meeting thrilled the country. The champions Maria Lenk and Piedade Coutinho, due to their brilliant performance, were acclaimed by the people of Rio de Janeiro, and by President Vargas.[52] All this was in accord with the political atmosphere of fascism in the 1940s, during which, sport was exalted as an integral part of fascist ideology.[53]

THE CAREER OF MARIA LENK

It is time now to consider the career of the foremost of these new Brazilian heroines – Maria Lenk. Lenk was born in 1915 in São Paulo. As mentioned earlier, she was the first representative of South American women in the 1932 Olympic Games in Los Angeles, and a pioneer, along with Marina Cruz. Earlier, together, they were involved in a series of settings such as participation in the inauguration of the Athletic Association's first official swimming pool in São Paulo, Brazil, in 1930, a moment that marked the increasing involvement in women's swimming events.[54] Lenk, in her *Braçadas e Abraços*,[55] recalls the struggle of her small and select group

> of young women of German descent, to overcome the high barriers of custom and local discrimination, when they attempted to swim in public, dressed in highly ornamented swimsuits, full of pleats and frills. Fortunately the domestic restrictions imposed on these young women at home were not strong because of their European Germanic cultural heritage which valued physical fitness and natural beauty. Besides swimming had the happy reputation of ensuring gracefulness, not muscularity, and as such, did not challenge the feminine virtues of graceful frailty required by male hegemony.[56]

Lenk took part in the First Interstate Women's Meeting, held in Botafogo Cove, on 25 April 1931, in competition with athletes from Rio de Janeiro and São Paulo. She won first prize, and was honoured by her club, the São Paulo Athletic Association. It is recorded that: 'Back in São Paulo, the athlete had a clamorous reception and, more importantly, her performance influenced the participation of an increasing number of female newcomers in swimming competitions.'[57]

In short, Lenk effectively contributed not only through her books,[58] but mainly through her example, to a reconsideration of the role of women in Brazilian sport, to an alteration of belief, to freeing the Brazilian woman's body from traditional prejudice and taboos, from *naturalized* impositions as well as overt and covert ideology. She was more than a pioneer amateur swimmer. She was a gender role model. With a determination, which set an example to future generations, she influenced young women across Brazil and indeed throughout South America, and encouraged the transformation of social representations that restricted women's participation in sport, in particular in swimming. She built for herself an image as *the* feminine icon in the emancipation of women's sport in Brazil and Latin America, in a situation, in effect, highly unfavourable to women's sport.

The first assertion in this chapter is that the individual performances of leading Brazilian female athletes greatly contributed to the transformation of long-established social attitudes associated with women's athletic activities. The chapter also reveals that family support was crucial to women's participation in sport. In fact, without family support, a young woman even from the élite, faced with severe prejudice, had to overcome serious obstacles, which more often than not barred her entry to sport. Inhibiting, together with discouraging attitudes and hostile behaviour, understandably sapped the initiative, on the part of young women, to take up such activities and consequently excluded sports from their lives, sometimes permanently.

Now an attempt will be made to map out the specific challenge to traditional social representations and the impressive athletic successes of Lenk as the foremost pioneer of Brazilian women's sports, which resulted in her becoming an icon of inspiration and of change. Lenke became a source of information and an instrument of education within the élite circles in which she moved. She is undeniably a prototypical representative of those fearless women who entered the world of sport at a time when the visibility of feminine physical activities was becoming steadily apparent, she contributed substantially to this visibility.

Maria Penna Lenk was of German descent. Her parents, keen athletes, came to Brazil in 1912, became Brazilian citizens, and spent the rest of their lives in Brazil: 'My parents were enthusiastic about Brazil,' she declared.[59] 'For that reason, we used sport to promote the country, and this was the purpose of all our efforts.'[60] Maria Lenk started swimming following medical advice. Apropos of this she also remarked:

> My father was a great athlete, a Brazilian gymnastics champion. I was one of those frail little girls, suffering all possible child diseases that culminated in pneumonia. As I did not care much for gymnastics, my father introduced me to swimming, gave me lessons and I learnt how to swim in one month. That was in 1930.[61]

From 1930 to 1938 Lenk took part in two Olympic Games, Los Angeles and Berlin, and continued to break national and continental records in swimming, as in 1935, in the First South American Women's Championship.[62]

Lenk arrived in Rio de Janeiro in 1938, invited by the Ministry of Education to teach at the brand-new National School of Physical Education. She has reported that her involvement in sport followed a smooth path since her parents did not object to her initial and subsequent incursions. Of German and Brazilian cultures, she has remarked that the latter is more conservative and sexist. She has stressed that her parents were very supportive, as, 'they had a European mentality, different from that of Brazilians at that time', and adds that, 'due to their German descent, they were not narrow-minded like most Latin Americans'.[63] They thought nothing of their daughter taking up swimming.

Lenk's criticism of Brazilian sexism of that period, from the perspective of a European attitude, is powerful and revealing. She observed and commented on the behaviour of Brazilian and Latin American men at the start of her sporting career: 'The Latin man is, above all, sexist and vindictive toward anything women do.'[64] The sexist culture in Brazilian society, reinforced by patriarchy and by means of a 'hygienic' ideology, is caught in Lenk's words. This culture had a forceful and significant part to play in the evolution of women's sport in Brazil. Lenk confronted and to a degree ensured the capitulation of the ideological view that a woman's place was in the home as the angel of the hearth with husband and children. This view is not to be denied. It was a powerful pressure which kept many women within the domestic sphere, dictated their public dress and reduced their participation in sport. In the words of Lenk reviewing her childhood:

> Women only wanted to get married and raise their children since that was the highest ambition of a girl in those days. Furthermore, the boys did not want to marry a girl who exposed herself in public. As a girl turned into a woman and had her first dates, the first thing her boyfriend did was to prohibit her from swimming.[65]

Therefore, sport provided woman with a new image; she was revealed not only as gracious, worth looking at and desirable, but now as someone to be admired for her achievements. Men, who were brought up in the normality of possession of, and dominance over, a woman's body, were opposed to this new image. For this reason, they did not permit their girlfriends to swim. They said they would condemn them to spinsterhood – a fate, at the time, considered almost worse than death.

Lenk was aware of her importance as a pioneer in the movement for the integration of women into sport, as a fearless role model when facing criticism for her public appearances, when wearing swimming suits in public. She was also aware of her position as the precursor of women's swimming in Brazil. She has spoken proudly of the way she confronted the social values of the time and the manner in which society, generally, reacted to the idea of girls taking part in sports in the 1920s and 1930s: 'I'm proud to be a Brazilian pioneer in women's swimming. I was not afraid of the critics because I was naive. I helped put an end to the prejudices of the time when I showed up in a swimming suit. We introduced women's swimming to Brazil.'[66] Lenk, to her credit, does not seek the whole glory for emancipatory trend in women's swimming. Lenk gives fulsome praise to another pioneer, Violeta Coelho Neto, a singer and the daughter of the writer Coelho Neto.[67] Violeta wore a swimming suit in a 1922 presentation, during festivities associated with swimming at Urca's swimming complex.[68] Violeta Coelho Neto's bold gesture represented a new, defiant attitude on the part of women towards the public display of their own bodies, despite the fact that the event in question had no links with competitive swimming.

Later, in the 1930s, in an interstate meeting, competitive swimming was officially introduced in Brazil.[69] 'In fact, we were the true precursors of serious competitive women's swimming. We can say that it all started in 1930, with the First Interstate Women's Swimming Meeting, between Rio de Janeiro and São Paulo, held in Botafogo Cove, Mourisco, with Marina Cruz and I representing São Paulo.'[70]

Lenk's most glorious moment involved the breaking of the taboo which prevented Brazilian and Latin American women from competing in international sports events. In 1932, the Olympic Games in Los Angeles witnessed her supreme act of defiance, against women's passive attitude in sport.[71] 'I was the only female representative from Brazil and South America, at the age of 17, and it was then that the taboo of female passivity in sport was broken in South America.'[72]

With this statement, Lenk shows that she was perfectly aware of what her contribution through swimming meant to Brazilian and South American women. Then when asked about how it was to travel without a chaperone to Los Angeles at the age of 17, which, for a young Brazilian girl, was uncommon and highly irregular, her answer demonstrated the avant-garde character of her family: 'Of course my father made it clear that I would be in good hands as I was in the care of the head of the delegation. Piedade Coutinho never travelled unaccompanied.'[73]

In reply to comments that she was the first and only woman in the delegation without a chaperone she said: 'It's the influence of my progressive family.' It is quite clear that the progress in sport was helped, not hindered by the unconditional support of her family of German descent: 'Physical activity is very important to the German people. They have also been the precursors in scientific aspects of sport; in sports medicine, and all things that made sports beautiful.'[75]

The first South American Women's Swimming Championship in pools was held in 1935. Two other Brazilian swimming stars appeared at that time, Lenk's sister Ciglinda, the backstroke champion, and Piedade Coutinho, the freestyle champion. 'We were the champions of the South American Meeting, together with other swimmers not so well qualified.'[76] In 1936, at the Eleventh Olympic Games in Berlin, there were six female swimmers in the Brazilian delegation. They were Helena Salles, Sila Venâncio, Marina Cruz, Ciglinda Lenk, Piedade Coutinho and Maria Lenk. Piedade Coutinho had the best result, fifth place in the 400 metres freestyle final. Later, Lenk spoke of the difficulties they faced during the trip. They travelled from Brazil in a cargo ship, which definitely put them at a disadvantage.

OTHER CLAIMS OF MARIA LENK

Lenk has a number of claims to fame beyond her achievements in National, South American and Olympic tournaments. For example, she introduced Brazilians to butterfly swimming. In her own words:

> Butterfly swimming first took place in these games (the Olympic Games in Berlin), and I brought the style to Brazil due to a contact I had with an American swimmer, when I came back from Berlin. In October 1939, I set the butterfly world record with the time of 6.16 minutes, at Botafogo swimming complex.[77]

Setting South American and world records was, and still is, a characteristic of Lenk. In November 1939, for example, in the pool of Fluminense Football Club, she set the 200 metres world record, with the time of 2.56 minutes. In 1998, during the Masters World Swimming Championship in Morocco, she once more got gold medals. However, her greatest wish – to earn an Olympic medal did not materialize, because when she was in her best form and fully prepared for the 1940 Olympics, the Games were cancelled because of the outbreak of the Second World War: 'My dream was to see the Brazilian flag on the Olympic podium. But that was not possible since the 1940 Olympic games were cancelled.'[78]

After the war Lenk, at the peak of her powers, was frequently invited to take part in swimming events all over the world. However, she decided to retire, without waiting for the onset of natural physical decline: 'It is a drastic decision to make, but there are some advantages. The days of glory are held in my memory as well as in the public memory. Physical decadence would be inevitable, so I stopped in 1951 and I was honoured[79] by the Brazilian government.'[80]

Her career as a competitive swimmer over, Maria Lenk began work in a school, got married and had children, at last combining a professional career with the responsibility of raising a family. While she had to work in order to help support her family, she could now see her influence at work, and witnessed with satisfaction, the rise of much new female swimming talent through public competitions.[81]

Lenk is a living illustration of how gradually women's social situations changed and how women were able eventually to show their competence in sport. She gives us an accurate and important account of the values women gradually internalized with regard to sport in the 1920s and 1930s and the barriers they had to overcome. In passing, it might be noted that the first athletic activities enjoyed by middle-class females in Brazil were tennis and cycling. There were good reasons for this: 'Women's first entry into sport was through tennis, probably because tennis outfits covered women's bodies adequately. They looked like ordinary dresses that could be worn in everyday social life. Tennis opened the way to women's participation in sport. Cycling emerged as another physical activity among women. There was even a special bicycle for women that allowed them to wear long skirts.'[82] No social taboos were thus infringed.[83]

Lenk considered that the gradual acceptance of women in other sports paved the way for acceptance of swimming. It gradually gained ground. It started on the beaches, with swimming costumes that covered all, then came swimming costumes which gradually became smaller, but 'modest', femininity was still emphasized and protected. So swimming became acceptable.

One of the virtues of Lenk's experience is that it demonstrates that the introduction of Brazilian women to sport was closely related to exposure in public. It also highlights the public reaction to this. Various factors shaped changing public attitudes to this exposure. Among these, North American trends played a part, but above all, by far the most dominant influence was the rise of the 'hygienic' movement begun by Brazilian physicians at the beginning of the twentieth century.[84]

It is of the outmost importance that it is appreciated that the contributions of Maria Lenk to women's emancipation in sport are not restricted to her performance as an athlete. There were other issues she wanted to fight for:

> I was a member of the National Sports Council. I remember it well, it was in 1965 or 1968. I advocated that women should be free to choose any sport they liked. At that time, soccer and boxing, for example, were forbidden to women. There are documents of mine lodged with the National Sports Council, which advocate women's freedom of choice.[85]

Lenk was a resolute advocate of the complete liberation of women in sport. Despite her valiant efforts, in reality, many sporting activities remained denied to women until the 1970s. This was finally achieved in 1975: 'The patriarchal culture protected women: "oh, the poor one is going to hurt her knees, her breast", and all that nonsense. But in the 1970s all kinds of sporting practices were finally made available to women.'[86]

Lenk did not consider herself an ideological feminist: 'much of my feminist attitude was due to the circumstances I had to face'. She was not involved in women's political issues or the feminist movement. She simply supported women's right to opportunities in sport.[87] In addition to being a top athlete, Lenk had a career, was a housewife and a mother. According to her, it was not easy to accommodate all these demands. Lenk did, in the 40s, what women are doing today, without any of the technological benefits of modern of life. Furthermore, she has never had any sponsors. Once she had retired she kept herself continually up-to-date in the field of physical education. Today, she is her own coach. In view of all this, Lenk exudes some bitterness toward the professionalism in modern sport. According to her, the athletic ideal has changed radically for the worse:

> The general mentality of the athlete has changed a lot. Nowadays people do not practise sport for the sake of sport, for the sake of one's country. Today, athletes want to win to get sponsorship. With this materialistic attitude, athletes will do anything, even take drugs, in order to finish with an advantage of a hundredth of a second, so as to win the competition, so as to get rich rewards.[88]

Lenk's view, perhaps a little too simplistic, is that the patriotism of the past was preferable to the materialism of the present.

We formed a group, for the first time a South American group that went to the United States. And there I competed with the best athletes in the world. And I said to my companion: 'Look, when you realize that I am in a tough situation, if you see that the competition is hard, wave the flag.' And he waved a flag and I was 25 metres ahead, but he wanted me to set a record. So, you see, the flag for us was a concept, a sacred thing, that we fought for. It was quite different.[89] Today money is the ambition, not patriotism.[90]

Perhaps she views the past through a rose-tinted haze. To this day, Lenk greatly regrets that the Olympic Games were not held in 1940, when she considered herself to have been at her best form. 'Then I had broken those two world records, the 200 and 400 metres, and there was nobody better prepared for the Olympic Games but they did not take place, and it was the end of my career.'[91]

The athlete, teacher, participant and observer insists that the evolution of women's sport was very slow. She considers the two world wars jointly responsible for the eventual visibility of women in the public arena. 'It was a difficult evolution, and if it had not been for the wars, maybe the presence of women in sport would not have come so quickly. The wars sent men away and women had to replace them.'[92]

When her active swimming career was over, Lenk became the first woman to serve on the National Sports Council. Once again, she was a pioneer, and an inspirational role model. 'In my pioneering move I took pride in being the first female member of the National Sports Council, and had the pleasure of working side by side with its president.'[93] Then, she was appointed as the first Director of the National School of Physical Education. In short, Lenk's life was a series of confrontations with convention. She kept on breaching taboos, overcoming obstacles and changing perceptions.[94]

At one other level Lenk certainly denied prejudice – at the level of the relative professional status and respect attributed to the medical and the physical education professions. 'They established a difference between doctors (physicians), who taught physiology and anatomy, and the others, who taught sport, athletics, volleyball, soccer, basketball, swimming and so on. The latter were regarded as teachers of practice, and were hired for three years. In case of any physical deterioration their contract was not renewed.'[95] In other words, the physical fitness of physical education teachers was considered fundamental to the practice of their profession. Unless they succeeded in obtaining a positive assessment, they were not re-appointed. Physicians, the teachers of 'theory', did not suffer this insecurity. In one other regard, teachers of physical education experienced discrimination. Physicians were allowed to take examinations to obtain the title of professor. Physical education teachers were not.

Lenk's response as the first woman Director of the National School of Physical Education was to join the battle between the physical education teacher and the physician, on the side of the teacher. She worked to overcome the inferior status assigned to physical education professionals in the Brazilian school system: 'Prejudice prevailed until we were able to become permanent teachers by means of bureaucratic battles of unimaginable dimensions.'[96]

In the face of extraordinary opposition, Lenk also made her mark as a pioneering disseminator of physical education throughout the interior of Brazil. 'I was one of the pioneering physical education teachers sent to the interior, where the bishop even wanted me excommunicated, because it was not a woman's role to give girls swimming classes.'[97] Lenk faced resistance at the hands of the school administration as well as the Church. She wanted both her male and female students to wear tracksuit bottoms to exercise: 'Because prejudice against women was even more pronounced in the interior, an essentially Catholic and even more backward environment, I made the girls wear tracksuit bottoms.'[98] Such brutal rejection of compromise in no way diminished her resolution or her success. Girls exercised.

In 1938 Lenk played an active part in the foundation of the Brazilian National School of Physical Education. She declared that: 'physical education strove to be accepted at the university level'.[99] However, the impetus behind the Brazilian National Project on Physical Education was, in fact, the poor physical conditioning of Brazilian men and women. It alarmed the military government and contravened fascist ideals of physical fitness for war. Fifty per cent of the army recruits were rejected due to their poor physical condition, with the result that the Brazilian National Plan was established. For the first time in South America, in all probability, Lenk has observed, physical education became part of the university syllabus. Lenk, and Brazil, led the way on the South American continent.

Lenk makes only indirect reference to Vargas' eugenic project to improve the race and the contribution that a National School of Physical

Education could give to this project: training strong men for war and healthy women for the production of strong men. Nevertheless, the war, certainly, was a factor that aided her in her own ambitions for Brazilian women.

It should not be overlooked that Lenk also exerted influence as a scholar and writer. In 1942, she published a book entitled *Natação* (Swimming).[100] Later in the same year she published *Natação Olímpica* (Olympic Swimming), a work focusing on training methods. In 1986, she wrote *Braçadas e Abraços* (Strokes and Embraces), in which she relates the most important moments in her career.

Finally, special mention should be made of Lenk as an administrator of physical education. As mentioned earlier, she was the first woman Director of the National School of Physical Education in the late 1960s, at a time when such positions were held exclusively by men. The situation set up to favour a male candidate clearly backfired. The name of the favoured candidate was included on the usual three-name short list with those of two women, one of whom was Lenk. She was, in fact, the chosen candidate.[101] This spoke volumes for her standing, her reputation and her record.

Lenk remarks that she turned the school upside down. She also maintains that the government gave her considerable support for her reforms. It was hardly surprising. It was practically falling apart. She recalls, 'I made them see that there was not even a ball with which to play soccer in the school.'[102] Her reform was so substantial that it ensured moving the site of the School. The President himself was present at the inauguration of the school on the new site, and the government embarked on a nation-wide sports provision project.

After the dedication Lenk had shown to the National School of Physical Education, during the years she was Director, and the steady support she won from the government, her exit could not have happened differently: 'I left as an Emeritus Professor. Yes, I was a professional with all my heart and soul.'[103]

CONCLUSION

It is incontrovertible that there was a significant increase in Brazilian women's involvement in sport because of icons like Maria Lenk. Women like her contributed, and still contribute, to the modification of restrictive, stereotypical, prejudiced and discriminatory representations of women in sport. In acting as inspirational agents of change, she and others have also had an impact on the wider social, intellectual and political emancipation of the Brazilian woman.

In addition, Lenk unquestionably made Brazilian women more aware of the importance – for themselves – of physical activity. She, and others, advised and guided women, choosing activities for them that ensured the maintenance and improvement of their health. Finally, she and others, helped to dismantle the subtle and unsubtle mechanisms limiting their mobility, their opportunities and their freedom.

She, and others, challenged the attitudes and behaviour of a male-dominated society. She, and others, helped dismantle the means and mechanisms by which that patriarchy maintained its dominance over its women. She, and others, opened the doors to female emancipation – culturally, socially *and* in the world of sport. Finally, Maria Lenk provided an initial vision of an equality of opportunity which inspired women then – and still inspires them to-day – to be visible participators in Brazilian sport and society.

NOTES

1. A. Prost and G. Vincent, *História da vida privada*, Vol.5 (São Paulo, 1992), p.98.
2. For a more detailed analysis of Lenk's career, see Ludmila Mourão, *The Social Representation of the Brazilian Woman in Physical and Sportive Activities: from Segregation to Democratisation* (Rio de Janeiro, Gama Filho University, Ph.D. dissertation, 1998).
3. Following J.A. Mangan and Roberta J. Park, in *From 'Fair' Sex to Feminism* (London, 1987), p.3, 'It was in the nineteenth century that social, industrial and technological changes, and an accompanying ideological ferment, gave rise to modern sport. As a consequence, an increasingly substantial and sophisticated picture of male sports has emerged from which mid-range generalizations can be advanced. The picture regarding women, however, is still very hazy. It is becoming apparent that many were far more involved in a wider range of 'athletic' activities than had hitherto been assumed.'
4. Denise Jodelet, *Les représentations sociales* (Paris, 1989).
5. C. Araujo *et al.*, 'Curso de medicina do exercício, aspectos toxoginecológicos do exercício', *Revista Brasileira de Ciência do Esporte*, 3 (1981), 5–15; Walter Areno, 'Os desportos femininos; aspectos médicos', *Educação Physica*, 62/63 (1942), 22–4; Walter Areno, 'Considerações médico-desportivas sobre atletismo feminino', *Arquivos da Escola Nacional de Educação Física e Desportos*, 1 (1945), 24–9; Walter Areno, 'Desportos para a mulher', *Revista Brasileira de Educação Física*, 34 (1947), 31–3; 'Fundamentos biológicos da educação física feminina', *Arquivos da Escola de Educação Física e Desportos*, 17 (1962) 55–70.
6. R. Araújo, *A vocação do prazer: a cidade e a família no Rio de Janeiro republicano* (Rio de Janeiro, 1995); see also sociological considerations in Fernando Azevedo, *Da educação física*, Vol.1 (Rio de Janeiro, 1920), and especially in *A evolução do esporte no Brasil* (São Paulo, 1930).
7. The Brazilian family was highly controlled by the Church, as can be seen in R. Azzi, 'Família, mulher e sexualidade na Igreja do Brasil (1930–1964)', in M. Marcilio (org), *Família, mulher, sexualidade e Igreja na história do Brasil* (São Paulo, 1993). pp.101–34, and in I. Raming, 'Da liberdade do evangelho à Igreja estratificada de homens: sobre a origem e desenvolvimento da dominação masculina na Igreja', in E. Carol, R. Laretin and M. Agudelo, *A mulher numa estrutura eclesial masculina* (Petrópolis, 1980), pp.5–15.

8. Tania Azevedo analyses discrimination against women in sport since the 1930s, in 'Women in Physical Education and in Sport (1932–1987)' (Dissertação de Mestrado em Educação, Niterói, 1988). The influence of Positivism is analysed in M.M. Carvalho, 'A imagem e a educação da mulher no positivismo; um estudo da condição feminina na filosofia de Augusto Comte' (Dissertação de Mestrado em Educação) (São Paulo, Faculdade de Educação da Universidade de São Paulo, 1991).
9. On the strict control of the Brazilian Empire on private life, see M.J. Carvalho, *A construção da ordem: a elite política imperial* (Brasília, 1981). Medical contribution to this state of affairs is nicely addressed by Jurandir Freire Costa, *Ordem médica e norma familiar* (Rio de Janeiro, 1983).
10. The Brazilian Communist Party was founded at the beginning of the 1920s, and since then has been a very strong force in Brazilian politics. Luis Carlos Prestes, mentioned later as the leader of Coluna Prestes, has lived for a long time in the former Soviet Union, representing Brazilian communists.
11. The Week of Modern Art, Semana da Arte Moderna, took place in 1922.
12. On 25 July 1924 military dissident troops of the State of São Paulo joined a group of insubordinate lieutenants from the State of Rio Grande do Sul, under the leadership of Luiz Carlos Prestes. Having made a long march of 25,000 kilometres, throughout Brazilian territory, the troops met and totalled 8,000. This march, known as Coluna Prestes, aimed to denounce the political situation of the country and organize a broad revolutionary movement. Nevertheless, in 1926 the group was reduced to only 800 men, who were not getting the expected response from Brazilian people. One year later, the last remnants of Coluna Prestes went into exile, in Bolivia.
13. The coffee crisis was a direct effect of an American crisis at the end of the 1920s. Millions of tons of Brazilian coffee were burned, at that point, with devastating effects on Brazil's social and economic life.
14. Brazilian Women's Suffrage Movement won voting rights for women in 1925, starting in the State of Ceará, in the north-east part of the country.
15. In Brazil, the period between the world wars was marked by the decline of coffee agriculture, by the advancement of industrialization and by the crisis of Old and first Republic, which came to an end with the Revolution of 1930, with the ascent of Getúlio Vargas and the fall of the regime of Washington Luiz. One of the major effects of this revolution was the launch of the project of modernising Brazilian society. The political battle which ensued in Europe, between conservative and communist forces, was also reflected in Brazil, with a communist insurrection (Intentona Comunista), that occurred in Rio de Janeiro, in 1935. Vargas inaugurated 'populism', a new style of governing the country, always addressing himself to the proletariat, seeking support to continue to ensure his political power. In 1945 Vargas left the government, overtaken by a military coup. Five years later, by popular vote, he returned to power.
16. See R. Araújo, *A vocação do prazer: a cidade e a família no Rio de Janeiro republicano* (Rio de Janeiro, 1995); M.M. Carvalho, 'A imagem e a educação da mulher no positivismo; um estudo da condição feminina na filosofia de Augusto Comte' (Dissertação de Mestrado em Educação, Faculdade de Educação da Universidade de São Paulo, 1991); M.J. Carvalho, *A construção da ordem: a elite política imperial* (Brasília, 1981); L.E. Costa, *O Rio de Janeiro de meu tempo*, Vol.3 (Rio de Janeiro, 1938); M. Del Priore, *Ao sul do corpo: condição feminina, maternidades e mentalidades no Brasil colônia* (Rio de Janeiro, 1995), and Gilberto Freyre, *Casa grande e senzala* (Brasília, 1963).
17. These ideas about the beginning of feminist movements in Brazil can be seen especially in M. Del Priore, *Ao sul do corpo: condição feminina, maternidades e mentalidades no Brasil colônia* (Rio de Janeiro, 1995), and in M. Del Priore (org.), *História das mulheres no Brasil* (São Paulo, 1997).
18. See F. Genevière and M. Perrote (orgs.) *A história das mulheres no Ocidente: o século XIX*, Vol.4 (Porto, 1991); E. Hobsbawm, 'A nova mulher' in: E. Hobsbawm, *A era dos impérios 1875–1914* (Rio de Janeiro, 1988), pp.271–306; M.M. Leite (org.), *A condição feminina no Rio de Janeiro no século XIX* (São Paulo, 1984); M.M. Leite and M. Massani, 'Representação do amor e da família', in M.A. D'Incao (org.), *O amor e a família no Brasil* (São Paulo, 1989); Rose Marie Muraro, *Sexualidade da mulher brasileira: corpo e classe social no Brasil* (Rio de Janeiro, 1996); A. Peixoto, *A educação da mulher* (São Paulo, 1936); T. Quintaneiro, *Retratos de mulher. O cotidiano feminino no Brasil sob o olhar de viageiros do século XIX* (Petrópolis, 1995); M. Rago, *Do cabaré*

ao lar: a utopia da cidade disciplinar no Brasil, 1890–1930 (Rio de Janeiro, 1985); J.H. Rodrigues, *Independência: revolução e contra-revolução: economia e sociedade* (Rio de Janeiro, 1975); N. Sevcenko, *Orfeu extático na metrópole*. São Paulo sociedade e cultura nos frementes anos 20 (São Paulo, 1992) and F. Tabak, *A mulher brasileira no Congresso Nacional* (Brasília, 1989).

19. From the middle of the nineteenth century, the discussion about which sports should be recommended to women came under the spotlight. See, for example, P.C. Frances, 'Ladies' amusements', *Every Saturday* (1870), and F. Genevière and M. Perrote (orgs.), *A história das mulheres no Ocidente: o século XIX*, Vol.4 (Porto, 1991).

20. A total of 127 women took part in these Games in events such as track and field (100 and 80 metre hurdles, 4x100 metre relay, high jump, discus and javelin throw), fencing, swimming (100 and 400 metre freestyle, 100 metre backstroke, 200 metre breast-stroke, 4x100 metre freestyle relay) and platform jumping. In 1936, in Berlin, from 1 to 16 August six of the 328 women were Brazilian. The events were track and field (100 and 80 metre hurdles, 4x100 metre relay, high jump, discus and javelin throw), fencing, gymnastics (combined exercises), swimming (100 and 400 metre freestyle, 100 metre backstroke, 100 metre backstroke, 200 metre breast-stroke, 4x100 metre freestyle relay) and springboard diving. In 1948, in the United Kingdom, 11 of the 385 women were Brazilian. They competed in track and field (100 metre dash, 200 metre, 4x100 metre relay, 80 metre hurdles, long and high jump, discus and javelin throw and shot put), canoeing (simple kayak), fencing, gymnastics (combined exercises), swimming (100 and 400 metre freestyle, 200 metre breaststroke, 100 metre backstroke, 4x100 metre freestyle relay) and platform diving. In 1952, in Helsinki, Finland, from 19 July to 3 August, 518 women, only five of them Brazilian, took part in competitions such as track and field (100, 200 and 80 metre hurdles, 4x100 metre relay, high and long jump, javelin and discus throw and shot put), canoeing (simple kayak), fencing, gymnastics (balance beam, uneven bars, vault, floor exercise, combined exercises and GRD), swimming (100 metre freestyle, 100 metre backstroke, 400 metre freestyle, 200 metre breaststroke, 4x100 metre freestyle relay).

21. J.A. Mangan and R.J. Park (eds.), *From 'Fair Sex' to Feminism: Sport and Socialisation of Women in the Industrial and Post-Industrial Eras*, present a pioneering analysis and discussion of women and sport in Europe and elsewhere, with a focus on British, Commonwealth and American perspectives. Part one: Overview is especially relevant for the concerns of women's emancipation from medical and educational constraints. Carroll Smith-Rosenberg and Charles Rosenberg deal with 'The Female Animal: Medical and Biological Views of Women and their Role in Nineteenth-Century America'. Paul Atkinson addresses 'The Feminist Physique: Physical Education and Medicalisation of Women's Education'. Roberta J. Park analyses 'Sport, Gender and Society in a Transatlantic Victorian Perspective'.

22. In the 1920s Violeta Coelho was the first Brazilian swimmer to appear in a public event, in the basin of Urca, in 1922. Anésia Coelho and Alice Possalo were the first women to cross the Guanabara Bay, a 5km distance, in 1925. In the 1930s, Maria Lenk was followed by Marina Cruz, champion in the crawl, at the first Women's Swimming Meeting in a swimming pool, in São Paulo Athletic Association, and Thora Melbourne.

23. Change was slow with practice, theories and ideas all mutually influencing each other.

24. See, especially: J.M. Teixeira, *Mortalidade na cidade do Rio de Janeiro* (Rio de Janeiro, 1876); J.M. Teixeira, *Causas da mortalidade das crianças no Rio de Janeiro* (Rio de Janeiro, 1888); L. F. Alencastro (1997). 'Vida privada e ordem privada no Império' in L.F. Alencastro (org.), *História da vida privada no Brasil Império: a corte e a modernidade nacional* (São Paulo, 1997), pp.11–94.

25. See C. Araujo *et al.*, 'Curso de medicina do exercício, aspectos toxoginecológicos do exercício'. *Revista Brasileira de Ciência do Esporte. Rio de Janeiro*, 3 (1981), 5–15; R. Araújo, *A vocação do prazer: a cidade e a família no Rio de Janeiro republicano* (Rio de Janeiro, 1995); Walter Areno, 'Os desportos femininos; aspectos médicos', *Educação Physica. Rio de Janeiro*, 62/63 (1942), 22–4; Walter Areno, 'Considerações médico-desportivas sobre atletismo feminino', *Arquivos da Escola Nacional de Educação Física e Desportos. Rio de Janeiro*, 1 (1945), 24–9.

26. From the Faculty of Medicine, see A. Armonde, *Da educação física, intelectual e moral da mocidade do Rio de Janeiro e da sua influência sobre a saúde* (Rio de Janeiro, 1874); J. da Matta Machado, *Da educação physica, moral e intellectual da mocidade no Rio de Janeiro e da sua influencia sobre a saúde* (Rio de Janeiro, 1874). The twentieth century is also considered by M. Del Priore, *Ao sul do corpo: condição feminina, maternidades e mentalidades no Brasil colônia* (Rio

de Janeiro, 1995); Nísia Floresta, *Opúsculo humanitário* (São Paulo, 1853), and Gilberto Freyre, *Sobrados e mucambos* (Rio de Janeiro, 1961).

27. Nísia Floresta was a leader of new education for girls, with emphasis on freedom of physical movements and ideas. Her book, *Opúsculo Humanitário*, from 1853, depicts the scenarios of restrictions against women at that period. Many men, acting as educators, entered the movement favouring physical education for women, such as A. Peixoto, *A educação da mulher* (São Paulo, 1936); O. Rangel Sobrinho, *Educação physica feminina* (Rio de Janeiro, 1930), and J. da Matta Machado, *Da educação physica, moral e intellectual da mocidade no Rio de Janeiro e da sua influencia sobre a saúde* (Rio de Janeiro, 1874).

28. See J. Ezagui, 'Educação fisica feminina', *Educação Física*, 78 (1853), 16–17; M.E.B. Mayne, 'O sistema sueco baseado na ginástica de Ling, adaptado ao sexo feminino, na Argentina', *Boletim de Educação Física*, 10 (1944), 73–8; Walter Areno, 'Considerações médico-desportivas sobre atletismo feminino', *Arquivos da Escola Nacional de Educação Física e Desportos*. Rio de Janeiro, 1 (1945), 24–9; S.F.M. Guérios, 'Educação fisica feminina; exercícios preventivos ou corretivos e de relaxamento', *Revista de Educação Física da Escola de Educação Física do Exército*, 15 (1948), 14–17; Inezil P. Marinho, 'Ginástica feminina moderna', *Arquivos da Escola Nacional de Educação Física e Desportos, Rio de Janeiro*, 9 (1956), 35–52, and E. M. Rezende, 'Ginástica rítmica desportiva', *Revista de Educação Física da Escola de Educação Física do Exército*, 104 (1978), 55; and E. Romero (org), *Mulheres em Movimento* (Vitória, 1997).

29. J. Ramos, 'Educação fisica feminina', *Revista de Educação Física da Escola de Educação Física do Exército*, 5 (1937), 35–38.

30. See the continuous presence of Walter Areno, in 'Os desportos femininos; aspectos médicos', *Educação Physica*, 62/63 (1942), 22–4; Walter Areno, 'Considerações médico-desportivas sobre atletismo feminino', *Arquivos da Escola Nacional de Educação Física e Desportos*, 1 (1945), 24–29; Walter Areno, 'Desportos para a mulher', *Revista Brasileira de Educação Física*, 34 (1947), 31–3, and Walter Areno, 'Fundamentos biológicos da educação fisica feminina', *Arquivos da Escola de Educação Física e Desportos. Rio de Janeiro*, 17 (1962), 55–70. See also C. Araujo *et al.*, 'Curso de medicina do exercício, aspectos tocoginecológicos do exercício, *Revista Brasileira de Ciência do Esporte*, 3 (1981), 5–15.

31. Tania Azevedo, *Women in Physical Education and in Sport (1932–1987)* (Niterói, 1988), p.98. The author attempts to analyse and question sexual discrimination related to women, in the realm of school sport and physical education.

32. *Educação Physica Técnica do Basketbal*, A4, n. 1, Rio (1932), 99–100. The basketball rules were the same as for men, except that the duration of the quarter was reduced from twenty minutes to ten. The winner was City Bank Club.

33. Conselho Nacional dos Desportos, 'National Sports Council' Deliberation 7, 1965.

34. According to Anita DeFrantz, 'La evolución del papel de la mujer en los Juegos Olímpicos', *Revista Olímpica*, XXVI (1997), 18–21.

35. Ibid.

36. The winner was Babe Didrickson, the first idol of German feminine sport.

37. Since then, the International Federation of Women's Sport has organized Parallel Games, in Europe, which continued until 1960.

38. It was only in 1960, at the Rome Olympic Games, that 800 metres returned as a distance limit for women.

39. Tania Azevedo, 'Women in Physical Education and in Sport (1932–1987)', 23.

40. On the contrary, following Inner London Education Authority, *Providing equal opportunities for girls and boys in physical education* (Philadelphia, 1979), there is evidence that 'women's trainability is similar to that of men, for aerobic effort; and 'Women's maximum aerobic potential in long distance events tends to be close to that of male athletes in the same speciality.'

41. Gertrud Pfister, in *The State of Knowledge and Current Research on Sport and Gender* (Rio: Universidade Gama Filho, 1999) shows that Mathilde Vaerting in the 1920s had already pointed out that men's and women's roles are dependent on their respective cultures. These, as a result of the power balance, are therefore not 'natural' but changeable. Vaerting, however, had little influence on mainstream thinking in those societies which were based on gender roles, particularly not on the unpaid housework and child care by mothers.

42. Walter Areno, 'Os desportos femininos; aspectos médicos', *Educação Physica*, 62/63 (1942),

22–4; Walter Areno, 'Considerações médico-desportivas sobre atletismo feminino', *Arquivos da Escola Nacional de Educação Física e Desportos*, 1 (1945), 24–9; Walter Areno, 'Desportos para a mulher', *Revista Brasileira de Educação Física*, 34 (1947), 31–3; and Walter Areno, 'Fundamentos biológicos da educação física feminina', *Arquivos da Escola de Educação Física e Desportos*, 17 (1962) 55–70. See also S.F.M. Guérios, 'Educação física feminina; exercícios preventivos ou corretivos e de relaxamento', *Revista de Educação Física da Escola de Educação Física do Exército*, 15 (1948), 14–17.

43. For a more detailed analysis of these ideas, see Tania Azevedo, 'Women in Physical Education and in Sport'.

44. For further clarification, see C.H. McCloy, 'A study of landing shock in jumping for women', *Arbeitsphysiologie*, 5 (1931), 100.

45. See C. Araujo *et al.*, 'Curso de medicina do exercício, aspectos toxoginecológicos do exercício', *Revista Brasileira de Ciência do Esporte*. Rio de Janeiro, 3, 1 (1981), 5–15.

46. See A.M. Hardman, 'Women in sports: a review of the physiological factors', *Physical Education Review*, 1 (1979), 9–44, and Inner London Education Authority. *Providing equal opportunities for girls and boys in physical education* (Philadelphia, 1979).

47. As Fluminense Football Club, Club Esperia, Athletic Association of São Paulo and Minas Tênis Club.

48. This statement is taken from a segment of a video produced by Globo Television Network in 1997, directed by Nelson Mello e Souza.

49. S. Lancellotti, *Olimpíadas 100 anos: a história completa dos jogos* (São Paulo, 1996).

50. In 1936 she won a gold medal from the journal *Diário de São Paulo* for having been voted the most popular sportswoman in Brazil – alongside the soccer player, Arthur Friedenreich, who was the most popular male sporting personality. She received the title 'Great Pioneer of Brazilian Women's Swimming'.

51. The New State was supposed to replace the Old Republic, following Vargas' words. It lasted until 1945.

52. In 1940, during the celebrations to mark the inauguration of the Pacaembu Stadium, in São Paulo, the Argentinean Federation of Swimming gave her a trophy with the words: Símbolo de Vinculacion Sudamericana (Symbol of South American Integration).

53. Brazilian fascist ideology promoted the exaltation of sport as a tool for race regeneration and as a preparation for war.

54. Marina Cruz was another famous Brazilian swimmer, a contemporary of Maria Lenk.

55. Maria Lenk, *Braçadas e Abraços* (São Paulo, 1986), p.17.

56. Apparently, there is some contradiction in Lenk's text; however, we can interpret it in a way that would show that German families were more liberal while Brazilian families were more sexist; or, that German families are both liberal and aware of the prejudice found in Brazilian society.

57. See *Braçadas e Abraços* (1986), p.23. This contributed to the evolution of women's swimming which called for a domestic championship. The first championship in São Paulo was held on 10 April 1932, sponsored by the São Paulo's Federation of Rowing Societies.

58. To be referred later.

59. M. Lenk, in an interview given to Ludmila Mourão, June 1998.

60. Lenk refers to her family's contribution to the development of sport.

61. M. Lenk, in an interview given to Ludmila Mourão, June 1998.

62. Following the 1932 Los Angeles Olympic Games, Maria Lenk was succeeded by a series of brilliant female swimmers. In the First South-American Women's Championship, in 1935, Lenk was in the company of very young swimmers, such as Helena Salles (second place, 100/400 metre freestyle); Piedade Coutinho (third place, 100/400 metre freestyle); Lenk, Piedade, Helena and Scylla Venancio were champions in 4x100 metre freestyle relay). In the 1936 Berlin Olympic Games, Maria Lenk (twelfth place among 23 swimmers, breast-stroke), was in the company of Piedade Coutinho (eighth place, 100 metre freestyle), Scylla Venancio, Siglinde Lenk, and Helena Salles. The Second World War prevented the next Olympic Games. Between 1936 (Berlin) and 1948 (London) the Pan-American Championships were also interrupted till 1951. In the South-American Women's Championship of 1941, in Chile, Brazilian swimmers were winners in all of the styles. Maria Lenk and Edith Heimplel took first

and second places in the 100 and 200 metre breast stroke. Ciglinde Lenk and Cecilia Helborn were first and second the 100 and 200 metre back-stroke. Lieselotte Kraus was second following Piedade, in the 100 and 400 metre freestyle. Maria Lenk, Siglinde Lenk, Piedade and Lieselotte were champions of 4x100 metre freestyle relay. In the Olympic Games of London, 1948, Brazil's competitors were Edith Groba, Eleonora Margarida Schmidt, Piedade Coutinho, Maria Angelica Leão Costa, and Talita de Alencar. In the First Pan-American Women's Championship, in Buenos Aires, 1951, Brazil was represented by Piedade Coutinho, Talita Rodrigues, Anna Santarita, Talita de Alencar, Idamis Busin, and Piedade Coutinho. In the Olympic Games of 1952, in Helsinki, the Brazilian swimmers were Piedade Coutinho and Edith Groba.

63. M. Lenk, in an interview given to Ludmila Mourão, June 1998.
64. Ibid.
65. Ibid.
66. Ibid.
67. Violeta Coelho Neto challenged the values of the society of Rio de Janeiro, by her pioneering gesture of wearing a swimsuit in public.
68. The 'swimming complex' of Urca was basically a rudimentary tank, full of water, in which people used to swim. The first swimming pool, as already mentioned, was inaugurated in São Paulo, in 1930.
69. Maria Lenk is referring to the group of girls of German descent, as well as those of Brazilian extraction, such as Marina Cruz and Piedade Coutinho.
70. M. Lenk, in an interview given to Ludmila Mourão, June 1998.
71. In the 1932 Olympic Games, Lenk made the semi-finals with relative success. She was encouraged because for the first time she saw training methods. She competed in her strongest style – breast-stroke – but she also entered the backstroke and the freestyle competitions.
72. M. Lenk, in an interview given to Ludmila Mourão, June 1998.
73. Ibid.
74. Ibid.
75. Ibid.
76. Ibid.
77. Ibid.
78. Ibid.
79. Lenk received two awards: Ordem do Mérito Esportivo and Cruz do Mérito Nacional.
80. M. Lenk, in an interview given to Ludmila Mourão, June 1998.
81. These new female swimming talents were revealed to the public both in national and international competitions and included Helena Salles, Piedade Coutinho, Scylla Venancio, Edith Heimplel, Cecilia Helborn, Lieselotte Kraus, Edith Groba, Eleonora Margarida Schmidt, Maria Angelica Leão Costa, Talita de Alencar Rodrigues, Anna Santarita and Idamis Busin.
82. M. Lenk, in an interview given to Ludmila Mourão, June 1998.
83. She refers to authors as P.C. Frances, 'Ladies' amusements', *Every Saturday* (1870), H. Slocum, 'Lawn tennis as a game for women', *Outing*, 14 (1889), and R.A. Smith, *A social history of the bicycle: its early life and times in America* (New York, 1972).
84. See, especially T.L. Madel, *As instituições médicas no Brasil: instituição e estratégia de hegemonia* (Rio de Janeiro, 1986); Ministério da Educação e Cultura, *Medicina e ordem política brasileira: políticas e instituições de saúde (1850–1930)* (Rio de Janeiro, 1982); *Revista de Educação Física*. Órgão da Escola de Educação Física do Exército, 2 (1933), and M. Del Priore (org.) (1997). *História das mulheres no Brasil* (São Paulo).
85. M. Lenk, in an interview given to Ludmila Mourão, June, 1998.
86. Ibid.
87. However, her participation in sport deeply influenced the gradual change in women's attitudes toward sport. At present, in her frequent appearances on television, she has assumed a more feminist tone as she reflects upon the meaning of her own career for the emancipation of women.
88. M. Lenk, in an interview given to Ludmila Mourão, June 1998.
89. The veteran athlete describes all the difficulties an athlete had to overcome in Brazil in the

1930s, including the lack of decent swimming facilities. There were very few pools and those that existed were unheated. She trained for the Olympic Games in temperatures of 12°–15°C at Tietê Sailing Club, in São Paulo. There was an Olympic pool, but it was never heated. No one thought of heating the water in a swimming pool.

90. M. Lenk, in an interview given to Ludmila Mourão, June 1998.
91. Ibid.
91. Ibid.
93. Maria Lenk refers to General Elói Menezes, then the President of the National Sports Council.
94. M. Lenk, in an interview given to Ludmila Mourão, June 1998: 'I was criticized as a swimmer for the fact that I would never have children, because this very strenuous activity would destroy not only all my feminine traits but the physiological ones too.'
95. M. Lenk, in an interview given to Ludmila Mourão, June 1998.
96. Ibid.
97. Maria Lenk refers to the City of Amparo, in the interior of the State of São Paulo.
98. M. Lenk, in an interview given to Ludmila Mourão, June 1998.
99. Ibid.
100. *Natação* was published in 1942, in São Paulo, by Editora Melhoramentos.
101. M. Lenk, in an interview given to Ludmila Mourão, June 1998.
102. Ibid.
103. Ibid.

10

In Pursuit of Empowerment: *Sensei* Nellie Kleinsmidt, Race and Gender Challenges in South Africa

DENISE E.M. JONES

YIN AND YANG[1] OF THE GRANDMOTHER OF KARATE IN AFRICA

Petronella (Nellie) Kleinsmidt, is both affectionately and respectfully called *Sensei* Nellie or *Sensei*, meaning instructor, by her colleagues and students. *Sensei* Nellie is regarded as the 'Grandmother of karate in Africa' and at the age of fifty-nine is recognized as the most senior female *karate-ka* (a person practising karate) on the African continent.

As a woman of colour[2] in South Africa, Nellie Kleinsmidt's life and karate career have been significantly shaped by the apartheid legislation in the country. In February 1965, at the age of twenty-five, the eldest daughter of a boxer father and sister of a weightlifter brother, she joined the karate school of Hugh St John Thomson in the centre of Cape Town. In the same year, she had the distinction of receiving advanced training under two world class Japanese[3] karate masters, *Shihans*, who were visiting South Africa, namely *Sensei* Kasè and *Sensei* Shirai. *Sensei* Nellie practises the *Go-Ju Ryu* (hard-soft style) of karate. This is one of the four major and most popular systems in the world.

In 1973 Nellie Kleinsmidt joined Johan Roux, a white male, at his Goodwood *dojo* (training hall). In 1982 they were founder members of the Karate-Zen organizations in which they are still actively involved. Kleinsmidt received her first black belt (Shodan) in March 1977. She felt enormous pride at this achievement and claimed that it was the highlight of her career. The other black belts followed as she shifted from being a 'scholar' to a '*sensei* of karate'. In 1982 *Sensei* Nellie became a full time karate instructor with Karate-Zen. This marked the beginning of her initiative to take karate to the marginalized coloured and African communities with the result that today her name is synonymous with karate, especially in the coloured townships of the Western Cape. In 1992 with the unification of karate in South Africa, Nellie Kleinsmidt began to extend her involvement to refereeing. She has subsequently become a South African national referee and has earned the status of continental judge with the Union of African Karate Federation (UFAK). Recently, she was appointed to the Referee's Board of South Africa. She is the first and only woman of colour to have been appointed.

Sensei Nellie's other administrative responsibilities have included Treasurer of Karate-Zen International, Treasurer of the National Olympic and Sports Congress (NOSC) in the Western Province, Treasurer of the National Sports Council (NSC) in the Western Cape, Treasurer of the National Women's Karate Forum, Vice-Chairperson of Women's Forum for Karate Association of Western Province (KAWP). She has also played a major role in the establishment of both the National Sports Council (NSC) and the Women's Karate Forum in her province.

Nellie Kleinsmidt, who was a primary school teacher[4] at a convent school for twenty-four years, views karate as the *yang*[5] side of her life, while her piano playing and flower arranging comprise the *yin* side. It is this *yang* side of her life which has transported her on a proactive path towards her own personal empowerment and enabled her to create opportunities for others. Her own empowerment, her ability to empower others and her struggle to free the female body, in and through karate, needs to be understood within the context and nature of South African karate.

In karate the liberation of the body goes hand in hand with the freeing of the mind. Consequently, freedom in karate is as much a state of mind as it is a state of being. In order to attain this freedom, like other *karate-ka*, Kleinsmidt has had to engage in a lengthy process of acquiring and mastering the relevant knowledge, skills and techniques.

The proficiency of a *karate-ka* increases as one earns more black belts. It takes, on average, approximately thirty-two years of hard and consistent work to progress from a first Dan back belt (*Shodan*) to the eighth dan (*Hachidan*). Kleinsmidt, who began her karate career in 1965, would certainly have obtained a higher grading had it not been for the apartheid system in South Africa and the sports moratorium[6] on international sporting contacts introduced in the country at that time. In

April 1998 she was awarded her sixth Dan Black Belt (*Rokudan*). This is a remarkable achievement given her age and the constraints she has had to overcome. Such mastery is a form of personal power.

Empowerment in and through karate can have its origins at any of the following levels: as a *karate-ka* (practising and/or competing); as an instructor and coach; and at the level of officials as an administrator, manager, referee and judge. Not only is Nellie Kleinsmidt active in each of these areas, she has also received recognition for her achievements in them. She is one of only three women in Africa to have been awarded the sixth Dan Black Belt.

Individual empowerment makes it possible for Kleinsmidt to access other types of power both within karate and beyond karate. These include economic, political, psychological, social and financial power. Karate gives access to these through representing the *dojo*, the province and/or country; achieving health benefits which are inherent in exercise; by being part of the administration such as official, instructor, manager, referee and/or policy maker, especially when one's competition days are over. In addition, karate can lead to various job opportunities. *Sensei* Nellie's achievements in karate have given her access to all of these except the opportunity to represent her country. Consistent with apartheid policy, she was denied this right because of her colour.[7] By the time the democratization process had begun in South Africa in the early 1990s, she had shifted her focus away from competing to instruction and refereeing. She now coaches *karate-ka* at all levels, preparing them for tournaments and championships. She is a highly rated judge, referee, administrator and manager. Nellie Kleinsmidt has acquired and developed both leadership and organizational skills. Her involvement in various committees and councils bear testimony to this.

Among her various impressive achievements, Kleinsmidt was the co-founder of the Women's Karate Forum in her province. She says that the purpose of the forum is for various female instructors of different karate organizations to share their expertise and to remain involved and advance the sport further. There are also self defence sessions. She claims that 'the big thing is to ensure that the women and girls are given the opportunity to express themselves, to participate, and to develop their karate because of the problem we have with men pushing women out'.[8] This important forum has the task of providing an affirming environment for women and girls to experience the strengths of their own bodies, to express themselves and to acquire the skills and knowledge to compete and improve their grades. It also provides an opportunity 'to deal with other issues like rape and sexual harassment'.[9] Furthermore, *Sensei* Nellie plans to use the forum to increase the number of female coaches and administrators.

It will be helpful in the light of this volume to explore the ways in which *Sensei* Nellie Kleinsmidt has negotiated discriminatory practices and overcome race and gender-related struggles, including the struggle to free the female body, in pursuit of empowerment. The chapter therefore explores the constraints and frustrations she has experienced, as well as the many contributions she has made to women's karate in South Africa and her future ambitions.

APARTHEID – THE FIRST MAJOR STRUGGLE

The beginning of Nellie Kleinsmidt's karate career coincided with the early development of South African karate, which must be viewed against the backdrop of the emergence of the non–racial[10] sporting organizations; the sports moratorium imposed by South African Council on Sport (SACOS); and the international boycott[11] of South African sportsmen and women, as well as apartheid legislation[12] such as the Separate Amenities Act, Mixed-marriages Act, Immorality Act and Group Areas Act.[13]

In 1966 the Group Areas Act, which divided the country into areas of occupancy and residency according to race, was extended by the South African government.[14] Hugh St John Thomson was advised to get rid of the students of colour or the authorities would close his *dojo*. As a woman of colour this affected Kleinsmidt. Determined not to give up, she explains that she and other students of colour 'practised on Friday evenings and Sundays when nobody else was there and the doors were closed. We then had to find another venue and eventually moved to the homes of individuals.'[15]

The lack of adequate training facilities and regular coaching made the opportunities for grading problematic. Kleinsmidt received little formal instruction between 1966 and 1973. Soon after she met Johan. As she explained: 'I battled to get into another dojo because of my skin colour. One day I saw a car with a karate sticker and I approached the driver and asked him [Johan] whether he accepted coloureds.'[16] Joining Johan's Goodwood karate school in 1973 provided Kleinsmidt with a regular venue for training, but it again brought with it the oppressive realities of apartheid. The Group Areas Act restricted residency in the conservative Afrikaner suburb of Goodwood to whites only, and any interaction between people of colour and whites was forbidden.

The invasion of the karate school by government officials was a frequent occurrence. Johan Roux, Nellie Kleinsmidt and the karate students were under constant threat of being forcibly removed from the *dojo* and imprisoned. Together, Kleinsmidt and Roux organized defiance campaigns, resisting the pressures from government to close their *dojo* because of its non-racial policies. Kleinsmidt was on the security list and 'considered to be a danger to the government'.[17] Government security guards waited outside the *dojo* in case something illegal was being planned. 'It was upsetting and frustrating. The situation we were in ... and the fact that Johan could be arrested.'[18]

WE HAD A MORAL OBLIGATION AND SUPPORTED THE MORATORIUM

During the 1970s and 1980s *Sensei* Nellie's karate career coincided with the emergence of the non-racial sporting organizations – associations which had rejected the apartheid government's policies and refused to affiliate to white sports federations. The most noteworthy was SACOS. Its slogan was *No normal sport in an abnormal society*[19] and a moratorium was instituted which prohibited contact with international sports organizations. This not only restricted white sportspersons, but also negatively impeded the growth of blacks who were already marginalized and disadvantaged by the country's apartheid legislation. Karate-Zen did not affiliate to SACOS; however, Kleinsmidt says they felt a 'moral obligation to support the moratorium'.[20] She claims that this accounts for the lack of progress made by black *karate-kas*, instructors and administrators. In fact *Sensei* Nellie feels that 'this is why we ended up being so far behind the whites'.[21] Those who ignored it, ran the risk of being blacklisted.[22]

The moratorium lasted until the early 1990s when SACOS was rivalled by the NOSC which was considered to be more representative of the new alliances forming in the country at that time.[23] By then South Africa had been expelled from the Olympic Games, and banned from many international organizations. The NOSC later became known as the National Sports Council (NSC). These developments, which coincided with the democratic transformations in South Africa, gave rise to the unification processes of the government sports bodies and the non-racial sports organizations. This provided the springboard for *Sensei* Nellie to pursue other aspects of her karate career and to address inequalities which existed within South African karate.

GENDER DISCRIMINATION: THE OTHER STRUGGLE

Nellie Kleinsmidt has experienced a lifetime of prejudice and discrimination because of the colour of her skin. Her struggle for personal and social empowerment at the broader political level was against the apartheid government because it labelled and categorized her as a *coloured* woman. Freeing her body at that level involved the abolition of the race categories and all other apartheid legislation which impacted on her life choices and experiences. Initially this struggle and that of freeing her female body occurred simultaneously. Unfortunately, while Kleinsmidt could work towards the freeing of her body within the context of karate, she could not translate this into freedom in South African society itself. The race categories were binding and limited her access to resources. While struggling against gender discrimination, it was in karate that she could strive for personal empowerment. Accessing the various levels of karate involved claiming physical and symbolic space on the *dojo* floor as well as in the committee room.

The overlapping and ongoing struggles in Kleinsmidt's karate career have required 'fighting and challenging on two fronts'. Initially she says that 'the racial discrimination was a more frightening issue' because of legislation and the associated power which the government had over black people – but even during all this one was a female first and foremost, 'the men never let you forget it'.[24] This situation was, and is, exacerbated by the overwhelming number of male instructors perpetuating the notion that the martial arts are inherently male sports.

In the initial stages of the transformation and democratization of South African karate, racism was still evident. The rank and seniority of black *karate-ka* was not always acknowledged and respected. This was due to a number of reasons. Firstly, the power struggle between the apartheid sports structures and the non-racial sports bodies. For example, some white male instructors, ignoring *Sensei* Nellie's rank and seniority, were inclined to refer to her by her first name and not by the title she had earned, exemplifying the double discrimination of race and gender. Refusing to be intimidated she resolved to reciprocate similarly whenever the occasion arose. Another reason was the failure on the part of some white male instructors to acknowledge the grades obtained during the apartheid era by members of non-racial organizations such as Karate-Zen. '.... because as I told you, the moratorium of SACOS meant no international exposure since 1973'.[25] Karate-Zen has always predominantly served people from historically disadvantaged communities.

Now most of Nellie Kleinsmidt's energies are focused on ensuring that women also have access to the power available at decision-making levels because decisions made at the executive level impact on all areas of karate. It is here that advancement of women's karate can be undermined. To this end Kleinsmidt ensures that she is familiar with the details of all relevant policies and constitutions and that there is always a female representative on the National Karate Executive Committee.

'TREAT THE FEMALES AS *KARATE-KA*'

When Nellie Kleinsmidt first began her karate career, the site of the struggle was the body and the place was the *dojo* floor. Being a woman often meant 'one was excluded in classes'. The male *karate-kas* avoided working with the women and female *karate-kas* were overlooked and ignored.[26] There were even occasions when male *karate-kas* refused to train with the women. At that stage, karate classes comprised both men and women. According to Kleinsmidt the instructors treated the women differently from the men, and male *karate-kas* were sexist. The male instructors who were accused of pampering the women claimed that the women used to cry if they fell too hard.[27]

Nellie reported that the male instructors used to embarrass them and gave them easier alternatives to some exercises. Characteristically, she took the lead in this struggle. The male instructors were told to 'treat the females as *karate-ka*'[28] rather than as different to the males. She then turned her attention to the women. Her view was that if they were unable to cope with the demands of karate, then they should not be doing it. She believes that in order to be taken seriously, women should not be treated differently. She made it clear that 'bowing out was not acceptable'.[29]

Even though karate is a contact sport, women are no more prone to injuries than men, providing discipline and self control are exercised.

However, continual focus on physical differences between men and women has been used to question the abilities and capacity of females to cope with the rigours of karate.[30] In this way female *karate-kas* can be marginalized and continually excluded from developing and demonstrating their knowledge, skills and control.[31] Resistance to the creation of a *kumite* section (free fighting) for female *karate-kas* is a useful illustration. This struggle was only won in 1992, due to the tireless efforts of women like Nellie Kleinsmidt and Sanette Smit.[32] They used to argue that 'After all, the women are the ones who need to defend themselves. They cannot become fighters if we do not teach them to fight.'[33] Excluding female *karate-kas* from the *kumite* was based partly on misconceptions regarding the vulnerability of the female body including fears that the reproductive organs will be damaged.[34] However, these myths[35] have in many instances been used to omit women from the *kumite* section of karate, which until 1992 had been the exclusive right of males.

Women might have the physical skill but from time to time some male *karate-kas* have felt it necessary to demonstrate their physical strength by intentionally hurting a female *karate-kas* during a practice session. Nellie Kleinsmidt has experienced this herself. 'Sometimes when you practise with men they want to show you that they are better than you and they hurt you. So I asked to have permission to *stand my man* so to speak, to be able to hit wherever I want.'[36] It was *Sensei* Nellie's philosophy to 'give as good as I got ... I became quite tough in attitude towards those who would deliberately hurt me so as to discourage me.'[37] There is little support these days for the abuse of physical strength in karate to demonstrate superiority.

Sensei Nellie is aware that in reality, many people still do entertain the belief that karate is potentially dangerous for women and girls. Well-respected and qualified instructors like her have a crucial role to play in dispelling such notions, while simultaneously highlighting the self-defence and other empowering features of karate. Nellie Kleinsmidt and others have promoted the view that women and girls will only get injured if there is no control' and that 'self-discipline as an inherent quality of karate, must be reinforced in the *dojos*'.[38]

FIGURE 10.1

KARATE IS THE YANG SIDE OF *SENSEI* NELLIE'S LIFE

FIGURE 10.2

THE GRANDMOTHER OF KARATE IN AFRICA

IT IS NOT WHAT THE BODY 'IS' IN KARATE, BUT WHAT IT 'DOES'

The body in karate has a dual function. On the one hand it is a generator of *ki*, energy-power, necessary for the individual to defend him/herself. On the other hand, the body is also the target of that defence. All movements in the various *katas* (routines) have self defence techniques and strategies as the focal point.[39] Her thirty-four years in karate have taught *Sensei* Nellie that one does not free the body without freeing the mind. Her ability to generate *ki* is determined by the capacity of her body and mind to perform as one. She constantly reminds her students that continual and regular practice is the only way to achieve this. Freedom in karate is therefore not only a state of mind, but also a state of being, at which dedicated *karate-kas*, like Nellie Kleinsmidt aim.[40] Women are often judged by the way they look and not by their achievements, but in karate, the opportunity exists for the body to be evaluated differently. The uniforms which all *karate-kas* wear, downplays femininity[41] and the focus is on one's ability to perform.[42] The emphasis in karate is on what the body 'does' and not what it 'is'. *Sensei* Nellie's successes in karate are assessed by her ability to perform and not by her physical appearance.

Karate has contributed to the freeing of Nellie Kleinsmidt's body by providing her with the mental and physical skills to control her fears for personal safety. The self-defence techniques acquired in karate allow for the development of a sharp mind, an awareness of and sensitivity to danger, and the ability to deal with it, should the need arise. The freedom derived from this empowerment has given Kleinsmidt a greater sense of self-confidence and a positive body image and higher self-esteem. Of course it is not only women and girls who lack confidence and experience low body and self-esteem. However, given the emphasis on the ideal female body shape, together with less involvement than males in activity programmes during childhood, females need to 'get to know their bodies' in ways men and boys take for granted.[43] Karate is a means for achieving this individual empowerment.

Females have been known to express concern that in karate they might develop overly muscular bodies and lose their femininity by displaying aggressive and competitive characteristics. Currently, this is not a cause for concern, partly due to the image which Kleinsmidt represents. At the age of fifty-nine her strong and toned body is an inspiration to both young and old. Many older women are attracted to karate with a desire to 'grow old' like her. Kleinsmidt has demonstrated that female athletes can become strong without the development of huge muscles. Myths about the development of 'masculine qualities, muscular bodies' do impact on karate as a choice for females. Plans for addressing these are in the conceptual stages. *Sensei* Nellie is optimistic that they will be operational in the near future.

THE BARGAINING POWER OF QUALIFICATIONS

The status of male *karate-kas*, instructors and administrators is enhanced by an underlying principle of respect based on seniority and rank. This is essentially sustained by a common understanding and recognition of what the process of disciplining and training the body and mind in karate entails. The result is that qualifications and achievements are held in high esteem and valued. The assumption is that this earns all *karate-ka*, including women who have qualified as referees, judges, administrators, managers and coaches – respect, status, and power. Unfortunately, this is not so. The personal power which female *karate-kas* derive from their qualifications does not automatically translate into forms of bargaining power. As mentioned earlier, Nellie Kleinsmidt and other female *karate-kas*, have experienced disregard for rank and seniority from both men and women. Sanette Smit has also experienced this lack of respect. 'Even though some men will say *Sensei* to me, they are only saying the words because it is part of the etiquette of karate'.[44] There was even an incident when a female referee was told 'you are only allowed to referee junior males not seniors ... because the men would feel awkward if a woman controlled the fight'.[45] Kleinsmidt says that such sexist behaviour is unacceptable and even hurtful. It is expected that *karate-kas*, especially those who are highly ranked, respect and acknowledge the achievements of others. Disempowering women in this way serves to maintain the gender inequalities in karate and to restrict the participation of females at the student *karate-ka* level.

Rank and seniority in karate are acknowledged as being important, However, if women allow themselves to be intimidated by these at all levels of karate, then the status quo will remain. According to Kleinsmidt, seniority and rank govern behaviour on the *dojo* floor and when performing or refereeing at tournaments and competitions, but they have far less influence in other situations such as at committee meetings and where policy decisions are made. The respect remains but the authority of the individual diminishes at the administrative levels where seniority and rank play out differently. What some women are unable to do is separate the two spaces. They cannot transfer the power gained at the floor level into the committee room. *Sensei* Nellie is about to launch a new project in Karate-Zen aimed at empowering the women at committee level. This is an ambitious but necessary venture because she claims: 'Feelings of inferiority are not easily dispelled.'[46]

The legacy of apartheid is evident in the reluctance of black women to challenge authority. This is seemingly an interesting contradiction. Women of colour were prepared to undertake the broader struggle against institutionalized racism, but are experiencing difficulties in shaking off some of the effects of apartheid in more personal capacities. 'This is also true for men of colour';[47] they, however, often benefit from the marginalization of women, as this creates space for them in the higher valued positions in karate. Under such circumstances, the value of a visionary and influential leader who has the support of a credible organization is incalculable.

'WOMEN MUST WORK TOGETHER TO CHALLENGE SEXISM'

Sensei Nellie's struggle for empowerment has always taken place within the broader struggles against racism and sexism, which have sustained each other and become her frames of reference. She worked with marginalized youth during her twenty-four years of teaching in a convent school and had considered becoming a nun before karate became a way of life for her. She has a capacity for forgiveness, tolerance and compassion which has helped her to deal with her feelings of resentment and indignation at the racial discrimination she has experienced most of her life. She says: 'It is in the past. We have to move on. It is possible to put it behind me when the women work together.'[48] While acknowledging the help of sympathetic male *karate-kas* and administrators, especially those with status and seniority, Nellie Kleinsmidt is also critical of her female counterparts. She recognizes the need for a critical mass of women in karate and continually emphasizes the necessity for 'women to work together'.[49] She is aware that men will continue to control the future of women's karate unless women's voices are heard and supported by other women.

There is evidence to suggest that homophobia is threatening to undermine the progress made thus far in women's karate. Kleinsmidt has already made efforts to address the issue. 'They are focusing on lifestyles of some women instead of recognizing what they have done for women's karate. We should just say we are all women and get on with the job. In fact discriminating against people because of their life style is against the law in South Africa.'[50] She claims that at the very least women should support each other, especially those who are dealing with power struggles at decision-making levels.

Nellie Kleinsmidt has a reputation for leading by example and many women look to her for guidance. She believes that women of colour have potentially more power to challenge gender inequalities than their white counterparts. This is not surprising given the apartheid history of South African sports and the current focus on redressing racial imbalances in the country. However she is quick to recognize the work of others irrespective of race and politics, and has established an amiable working relationship with Sanette Smit. 'We at Karate-Zen support the work Sanette is doing. ...We have the same mission.'[51] In 1992 Nellie Kleinsmidt and Sanette Smit initiated a move to establish a Women's Karate Forum for the Western Cape, pooling their strengths and resources.

The establishment of the forum coincided with the initial stages in the unification of the various sports federations which had emerged as a consequence of apartheid. There were two main camps: Those organizations which had aligned themselves with the government sports structures, referred to as *establishment sports*. The other sports organizations were referred to as *non racial sports* and had been formed in resistance to the continual exclusion and marginalization of sportspeople of colour. Kleinsmidt like many other sportsmen and women of colour had aligned herself to this second camp, although the organizations were not racially exclusive.

The process of establishing the Women's Karate Forum became the site for yet another power struggle. Kleinsmidt found the women in the old government sports structures 'ambitious and resistant to change'.[52] These days much progress has been made in women's karate and the women are working together. 'We are straight about things, and accommodate each other.'[53] This battle for power in decision-making areas was consistent with developments in other realms of South African society. Kleinsmidt felt distrust towards those who had been advantaged by the apartheid system and now appeared reluctant to change. She claims that the discipline, self control and tolerance she acquired through her many years of practising karate, helped her during this difficult time.

Nellie Kleinsmidt and Sanette Smit are an example to women who were aware that although they had begun their karate careers in different political camps, they were now prepared to put their differences aside. Their partnership was cemented by a determination to make South African karate less male dominated. In the current climate of change the forum has proved to be a significant site for the empowerment of women in and through karate.

THE ADMINISTRATIVE STRUGGLE

One of *Sensei* Nellie's goals has been to become 'the first *coloured* woman in Africa to receive international referee status'.[54] Another is 'to pave the way for women ... to open the road for them ... to do this for the future female referees in South Africa'.[55] Nellie Kleinsmidt recently achieved her first goal and this personal victory has opened up new possibilities for all women in karate. Today she holds the positions of South African National Referee and Continental Judge for Africa, and is a member of the Referee's Board of South Africa. These are outstanding achievements.

In 1992 when South Africa was re-entering the world of international karate, a team of potential referees was selected to attend an international seminar for referees in Spain. No women were included in the team. Kleinsmidt had set her sights on this tour and had been preparing herself by attending, at her own expense, all local referee courses in karate. Realising that she qualified on rank and seniority yet had been excluded, she quietly but firmly stated: 'I am not standing for this.'[56] With the help of highly-ranked men in her organization, Kleinsmidt challenged the decision and it was overturned. When she arrived in Spain in 1992 to do the referee's exam, she was surprised to discover that she was the only woman among approximately 150 men from countries around the world. On enquiring about this, she was informed that decisions come from the countries themselves. It is her conviction that women throughout the world are being discouraged from obtaining referee status. She says that 'The attitude and body language [of the men] is the same as before'[57] even though discrimination based on sex is unconstitutional.[58] Kleinsmidt believes that constitutions can be useful tools in the gender equity struggle. She has set her sights on ensuring that the karate constitution of South Africa fulfils this function. The constitution has recently been amended to reflect a more gender sensitive and equitable approach to karate. The next struggle lies in ensuring that this translates into practice.

EVERY VICTORY HAS REQUIRED A STRUGGLE

Every victory gained by female *karate-kas* in accessing the different realms of South African karate has involved some struggle. Yet, despite the many overlapping and ongoing race and gender-related struggles which Nellie Kleinsmidt has experienced, she has always found opportunities in karate for freeing her female body. As the first and only women of colour to have been appointed to the Referee's Board of South Africa and as the only women of colour in Africa to have been awarded the sixth Dan Black Belt, *Sensei* Nellie is an inspiration to all women. Successful athletes like her are empowered at all levels in karate, as well as in their personal and public capacities. It is what they choose to do with this power and the extent to which they have struggled in pursuit of their goals that gives them the status of inspirational icon. Will she retire? *Sensei* Nellie Kleinsmidt says: 'I want to study karate until I am 95 years old. Karate becomes a way of life after a while. If I miss out on one day's training, it is like something is missing from my life.'[59]

NOTES

1. A. Henderson, *Qualitative Approach to Recreation, Parks, and Leisure Research* (Pennsylvania, 1991), p.5 describes the yin-yang as a 'symbol of polar energies in harmony with one another'. It is referred to as opposites and is broadly related to any dualism such as 'feminine–masculine'or 'subjective–objective, question–answer, space–time'. The one concept is interdependent on the other. Counterforce and major force interact to create a balance. The concept of yin-yang unites all opposites.
2. In this chapter the term *women of colour* has been used in the same way as the term *black*. It is an inclusive term for all persons not classified as *white* during the apartheid era in South Africa. The words *Indian, Coloured, African and White* will be used when it is necessary to make a distinction. Nellie Kleinsmidt is a *coloured* person, meaning someone of mixed descent. In this chapter, when necessary she identifies herself as *coloured*. Otherwise she uses the more inclusive term and refers to herself as *black* or as a *woman of colour*.
3. The harsh realities of apartheid were extended to visitors to South Africa. As people of colour, the Japanese karate masters were categorized as *honorary* guests. Although they outranked *karate-kas* in South Africa, they were not permitted to act in any official capacity at karate competitions and tournaments during their visit.
4. Compulsory segregation in the South African Education system was institutionalized by various Education Acts between the 1950s and 1970s. They contributed to enormous disparities between the various race groups in South Africa regarding the provision of facilities, training opportunities, salaries and employment opportunities. The result was what it is still

referred to as 'gutter' education, meaning inferior education. Nellie taught within that 'gutter' education system for 24 years. Refer to D.E.M. Jones, 'The Emergence of a Non-Alternative Physical Education for females in South Africa', *Sport as Symbol, Symbols in Sport*, ISHPES Studies Series, IV (1996) for further illustrations of the impact of the Education Acts on the lives of South African women.

5. E. Farkaf and J. Corcoran, *Dictionary of Martial Arts* (New York, 1983) point out that in the context of karate, the Japanese, refer to the *yin* as all the 'passive' or 'negative' elements. While the *yang* is considered to be the 'active' and 'positive'. The balance between the two is believed to be the centre of existence. In the *Go-Ju* style of karate which Nellie Kleinsmidt practises, the hard–explosive movements are interdependent and united with the soft-flowing movements, thereby creating a balanced performance. Kleinsmidt has translated to her own life, the hard–soft and passive–active dualisms inherent in her karate style. In this way she unifies and balances the significant aspects of her life.

6. In the early 1980s SACOS campaigned for the international isolation of *both* the government sports bodies as well as non-racial sports, until such time as South Africa was democratic. This meant a self-imposed international moratorium on sports tours to and from South Africa.

7. M.L. Krotee, 'Apartheid and Sport: South Africa revisited' *Sociology of Sport Journal*, V (1988), 125, points out that the announcement in 1956 by Dr T.E. Donges, the Minister of Interior, was the first official government statement on mixed sport. At the time the derogatory term 'non-white' was used instead of black. He stated clearly that although the government had no control over sport, whites and blacks should organize sport separately, that no interracial competition should take place within South Africa, and the mixing of races should be avoided. He went on to say that the government would withhold support from any black sports bodies seeking international recognition and would withhold the granting of passports to blacks guilty of such 'subversive intentions'.

8. N. Kleinsmidt, interview, 16 March 1999.

9. N. Kleinsmidt, interview, 7 August 1996.

10. The non-racial sports bodies emerged as a form of resistance against the continual marginalization and discrimination in South Africa of all sports people of colour. The most well known of these non-racial structures was South African Council on Sport (SACOS) which evolved in 1973 from South African Non-racial Sports Organization (SASPO). In 1970 the latter continued the work of the exiled South African Non-Racial Olympic Committee (SAN-ROC) which, in turn, had replaced the South African Sports Association (SASA) in 1963. The establishment of SASA in 1958 marked the beginning of the non-racial sports movement and paved the way for the non-racial principle. The non-racial principle means a non-reference to race or skin colour. Non-racial organizations did not exclude whites. Refer to S. Ramsamy, *Apartheid: The Real Hurdle* (International Defence and Aid Fund for Southern Africa, London, 1982); C. Roberts, *SACOS 1973–88: 15 Years of Sports Resistance* (1988) and SACOS, *Sacossport Festival: A Commemorative Volume* (Cape Town, 1988).

11. SAN-ROC was successful in getting South Africa expelled from the 1968 Mexico Olympics. In 1970 South Africa was expelled from the Olympic Movement. In 1977, as a result of the Gleneagles Agreement, South Africa was expelled from the Commonwealth Games. In the same year The General Assembly of the United Nations also adopted a declaration to isolate South Africa from the international sporting arenas. South Africa was only readmitted to the Olympic Movement in 1992 and participated in the Commonwealth Games in 1994. Refer to J. Brickhill, *Race against Race: South Africa's Multinational Sport Fraud* (London, 1976) and P. Hain, 'The Politics of Sport and Apartheid', in J. Hargreaves, *Sport, Culture and Ideology* (London, 1982).

12. Refer to R. Archer and A. Bouillon, *Sport in South African History in The South African Game: Sport and Racism* (London, 1982) and G. Jarvie, Sport, Power and Dependency in Southern Africa (Chapter 8) in E. Dunning and C. Rojek, *Sport and Leisure in the Civilising Process* (Toronto, 1992) for an account of the way in which apartheid legislation affected sport in South Africa. Initially there was no specific sport legislation which forbade mixed sport. The various apartheid laws made it virtually impossible for black and white sportsmen and women to compete or practise against each other. They were not permitted to mix socially without special permission.

13. It is important to appreciate the indignity of the apartheid system and the misery it bestowed on people of colour. For example, in 1978 Nellie Kleinsmidt illegally set up home with Johan Roux. He was to become her chief karate instructor and life-long companion. In doing so, she defied the Separate Amenities, Mixed-marriages, Immorality and Group Areas Acts.
14. Nellie Kleinsmidt's family was one of many to be affected by the process of forced removals instigated by the Group Areas Act.
15. N. Kleinsmidt, interview, 26 August 1996.
16. N. Kleinsmidt, interview, 30 March 1999.
17. N. Kleinsmidt, interview, 3 September 1996.
18. Ibid.
19. The view was that one could not have the system of apartheid on the statute book and simultaneously expect that sport be non-racial. In other words it was not possible to have *normal sport in an abnormal society*. Refer to S. Ramsamy, *Apartheid: The Real Hurdle* (London, 1982); C. Roberts, *SACOS 1973–1988: 15 Years of Sports Resistance* (1988).
20. N. Kleinsmidt, interview, 26 August 1996.
21. Ibid.
22. The struggle for non-racial sport in South Africa was viewed as being part of the broader political struggle, therefore representing South Africa was viewed as expressing support for white domination, apartheid and racial discrimination in the country. Players and administrators who did so were not upholding the non-racial principle in sport and would be considered to be guilty of practising double standards. Refer to C. Roberts, *SACOS 1973–88: 15 Years of Sports Resistance* (1988) and SACOS, *Sacossport Festival: A Commemorative Volume* (Cape Town, 1988).
23. Refer to The Sports Movement of the Future: The Playground, Emergence and Policy of the National Olympic and Sports Congress (NOSC) (c.1992).
24. N. Kleinsmidt, interview, 26 August 1996.
25. N. Kleinsmidt, Interview, 9 March 1999.
26. N. Kleinsmidt, Interview, 7 July 1996.
27. Ibid.
28. N. Kleinsmidt, interview, 26 August 1996.
29. Ibid.
30. M. Boutiller and L. SanGiovanni, *The Sporting Woman* (Illinois, 1983), p.103 offer two ways of viewing men's resistance to the apparent intrusion of women in what men consider to be their sports: Firstly, it will 'masculinize' the women , 'stripping them of their unique female qualities'. Alternatively, the resistance could be attributed to men's deeper fear of the 'femininization' of men's sports.
31. L. Bryson, 'Sport and the Maintenance of Masculine Hegemony', *Women's Studies International Forum*, X (1987), 349 is of the opinion that continuous negative feedback about the sporting ability of females is an exclusionary practice adopted by men and results in women themselves believing and accepting that men are more capable than they are.
32. Sanette Smit, a white female, is a long time campaigner for gender equality in South African karate. She and Nellie Kleinsmidt co-founded the Women's Karate Forum in the Western Cape. Like Kleinsmidt, Smit is also a holder of the 6th Dan Black Belt. She owns and manages a karate school and a self-defence workshop business.
33. S. Smit, interview, 28 July 1996.
34. According to S. Scraton, 'Images of Femininity and the Teaching of Girls' Physical Education', in J. Evans, *Physical Education, Sport and Schooling* (London, 1986), p.87, the 'need for protection of the female body relates specifically to the damage that might be caused to the reproductive ability'. This is a commonly used explanation for discouraging women from participating in contact sports.
35. C. Wells, *Women, Sport, and Performance: A Physiological Perspective* (Illinois, 1991) p.266 points out that men are more 'in danger of injuries to their reproductive organs than women because their organs are exposed and relatively unsupported'.
36 . N. Kleinsmidt, interview, 9 March 1999.
37. Ibid.
38. N. Kleinsmidt, interview, 30 March 1999.

39. J. Roux, 'KATA' *Boxing World* (May 1995), 38 co-founder of Karate-Zen with Nellie Kleinsmidt, offers an insightful view of what a *kata* is. He says: 'The art and the beauty of karate is expressed through the *kata*, which can be described as an experience – a type of meditation where the rest of the world is cut off, a state of total absorption'.

40. E. Cave, 'Zen and the Martial Arts Warrior', *Boxing World* (October 1995), 37 offers an enlightening view regarding the link between the 'state of being' in karate and freeing of the body.

41. R. Connell, *Gender and Power: Society, the Person and Sexual Politics* (Stanford, 1987), p.187 discusses the relationship between 'emphasized femininity' and the dominance of heterosexual men. J. Hargreaves, *Sporting Females: Critical Issues in the History and Sociology of Women's Sports* (London, 1994), p.172 refers to the way in which 'heterosexual femininity is the "emphasized" image of femininity in sports'.

42. Hargreaves, *Sporting Females*, p.159 refers to labelling of sports such as gymnastics, aerobics and synchronized swimming as 'feminine-appropriate' because they make visible the 'form and sexuality of the female body'. They affirm and 'emphasize' a popular image of femininity. This is also true of clothes worn by female track athletes. Karate does not provide this opportunity because of the uniform worn by all *karate-kas*. Hence my comment that it 'downplays' femininity and shifts the focus to performance.

43. P. Edwards, *Self-esteem, Sport and Physical Activity* (Ontario, 1993), p.19 points out that physical appearance and body image play a significant role in developing a young woman's sense of worth. She comments further that many females are not able to enjoy the power, self-knowledge and body awareness which results from 'unencumbered exploration' of physical activities in sport.

44. S. Smit, interview, 28 July 1996.
45. Ibid.
46. N. Kleinsmidt, interview, 30 March 1999.
47. Ibid.
48. N. Kleinsmidt, interview, 9 March 1999.
49. Ibid.
50. Ibid.
51. N. Kleinsmidt, interview, 26 July 1996.
52. N. Kleinsmidt, interview, 3 September 1996.
53. Ibid.
54. N. Kleinsmidt, interview, 30 March 1999.
55. Ibid.
56. N. Kleinsmidt, interview, 16 March 1999.
57. Ibid.
58. Nellie Kleinsmidt reported that she was eventually joined by a Canadian, Norma Foster, who was the only internationally qualified female judge at that seminar.
59. *South Newspaper* (February 1992).

Prospects for the New Millennium: Women, Emancipation and the Body

J.A. MANGAN

In *Daughters of Time: Women in the Western Tradition*, Mary Kinnear claims, hardly with originality, that to understand and explain the present, it is helpful to explore the past and she sets out to do just that. *Freeing the Female Body: Inspirational Icons* has the same end – but a different starting point. Unlike Kinnear, it has not sought to discover the broad social, economic, cultural and political foundations for the status of women in modern times[1] but has sought to discover more precisely how some women in modern times, through a re-evaluation, reconstruction and rehabilitation of their *bodies* and women's bodies in general, have influenced and determined, directly and indirectly and to a lesser or greater extent, the status of many modern women of the modern 'global village'. What the chosen women of *Freeing the Female Body* have all demonstrated and to a degree determined through their determination, is that, despite historical belief, assertion and demand, women are not to be 'relegated' primarily or predominantly to reproduction,[2] nor to subscription to the uterine tradition that defines women's bodies according to their reproductive potential.[3]

The rediscovery and re-evaluation of women of the past, should be energetically tackled, as Kinnear demands with unassailable good sense,[4] and *Freeing the Female Body* has taken up the challenge. It has dealt directly with influential, exceptional and extraordinary women, but it has been concerned just as much with their influence on unexceptional and ordinary women.

Kinnear remarks, perhaps with too much optimism, that social history now uses interdisciplinary perspectives, has witnessed a shift in historical focus from public event to private experience and from a consideration of separate events to long term patterns, and that women's history in the wake of these developments is now essentially a study of the relations between the sexes: economic, political, social and sexual,[5] and is therefore very much concerned with the related status of women.[6] Furthermore, she argues, that as a consequence of these developments, among other things, women increasingly render themselves, and are rendered by the commentator, more visible in history. All this, implicitly if not always explicitly, is certainly true of *Freeing the Female Body*.

Kinnear has further sensible observations to make, not least that women, like men, have never comprised a single monolithic and homogeneous group.[7] Thus women should always be compared, not only with men, but with other women. In *Freeing the Female Body* comparison reveals that, whilst its women were often very different in their individual lives, circumstances and experiences, interestingly they mostly appear to have had certain things in common. These iconic inspirationalists were mostly middle class and mostly possessed the invaluable asset of strong family support. In a real sense often their family – parent or parents and on occasion siblings – made them. There is scope here for further and deeper inquiry into sport, women and emancipation.

In the final analysis, however, in contradiction of Kinnear's claim that the study of women in Western civilization is a study fraught with ambiguity, there has been perhaps too little ambiguity in the approaches of the contributors to *Freeing the Female Body*. The 'Woolfian Woman',[8] that 'very queer composite being' as described by Virginia Woolf – in a passage that appears to be a regression to the language of the Aesthetic Movement in which words obscure the things described and the writer appears more interested in what is said rather than what is seen[9] – has little relevance to the individual studies of the characters of this book.

But one thing is certainly true: if Woolf used words as embroidered altarcloths, the women of *Freeing the Female Body* used actions as plain tablecloths. The contributors have made it abundantly clear that their women lived through performance not fantasy; lived not in fiction but in fact; were slaves only to their own convictions and ambitions.

What, however, of future studies beyond *Freeing the Female Body* on the theme of sport, women and emancipation? Malia B. Formes remarks that historians of women are 'fundamentally concerned with power relations, primarily those between the sexes'.[10] These historians now view gender, she maintains, as the main means leading to an understanding of all historical social relations.[11] If nothing else this assertion certainly brings gender to centre stage. Formes, for her part, is more narrowly concerned with the relationship between gender and imperialism. In her discussion of this relationship she makes thoughtful points about approaches to feminist history that merit thoughtful attention here. She argues first and foremost that the complexity of colonial relationships has been inadequately considered.[12]

The same may be said of the complexity of the relationships between modern sport, female emancipation and power. One danger in any discussion of this triadic relationship is to fall prey to the weaknesses of a rigid dichotomous approach[13] involving, for example, women as victims and men as oppressors. Clearly simplistic and too pervasive stereotyping of this kind is to be avoided in the interests of reality.[14] Another danger is the tendency for men to recede into the background and become '*monolithic* supporting players'[15] to women-centred studies. The dangers of such simplifications are obvious: naïve male stereotyping, reduction of complex realities and inter-relationships and the failure, calculated or careless, to fully assess womens' actual power, covert and overt, in male and female relationships whatever the *ostensible* formal, institutional, cultural and political frameworks.

Apropos the complexity of male and female relationships, it could be helpful to consider carefully the shrewd observations of Olwen Hufton. She warns of the dangers of reading 'ego documents' – autobiographies, memoirs, letters, diaries, lawsuits and such like – which have been exploited extensively to reveal the constraints of culture on the lives of individual women. These dangers include the difficulty of transferring 'this approach on to a broader canvas without straying into the realms of conjecture' with the associated risks to which many social historians, she claims, have fallen prey, of over-speculation, the creation of the 'generic' woman and man and corresponding versions of womanhood and manhood, at the expense of the experiences of real people. Then there is the further risk that in some cases the search for polarised gender attitudes and the associated belief that individuals were made not born, have tended to discount biological differences between women and men and led to an insistence on gender solely as a cultural construct. Finally, there is the risk that 'in attempting to understand ... cultural rules, insufficient attention has been given to the material constraints which determined the lives of the vast majority of people' – women *and* men. In recorded history most of both sexes have been oppressed.

In support of her caveats, Hufton casts a cool eye over the influential work of Alice Clark, who wrote in the early twentieth century about the seventeenth-century Englishwoman. Clark, claims Hufton, compared

> the sturdy farmer's and artisan's wife whom she discovered through considerable archival work with the useless woman of later literature, conspicuous for her lack of meaningful activity, and she laid the responsibility for this metamorphosis at the feet of encroaching capitalism. She also idealized the working home of the seventeenth century, where she assumed husband and wife toiled as partners, and compared this situation with the later harshly severed world of work and home. Clark was in many ways writing the predicament of many of her contemporaries into the script. More dangerously, to advance her thesis of the serial decline from healthy activity to idleness and or exploitation (depending on class) she had recourse to prescriptive literature and assumed that the ideology was strong enough to produce the reality.[16]

Reality, in reality, has a tendency to be less than amenable to such simplification.

It is as well also to be aware of the fact that freedom is not an inexorable linear progression. At the present time when young women drink alcohol increasingly free from social inhibition or restriction – a fact that is causing medical concern due to the associated rise in female alcoholism – the comment of the French diarist Henri Misson on women in London in the eighteenth century to the effect that they held their own with men in drinking bouts is both interesting and possibly illuminating.[17] Equally dangerous for the historian is polemical commitment to the villain versus heroine model of explanation, with women triumphing over the circumstances contrived by men to maintain a status quo of superiority and inferiority. Such polarization, to use a meaningful expression of Formes, 'masks the complexity and fluidity of social experience'[18] and, it may be added, the realities of human interaction.

It is as well then not to be bound by simplistic dichotomies. Apart from the caveats issued above, of course, there is the matter of women's relationships with women, which are not all accord, harmony, equality and support, not to mention cultural variations in patterns of masculinity and personal flexibility in the face of formal convention that is a feature of individuals in all cultures to a greater or lesser degree. In her critique of Helen Callaway's *Gender, Culture and Empire: European Women in Colonial Nigeria* and Callaway's espousal of the villain versus heroine view of history in a colonial setting, Formes draws attention to the studies of Antoinette Barton and Barbara Ramsack, which reveal that period feminist concern with social reform in imperial India was, at one and the same time, 'a feminist expression of cross-racial sisterhood *and* (emphasis added) an imperialist demonstration of British superiority'.[19] In other words, there is a clear need to recognise, as Formes remarks, quoting Barton, 'that feminism(s) are and always will be as much quests for power as they are battles for rights'[20] and power over other women as much as power over men!

Formes, in her own dispassionate quest for accuracy, is critical of Barton in her recourse to an unsophisticated complicity versus resistance metaphor which Formes quotes:

> British feminists ... were trapped within an imperial discourse they did not create and perhaps which they could not escape. That they collaborated in the ideological work of empire implicates them and the legacy of Western feminism we have inherited from them.[21]

Formes observes rightly that Barton's feminists 'turn into one dimensional villains by her use of the word 'collaborated' and at the same time by using the verb 'trapped' in imperial discourse not of their making, she [Barton] portrays these women as victims – thus they become both villains and victims'.[22]

This comment by Formes has the virtue that subtlety of perspective is at least approached. A greater subtlety might have been arrived at if she suggested quite specifically that these women were not necessarily nor invariably 'trapped' in 'imperial discourse', nor simply 'collaborated with' in imperial ideology, but certainly in some cases were willing, knowing and sincere subscribers to it! To deny them the capacity for independence of thought and action demeans them. The truth is that Barton and Formes both fail to allow 'for the more ambiguous interjections ... that characterize actual social experience'.[23] In other words, simplistic dichotomous contrasts between power and powerlessness, the trapped and the free, collaborators and resistors, can leave much to be desired by way of an adequate analysis of the complexity of reality.

It is, therefore, surely time to adopt a Foucaultian analytical approach and acknowledge the diversity of interaction between men and women, reject inflexible categorization and 'conceive of power ... as a force which is dispensed throughout society and may be exercised, although unequally, by people of all statuses'.[24] The reality of relationships is complex, convoluted and changing. Conflicting and changing identities characterize all human relationships in their interactions and it is precisely for this reason that people, including academics, invent rigid categories and boundaries to simplify their lives and in the case of some academics, to present in their writing, polemical theories rather than the perplexing actualities.[25]

There are others who press for subtlety of analysis in women's history. As Marjorie Theobald has illustrated 'the woman at the piano' was an icon of nineteenth-century education – 'a woman of accomplishments in music, art, modern languages, literature and the natural sciences'.[26] And as Theobald remarks, 'this form of education has been overlooked or dismissed by both mainstream and feminist historiography'.[27] Theobald requests a reconsideration of that sacred cow of feminist theory, the man and science, women and culture dichotomy. Theobald seeks to rein back the strident feminism that peddles 'a persistent orthodoxy in the historiography of women's education' which still enshrines 'a watershed thesis' which claims that 'most educational provision for middle-class women before the 1860s was meretricious and misguided'.[28] In this view 'girls are deemed to have been educated by default or not at all'.[29] She shows this was far from being the case.

It is important that subtlety is sought and achieved, otherwise the danger of distortion is real. 'A common complaint of the old, battling feminists of the 1960s and 1970s was that marriage enslaved women, turning them into succubi; meek, passive ghosts of the vivid characters they might otherwise have become',[30] comments Jane Shilling and suggests that this polemical generalisation requires challenging in the interests of the recognition of its somewhat fanciful and certainly extreme nature. Shilling challenges it herself. She remarks: '... unpalatable as it is to admit, for every frustrated female bitterly serving out her domestic sentence there are plenty of others: intelligent, thoughtful women, as well-qualified as their go-getting husbands, who have found an unambiguous satisfaction in the confining roles of housekeeper and nursery maid'.[31] She further remarks perceptively: 'passivity is not to be confused with *powerlessness* (emphasis added): ... the weapons of the martyr and victim are just as potent in their way as those of more visible transgressors'.[32] To this comment should be added that the assumption that self-chosen or even conventionally required domesticity *necessarily* carries the negative connotation of 'victim' and 'martyr', adds insult to injury.

In this context surely it is time *inter alia* for subtle, careful and balanced explanations of women and power in the family and home and their not infrequent dominance in this setting – covert and overt. The nineteenth century and later 'Master in his own Home', depicted so frequently in feminist literature, is overdue for more precise scrutiny. It has been noted shrewdly that:

> Since monogamous marriage was at the heart of the western European social system, something most men and women experienced, it was also the key to western humour. The contrast between ideal marriage and real life afforded scope for irony, parody, satire, and had a resonance in the minds of all who heard or read or viewed it. It purported to disclose what was (emphasis added), rather than what should be.[33]

A glimmer of the reality of human existence to offset images of overwhelming oppression, submission and victimization peeps through the Kinnear text when, in her Postscript, she admits that within the family 'women have been able to exercise authority'[34] and when she accepts a little later that while the monarch exacted unquestioning obedience from the subject, within the family the lady lived by exactly the same formula of deference and submission to her lord, yet these prescriptions of womanly obedience were not universally followed.[35] Precisely.

Nicole Ann Dombrowski in *Women and War in the Twentieth Century*[36] bravely admits to a Pauline conversion from the espousal of the simplistic to an espousal of the sophisticated in her attempt to comprehend matters of war and peace and male and female involvement. With maturity, she abandoned an initial subscription to naïve dichotomy. At first, she considered military women collectively 'a misguided lot for placing their bodies at the behest of the state',[37] but subsequently acknowledged a diversity of motivation and recognizing that 'they are no more of a piece than are civilian women'.[38] Likewise she was initially of the opinion that 'military men were little more than a gang of grown-up boys with deadly toys'[39] but advanced to greater maturity when she realized that many seek ways to constrain and limit violence and find nuclear weapons repulsive! Remarkable perspicacity!

Dombrowski has commonsense comments to make on her conversion to complexity, namely that contemporary social science is too often ill-equipped to comprehend the sophisticated nature and role of symbol, myth, metaphor and rhetoric and falls back too readily for reassurance on abstract models, and it might be added, glib generalization, despite the fact that to ensure that subtlety is not overlooked, it is necessary to remain open-minded rather than impose a prefabricated formula on diverse, complex and paradoxical material.[40] In short, it is helpful to observe behaviour in its variety and analyse it in these terms. Thus she challenges, among other things, a naïve feminist dichotomy of women as life givers[41] and men as life takers, and writes of women who seek their own honour, glory and status in Spartan motherhood or, less frequently, front-line battle and she ruminates usefully on men as conscripted, compassionate and just warriors. On 'Spartan Motherhood', incidentally, Genevieve Lloyd has commented correctly that:

> Surrendering sons to significant deaths becomes a higher mode of giving birth. Socially constructed motherhood, no less than socially constructed masculinity, is at the service of the ideal of citizenship ...[42]

She then adds, oddly and incorrectly, that in giving up their sons to society's wars 'women are supposed to allow themselves to become real men'. In fact, of course, they are self-evidently declaring themselves 'real women'.[43]

Kinnear concludes that 'as more historians unravel more of women's experience in the past, we shall discover in greater measure what our cultural resources are'.[44] *Freeing the Female Body* has certainly attempted to contribute to that endeavour, but perhaps it also points the way in its certainty of conviction to the necessity of more qualificatory analyses in the future along the lines indicated earlier. What is required, of course, is acute sensitivity to reality, a proper acknowledgement of the variety of human need, choice and action, a recognition of human powers of overt *and* covert adjustment, adaptation and reconstruction and a subscription to the accurate recording of the variety of female (and male) response to circumstance.

In the 1980s, after a considerable period of distrust regarding the body, Elizabeth Grosz has noted that feminism became increasingly interested in the role the body plays in the social construction of sexual identity.[45] The female body was to be placed, she argued, 'within a network of socio-historical relations instead of being tied to a fixed essence'. Whether her sense of timing is sound, her request certainly is. The concern in *Freeing the Female Body* is, of course, with female inspirationalists who justifiably and properly challenged and overcame convention, custom and prejudice in various social networks. However, in the past, while to an extent (but to what extent?) men determined the identity of women, dictated what was desirable and undesirable, demanded what was acceptable and denied what was unacceptable, in that concrete world of men and women as distinct from the abstract world of political publication, women also made their own demands of other women – *and* of men. These realities receive far less attention from feminism but they are crucial to a subtle analysis of the power relations between women and men and women and women.

To return to an earlier point, briefly, and to return to Grosz:

> Women's bodies are not only used as fixed elements to dictate 'efficient' or adaptive roles for women in culture, they are also used to reduce women to a pseudo-evolutionary function in the reproduction of the species, which supposedly acts as a compensation for women's social powerlessness. It supposedly assures women of a socially recognised and validated function – maternity. Women's biologies, it seems, are distinguished from men's insofar as only women's reproductive organs and activities characterise them (doctors dealing with so-called 'women's problem', for example, are gynecologists or obstetricians). The allocation of only a reproductive specificity, at the expense of other functions and capacities, once again confirms the presumption that somehow (because of particular biological, physiological and endocrinological transformations that they involuntarily undergo), women are closer to biology, corporeality and nature than men.[47]

Grosz calls this manifestation of a demand for a 'fixed essence', masculine 'essentialism'. She issues a caveat which can be added usefully to those set out earlier, on the creation of gender identity in culture – local, regional and global, namely that: 'if feminists are to escape "a reverse essentialism", in which a determinate form of femininity is universalized, providing a female "version of humanity" then concepts, which explain both the commonness women share cross-culturally, and their cultural and individual specificities are necessary for women's positive self definition'. Put simply, this jargonized but sensible warning

means that cultural pluralism in *gender* (women and men) issues is both
to be accurately observed and carefully recorded. What is required in
studies of women (and men) and their bodies is a recognition of what is
universal and what is particular at a number of levels, for the simple
reason that concepts of the body are considerably culturally determined
and individually interpreted and there are many cultures and many
layers within cultures, and numerous individual women and men. *Any*
'essentialism' is to be avoided – including a feminist 'essentialism' of
masculinity.

Thus studies going beyond a concern with the challenge modern
women have rightly issued to past cultural traditions of the female body
as essentially reproductive as exemplified by the women in *Freeing the
Female Body*, need now to be supplemented by a sophisticated
Berlinesque pluralism dealing with cultural differences and similarities
and involving inquiry into challenge – but also accommodation,
adaptation and compliance and embracing cultural, class and racial
'specificities',[48] both historical and contemporary. Perhaps even more to
the point, more studies similar to *Shaping the Superman*[49] but concerned
with the *political* role of the female body, past and present, are called for.
One obvious need, for example, is a long-overdue exploration of Chinese
women, their physical exertions, courage and stamina in the famous
Communist Long March and the impact on their subsequent image and
the later political resonances for the Peoples' Republic of China.[50]

In the present era of astounding transformation for women, at least
for middle-class women in modern technological societies, more than
ever has biology to be regarded in conjunction with evolving social,
psychological, cultural and *political* continuities *and* changes and the
human capacity at an individual level to reconstruct, redefine,
reinterpret and reorder cultural norms.

If cultures give meaning to individuals,[51] as *Freeing the Female Body*
clearly demonstrates, individuals give meaning to cultures as it also
clearly demonstrates. If a political, cultural and psychological pluralism
born of democracy and its inherent respect for the individual and
individuality gains ground in at least some new places, and indeed some
old places, in the twenty-first century, so a feminist, sometimes
exaggerated, frequently negative and simplistically dichotomous
preoccupation with men and women and associated concepts of
patriarchy, exploitation, victimization and oppression associated with
the female body (and mind and emotions) will be, and should be

augmented by more complete and sophisticated studies of the female body (and mind and emotions) in society and more realistic inquiries as to the nature of women's power and powerlessness, through and beyond their bodies, within and across cultures – past and present. One possibility has been aired by Grosz in her somewhat heavy-handed way with language:

> Feminists have increasingly recognised that there is no monolithic category, 'the body'. There are only particular kinds of bodies. Where one (the youthful, white, middle-class male body) functions as a representative of all bodies, its domination must be overcome through a defiant affirmation of the autonomy of other kinds of bodies ... It may turn out that a subversion is accomplished by the proliferation of a number of different types of ideals or representatives for the range and type of bodies.[52]

It could be argued with greater validity, of course, that in Westernized contemporary cultures youthful female bodies of various colours dominate representationally and there should be defiant affirmation of the autonomy of other kinds of bodies – both female and male! The essential point is, however, that subtle inquiries into power through the body are certainly overdue.

Elizabeth Gross raises the theme of pluralism in the Conclusion to *Feminist Challenges*[53] with a demand of academia. She reasonably and perspicaciously requests of feminist themes 'a proliferation of voices ... a plurality of perspectives and interests ... new kinds of questions and different kinds of answers'.[54] No one form would then be privileged as the truth, the correct interpretation, the right method with the result that knowledge, method and interpretation would be used according to their appropriateness to specific settings, strategies and effects.[55] Rather oddly, however, for a feminist in laudable pursuit of pluralistic interpretations in the interest of full comprehension, she appears to allow freedom to write on feminist issues in this subtle way only to women![56] 'Feminist theory seeks a new *discursive* space, a space where women can write, read and think *as women*.' Her recommendations self-evidently make considerable sense for *all* who reflect, among other things, on the important issue of emancipation and the body. If history is 'too important to leave to patriarchal methodologies',[57] equally it is too important to leave to such 'feminist methodologies'. Gross also argues, as has been argued in this Epilogue, for a rationality not divided from experience, nor from particularity nor specificity. In short, she requests a rationality 'not beyond or above experience, but based on it'[58] the central request of this Epilogue.

Finally, as for the analysis of the body, so too for the analysis of power, a pluralistic approach, *among other things*[59] would involve an extensive and extended inquiry into the means by which *women's* power through the body is achieved – in the realm of sexuality, for example, how this is enhanced, how this is maintained and how this is retained. It will then become increasingly clear that tendencies to simplistic dichotomous analyses of power and powerlessness in the past and the present, increasingly will be found wanting.

NOTES

1. Mary Kinnear, *Daughters of Time: Women in the Western Tradition* (London, 1998) pp.1–2.
2. Ibid., p.2.
3. Jill Julius Matthews, 'Building the Body Beautiful', *Australian Feminist Studies*, 5 (1987), 17.
4. Olwen Hufton is unquestionably correct: 'The history of women as a field of enquiry emerged in the late 1960s as an offshoot of the women's movement and the demands for civil rights. The conspicuous absence of women from the historical record, unless they belonged to a few small categories – queens, consorts, famous mistresses of yet more famous men, courtesans or saints – meant that history was unbalanced. Their absence was also seen in the 1960s as pointing either to a grave sin of omission or to a flagrant suppression of the evidence, and hence to a distortion of the record by the historians of former times. Whether the omission was unconscious or deliberate, the result was the same: women, with a few notable exceptions, had been denied a history.' Olwen Hufton, *The Prospect Before Her: A History of Women in Western Europe, Vol. 1, 1500–1800* (London, 1995), pp.1–2.
5. Kinnear, *Daughters of Time*, p.3.
6. Ibid.
7. Ibid., p.5.
8. Ibid.
9. See Jan Marsh, *Edward Thomas: A Poet for his Country* (London, 1978), p.43.
10. Malia B. Formes, 'Beyond Complicity Versus Resistance: Recent Work on Gender and European Imperialism', *Journal of Social History*, 28 (1995), 629–41. This is a thoughtful and intelligent paper that deserves the closest attention.
11. Ibid.
12. Ibid.
13. Such an approach might be termed the 'Friedan Fallacy' after Betty Friedan in *The Feminist Mystique* who 'seems to believe that men have done the more important things, the mental things; women have been relegated in the past to the less important human tasks involving bodily functions ...' (See Elizabeth V. Spelman, 'Woman as Body: Ancient and Contemporary Views', *Feminist Studies*, 8 (1982), 122. It is interesting to note that the more feminist history is written, the more this simplified view has to be adapted. Spelman does inject a note of sophistication into the discussion of women's bodies and emancipation, when she points out that 'various versions of women's liberation may themselves rest on the very same assumptions that informed the deprecation and degradation of women, and *other* groups (emphasis added) in the past. Those assumptions are that we must distinguish between soul and body, and that the physical part of our existence is to be devalued in comparison to the mental.'
14. A good example of this is Edward Shorter, *A History of Women's Bodies* (London, 1983). Shorter confidently presents a moving, but hugely generalized, argument that women's

(implicitly all classes, all cultures, all periods) historical subordination was essentially the outcome of continued pregnancies producing disease, exhaustion and often premature death, caused essentially by brutal insensitive men insisting on sexual access. He offers selected examples from recent recorded history! There appear to be no loving, caring, considerate men or marital relationships in his history – only a pervasive omnipresent 'male unconcern for the welfare of women'! (p.4). It is not only, on his own admission, his title which is lurid, but his argument. Not without an important element of truth, it rides roughshod over individual response, will and personality and over cultural variety, and social differences in concepts of, and attitudes towards, masculinity and femininity at different moments in time, in different places. Feminity, argues Shorter, with what can be called a staggeringly confident insight across aeons of time and an incredible number of individuals of different races, classes and cultures 'was basically a negative concept for most women ... a burden with which God had saddled them since Eve was expelled from the garden' until about 1930! Of those women, east, west, north and south, who knew nothing of Eve's expulsion, we learn nothing, but implicitly they seem drawn into a series of remarkably confident generalizations. In this context, it is interesting to note the ethnocentric confidence of the title, *A History of Women's Bodies*, while his statistics, as his examples, cover parts of Europe and America mostly in the nineteenth and twentieth centuries!

15. Ibid., p.630.
16. Hufton, p.23.
17. See Rose Tremain, review of Maureen Waller, *1700: Scenes from London Life* (London, 2000), *Daily Telegraph*, Arts and Books, 12 February, A3.
18. Formes, 'Beyond Complicity...', p.632.
19. Ibid., pp.632–3.
20. Ibid.
21. Ibid.
22. Ibid.
23. Ibid., p.634.
24. Ibid.,.p.635.
25. Ibid., p.637.
26. Ibid.
27. Marjorie R. Theobald, 'The Sin of Laura: the Meaning of Culture in the Education of Nineteenth Century Women', *Journal of the Canadian Historical Association*, 1 (1990), 351.
28. Ibid., 264. Equally inadequate in its sweeping generalization is the statement by Jill Julius Matthews, 'It was during the inter-war years that the modern feminine body became popular. Desire became flesh' ('Building the Body Beautiful', 19). Only then? How modern is modern?
29. Ibid.
30. Susan Shilling in a review of Joanna Trollope, *Marrying the Mistress* (London, 2000), *Sunday Telegraph*, 30 January 2000, Reviews, p.15.
31. Ibid.
32. Ibid.
33. Kinnear, *Daughters of Time*, p.45.
34. Ibid., p.187.
35. Ibid., p.188.
36. Nicole Ann Dombrowski (ed.), *Women and War in the Twentieth Century* (London, 1999).
37. Ibid., p.xi.
38. Ibid.
39. Ibid.
40. Ibid.
41. Ibid., p.xiii.
42. Genevieve Lloyd, 'Selfhood, war and masculinity' in Carole Pateman and Elizabeth Gross (eds.), *Feminist Challenges* (London, 1986), p.63.
43. Ibid., p.63
44. Kinnear, *Daughters of Time* ..., p.189.
45. Elizabeth Grosz, 'Notes towards a corporeal feminism', *Australian Feminist Studies*, 5 (1987), 21.

46. Ibid.
47. Ibid., p.6.
48. Ibid., p.2.
49. See J.A. Mangan (ed.), *Shaping the Superman: Fascist Body as Political Icon – Aryan Fascism* (London, 1999).
50. See Fan Hong, *Footbinding, Feminism and Freedom: The Liberation of Women's Bodies in Modern China* (London, 1998) for one approach to Chinese politics and the female body, but not specifically the Long March.
51. Grosz, 'Notes', p.8.
52. Ibid., p.9.
53. Pateman and Gross (eds.), *Feminist Challenges*, p.204.
54. Ibid.
55. Ibid.
56. Ibid.
57. Judith Allen, 'Evidence and Silence: Feminism and the Limits of History' in Pateman and Gross (eds.), *Feminist Challenges*, p.181.
58. Gross, 'Confusion' in Pateman and Gross, *Feminist Challenges*, p.203.
59. Elizabeth Grosz has a long list of suggestions but the language is so strained and convoluted at many points they verge on incomprehensibility. See Grosz, 'Notes' 10–13 especially.

Select Bibliography

Prologue: Freeing Bodies: Heroines in History
FAN HONG

J. Hargreaves, *Sporting Females: Critical Issues in the History and Sociology of Women's Sports* (London, 1994).

J.A. Mangan and Roberta J. Park (eds.), *From 'Fair Sex' to Feminism: Sport and the Socialisation of Women in the Industrial and Post-Industrial Eras* (London, 1987).

J.A. Mangan and J. Walvin (eds.), *Manliness and Morality: Middle-Class Masculinity in Britain and America, 1850–1940* (Manchester, 1987).

M. Ann Hall, *Feminism and Sporting Bodies: Essays on Theory and Practice* (Champaign, IL, 1996).

P.A. Vertinsky, *The Eternally Wounded Woman: Women, Doctors and Exercise in the Nineteenth Century* (Manchester, 1990)

'All the freedom of the Boy':
Elizabeth Cady Stanton, Nineteenth-Century Architect of Women's Rights
ROBERTA J. PARK

L.V. Banner, *Elizabeth Cady Stanton: A Radical for Woman's Rights* (Boston, 1980).

E. Griffith, *In Her Own Right: The Life of Elizabeth Cady Stanton* (New York, 1984).

I.H. Harper, 'Elizabeth Cady Stanton', *American Review of Reviews*, 26 (1902).

R.J. Park, '"Embodied Selves": The Rise and Development of Concern for Physical Education, Active Games, and Recreation for Amerian Women, 1776-1865', *Journal of Sport History*, 5 (1978).

E.C. Stanton, *Eighty Years and More: Reminiscences, 1815–1897* (New York, 1898).

E.C. Stanton, S.B. Anthony and M.J. Gade (eds.), *Woman Suffrage* (New York, 1881–[1922]).

T. Stanton and H.S. Blatch, *Elizabeth Cady Stanton* (New York, 1969).

E.C. Stanton, 'The Other Side of the Woman Question', *North American Review*, 128 (1879) 432–439.

'Sunflower' [Elizabeth Cady Stanton], 'Man Superior to Woman', *The Lily* April (1850).

A Martyr for Modernity Qui Jin –Feminist, Warrior and Revolutionary
FAN HONG and J.A. MANGAN

Fan Hong, *Footbinding, Feminism and Freedom: The Liberation of Women's Bodies in Modern China* (London, 1997).

Guo Yanli, *Qiu Jin nianpu* (A Chronicle of Qiu Jin's Life) (Jinan, 1983).

Qiu Zhongzhang, 'Liu liu si cheng', *Dongnan ribao – Wuyue chuenqiu* (South-East Daily – Zhejiang's Spring and Autumn) (1934).

Zhonghua shuju (ed.), *Qiu Jin Ji* (Shanghai, 1960).

Qiu Canzhi, *Qiu Jin gemingzhuan* (Biography of Qiu Jin) (Taibei, 1984).

Qiu Canzhi (ed.), *Qiu Jin nuxia yiji* (Selected Works of Qiu Jin) (Shanghai, 1929).

M.B. Rankin, 'The Emergence of Women at the End of the Ch'ing: The Case of Ch'iu Chin', M. Wolf and R. Witke (eds.), *Women in Chinese Society* (Stanford, 1975).

The Chinese People's Political Consultative Conference (ed.), *Xinhai gemin huiyi lu* (Collections of the 1911 Revolution) (Shanghai, 1961–64).

Yao Tinhua, 'Datong xuetang kao' (Datong Normal College Textual Research), *Zhejiang tiyu shiliao* (The Historical Materials of Zhejiang Sports History), 1 (1984).

J.D. Spence, *The Gate of Heavenly Peace* (London, 1981).

A Militant Madonna:
Charlotte Perkins Gilman – Feminism and Physical Culture
PATRICIA VERTINSKY

I. Diamond and L. Quinby (eds.), *Feminism and Foucault. Reflections on Resistance* (Boston, 1988).

B. Johnson, *The Feminist Difference. Literature, Psychoanalysis, Race and Gender* (Cambridge, 1998).

C.P. Gilman, *The Living of Charlotte Perkins Gilman: An Autobiography* (Winsconsin, 1935).

M.A. Hill, *Charlotte Perkins Gilman: The Making of a Radical Feminist, 1860–1896* (Philadelphia, PA, 1980).

A.J. Lane, 'The Fictional World of Charlotte Perkins Gilman', *The CPG Reader* (1980).

S.L. Post, 'His and Hers: Mental Breakdown as Depicted by Evelyn Waugh and Charlotte Perkins Gilman', *Literature and Medicine* (1990).

G. Scharnhorst, *Charlotte Perkins Gilman: A Bibliography* (New Jersey, 1985).

C. Smith-Rosenberg, *Disorderly Conduct: Visions of Gender in Victorian America* (New York, 1985).

P. Vertinsky, *The Eternally Wounded Woman: Doctors, Women and Exercise in the Late Nineteenth Century* (Manchester, 1990).

A Lifetime of Campaigning:
Ettie Rout, Emancipationist Beyond the Pale
JANE TOLERTON

E. Hornibrook, *The Morality of Birth Control* (London, 1925).

E. Hornibrook, *Safe Marriage: a Return to Sanity* (London, 1922).

E. Hornibrook, *Sex and Exercise: a Study of the Sex Function in Women and its Relation to Exercise* (London, 1925).

E. Hornibrook, *Two Years in Paris* (London, 1923).

F.A. Hornibrook, *Without Reserve* (London, 1935).

J. Tolerton, *Ettie: A Life of Ettie Rout* (Auckland, 1992).

Breaking Bounds: Alice Profé, Radical and Emancipationist
GERTRUD PFISTER

C. Eckelmann, *Ärztin in der Weimarer Zeit und im Nationalsozialismus. Eine Untersuchung über den Bund Deutscher Ärztinnen* (Wermelskirchen, 1992).

G. Pfister (ed.), *Frau und Sport. Frühe Texte* (Frankfurt, 1980).

G. Pfister and H. Langenfeld, 'Die Leibesübungen für das weibliche Geschlecht – ein Mittel zur Emanzipation der Frau?', in H.

Ueberhorst (ed.), *Geschichte der Leibesübungen*. Bd. 3/1 (Berlin, 1980).

G. Pfister and H. Langenfeld, 'Vom Frauenturnen zum modernen Sport – Die Entwicklung der Leibesübungen der Frauen und Mädchen seit dem Ersten Weltkrieg', in H. Ueberhorst (ed.), *Geschichte der Leibesübungen*, Bd. 3/2 (Berlin, 1982).

G. Pfister, 'Der Internationale Frauensportverband und die Olympischen Frauenspiele', *Jahrbuch des Sportmuseums* (Berlin, 1999).

G. Pfister, 'The Medical Discourse on Female Physical Culture in Germany in the 19th and Early 20th Centuries', *Journal of Sport History*, 17 (1990).

A. Schaser and H. Lange in: H. Huisbergen (ed.), *Stadtbild und Frauenleben. Berlin im Spiegel von 16 Frauenporträts.* (Berlin, 1997).

B. Ziegeler, *Weibliche Ärzte und Krankenkassen: Anfänge ärztlicher Berufstätigkeit von Frauen in Berlin 1893–1935* (Weinheim, 1993).

At the Heart of a New Profession:
Margaret Stansfeld, a Radical English Educationalist
RICHARD SMART

Bedford Physical Training College, *Margaret Stansfeld* (Bedford, 1953).

S. Fletcher, *Women First: The Female Tradition in English Physical Education, 1880–1980* (London, 1984).

J. Hargreaves, *Sporting Females: Critical Issues in the History and Sociology of Women's Sports* (London, 1994).

J. May, *Madame Bergman-Osterberg: Pioneer of Physical Education and Games for Girls and Women* (London, 1969).

R. Smart, *On Others' Shoulders: An Illustrated History of the Polhill and Lansdowne Colleges, now De Montfort University Bedford* (Bedford, 1994).

M. Squire, 'Teaching a Way of Life', in *Nine Pioneers in Physical Education* (London, 1964).

K.J. Street, 'Female Culture in Physical Education Colleges' (unpublished Ph.D. thesis, De Montfort University, 1999).

J. Tey, *Miss Pym Disposes* (London, 1957).

Alexandrine Gibb: In 'No Man's Land of Sport'
M.A. HALL

A.Gibb, 'Canada at the Olympics', *MacLean's Magazine*, 1 October 1928.

R. Hotchkiss, '"The Matchless Six" Canadian Women at the Olympics, 1928', *The Beaver*, 73 (1993).

B. Kidd, *The Struggle for Canadian Sport* (Toronto, 1996).

A. Lytle, 'Girls Shouldn't Do It', *Chatelaine*, May 1933.

P. Olafson, *Sport, Physical Education and the Ideal Girl in Selected Ontario Denominational Schools, 1870–1930* (Master's thesis, University of Windsor, 1990).

G. Pallett, *Women's Athletics* (London, 1955)

N.R. Raine, 'Girls invade track and diamond', *MacLean's Magazine*, 15 August 1925.

K. Rex, *No Daughter of Mine: The Women and History of the Canadian Women's Press Club 1904–1971* (Toronto, 1995).

F.A.M. Webster, *Athletics of Today for Women: History, Development and Training* (London, 1930).

Ignoring Taboos: Maria Lenk, Latin American Inspirationalist
SEBASTIÃO VOTRE and LUDMILLA MOURÃO

F. Azevedo, *Da Educação Física*, Vol.1 (Rio de Janeiro,1920).

F. Costa, Jurandir, *Ordem Médica e Norma Familia*, 3rd edn (Rio de Janeiro, 1983)

M. Del, Priori (Org), *História Das Mulheres No Brasil* (São Paulo, 1997).

N. Floresta, *Opúsculo Humanitário,.* 2nd edn (São Paulo, 1853).

G. Freyre, *Sobrados E Mucambos.* (Rio de Janeiro, 1961).

M. Lenk, *Braçadas & Abraços*, 2nd edn (São Paulo, 1986).

T.L. Madel, *As Instituições Médicas No Brasil,* Instituição E Estratégia De Hegemonia. 3rd edn (Rio De Janeiro, 1986).

I.P. Marinho (S.D.). *História Da Educação Física No Brasil* (São Paulo).

A. Peixoto, *A Educação Da Mulher* (São Paulo,1936).

D.B. Sant'anna, De. (Org.) *Políticas Do Corpo* (São Paulo, 1995).

H. Spencer, *Da Educação Moral, Intelectual E Physica* (Lisbon, 1887).

In Pursuit of Empowerment:
Sensei Nellie Kleinsmidt, Race and Gender Challenges in
South Africa
DENISE E.M JONES

T. Gilpin, *Match Makers: A Case for South African Sport* (Cape Town, 1999).

J. Hargreaves, 'Women's Sport, Development and Cultural Diversity: The South African Experience', *Women's Studies International Forum*, 20, 2 (1997).

D. Black and J. Nauright, *Rugby and the South African Nation* (Manchester, 1998).

C. Roberts, *Challenges Facing South African Sport* (Township Publishing Co-operative, 1990).

C. Roberts, 'Black Women, Recreation and Organised Sport', *Agenda*, 17 (1993).

Epilogue:
Prospects for the New Millennium – Women,
Emancipation and the Body
J.A. MANGAN

N.A. Dombrowski (ed.), *Women and War in the Twentieth Century* (London, 1999).

M. Kinnear, *Daughters of Time: Women in the Western Tradition* (London, 1998).

M.B. Formes, 'Beyond Complicity Verus Resistance: Recent Work on Gender and European Imperialism', *Journal of Social History*, 28, 3 (1995).

E. Grotz, 'Notes towards a corporeal feminism', *Australian Feminist Studies*, 5 (1987).

O. Hufton, *The Prospect Before Her: A History of Women in Western Europe, Vol.1 1500–1800* (London, 1995).

Notes on Contributors

Fan Hong is a senior lecturer in the School of Physical Education, Sport and Leisure at De Montfort University in England. She was an editor of the *Journal of Sports History and Culture* published by the Sports Ministry in Beijing in the 1980s. Her main research interests are in the areas of body, gender and sport, with particular reference to China. Her latest book is entitled *Footbinding, Feminism and Freedom: the Liberation of Women's Bodies in Modern China.* She is a member of the Editorial Board of *The International Journal of the History of Sport* and the *International Encyclopaedia of Women and Sport* and a member of the Gender, Equality and Sport Commission of the Fédération Internationale d'Education Physique.

Gigliola Gori has a doctorate in social science and teaches the History of Physical Education and Sport in the Faculty of Motor Sciences at the University of Urbino, Italy. She studied initially at the National Dance Academy of Rome and later at the University of Urbino. She has written a number of papers, essays and books on early Italian sport, Futurism, Fascism and the 'fair sex'. She is a member of the International Society for the History of Physical Education and Sport (ISHPES), and serves on the editorial board of the *European Sports History Review* and *Acta Kinesiologiae Universitatis Tartuensis.* She is also a founder member of the European Committee for Sport History (CESH).

M. Ann Hall is a Professor Emeritus at the University of Alberta in Canada and a Visiting Research Fellow at De Montfort University in England where she occasionally lectures. She has written extensively on the topic of women in sport and has given presentations at dozens of conferences internationally. Her most recent books are *Honoring the Legacy: Fifty Years of the International Association of Physical Education and Sport for Girls and Women* (with Gertrud Pfister, Smith College, 1999) and *Feminism and Sporting Bodies: Essays on Theory and Practice* (Human Kinetics, 1996). She is at present completing a new book called *The Girl and the Game: A Century of Women's Sport in Canada* to be published by Broadview Press. She also serves on the editorial board of several academic journals, and is co-editor of the 'Sport and Culture' book series published by the University of Minnesota Press.

Denise E.M. Jones is a part-time lecturer in the Department of Human Movement Studies at the University of the Western Cape, South Africa, and consultant/researcher on South African Sport and Recreation for Recreactive, South Africa.

J.A. Mangan is Director of the International Research Centre for Sport, Socialisation and Society at the University of Strathclyde, Glasgow, and author and editor of many books. He is founder and General Editor of the Cass series Sport in the Global Society and founding and executive academic editor of the Cass journals *The International Journal of the History of Sport, Culture, Sport, Society, Soccer and Society* and *The European Sports History Review*. His internationally acclaimed *Athleticism in the Victorian and Edwardian Public School* and *The Games Ethic and Imperialism* have recently been reprinted by Frank Cass.

Ludmila Mourão teaches Physical Education at Universidade Gama Filho, Rio de Janeiro, Brasil. She has a Ph.D on Gender and Sport, with *Social Representation of Brazilian Woman in Physical Sporting Activity*.

Roberta J. Park, Professor Emeritus, Department of Integrative Biology, University of California, currently teaches in the American Studies Program. A member of the faculty since 1959, she served as the Chair of the former Department of Human Biodynamics from 1982 to 1992. Professor Park has been President of the American Academy of Kinesiology and Physical Education, a Vice-President of the International Society for the History of Physical Education and Sport, and has served on the editorial boards of numerous journals. Among her several honours, she has been the American College of Sports Medicine's D.B. Dill Lecturer, the Catholic University of Leaven's Michael Oysten M.D. Lecturer, and Alliance Scholar of the American Alliance for Health, Physical Education, Recreation, and Dance. In 1999, she was named Crocker Lecturer at the International Olympic Centre, University of Western Ontario.

Gertrud Pfister studied Latin, physical education, history and sociology. Since 1981 she has been Professor of Sports History at the

Free University in Berlin; she is President of the International Society for the History of Physical Education and Sport, Vice-President of the German Gymnastic Federation and convenor of the Scientific Committee of the International Association for Physical Education and Sport for Girls and Women. She has published several books and more than 200 articles. Her main area of research is gender and sport. She loves all kinds of sporting activities, especially skiing, tennis and jogging.

Richard Smart LTCL, MA, MEd, FRSA is Head of History at De Montfort University Bedford. He read History at Oxford and taught in a wide variety of schools, from Junior to Grammar, before arriving in Bedford in 1970 as history lecturer at the 'other' of the two training colleges in the town, whose origins lay in the training of teachers in Froebel's kindergarten system. The discovery of boxes of archive materials there dating from the 1880s led to his research interest in the development of kindergarten methods within the English and Welsh educational systems. When in 1976 the old kindergarten college became part of Bedford College of Higher Education, together with the Bedford College of Physical Education, he became interested in this too, and not least in the remarkable career of Margaret Stansfeld. In 1994 he wrote a joint history of both colleges, which now form De Montfort University Bedford.

Jane Tolerton is the author of *Ettie: A Life of Ettie Rout*, published by Penguin in 1992 which won a New Zealand Book Award and PEN Best First Book award. She is also the author of the bestselling oral history *Convent Girls*, and *Sixties Chicks: hit the nineties* and co-author of *In The Shadow of War*, an oral history of New Zealand soldiers in World War One. She lives in Wellington, New Zealand, where she is a freelance writer.

Patricia Vertinsky is Professor and Head of the Department of Educational Studies at the University of British Columbia. She is Past-President of the North American Sport History Association (NASSH), Board member of ISHPES and an International Fellow of the American Academy of Kinesiology and Physical Education. Dr Vertinsky is a social and cultural historian of health, physical activity and sport with a particular focus on representations of the body. Her many publications include *The Eternally Wounded Woman: Doctors, Women and Exercise in the Late Nineteenth Century*, and her research has focused on a multifaceted study of the female body in exercise and sports, the marking of race and gender on the body and, most recently, disability, normalcy and the body.

Sebastião Votre teaches Semiotics and Sport in the Post-Graduate Program of Physical Education at Universidade Gama Filho. He has published extensively on Discourse Analysis and Sport, and on Gender and Sport. He organized *Social Representation of Woman in Sporting Activity* in 1998.

Index

abolition (of slavery), 7–8, 11–12
abortion, 86, 187
Abrahams, Harold, 154
Alcott, Bronson, 15
Aldred, Guy, 86
Allen, Janet, 155
Amateur Athletic Union of Canada (AAU of C), 152–3, 155–7, 161, 163–4
amateurism, 158
Amendola, Eva Kuhn, 181
American Equal Rights Association, 19
American, Journal of Education, 17
American Review of Reviews, 23
Anstey Physical Training College, 126, 130, 141, 144
Anstey, Rhoda, 126, 144
Anthony, Susan B., 8, 15, 18–20, 22–3
apartheid, 219–23, 230–1
archery, 37, 190
Areno, W., 198–200
Association of German Women Physicians, 104
athletics, 105–6, 151–3, 155–6, 159, 160–1, 174, 190, 199–20
Atlantic Monthly, 19
Augusta School, 102, 105, 112–13
Azevedo, T., 199–200

Banner, Lois, 7, 10
Barnard, Henry, 17
Barr, James, 86
Barton, Antoinette, 241
baseball, 155, 199
basketball, 150–2, 155, 158–9, 190, 199, 201
Basuk, Ellen L., 64
Bath Street Board School, 120–2, 124, 127
Beale, Dorothea, 139
Beard, George, 61
Bedford High School, 125, 136
Bedford Physical Training College, 126–44; Old Students' Association, 140
Bedford County Council, 143
Beecher, Catharine, 56–7
Beinhorn, Elli, 98
Bell, Marilyn, 168
Bellamy, Edward, 67–8
Bennett, Arnold, 87
Bergman-Osterberg, Madame (Martina), 122, 124, 136, 141, 143–5

Bickerton, Alexander, 91, 95
Birkbeck College, 122
birth control, 1, 8, 82–7, 92, 94, 96, 186–7
birth rate, 186, 192
Bjorksten, Elli, 137
Blackwell, Elizabeth, 15–16
Blaikie, William, 67
Blatch, Nora Stanton, 23
Bloomer, Amelia, 17
body, the, 1–5, 8, 15, 19, 28–9, 37, 57–8, 83, 88, 98, 190–1, 197, 199, 202, 204–5, 220–1, 224–6, 228, 237, 144–8
Bordo, Susan, 65
Boxer Rebellion, 32–3
boxing, 208
Braçadas e Abraços, 202, 211
Brazil, 196–212; National Plan, 210; National School of Physical Education, 203, 209–11; National Sports Council, 201, 208–9
Brazilian Communist Party, 197
Bresciani, Cesarini, 181
British Empire Exhibition (1924), 90
British Empire Games (1934), 160, 163
Brownell, Susan, 4
Bueno, Maria Ester, 196
Buss, Frances Mary, 139

Cady, Daniel, 8
Cady, Eleazer, 9
Cady, Margaret Livingston, 8
callisthenics, 56, 59, 124
Callaway, Helen, 241
Canada, 149–69
Canadian Amateur Basketball Association, 151
Canadian Ladies Athletic Club, 154–5
Canadian Olympic Committee, 156, 160
Carpenter, Edward, 86
Catholic Church, 179, 184, 190–1, 210
Central Committee for Traditional and Youth Games (Germany), 103, 108; Congress of (1912), 110
Central Council for Physical Recreation, 130, 144
Central Council for Recreative Physical Training, 130
Chadwick, Edwin, 123
Chadwick, Florence, 168
Chariots of Fire, 154

Chelsea Physical Training College, 130, 141, 144
Cheltenham Ladies' College, 127
Cheng Fan, 38
Cheng Tianhua, 39
China, 4, 27–49; People's Republic of, 246; The Long March, 246
Chinese Women's Journal (Zhongguo nubao), 42
Christchurch Exhibition, 90
Cixi, Empress of China, 32
Clark, Alice, 240
Clark, Ann, 163
co-education, 7, 10, 18, 21
Colonial Office Conference (1930), 90
Colson, Phyllis, 130,144
Coluna Prestes, 197
Colwill, Freda, 136,138–40
Combe, Andrew, 16
Comitato Olimpico Nazionale Italiano (CONI), 184
Committee for Women's Physical Fitness (Germany), 103
communism, 185–6
Conference on the Physical Education of German Women (1925), 103
Conference on Women's Gymnastics and Sport (1929), 104
Constitutional Movement (One Hundred Days Reform), 31–3, 40
Coo, Lillian 'Jimmy', 157
Cook, Myrtle, 157
Coubertin, Pierre de, 199
Coutinho, Piedade, 201, 205–6
Cranz, Christl, 98
cricket, 125, 138–9, 150
Criminal Law Amendment Bill (1920), 82
croquet, 124
Cruz, Marina, 202, 205–6
Culture of the Abdomen, 87–8
cycling, 22, 98, 133, 207

Daily Herald, 92
Dame Alice Owen School, 125–6
dance, 88–90, 94, 123, 131, 136–8, 143–4
Dartford Physical Training College, 125–6, 130, 141, 143
Datong Normal College, 42–3
Daughters of Time: Women in Western Tradition, 237
Davies, Emily, 139, 141
Davis, Kathy, 1
Davis, Paulina Wright, 14
DeFranz, A., 199
DeGruchy, John, 156
Demsey, Lotta, 169

Deutsche Turnerschaft (German Gymnastics Association), 104, 112
Dial, The, 15
Dibble, Harry, 151
diet, 28, 91–2, 96
divorce, 7, 18, 96
Dombrowski, Nicole Ann, 243–4
domesticity, 8, 57, 60, 173, 185, 242–3
Donati, Ines, 183
Donne Fascisti, 189
Dostoevsky, F.M., 66
Double, The, 66
Douglass, Frederick, 11
dress, 7–8, 12, 16–17, 59, 73, 75–6, 98, 108, 111, 135–7, 145, 150, 196, 204–5, 207, 210, 228
drill, 121–2
Duncan, Isadora, 89, 136
Dunnell, Milt, 168–9
Du Pu, 30

Eaton, Daniel, 12
Edinburgh, Duke of, 168
Edmonton, Grads, 152
Edmonton Journal, 157
Eighty Years and More: Reminiscences, 1815–1897, 9
elementary schools, 120, 127–8
Elizabeth, Princess, 168
Elliott-Lynn, Sophie, 154
Ellis, Havelock, 85
emancipation of women, 3–5,13, 29, 34, 36, 41–3, 73, 98, 178–9, 181, 192, 196, 202, 212, 238–9, 247
Emerson, Ralph Waldo, 15
Eternally Wounded Woman: Women, Doctors and Exercise in the Nineteenth Century, The, 3
Ethiopia, 180, 188
eugenics, 91, 133–4, 179, 190, 192, 210
Evening Telegram, 152
Exercises for Women, 92
Ezagui, J., 198

Family Limitation, 86
family support, 9–12, 30, 56–7, 73, 100, 173–4, 202–4, 238
Fan Hong, 4
Fasci di Combattimento, 179–81
Fasci Femminili, 181
Fascism, 173–4, 176, 178–93
Federation of Labour (New Zealand), 77
Fédération Sportive Féminine Internationale (FSFI), 93, 105, 153
Federazione Italiana d'Atletica Femminile, 184
femininity, 48, 60, 110, 159, 174, 185, 190, 192, 199, 202, 228, 245

feminism, 1–4, 7, 28–9, 41–3, 48, 55–6, 58,
    68–9, 75, 77, 120, 145, 159, 180, 182, 185,
    208, 241–2, 244–7
Feminism and Sex-Extinction, 133
*Feminism and Sporting Bodies: Essays on
    Theory and Practice*, 4
fencing, 37, 190
Ferguson, Elmer, 168
Festival of Youth (1937), 127, 130
Fitzpatrick, E., 10
Flexner, E., 10
Fondelli, Piera, 181
footbinding, 28, 32, 36–7, 42, 46
Formes, Malia B., 238–41
Fortschrittliche Volkspartei, 102
Frauenbildung – Frauenstudium, 102
Frayne, Trent, 168
Freethinker, 95
Froebel Training College, 125–6
*From 'Fair Sex' to Feminism: Sport and the
    Socialization of Women in the Industrial and
    Post-Industrial Eras*, 2
Fuller, Margaret, 15
futurism, 181

Gage, Matilda, 15
Galton, Francis, 134
games, 100, 103, 138–9, 143–5, 150;
    children's, 9, 15
games mistress, the, 142–3
Garrison, William Lloyd, 11–12
gender, 56, 224–6, 229–33, 246
*Gender, Culture and Empire: European Women
    in Colonial Nigeria*, 241
George VI, 130
German College of Physical Exercise, 105
German Ladies' Rowing Association, 105
German Physicians' Association for the
    Advancement of Physical Exercise (DÄB),
    104
German Society for Health and Hygiene at
    School, 102
German Women and Physical Education, 111
Germany, 98–115, 180
Gibb, Alexandrine, 149–70
Gibb, John, 149–50
Gibb, Sarah Sparks, 149–50
Gilman, Charlotte Perkins, 55–70
Giovanni Fascisti, 189
Gioventù Italiana del Littorio (GIL), 189
Girolamo, Antonietta, 185
Girton College, 139, 141
Globe & Mail, 157, 168
golf, 150, 152
Goodrich, Joan, 138
Greeley, Horace, 14

Greenwood, Grace, 19
Griffith, Elisabeth, 8, 13
Griffiths, Phyllis, 157, 161
Grimké, Angela, 11
Grimké, Sarah, 11
Grosz, Elizabeth, 244–5
Gruppi Universitari Fascisti (GUF), 176,
    190
Guangxu, Emperor of China, 31–2
Guérios, S., 198
gymnastics, 56, 58, 103, 106, 108–11, 114, 120,
    123–5, 136, 143–4, 150, 190–1

Hall, Ann, 1, 4–5
Hampstead Gymnasium, 124
Hargreaves, Jennifer, 3
Harper, Ida Husted, 23
Havergal College, 150
Health, 28, 55–6, 58–64, 67–9, 73, 76, 78, 87,
    102, 106–8, 112, 134, 185–7, 208, 212, 221;
    see also birth control, diet, physical exercise,
    venereal disease
Health for All, 89
Health and Strength League, 87
Herbert, A.P., 87
Herland, 68, 70
Hewitt, W.A., 157
Heyerdahl, Thor, 91
Higginson, Thomas Wentworth, 19, 21
hiking, 98, 115
Hinder, Olive, 160
hockey, 125, 133, 138–9
Hohepa Te Rake, 90–1
Hollingsworth, Patricia Page, 157
homophobia, 230–1
Hornibrook, Fred, 75, 80–2, 87–90, 94–6
Hosack, Simon, 9
Hospital of Women Doctors, 102
How to Get Strong and How to Stay So, 67
Hua Mulan, 40
Hubei Students Journal, 34
Hufton, Owen, 239–40
Humanitarian Society (Gongaihui), 38
Huxley, Aldous, 87
Huxley, Julian, 90
Huxley, T.H., 122
hygiene, *see* health

ice hockey, 150, 155
imperialism, 28, 173, 180, 188, 239, 241
International Amateur Athletic Federation
    (IAAF), 153
International Athletic Association, 105
International Council of Women, 21
International Olympic Committee (IOC), 105,
    153

International Swimming Federation, 198
Italy, 173–93

Jackson, Fred, 166
Japan, 34, 36, 39
Joan of Arc, 34, 40
Jordan, Diana, 138
Journal of Jiangsu, The, 34
Julian, George W., 19

Kang Youwei, 31–2
karate, 219–33
Karate Association of Western Province
    (KAWP), 220
Karate-Zen International, 220
Kasè, *Sensei*, 219
'Keep Fit' movement, 87, 130
Kelly, Joan, 56
Kenealy, Arabella, 133–4
Key, Ellen, 77
Kinnear, Mary, 237, 243–4
Kirchhoff, Arthur, 101
Kleinsmidt, Petronella (Nellie), 219–33
Knox, Walter, 153
Kollwitz, Hans, 114–15
Körper und Geist, 100, 103
Küstner, H., 107

Laban, Rudolf, 136, 138, 144
lacrosse, 125, 138
Lamb, A.S., 161
Lancet, The, 134
Lane, William Arbuthnot, 82, 85, 90
Lawrence, Margaret, 7
*Laws of Life, With Special Reference to the
    Physical Education of Girls, The*, 16
Lenk, Ciglinda, 206
Lenk, Maria Penna, 196, 201–12
Lewis, Dioclesian, 17
Liang Qichao, 29, 31
Lily, The, 14, 16–17
Ling Association, 119, 131, 144
Ling Hjalmar, 123
Ling, Per Henrik, 123, 136–7
Lin Zhongxue, 46
Lloyd, Genevieve, 244
London School Board, 122, 124, 143
London, University of, 119, 132, 143;
    Diploma in the Theory and Practice of
    Physical Education, of, 132–3
Looking Backward 2000–1887, 67
Lüders, Marie-Elisabeth, 114
Lueszler, Winnie Roach, 168
Lutz, Alma, 13, 16
Lytle, Andy, 160, 166
Lyttleton Times, 74

McBride, Mary Margaret, 93
MacLean's magazine, 157
McNair Report, 143
Maltoni, Rosa, 184
Mangan, J.A., 2
Maori Symbolism, 90–1, 95
Marinho, I.P., 198
Married Love, 82
Marsh, Lou, 156–7, 163, 166
Martial Arts Society (Tokyo), 37
masculinity, 27, 40, 110, 178, 241
Masters World Swimming Championship
    (1998), 206
Massaie Rurali, 189
maternity, 28, 40, 62, 68–9, 77, 98, 103, 134,
    156, 179–80, 182, 185–8, 190–2, 198–9, 244
Matthias, E., 114
Mauermayer, Gisela, 98
Maugham, Somerset, 87
Mayne, M., 198
Mead, Margaret, 91
medical theories, 55, 59, 61–3, 98, 106–7,
    134–5, 179–80, 199, 200
medicine, sports, 104, 188, 206
medicine, study of, 101
menstruation, 112, 134, 192
militarism, 38, 49, 243–4
militarization, 180, 189
military training, 31–2, 42–3
Miller, Elizabeth Smith, 16–17
Milliat, Alice, 98, 153
Min bao, 46
Misson, Henri, 240
Mitchell, S. Weir, 61–4
modernity, 173, 181, 184–5
Montreal Daily Herald, 157
Montreal Star, 157
Morris, Margaret, 89
Mott, Lucretia, 12–14
movement, 137–8
Moving the Mountain, 68
Mussabini, Sam, 154
Mussolini, Benito, 173, 185–6, 188–9, 191–3
Mussolini, Edda, 185
Mussolini, Rachele, 185

Natação, 211
National American Woman Suffrage
    Association, 22
National Antislavery Society (USA), 12
National Council of Girls' Clubs, 130
nationalism, 201; *see also* patriotism
National Karate Executive Committee (South
    Africa), 225
National Olympic and Sports Congress
    (NOSC) (South Africa), 220, 223

National Secular Society, 85
National Socialism, 111, 114
National Sports Council (NSC) (South Africa), 220, 223
National Woman Suffrage Association (USA), 20–1
National Women's Karate Forum (South Africa), 220
Native Diet, 91
netball, 138
Neto, Coelho, 205
Neto, Violeta Coelho, 205
Neuendorff, Edmund, 112
neurasthenia, 61–4
New England Magazine, 64
New Generation, 85, 95
New People's Journal, 34
New York State Teachers' Association, 18
New York Tribune, The, 14–15
New Zealand, 74–5, 77, 80, 95–6
New Zealand Listener, 95
New Zealand Volunteer Sisterhood, 77, 81
Norchi, Elda, 181
Novo, Estado, 201

Ontario Athletic Commission, 163–4
Ontario Ladies' Basketball Association, 151
Ontario Ladies' Hockey Association, 155
Ontario Ladies' Softball Association, 156
Opera Nazionale Balilla (ONB), 176, 189, 191
Opera Nazionale Dopolavoro (OND), 176
Opera Nazionale per la Maternità ed Infanzia (ONMI), 186–7
Osservatore Romano, L', 190
Osterberg, *see* Bergman-Osterberg, Madame

Page, Percy, 152, 157
Park, Roberta, 2
Parker, Theodore, 13
Parkman, Francis, 21
Parks, Marie, 155, 161
patriotism, 33–4, 36–7, 41, 45, 48–9, 208
Peabody, Elizabeth, 15
Pende, Nicola, 190
Petit Parisien, 182
Pfister, Gertrud, 5
Philadelphia Press, 19
Phillips, Wendell, 11
physical culture, 67–8
physical education, 14–19, 28, 37, 43, 46, 56, 59, 103–11, 119–20, 122–46, 191, 208–11
Physical Education and the Preservation of Health, 15
physical exercise, 3, 8, 17–18, 31–2, 37, 56, 58–9, 75, 87, 92–4, 96, 98–9, 103, 107–12

Physiology and Callisthenics for Schools and Families, 57
physiotherapy, 130–1, 143–4
Pillsbury, Parker, 18
Pius XI (Pope), 177–8, 190
Poggi-Longostrevi, Giuseppe, 192
polo, 199
Popolo d'Italia, Il, 182
Post, S.L., 66
power, 3, 49, 229, 231–2, 238–9, 241–2, 245, 247
Practical Birth Control, 92
Principles of Physiology Applied to the Preservation of Health and the Improvement of Physical and Mental Education, 16
Profé, Alice, 99–116
Profé, Hanfried, 113
Profé, Heinrich Eduard, 100
professionalism, 208
property rights, 7, 18, 21
Prost, A., 196
Punch, 87
Putnam, George P., 16

Qing Liangyu, 40
Qiu, Jin, 5, 27, 29–49

racism, 224, 230, 233; *see also* apartheid
Ramos, J., 199
Ramsack, Barbara, 241
Rational Dress Association (Christchurch), 75
Ray, Mabel, 161–2
Read, Cicely, 130, 137
Referees Board of South Africa, 232
Reichsausschuss für Leibesübungen, 104
Reichsbahn-Turn-und Sportzeitung, 112
reproduction, 28–9, 107, 200, 237, 245–6; *see also* maternity, medical theories
Repubblica Sociale Italiana, 180
Restoration Army, 44
Restoration Exercises for Women, 93
Restoration Society, 38, 40–2, 44, 47
revolution, 29, 32, 34, 36–7, 39–46
Revolution, The, 18
Revolutionary Alliance, 38
Rezende, E.M., 198
Rizzioli, Elisa Majer, 181
Roberts, Elizabeth, 141
Robinson, Betty, 161
Rocco, Alfredo, 186
Roland, Madame, 34
Romero, E., 198
Roosevelt, Theodore, 7
Rosenfeld, Fanny 'Bobbie', 157, 161, 163
Rout, Ettie, 73–96
Rout, William John, 74

Roux, Johan, 219, 222
rowing, 105, 115
Roxborough, Henry, 157
Russell, Dora, 87
Ryder, Gus, 168

Safe Marriage, 83, 85–6, 92
Salles, Helena, 206
Sallis, Victoria, 161
Sandow, Eugen, 75
Sanger, Margaret, 86, 94
São Paulo Athletic Association, 202
Sarfatti, Margherita, 181
Sargent School of Physical Education, Boston, 150
Schneck, Jerome M., 66
Schöpp-Schilling, Beate, 65
Schröder, Els, 112
Seidel, Gertrud, 115
Sellheim, Hugo, 107
Serafini, Rina, 190
sex, 82–8, 91–3, 96
Sex and Exercise, 73, 88, 92
sexism, 203–4, 224–5, 229–32
Shao Youlian, 29
Sheng Jin, 33
Shilling, Jane, 242
Shirai (*Sensei*), 219
Showalter, Elaine, 63
Simple Language, 36
skating, 15, 112, 115, 190
Smit, Sanette, 226, 229, 231–2
Smith, Gerrit, 11, 17
Smith-Rosenberg, Carroll, 63
soccer, 199, 208
social class, 8, 29, 119–20, 123–4, 127–8, 131, 238, 246
socialism, 67–8, 185–6
Society of Internal Medicine and Paediatrics, 102
Society for the Prevention of Venereal Disease, 85
Society of Public Speech (Yanshuo lianxihui), 36
softball, 151, 155, 158
South Africa, 219–33; Group Areas Act, 222–3; Immorality Act, 222; Mixed-Marriages Act, 222; Separate Amenities Act, 222
South African Council on Sport (SACOS), 222–3, 225
South American Women's Swimming Championship (1935), 206
South American Women's Swimming Meeting (1930), 205
Spafford, Phyllis, 130

Sparks, James, 149
Sport, 1–5, 43, 46–7, 70, 98–9, 103, 106–7, 109, 111, 119–20, 145, 151–70, 184, 189–92, 200–6, 212, 238
Sporting Females: Critical Issues in the History and Sociology of Women's Sport, 3
Sports Medical Advice Centre for Girls and Women, Berlin, 104
Squire, Marion, 14
Stand Up and Slim Down, 93
Stansfeld, Janet, 120, 125
Stansfeld, Margaret, 119–46
Stanton, Elizabeth Cady, 7–23
Stanton, Harriot, 9, 21
Stanton, Henry Brewster, 12, 14, 20
Stanton, Theodore, 9, 21
Start und Ziel, 105
Stephens, Helen, 159
Stockholm Institute, 124
Stone, Lucy, 21
Stones of the Jing Wei Bird, 41
Stopes, Marie, 82–3, 85
Stowe, Harriet Beecher, 56
Subao, 38
suffrage, 7–8, 14–15, 19–21, 75, 102, 180–2
Sun Yat-sen, 38, 46
Swallow, Elizabeth, 144
swimming, 143, 112, 138, 150, 155, 196, 198, 201–7, 210
Switzerland, 101
Sydney Bulletin, 75

Tan Cichang, 33
target-shooting, 190
Teachers and Youth Leaders, 143
tennis, 125, 133, 138–9, 150, 190, 196, 207
Theobald, Marjorie, 242
Thomson, Hugh St. John, 219, 222
Tide of Zhejiang, The, 34
Times, The, 90, 92
Toronto Daily Star, 149, 152, 155–7, 160, 167–9
Toronto Ladies Athletic Club, 151–2, 158
Toronto private girls' schools, 150
Toronto Telegram, 157, 161
Toronto Star Weekly, 157
Toronto, University of, 155
Toronto Women's Softball Association, 161
Toronto World, 152
track and field, *see* athletics
Transcendentalism, 15
Túnis, J., 199
Turner, Bryan, S., 2

Ullmann, Lisa, 138
Una, The, 14

Uncle Tom's Cabin, 56
Underwood Trophy, 152
Union of African Karate Federation (UFAK), 220

Valla, Trebisonda 'Ondina', 173–9, 189, 191
Vancouver Sun, 157, 160
Vargas, Getúlio, 197, 201, 210
Vaz, Yara, 196
vegetarianism, 92, 96
Venâncio, Sila, 206
venereal disease, 78–83, 95–6
Venereal Disease Act (1917), 83
Vertinsky, Patricia, 3
Vincent, G., 196
Vindication of the Rights of Women, A, 14
volleyball, 201

Walasiewicz, Stanislawa (Stella Walsh), 159
Wang Fuchen, 30
Wang Zifang, 30, 35
Warninghoff, H., 117
Warren, John, 15
Webster, Fred, 154
Week of Modern Art (Brazil), 197
weightlifting, 87, 199
Wells, H.G., 85–8, 90, 92, 95–6
Westlake, Alice, 123
Wheelman, The, 23
Whole-meal: with practical recipes, 92
Wiegels, W., 114
Wigman, Mary, 138
Wilkie, Dorette, 144
Willard, Emma, 10
Wilson, Ruth, 157
Winnipeg Free Press, 157
Witcop, Rose, 86
With Her in Ourland, 68
Wollstonecraft, Mary, 14, 18
Woman Suffrage, History of, 15
Woman Suffrage Association (USA), 19–21
Woman's Bible, The, 22
Women and Economics, 67

Women and War in the Twentieth Century, 243
Women's Amateur Athletic Association, 154
Woman's Amateur Athletic Federation of Canada (WAAF of C), 156, 159, 160, 162–4
Women's Amateur Athletic Union of Canada, 152, 154, 156
Women's Gymnastics and Sports Conference, Berlin (1929), 110, 114
Women's Karate Forum, 220–1, 231
Women's Military Training Alliance, 46
Women's Olympic Games, 105, 153
Women's Rights Convention (1848) 13, (1860) 18, (1866) 19
Woman's World (Nuzi-shijie), 38
Women's Zhejiang Northern Expeditionary 'Dare to Die' Regiment, 46
Woolf, Virginia, 238
Workers' Sport Association of Canada, 164
World Antislavery Convention (1840), 12
World Games (1930), 176, 191–2; (1933) 177, 191
World War I, 77–82, 131, 151, 180, 209
World War II, 92, 166, 180, 206, 209, 211
Wright, Frances, 15
Wright, Martha C., 13
Wu Mulan, 46
Wu Zhiying, 33, 46, 52
Wycombe Abbey, 127

Xin Qiji, 30
Xu Zihua, 41–2, 44, 46
Xu Zilin, 42–5

Yangjia nujiang, 40
Yellow Wallpaper, The, 56, 64–7
You Can't Be Too Careful, 95
Young Communist League, 164
Young, Freda, 141
Yue Fei, 44
Yun Weijun, 46

Zhejiang Sports Society, 42
Zhejiang Women's Military Regiment, 46

FREEING THE FEMALE BODY
Inspirational Icons

Editors: J.A. Mangan and Fan Hong

This book tells the stories of remarkable women who devoted their lives to the cause of women's physical liberation. They each shared the same ambition: to free women's bodies through sport. Scholars have studied the paradoxical importance of sport in both reinforcing the male-dominated status quo and emancipating women from traditional repression in both Western and Eastern worlds, but the role that individuals played in achieving the political and economic freedom of women through sport has been neglected. This collection records the bravery of these forgotten inspirational figures whose determination challenged and overcame convention, custom and prejudice to free women from the ranks of the sexualized, controlled and oppressed.

J.A. Mangan is Director of the International Research Centre for Sport, Socialisation and Society at the University of Strathclyde, Glasgow, and author and editor of many books. He is founder and General Editor of the Cass series Sport in the Global Society and founding and executive academic editor of the Cass journals *The International Journal of the History of Sport*, *Culture, Sport, Society*, *Soccer and Society* and *The European Sports History Review*. His internationally acclaimed *Athleticism in the Victorian and Edwardian Public School* and *The Games Ethic and Imperialism* have recently been reprinted by Frank Cass.

Fan Hong is a senior lecturer in the School of Physical Education, Sport and Leisure at De Montfort University in England. She was an editor of the *Journal of Sports History and Culture* published by the Sports Ministry in Beijing in the 1980s. Her main research interests are in the areas of body, gender and sport, with particular reference to China. Her previous book is entitled *Footbinding, Feminism and Freedom: The Liberation of Women's Bodies in Modern China*. She is a member of the Editorial Board of *The International Journal of the History of Sport* and the *International Encyclopaedia of Women and Sport* and a member of the Gender, Equality and Sport Commission of the Fédération Internationale d'Education Physique.

Cover illustration: *The Race* (1922) by Pablo Picasso. Reproduced by courtesy of the Musée Picasso, Paris.

Books of Related Interest

Footbinding, Feminism and Freedom

The Liberation of Women's Bodies in Modern China

Fan Hong, *De Montfort University*

> ' ... valuable for its survey of modern Chinese sports history and Chinese debates about women and physical activity – no English-language book has covered the subject so comprehensively.'
>
> *Choice*

352 pages   1997
0 7146 4633 4   cloth
0 7146 4334 3   paper
Sport in the Global Society No 1

Athleticism in the Victorian and Edwardian Public School

The Emergence and Consolidation of an Educational Ideology

J A Mangan, *University of Strathclyde*

Foreword by **Sheldon Rothblatt**, *Introduction by* **Jeffrey Richards**

Comments on the First Edition
'one of the four most important books published in the last twenty years on sports history.'
Allen Guttmann, Amherst College

'... original, exhaustively-researched and stimulating ...' **Francis Wheen, The New Statesman**

'... awesomely scholarly and meticulously documented ...' **Jeffrey Richards, The Listener**

Games obsessed the Victorian and Edwardian public schools. This obsession has become widely known as athleticism. When it appeared in 1981, this book was the first major study of the games ethos which dominated the lives of many Victorian and Edwardian public schoolboys. Written with Professor Mangan's customary panache, it has become a classic, the seminal work on the social and cultural history of modern sport.

408 pages 2nd revised edition 2000
0 7146 8043 5   paper
Sport in the Global Society No. 13

FRANK CASS PUBLISHERS
Crown House, 47 Chase Side, London N14 5BP, England
Tel: +44 (0)20 8920 2100 Fax: +44 (0)20 8447 8548 E-mail: info@frankcass.com
NORTH AMERICA
5824 NE Hassalo Street, Portland, OR 97213 3644, USA
Tel: 800 944 6190 Fax: 503 280 8832 E-mail cass@isbs.com
Website: http://www.frankcass.com

NORTHERN MICHIGAN UNIVERSITY

3 1854 007 194 627

Shaping the Superman: Fascist Body as Political Icon – Aryan Fascism

J A Mangan, *University of Strathclyde* (Ed)

> ' ... an authoritative, thought-provoking and readable discussion of an aspect of Fascist ideology which has received comparatively little attention.'
>
> *Culture, Sport, Society*

> 'Some superb insights into different aspects of this question.'
>
> *Contemporary Review*

One of the central images of masculinity in the Western cultural tradition is the murderous hero, the supreme specialist in violence. A string of warrior-heroes – Achilles, Siegfried, Lancelot, Rambo – popular European and American film and literature. Governments can use this connection between admired masculinity and violent response to threat to mobilize support for war. The most systematic case in modern history was the Nazis' cult of Nordic manhood, reaching its peak in the propaganda image of the SS-man. This book is a study of masculinity as a metaphor and especially of the muscular male body as a moral symbol. It explores the Nazis' preoccupation with the male body as an icon of political power, and the ideology and theories which propelled it.

232 pages   15 illus   1999
0 7146 4954 6   cloth
0 7146 8013 3   paper
Sport in the Global Society No 14
A special issue of The International Journal of the History of Sport

Superman Supreme: Fascist Body as Political Icon – Global Fascism

The Emergence and Consolidation of an Educational Ideology

J A Mangan, *University of Strathclyde* (Ed)

The Fascism of the 1930s was a major political force both within and outside Europe. It appealed to emotion and sentiment, to the love of adventure and heroism, the belief in action rather than words, self-sacrifice, the exultation of violence, even death. A neglected element of this international phenomenon is Fascism's projection of the martial male body as a symbol of state power. This sequel to the acclaimed *Shaping the Superman* shows that the idealised image of the Aryan Superman had a wide currency beyond Germany and reveals how Fascist movements in Europe, America and Asia made metaphorical and literal use of the male body for political purposes.

224 pages   38 illus   2000
0 7146 4955 4   cloth
0 7146 8014 1   paper
Sport in the Global Society No 15
A special issue of The International Journal of the History of Sport

FRANK CASS PUBLISHERS
Crown House, 47 Chase Side, London N14 5BP, England
Tel: +44 (0)20 8920 2100 Fax: +44 (0)20 8447 8548 E-mail: info@frankcass.com
NORTH AMERICA
5824 NE Hassalo Street, Portland, OR 97213 3644, USA
Tel: 800 944 6190 Fax: 503 280 8832 E-mail cass@isbs.com
Website: http://www.frankcass.com